Settler Anxiety at the Outposts of Empire

Kenton Storey

Settler Anxiety at the Outposts of Empire

Colonial Relations, Humanitarian Discourses, and the Imperial Press

UBCPress · Vancouver · Toronto

25 24 23 22 21 20 19 18 17 16   5 4 3 2 1

Printed in Canada on FSC-certified ancient-forest-free paper (100% post-consumer recycled) that is processed chlorine- and acid-free.

Library and Archives Canada Cataloguing in Publication

Storey, Kenton, 1980-, author
    Settler anxiety at the outposts of empire: colonial relations, humanitarian discourses, and the imperial press / Kenton Storey.

Includes bibliographical references and index.
Issued in print and electronic formats.
ISBN 978-0-7748-2947-2 (hardback). – ISBN 978-0-7748-2949-6 (pdf).
ISBN 978-0-7748-2950-2 (epub). – ISBN 978-0-7748-3078-2 (mobi).

    1. Colonists – New Zealand – History – 19th century. 2. Humanitarianism – New Zealand – History – 19th century. 3. Press – New Zealand – History – 19th century. 4. Britons – New Zealand – History – 19th century. 5. Great Britain – Colonies – New Zealand – Ethnic relations – History – 19th century. 6. Great Britain – Colonies – New Zealand – Social conditions – 19th century. 7. Colonists – British Columbia – Vancouver Island – History – 19th century. 8. Humanitarianism – British Columbia – Vancouver Island – History – 19th century. 9. Press – British Columbia – Vancouver Island – History – 19th century. 10. Britons – British Columbia – Vancouver Island – History – 19th century. 11. Great Britain – Colonies – British Columbia – Vancouver Island – Ethnic relations – History – 19th century. 12. Great Britain – Colonies – British Columbia – Vancouver Island – Social conditions – 19th century. 13. Indigenous peoples – Great Britain – Colonies – History – 19th century. I. Title.

JV1035.S76 2016   305.8009171'24109034   C2015-908484-9
                                                        C2015-908485-7

Canadä

UBC Press gratefully acknowledges the financial support for our publishing program of the Government of Canada (through the Canada Book Fund), the Canada Council for the Arts, and the British Columbia Arts Council.

This book has been published with the help of a grant from the Canadian Federation for the Humanities and Social Sciences, through the Awards to Scholarly Publications Program, using funds provided by the Social Sciences and Humanities Research Council of Canada.

The Institute for the Humanities at the University of Manitoba provided funding for the book's maps.

UBC Press
The University of British Columbia
2029 West Mall
Vancouver, BC V6T 1Z2
www.ubcpress.ca

For Meghan

Contents

Figures

Acknowledgments

THE GENESIS OF THIS BOOK occurred in 2003 when I happened upon a paperback copy of James Belich's *Making Peoples* while browsing the stacks of the Elizabeth Dafoe Library at the University of Manitoba. I was struck first by the evocative cover, then by Belich's vivid prose, and finally by his reflections that the histories of Canada and New Zealand were quite similar. I wondered immediately if someone else had explored this subject further. Reading the transplanted Kiwi historian Robin Fisher's book *Contact and Conflict* confirmed my suspicions that there was a story to tell about both colonial New Zealand and colonial British Columbia. With the encouragement of Adele Perry, Jarvis Brownlie, and Tony Ballantyne, I then embarked on a PhD at the University of Otago in 2008. Truly there is no greater testament to the power of a history book than a life changed!

At the University of Otago, both Tony Ballantyne and Angela Wanhalla encouraged my passion for nineteenth-century newspapers and guided me through their own engagement with the history of the British Empire. For financial support during my studies I am grateful to the Government of New Zealand for a New Zealand International Doctoral Research Scholarship and to the Social Sciences and Humanities Research Council of Canada for a doctoral fellowship. Further research and writing occurred while I worked as a sessional lecturer at Brandon University and then as a postdoctoral fellow in western Canadian social history at the University of Manitoba, supervised by Adele Perry. Thank you Adele for your mentorship and the opportunity to complete this book in good time.

In the course of writing *Settler Anxiety at the Outposts of Empire* I have been assisted by archivists and staff at British Columbia Archives, the Hocken Collections (University of Otago), the Alexander Turnbull Library, the Auckland War Memorial Library, the Auckland Public Library, Puke Ariki, and Archives New Zealand. I owe special thanks to Ross Harvey, who directed me to a hidden source, and credit him with path-finding research. My understanding of the history of Vancouver Island was enriched through the hospitality of Chris Arnett, John Lutz, Danielle and Curtis Harder, and Brad Morrison. Like many scholars before me, I have come to rely on Brad's encyclopaedic knowledge and generosity. Along the way, *Settler Anxiety at the Outposts of Empire* has been strengthened by the helpful advice of Alan Lester, Keith Carlson, Tom Brooking, Peter Dennis, John Stenhouse, Michael Stevens, David Haines, Michael Allen, Lachy Paterson, Brad Morrison, Mark Gingerich, Antje Lübcke, Christopher Burke, Dan Davy, Pete Dulgar, Davinia Thornley, Raymond Frogner, Jim Naylor, Adele Perry, and Jean Friesen. I am grateful to Darcy Cullen for her interest in the book and the team at UBC Press for their commitment to its publication. I also deeply appreciate the critical feedback offered by the book's anonymous reviewers.

An earlier version of material in Chapter 3 appears as "*Te Karere Maori* and the Defence of Empire, 1855–60," in Catharine Coleborne and Katie Pickles, eds., *New Zealand's Empire* (Manchester University Press, 2015). Part of Chapter 6 is published in "Colonial Humanitarian? Thomas Gore Browne and the Taranaki War, 1860–61," *Journal of British Studies* 53, 1 (2014): 111–35.

This book is dedicated to my partner, Meghan Storey. We have journeyed from Landmark to Dunedin to Brandon and now Winnipeg. The adventure symbolically began in 2007 when we built a house together and now continues with our children Corin and Quinn. You have sacrificed for this book, learning more about colonial Vancouver Island and New Zealand than you might have wanted. Love, Kenton.

Settler Anxiety at the Outposts of Empire

Introduction

"Horrid Massacre in New Zealand"

         – headline, *Pacific Commercial Advertiser*,
         14 April 1861

NEWS TRAVERSED THE British Empire slowly in the mid-nineteenth century, carried predominantly by horse, rail, sail, and steam transportation. Sometimes when communication occurred across great distance, rumour masqueraded as fact in an environment that lacked the context needed to understand the story/article. This occurred in Victoria, Vancouver Island, in May 1861, when the local newspaper, the *British Colonist,* reported fresh news of the Taranaki War in New Zealand dated to January and copied from a Hawaiian paper.[1] According to the *Pacific Commercial Advertiser* extract, Maori insurgents had launched a surprise attack on a British settler community south of Auckland, New Zealand's capital. The details were chilling:

> The Natives came down from the mountains in great numbers and surprised one of the settlements near Auckland, murdering in the most inhuman manner about 850 inhabitants. The most horrid barbarities were practiced by them in the attack, defenceless farmers butchered, women with child were cut open, and small innocent children had their hands and feet cut off, and in that miserable position left to perish.[2]

This description of Maori atrocities was reminiscent of widely reported accounts of the 1857 Indian Rebellion. Then British audiences had been shocked by the rape and murder of European women and children by rebel Indian sepoys at Kanpur. News about the Taranaki War resonated in Victoria and inspired colonists to prepare to defend themselves against local First Nations.

However, the massacre described above never actually occurred, and the story's origins are murky. Rumours abounded in wartime New Zealand, and this narrative may have expressed the darkest fears of Auckland settlers who, throughout the Taranaki War, feared a surprise attack. The *Pacific Commercial Advertiser*'s source, Captain F.H. Winslow of the whaling ship *Tamerlane*, had learned of the Maori attack second-hand while in port at the Chatham Islands located eight hundred kilometres east of New Zealand. Winslow was a veteran of the South Pacific, and as a news informant he represented one strand in a larger web of connections that facilitated the exchange of news across the Pacific. Indeed, the *Pacific Commercial Advertiser* had embellished Winslow's account by referring to an earlier report from the *Southern Cross*, an Auckland newspaper that, in late 1860, described the capability of Maori to overwhelm any settler community.[3]

Winslow's report seems to confirm this grim assessment. But the editor of the *Pacific Commercial Advertiser* misinterpreted the point of the *Southern Cross* – which was that the majority of Maori were not hostile and had no intention of taking advantage of their military strength. Ironically, Maori insurgents and colonial officials achieved a truce just as "Massacre in New Zealand" was reported across North America. Newspaper editors in New Zealand had tried to avoid this sort of hyperbole in order to prevent overseas comparisons between the Taranaki War and the Indian Rebellion, which was perceived as a war between races. As this example illustrates, though, interpreting news from afar was difficult. Journalists were challenged at both ends of a communications network (1) to craft narratives that could withstand the loss of context that occurred through transmission and (2) to report on news that was *new* but not necessarily *true*. This task was all the more difficult when writing about the fraught subject of racial violence.

Settler Anxiety at the Outposts of Empire examines public characterizations of settler relations with Indigenous peoples in the press communities and print culture of New Zealand and Vancouver Island and the related effect of these colonies' different positions within networks of news production and transmission. Through a contextualized reading of print and politics,

I examine how colonists in both locations dealt with profound anxiety related to interracial violence in the 1850s and 1860s and how humanitarian discourses energized public debates over the rights of Indigenous peoples. By showing how news production and transmission operated, I am able to indicate how news about both local and international events reshaped the culture of colonialism across the Empire and mediated understandings of race in particular colonial locations according to the imagined audiences of newspaper editors. This comparative approach, which is centred on the connections between the press, settler anxiety, and humanitarian discourses, allows us to examine the consequences of the clusters of rebellions and Indigenous resistance that challenged British rule around 1860.

The Origins and Relevance of Humanitarian Discourses

Settler Anxiety at the Outposts of Empire confirms recent work that argues that humanitarian discourses remained politically relevant across the nineteenth century.[4] But the story of the ongoing appeal of humanitarian philosophy in the press communities of New Zealand and Vancouver Island is controversial because it challenges a central tenet of the "new imperial history" of the British Empire. Prominent historians and historical geographers such as Ronald Hyam, Antoinette Burton, Catherine Hall, and Alan Lester argue that a long sequence of crises across the mid-nineteenth century – including the Matale Rebellion in Ceylon in 1848, the Xhosa cattle-killings of 1856–57, the Santhal insurrection of 1855–56, the Indian Rebellion of 1857–58, the New Zealand Wars of 1860–72, and the Morant Bay Rebellion of 1865 – facilitated the decline in the popularity of humanitarianism. These events are understood to have shaken the British Empire, hardening racial attitudes and encouraging the acceptance of scientific racial theories that stressed immutable racial difference.[5] This chronology associates the popularity of humanitarian discourses with events of the early nineteenth century, especially the campaign for the abolition of slavery. For these historians, the racial vitriol elicited during the colonial crises of the 1860s and the general failure to protect vulnerable Indigenous peoples in this era reveals that humanitarianism was a spent force.

Things played out differently on Vancouver Island and in New Zealand, though. Certainly the eighteen-month-long conflict that followed the British East India Company's rebellion in May 1857 was a global media event that heightened settler fears across the British Empire.[6] However, in New Zealand

and Vancouver Island, newspaper editors were cautious about highlighting the local relevance of the Indian Rebellion. The perceived racial savagery of this conflict was too dangerous. In these places, it continued to be politically strategic for settlers to employ humanitarian language to characterize their relations with Indigenous peoples. Humanitarianism was a flexible political language that could be harnessed for various ends: its ability to be adapted and appropriated energized a series of fierce debates, and these exchanges are at the heart of this book.

The origins of humanitarianism lie in both the eighteenth-century Enlightenment and Britain's evangelical revival. Humanitarianism's pre-occupation with social reform originated in the eighteenth century's "culture of sensibility," which drew upon the moral philosophy of the Scottish Enlightenment and redefined physical pain as objectionable, characterizing sympathy and compassion for previously despised elements of society as the tenets of a virtuous character.[7] At the same time, Britain's eighteenth-century revival came out of a theological paradigm shift that emphasized "the message of justification by faith."[8] According to this Arminian doctrine, Christian believers could experience the assurance of their salvation and be justified by their faith in Christ. This theological shift emphasized that grace was available to all, and it empowered evangelical Christians to focus on the salvation of foreign unbelievers.[9] Central to both humanitarianism and Christian missions, then, was a belief in the vulnerability of Indigenous peoples and their potential to achieve a measure of "civilization" through Christian conversion and cultural reform.

The foundations of this worldview are both biblical and historical. Humanitarians held the monogenist belief that the book of Genesis revealed the descent of all human races from Adam and Eve.[10] Of course, the Bible has little to say about the origins of racial difference or human diversity. Here the Scottish Enlightenment's "four-stage theory" of cultural development proved both useful and popular.[11] According to this stadial theory of history, human societies across the world had developed unevenly over time and could be categorized according to their subsistence practices into four recognizable stages from the most primitive to the most advanced – hunting and gathering, pastoralism and nomadism, subsistence agriculture, and mercantile capitalism. Indeed, theorists like Adam Smith identified how the history of Great Britain exemplified the working out of this four-stage theory.

Drawing upon both Classical sources and the work of John Locke, this secular discourse of "civilization" associates gentlemanly farming with cultural sophistication and argues that land ownership is bound up with agricultural labour.[12] Those closest to "nature," like Indigenous peoples, were believed to lack rights to the territory they occupied if they did not improve it with their labour.[13] Humanitarians, however, believed that Indigenous peoples could fast-forward the epochal process of civilization by converting to Christianity and becoming integrated into the British liberal political economy. As I show, assessments of the civilized status of Indigenous peoples varied widely in New Zealand and Vancouver Island, depending upon whether the assessor accorded higher significance to secular or to religious measures of "civilization." The stakes of these seemingly esoteric debates were significant for Indigenous peoples: Were they to be accorded the full rights of British subjects or were they to be deemed legal minors worthy of protection?

The humanitarian movement came to prominence in Great Britain in the late eighteenth and early nineteenth centuries through the campaign to end slavery across the British Empire. Middle-class evangelical Christians, from whom the abolition movement gained its strength, objected to how slavery contradicted "the liberty of moral choice and ethical behaviour."[14] In effect, slavery was a national sin. Humanitarians employed all the resources at their disposal, including modern print capitalism and the growth of the public sphere in Great Britain, to campaign for its legislative abolition, resulting in the end of the slave trade across the British Empire in 1807 and the abolition of slavery in 1833. What we must remember, though, is that Christian evangelicals would not have embraced the abolitionist movement had they not been thoroughly convinced that the Enlightenment principles of "benevolence, happiness, and liberty were the birth-right of all peoples."[15]

So with the success of the Abolitionist campaign, humanitarians like Thomas Fowell Buxton became interested in reforming the excesses of British colonialism in order to preserve the "atonement" that Great Britain had achieved. Most prominently, Buxton chaired the Parliamentary Select Committee on Aboriginal Tribes in 1835–36, which examined the injustices of British colonization around the world and suggested how settlement could occur with the least possible ill-effects on Indigenous peoples and at the lowest cost to Great Britain.[16] The committee's report emphasized that Christian missions and the idea of reforming Indigenous peoples by "civilizing" them went hand in hand. This belief in Indigenous potential was grounded in the Christian tenet that the unity of Creation meant that, spiritually, all human races were equal.[17] The *Report of the Parliamentary Select Committee on Aboriginal Tribes* has been interpreted as the high point of humanitarianism's political influence in Great Britain. It had significant ramifications for subsequent British colonization, especially in New Zealand and Vancouver Island, as it established an obligation to treat Indigenous peoples justly. Humanitarian discourses garnered enduring power in the nineteenth century by characterizing British imperialism as a beneficial force in the world. They were attractive to the Colonial Office because protecting Indigenous peoples offered a means for London to justify maintaining control over the process of settlement.[18] The irony, of course, as historian Elizabeth Elbourne observes, is that, alongside the discourses of liberalism, abolitionism, and humanitarianism, British imperialism "was in fact dependent on violence, coercion and property theft to extend its control over ever-increasing tracts of land."[19]

Humanitarian discourses are inclusive. Anyone could express sympathy for Indigenous peoples, and anyone could assess their progress towards civilization. Because of the widespread use of humanitarianism in colonial print culture, I distinguish between *rhetorical* and *evangelical* humanitarianism. *Rhetorical* humanitarianism refers to the strategic, and often cynical, use of humanitarian language to promote the interests of colonists while, at the same time, asserting the need to protect Indigenous peoples. *Evangelical* humanitarianism refers to a powerful strand of humanitarian thought that developed out of missionary work and that was driven by a commitment to protect all Indigenous peoples but especially those who embraced Christianity. Rhetorical humanitarians often appropriated the language of evangelical humanitarians because of concerns related to the metropolitan surveillance of colonial affairs and the understanding that colonial executives operated under a humanitarian mandate. This being the case, humanitarian language provided an idealized portrait of settler relations with Indigenous peoples. As I show, colonial editors hoped that the press environment in Great Britain, which lacked an adequate context for understanding news from the colonies, would enhance their credibility. At the same time, colonial editors sometimes supported humanitarian policy and advocated the recognition of Indigenous peoples' rights in order to conceal their anxiety regarding the threat of Indigenous violence.

Arguing against narratives of the precipitous decline of humanitarianism after 1837, I identify connections between humanitarianism, colonial anxiety, and debates over the rights of Indigenous peoples. From a common position of cultural superiority, colonial executives, newspaper editors, and missionaries all publicly invoked humanitarian themes, albeit with nuances in tone, content, and purpose. However, this is not a simple story about how rhetorical humanitarians thwarted the efforts of evangelical humanitarians to protect the rights of Indigenous peoples by usurping the language of sympathy. By its very nature humanitarian philosophy reified inequality within a hierarchy of races/cultures. And, with the emphasis on Indigenous peoples *becoming* civilized, their rights belonged to the future, not the present. Ironies and contradictions abounded. Sometimes rhetorical humanitarians fought for the rights of Indigenous peoples – to buy and sell land freely, to purchase and drink alcohol – in order to exploit them. Sometimes evangelical humanitarians did the opposite in order to (supposedly) protect them. But humanitarians of all stripes spoke a dialect of imperialism in that they all defended the British Empire's providential role in the world.

New Zealand and Vancouver Island in Comparison

New Zealand and Vancouver Island are useful sites for comparison not only because of the parallels in their historical development but because of their divergent locations within imperial networks of communication. Straddling the Pacific Rim, both regions were similarly distant geographically from Great Britain but occupied very different locations within the metropolitan imaginary. Settlers in New Zealand believed their affairs were closely scrutinized by metropolitan Britons, while settlers on Vancouver Island did not. This key difference provides a framework for my examination of how humanitarian discourses resonated in these two locales.

Both New Zealand and Vancouver Island were incorporated into British imperial networks through Captain James Cook's voyages of discovery in the 1760s and 1770s. Subsequent to European exploration, both regions were identified as sources of strategic resources and were sites of imperial contestation when visited by a variety of merchant shipping enterprises. Populous Indigenous communities lived in these spaces, and their martial cultures and excellent trading skills commanded respect from European newcomers.[20] Thus, when subsequent European commentators classified New Zealand's Maori and the Northwest Coast's First Nations peoples as

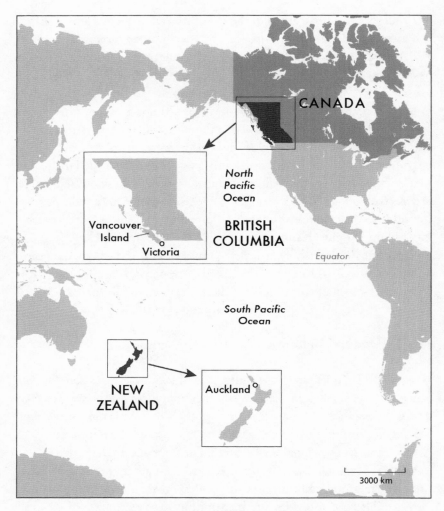

Figure 1 New Zealand and Vancouver Island

racially superior, they did so in reference to the ability of these communities to offer open resistance. This threat deepened as merchant shipping sold Indigenous peoples firearms that were employed in conflicts in both regions.[21] Indeed, when New Zealand and Vancouver Island officially became British colonies, both Maori and First Nations peoples were well supplied with firearms.[22] This military capacity unsettled notions of Indigenous racial inferiority and undermined the British military's ability to compel Indigenous acquiescence. The apparent threat of Indigenous violence pervaded the colonial societies of New Zealand and Vancouver Island, and this was heightened by rumour, anxiety, and cultural difference.

New Zealand officially entered the British Empire in 1840. In 1846, Great Britain confirmed its sovereign control over the fur trade territory of the Columbia District through the Oregon Treaty with the United States, which, in 1849, led to the creation of Vancouver Island as a formal British colony administered by the Hudson's Bay Company (HBC). A humanitarian ethos infused metropolitan debates over the establishment of both colonies.[23] For example, just prior to 1840, the Church Missionary Society (CMS), which had been resident in New Zealand since 1814, expressed its disapproval of the New Zealand Company's (NZC) plans to establish a settler colony. The CMS reiterated the concerns of the Aborigines Report in its opposition to British expansion, arguing that the establishment of a settler society would hasten the demise of Maori. In opposition, advocates of the NZC argued that their purpose was to benefit Maori.[24] But the Colonial Office intervened before the NZC could act, convinced, as Tony Ballantyne argues, "that the annexation of New Zealand and its formal incorporation into the empire was the most effective means of 'protecting' Maori."[25] Captain William Hobson established British sovereignty by negotiating the terms of the Treaty of Waitangi with Maori *rangatira* (tribal leaders). The treaty's recognition of Maori title to the territory of New Zealand has been attributed to the influence of humanitarian discourses within the Colonial Office.[26] Historian James Heartfield writes that the treaty "was the most singular outcome of the House of Commons' 1835 Select Committee on Aborigines" and was framed in the context of the Indigenous extinction that threatened Australia.[27] Likewise, in 1849, debates over the HBC's proposed administration of Vancouver Island centred on the company's fitness to oversee local First Nations based upon its legacy in the North American fur trade.[28] In this period, both advocates and critics of colonization framed their arguments in terms of the welfare of Indigenous peoples.

However, British colonization on Vancouver Island did not feature a founding treaty or the formal recognition of First Nations rights to the territory of Vancouver Island. Here we see the effects of debates over Indigenous title in Great Britain during the 1840s as well as of the absence of prominent evangelical humanitarians to help shape HBC policy. Both New Zealand and Vancouver Island featured systematic colonization schemes implemented by the NZC and the HBC. Systematic colonization was the brainchild of the political economist Edward Gibbon Wakefield, who sought to regulate fledgling colonial societies by setting a high price on land. In this way, colonists would be compelled to participate in the local labour market and monied capitalists would be guaranteed labour to work their estates. Wakefield and his supporters sought to correct what they perceived as an excess of free land in British North America.[29] As Damon Salesa shows, the NZC's prospectus included an important role for Maori as it sought to maintain the stratified class structure of Great Britain while integrating Maori and colonists through a process of racial amalgamation.[30]

Systematic colonization failed in both New Zealand and Vancouver Island but for divergent reasons. In New Zealand, both the Treaty of Waitangi and the opposition of CMS missionaries kept the NZC from controlling the terms of colonization. Indeed, the NZC experienced considerable financial difficulty in 1843 because its business model had been based upon appropriating Maori territory and then reselling this land to colonists at a profit.[31] As I show, much subsequent conflict originated in the NZC's failure to purchase land from Maori. In contrast, the HBC's scheme for systematic colonization did not attract many emigrants even though it consolidated the power of local HBC elites. Vancouver Island remained a colonial backwater for non-Indigenous settlement until the Fraser River gold rush in 1858.

In any case, while the Colonial Office expected the HBC to extinguish Aboriginal title generally, the HBC only wanted to recognize First Nations sites of occupation and cultivation.[32] Here the HBC echoed the findings of the 1844 House of Commons Select Committee on New Zealand, which had concluded that Indigenous peoples had "but a qualified dominion ... a right of occupancy only," which meant title to only their cultivated fields and villages.[33] This decision reflected a Lockean view of property rights, which associated land ownership primarily with occupation and cultivation. The view that the vast majority of territory on Vancouver Island had not been "improved" and therefore lay in waste ignored how Aboriginal peoples shaped the ecologies in which they lived and how they utilized a diversity of resources across their customary territories. In effect, the HBC's limited recognition of Aboriginal territorial rights implemented the policy that the NZC had originally envisioned for New Zealand but that the Colonial Office had rejected.[34] This back and forth over the nature of Indigenous land rights across the 1840s is revealing. Despite a long history of British settlement in both North America and the Pacific, the Colonial Office approached the issue of Indigenous land tenure with flexibility and, sometimes, disinterest. What occurred in situ depended very much upon local conditions, the beliefs of the agents enacting policy, and the degree of metropolitan surveillance.

Similarities in actual practice occurred on the ground, though. Between 1849 and 1854, Governor James Douglas effectively recognized Aboriginal title on Vancouver Island through fourteen territorial purchases.[35] In New Zealand in 1846, Governor George Grey resisted instructions from the colonial secretary, Lord Henry George Grey, to renege on the Treaty of Waitangi by limiting Maori title to their village sites and cultivations.[36] We see the consequences of Indigenous power in this pragmatic recognition of land title on the part of colonial executives. Simply confiscating Indigenous territory was too dangerous as both New Zealand and Vancouver Island lacked substantial military garrisons to back up settler bluster. Yet extinguishing Indigenous title both cheaply and quickly remained a significant challenge in both New Zealand and Vancouver Island. Indigenous land rights are at the heart of the story of settler colonialism as "the primary aim of the settlers was to get possession of the land."[37] I seek to understand how colonial journalists and governors utilized humanitarian language to advocate for land-hungry settlers in the face of both the threat of Indigenous resistance and a lack of money.

I stress the roles of both real resistance and settler anxieties about the possibilities of Indigenous violence in shaping editorial discourses and political policy. Settler anxiety was a constant in both Vancouver Island and New Zealand but it was (and is) also a controversial subject. The study of settler anxiety is intrinsically linked to the mutually constitutive categories of gender, race, and class. Anxiety was a subversive emotion: it contradicted Victorian scripts of manliness, racial superiority, and upper/middle-class prowess.[38] As public exemplars, editors trod very carefully when they wrote about their fears and the strengths of Indigenous peoples. Yet, in spite of these taboos, newspapers offer the best evidence of settler fears. Writing in real time, editors often reported on, and committed transgressive acts in the midst of, frightening circumstances. Their dedication to narrating breaking news compelled them to grapple with the challenges of assessing, diffusing, and channelling settler fears. Ultimately, this study reveals much more about the psyche of settlers than it does about the capacity of Indigenous peoples for violence. At the same time, acts of settler violence, coercion, and dispossession directed against Indigenous peoples were intrinsic to the colonial project, and they bred fear.[39] I engage with a rich New Zealand historiography – one that examines how the Crown's pursuit of Maori territory precipitated a decade of violence in the 1860s known as the New Zealand Wars. Lesser known is the extent to which the perceived threat of First Nations resistance guided debates over racial segregation in Victoria and, for a limited time, led to support for the recognition of Aboriginal title on Vancouver Island and in British Columbia.

I pay attention to the repercussions of New Zealand's and Vancouver Island's embedded positions within the British Empire. Rather than occupying proto-national environments, colonists in both spaces believed that Great Britain controlled local affairs in spite of its great distance and the Colonial Office's inefficiency. For New Zealand, this involves the study of colonial print culture during the New Zealand Wars and, especially, during the Taranaki War in 1860–61. The New Zealand Wars were a series of conflicts between Maori and the Crown, and they were fought over the control of land, the implementation of British sovereignty, and a defence of Maori *mana* (i.e., prestige, authority, and/or spiritual power). However, rather than interpreting the New Zealand Wars as conflicts between colonists and Maori, I bring into fierce relief the way in which they divided colonial society and the way in which perceptions of metropolitan surveillance and priorities shaped the debates surrounding them. Humanitarian philosophy flourished in this environment, as colonial executives and editors attempted to convince both metropolitan Britons and Maori of their good intentions. Indeed, the breadth of humanitarian discourses articulated by both opponents and supporters of the Taranaki War left metropolitan Britons confused. How could metropolitan readers discern the truth of competing narratives in a press environment that lacked an adequate context for doing so?

The argument that settler anxiety pertaining to the threat of Maori violence had significant repercussions is not controversial. More revolutionary is my premise that press discourses connected to the threat of First Nations violence on Vancouver Island were far more prevalent and significant than has been previously acknowledged. For this reason, I explore the origins and repercussions of editors' anxiety on Vancouver Island in detail. Indeed, I focus particularly on the period between 1853 and 1862, when thousands of First Nations people from all along the Northwest Coast travelled to Victoria to work and trade. I examine how Governor James Douglas's assessments of First Nations were influenced by anxiety and informed his use of what Cole Harris terms "the politics of terror."[40] In addition, I draw on records of reported First Nations violence involving fatalities to reveal how local editors emphasized the hostility of First Nations peoples. In this way, I build on pioneering scholarship by Adele Perry and Jean Barman that illustrates how First Nations, especially Aboriginal women, in Victoria were castigated by settlers as the sources of the community's vice and social disorder as well as work by Robin Fisher, Elizabeth Vibert, Carol J. Williams, and Paige Raibmon on the significance of colonial representations of First Nations peoples.[41] I show that the anxiety of editors had real effects, especially when local First Nations experienced a smallpox epidemic in 1862. Both the degree of reported violence in Vancouver Island and the character of the local press's coverage stand in stark relief when compared with New Zealand, a colony renowned for racial warfare but with no comparable reportage of Maori violence.

Through a study of colonial press discourses of Aboriginal violence, I offer a new understanding of why editors' support for the recognition of Aboriginal title had evaporated by the time Vancouver Island merged with the colony of British Columbia in 1866. This is a new perspective on what has been a central question – namely, why did colonial executives like Governor James Douglas and Governor Arthur Kennedy quit the treaty making practised in the 1850s to adopt the non-recognition of Aboriginal title in the 1860s?[42] Generally, Douglas is portrayed sympathetically by contemporary historians, who ignore Chris Arnett's research, which indicates that Douglas reneged on one last attempt at treaty making on Vancouver Island in 1862.[43] These narratives structure British Columbia's colonial history into pre- and post-Douglas eras, the former marked by mutual respect for First Nations and the latter by the decline of Aboriginal rights.[44] What is downplayed within such framings is the extent to which Douglas utilized violence and the threat of coercion to manage relations with local First Nations and how, in turn, the threat of Aboriginal violence itself influenced local editors' support for the recognition of First Nations title.

In this way, *Settler Anxiety at the Outposts of Empire* responds to Cole Harris's article "How Did Colonialism Dispossess?"[45] Here Harris criticizes the practice of discourse analysis prevalent in postcolonial literature, which emphasizes hegemonic strategies of representation rather than revealing the tangible processes that led to the dispossession of Indigenous territory. Harris's point is that "the cultural discourse of colonialism should begin to be contextualized." I accomplish this goal by writing about settler print culture on the imperial periphery, thereby illustrating not only how settlers secured Indigenous territory but also the fractured, contested, and changeable views about First Nations peoples that were voiced in the colonial press. Worth recognizing, too, is that these discursive strategies were grounded in local circumstances and did have power. They did spur on the eviction of First Nations from Victoria and they do detail changing and changeable attitudes towards the recognition of Aboriginal title over time.

Both Maori and First Nations participated vigorously in the settler economies of New Zealand and Vancouver Island, respectively, providing significant trade goods, agricultural production, and labour. Managing relations between settlers and Indigenous peoples was important in both colonies, especially when the writ of law was more imaginary than real across most of the hinterland. Both New Zealand and Vancouver Island featured the lived reality of legal pluralism during this period – the simultaneous existence of both British settler law and Indigenous customary law. The lack of effective jurisdictional control over Indigenous peoples challenged what Lisa Ford terms "perfect settler sovereignty," which rests on the conflation of sovereignty, territory, and jurisdiction.[46] As we will see, public debates over Indigenous land sales and social disorder were part of a broader campaign to achieve actual settler sovereignty. British contemporaries of the mid-nineteenth century believed that their knowledge and expertise were applicable to the administration of disparate Indigenous peoples across the Empire. Yet the differences between the Indigenous peoples of New Zealand and Vancouver Island also influenced the ways in which editors articulated humanitarian discourses in each locale. As I show, the racial language employed by editors changed when they conceptualized Indigenous peoples as interested readers.

Studying the Press

All men, now-a-days, who read at all, read Newspapers. Go where you will, you see the broad sheet that tells the Passing History of the World We Live In, and that reflects the real life – the feelings, the actions, the aspirations and the prejudices – the glory and the shame of the Men of To-Day. It shows us the world we can see, and walk over, and move amongst; the only world we can test by our personal experience and our outward senses. What wonder, then, that Newspapers have grown upon us until they have become a positive necessity of civilized existence – a portion, indeed, of modern civilization.[47]

In this passage the journalist and author F. Knight Hunt bears witness to the significance of the press in British society in 1850. I explore the power of the press by offering a close reading of communities of newspapers both on Vancouver Island and in New Zealand. I argue that the press occupied an iconic status in British society and that newspapers in both colonies captured cross-class support and functioned as vital forums for the exchange of ideas and information. People in the nineteenth century believed that the coming of cheap printed news had transformed the way in which their social world was represented and power was exercised.[48] Certainly in this period enormous volumes of newspapers, sometimes exceeding the number of letters, were transmitted across the British Empire via the mail. When regular communications links were present, such as those that tied New Zealand with Great Britain, editors understood that their manifestos might be reproduced verbatim overseas and that their opinions accrued representational power by virtue of their presence in type.

The role of the press, or the "Fourth Estate," in the nineteenth century was to reflect public opinion and to mediate relations between the ruling and ruled classes.[49] The press had slowly garnered this significant responsibility alongside the emergence of the public sphere in the eighteenth century.[50] But public opinion in this period was not simply an aggregate of individual opinions but, rather, as historian Jeffrey L. McNairn emphasizes, "the outcome of prolonged public deliberation among diverse individuals listening to and participating in the free, open, and reasoned exchange of information and argument."[51] The press itself played an active rather than a passive role in this process and was believed to be a quintessentially English institution, the enemy of tyranny, and an agent of the moral, social, and political transformation of the world.[52] This folk knowledge about the idealism and representational quality of the press co-existed with the understanding that newspapers actually reflected the specific interests of their owners and editors.[53] Colonial newspapers were first and foremost commercial enterprises that often also operated to advance the political careers of their owners. These hybrid institutions were consumed with party politics but were also oriented to a popular audience, resembling neither the purely political journals of decades earlier nor the more fully commercialized press of the late nineteenth century.[54] Newspapers did not articulate public opinion in a straightforward manner. Editors worked hard to balance financial pressures and political aspirations; they sought to shape public opinion while being alive to the currents of popular sentiment. This was a subtle and difficult enterprise, and it challenges the contemporary historian who seeks the boundaries between editorial agendas and public opinion. In isolation, a historic newspaper reveals a particular editor's vision of the world. A press community, however, reveals the breadth of discourse in a given place and much about the multiple audiences that competing editors addressed in common.

New Zealand and Vancouver Island were both geographically distant from Great Britain, but they occupied quite different locations in imperial communications networks. The press of New Zealand had more established connections with Great Britain than did its counterpart on Vancouver Island.[55] Not only were papers from New Zealand transmitted to Great Britain in large numbers but local editorial perspectives appeared frequently in Australian papers, which were also forwarded to Great Britain. Here we see evidence of Alan Lester's argument that London was the "meeting point of multidirectional, trans-imperial trajectories."[56] This conception of imperial communications networks critiques the core-periphery model of Empire and, instead, emphasizes how news travelled between imperial sites and to and fro from the metropole. Due to the strength of these ties, journalists in New Zealand tailored their characterizations of settler relations with Maori for a metropolitan audience, but a similar phenomenon is not discernable in the press of Vancouver Island. Indeed, I show how guidebook writers provided metropolitan Britons with a far different portrait of the First Nations peoples of Vancouver Island than did local editors in Victoria.

Settler Anxiety at the Outposts of Empire draws upon the communications scholarship of Harold Innis and James W. Carey. In his landmark *Empire and Communications*, Innis illustrates how communications technologies have been central to the organization of empires throughout history.[57] He emphasizes that "peculiarities of the medium" matter.[58] Communication technologies, from clay tablets, papyrus, parchment, to paper, have each had specific cultural effects and biases towards transmission through space or time. Looking at the antecedents of print culture in the nineteenth-century British Empire, Innis perceives that the growth in popularity of paper in early modern Europe had facilitated the growing authority of vernacular languages and the rise of nationalism and that it had led to the preservation of aspects of oral tradition. At the same time, Innis argues that paper, with its bias towards communication across space, facilitated imperialism by allowing information to be transmitted quickly and economically across great distance. Innis's greatest contribution as a cultural theorist is his "insistence on the crucial role of communication and transportation technologies in forming such spatial configurations of power."[59] Innis reminds us that the transmission of news in newspapers reinforced British imperialism and that a history of the press must include the study of newspapers as objects, printing technologies, communications infrastructure, and ideas.

On an interpersonal level, newspaper owners, editors, and correspondents were imbricated in far-reaching networks of commerce and politics. Newspapers from New Zealand and Vancouver Island travelled across multiple regional and international trajectories, resonating particularly in the press communities of the Australian colonies and the west coast of the United States. Here Tony Ballantyne's conceptualization of the British Empire as a web-like structure is helpful in visualizing how the colonial press traversed asymmetrical threads between colonies as well as between colonies and the metropole.[60] The propagation of colonial news was also shaped by editors' practice of cutting and pasting entire articles pertaining to foreign news into their own columns – something that led to the reproduction of ideas and arguments across the British Empire. When opposing perspectives of a particular news event were not transmitted across the world, this passive form of news acquisition could lead to interpretive monopolies. Indeed, Peter Putnis illustrates this effect when he argues that, across the globe, editorial responses to the Indian Rebellion were very much shaped by the way in which Anglo-Indian papers came together to portray the conflict as "civilization vs barbarism."[61] My central premise is that New Zealand's and Vancouver Island's divergent locations within networks of imperial information transmission mediated the metropolitan interpretation of news from each region.

The social meaning of the press extended beyond its delivery of facts; rather, news functioned as a medium for community building. James W. Carey, in *Communication as Culture*, shows how an analysis of the press must take into account both the *transmission* and the *ritual* views of communication.[62] According to Carey, communication is most commonly understood as "a process whereby messages are transmitted and distributed in space for the control of distance and people."[63] Against this transmission model, Carey suggests that the study of communication as ritual emphasizes how information, such as the news offered by the press, functions as a form of drama, which provides "a presentation of reality that gives life an overall form, order, and tone."[64]

Ideally, colonial editors presented readers with information through the provision of local/metropolitan news, commercial information, and editorial commentary, thereby connecting colonists to multiple communities through access to shared knowledge. It seems to me that Gordon M. Winder's argument that the internationalization of news "generated transnational geographic imaginaries of citizenship" holds true for this era.[65] By crafting manifestos that reflected shared British values, colonial editors affirmed the collective identity of colonists and metropolitan Britons. The use of humanitarian language was central to this quest to elicit sympathy for the settler project. The integration of newspapers into imperial networks occurred on multiple levels, too. Newspapers had institutional characters that mediated readers' perceptions of their editorial manifestos – the London *Times* spoke for a nation in a way that the *New Westminster Times* in British Columbia did not. The reputations of colonial papers did not always resonate in Great Britain to the same degree as did those of metropolitan papers in British colonies. The transmission of newspapers across great distance strained editors' ability to interpret news, and serving the needs of disparate audiences was immensely challenging.

News, then as now, was time-centric: it accrued or lost value in proportion to its freshness. Colonial editors exploited new communication technologies and competed to publish metropolitan news ahead of their peers. Here we must recognize that the mid-nineteenth century was a transitional period in communications technology. In the late 1850s and 1860s, sail power was displaced by steamships and railways in connecting the periphery of the British Empire to Great Britain.[66] Though the introduction of regular steamship packets to carry mail and newspapers occurred during this period, implementation proved problematic. Because of the high cost of fuel and their limited passenger capacity, steamships were ill suited to extended sea voyages.[67] While the first half of the nineteenth century featured diminishing travel times, communication between Vancouver Island/New Zealand and Great Britain still took several months in each direction. Actual telegraph connections did not eventuate until 1866 for Vancouver Island (via the United States) and 1876 for New Zealand (via the Australian colonies). While the telegraph played an influential role in expediting news of the Indian Rebellion to Great Britain and aided its suppression on the ground in India, it still only connected a small portion of the British Empire. And even where telegraph networks were available, because of their prohibitive cost they transmitted only a fraction of the total news.[68] Networks of information transmission in 1860s New Zealand and Vancouver Island were informal and relatively unstructured. This is in contrast to the press "systems" that Simon Potter argues took shape in the latter half of the nineteenth century as the development of new communications infrastructure (telegraph and undersea cables) facilitated the creation of press monopolies.[69]

My analysis is influenced by Kirsten McKenzie's suggestion that "colonial identity cannot be understood in isolation – it was connected under the constantly imagined gaze of the metropole."[70] The colonial press attempted to ameliorate anxiety by representing colonists to metropolitan Britons in a positive light. In this manner, the press constituted one element of what Peter Gibbons terms "the literature of invasion," which legitimized colonialism through its advocacy of "civilizing" (which was equated with "improving") and its symbolic importance as an embodiment of British liberty.[71] Implicitly related to this point is Carey's insistence that both the colonial project and the idea of communication were deeply inscribed with Christian symbolism and the extension of "God's kingdom on earth."[72] As I illustrate, colonial newspapers employed humanitarian language against their critics in order to defend colonialism's providential mission. Newspapers were the right medium for evangelizing this particular dialect of imperialism.

Methodology and Organization

My study of the connections between the colonial press, settler anxiety, and humanitarianism highlights the significance of mobility in the mid-nineteenth century and prompts us to consider how Britons perceived Vancouver Island and New Zealand in terms of their prior experiences. It is grounded in the new imperial history of the British Empire, which re-imagines the interconnections between class, race, and gender, showing how British imperialism moulded metropolitan social development. Originating in 1970s debates over British identity, this scholarship critiques arguments that the British Empire never mattered to Britons at "Home."[73] As Tony Ballantyne and Antoinette Burton argue, "One of the chief results of the new imperial history has been to reshape spatial understandings of empire and its geographies of power."[74] Scholars like Catherine Hall, Alan Lester, Zoë Laidlaw, and Julie Evans track the careers of British officers, missionaries, and colonial executives across the British Empire, illustrating how the movement of British persons connected disparate localities within an imagined British sphere.[75] *Settler Anxiety at the Outposts of Empire* is also caught up in a new wave of comparative work that seeks to broaden our under-standing of British imperialism by escaping the national parameters of colonial historiography.[76]

This book is organized into seven chapters. Chapter 1 provides a brief sketch of early European newcomer-Indigenous history in Aotearoa (Maori for "land of the long white cloud") New Zealand and the Northwest Coast of North America up until the mid-nineteenth century. The subsequent four chapters alternate their focus between Vancouver Island and New Zealand. Chapters 2 and 4 examine public discourses in Vancouver Island's Victoria press regarding the threat of Aboriginal violence and editors' sup-port for both the racial segregation of Victoria and the recognition of Aboriginal title. Chapters 3 and 5 detail press responses to the Taranaki War in the significant press communities of New Plymouth and Auckland, in-cluding an examination of *Te Karere Maori,* the bilingual paper published for Maori by the Native Department. Chapters 6 and 7 feature comparative analyses of Vancouver Island and New Zealand. Chapter 6 draws upon the personal and published papers of colonial humanitarians to examine the forces that drew together colonial executives and evangelical humanitarians. Chapter 7 considers the effects of New Zealand's and Vancouver Island's locations within networks of information transmission; their exchange of print culture, including guidebooks, with Great Britain; and the repercus-sions of the nearby press in the Australian colonies and California.

Through an analysis of the colonial press, I reconstruct the public debates that featured in New Zealand and Vancouver Island in the mid-nineteenth century. Explicitly, my interest in the colonial press reflects one of the legacies of colonialism – the privileging of settler voices over Indigenous voices, and of textual sources over oral sources. Moreover, colonial newspapers were predominantly operated by middle- to upper-class men. The voices of women and working-class colonists are not frequently articulated in these narratives, though editors did conceptualize working-class colonists in their imagined audiences. As Tony Ballantyne states regarding the "problematic" nature of archives, "historians need to rise to the challenge and recognize that our archives are important microcosms of the colonial processes that have moulded the development of modern New Zealand."[77] Newspapers provide a very particular representation of the colonial past – one that elides many voices.

Newspapers from the mid-nineteenth century are a challenging archival source because they do not usually reveal the context within which they were created and consumed. This intangibility is exacerbated when the researcher encounters the newspaper text only on microfilm or via a digital image. It is also often difficult not only to ascertain who wrote for particular papers during an era of anonymous journalism but also whether newspapers were profitable, or even popular, as almost no business records remain regarding them. Judging the social influence of a newspaper is a difficult and controversial task. For instance, even when we know a given newspaper was popular, we cannot take it for granted that its subscribers agreed with its particular editorial manifesto – perhaps they merely appreciated its commercial content. At the same time, I think that the colonial press has significant value for its preservation of "embalmed evidence."[78] Read against the grain, colonial newspapers offer insights not only into Indigenous perspectives but also into settler relations with Indigenous peoples. Reading through the rhetoric, we encounter the insecurities of editors. As the opening vignette, "Massacre in New Zealand," illustrates, journalists wrote articles in real time, and their misinterpretations are often very revealing. An analysis of the press, rather than showing editors transparently representing public opinion, shows them grappling with the issues of the day. Again, returning to the question of how editors conceptualized their imagined audiences, I indicate how they attempted to appeal to and speak for a broad segment of colonial societies rather than just local elites. To recognize this broad appeal is not to accept that editorial manifestos captured or reflected public sentiment. In New Zealand and Vancouver Island, editors' characterizations of Indigenous peoples were central to the colonial project, and they were defined by both real and imagined interactions between colonists and Indigenous peoples.

Terminology

It is important to recognize the significance of naming practices, both historical and contemporary, and their inscribed meanings within texts. Throughout *Settler Anxiety at the Outposts of Empire*, I utilize the term "Indigenous" when referring to both Maori people of Aotearoa New Zealand and First Nations people of the Northwest Coast of North America. Whenever possible I employ the contemporary names of Indigenous groups in both New Zealand and British Columbia alongside their customary designations within historic texts. I also alternate between the contemporary terms "Aboriginal" and "First Nations" in the context of British Columbia.

I utilize a variety of naming strategies when referring to the newcomer populations of New Zealand and Vancouver Island, depending on the context, including: "whites," "Euro-Americans," and "settlers/colonists." Each term has strengths and weaknesses. The term "white" is monolithic and does not capture the range of cultures and ethnicities that comprised settler societies. The term "Euro-American" is useful with reference to British Columbia, where a large portion of the newcomer population was not of Anglo-Saxon descent and also included a significant community of black settlers formerly from the United States. While the terms "settler" and "colonist" are useful for New Zealand, they are not always applicable to British Columbia, where so many Euro-American newcomers were gold seekers rather than settlers. Finally, when appropriate, I employ the terms "Métis" and "mixed-race" hesitantly, with the knowledge that their tendency to essentialize cultural identities is problematic.

1

A Short History of New Zealand and Vancouver Island

MY FOCUS IS ON THE mid-nineteenth century, when New Zealand and Vancouver Island were newly minted British colonies. These settler societies were in their infancy, but, by the 1850s, the Indigenous populations of both regions had been in sustained contact with European newcomers for almost one hundred years. And Indigenous-newcomer relations during the era of informal European imperialism affected the colonial period. The Indigenous histories of Aotearoa New Zealand and the Northwest Coast of North America; the shape of early European trade, settlement, and Christian missions; and these colonies' positions within the communications networks of the British Empire are all a critical backdrop to my comparative analysis of empire.

Indigenous Histories

When European newcomers arrived in Aotearoa and the Northwest Coast at the end of the eighteenth century, they encountered dynamic, sophisticated, and populous Indigenous communities. As the Introduction details, European newcomers like Captain James Cook were impressed by the martial skills and trading acumen of Indigenous peoples in both places. Of course, there are many more commonalities and differences between First Nations and Maori and the regions they inhabit. This sketch merely details relevant highlights and has no pretense to being exhaustive.

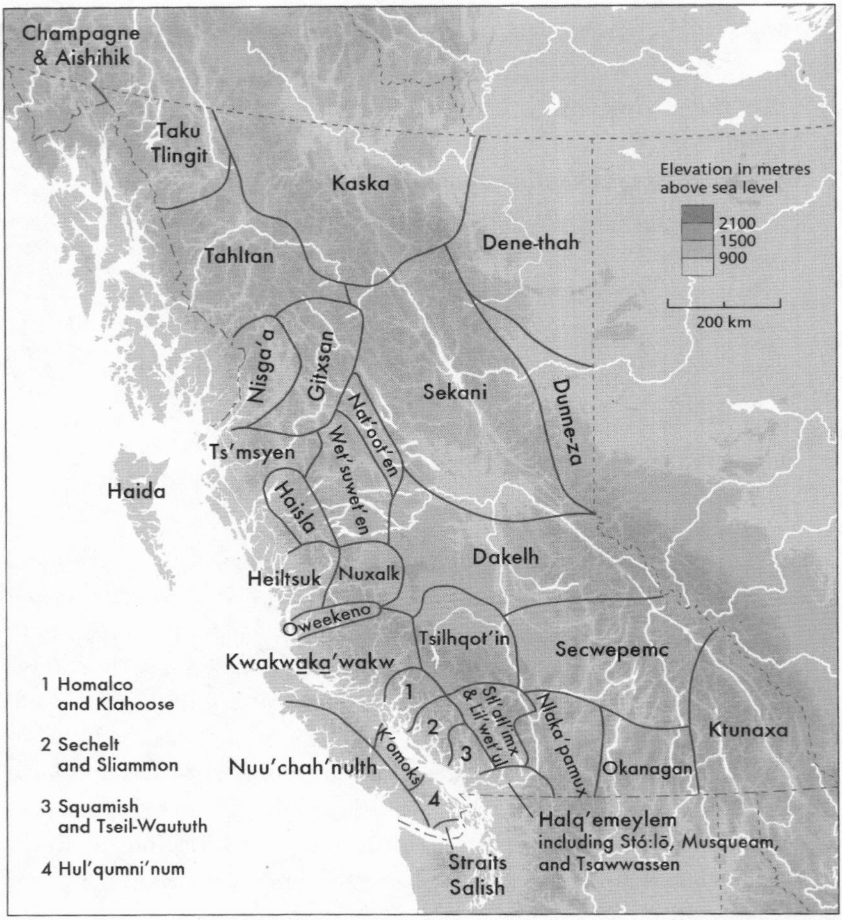
Champagne
& Aishihik
Taku
Tlingit
Kaska
Elevation in metres
above sea level
2100
1500
900
200 km
Tahltan
Dene-thah
Nisga'a
Gitxsan
Sekani
Dunne-za
Nat'oot'en
Wet'suwet'en
Ts'msyen
Haida
Haisla
Dakelh
Heiltsuk
Nuxalk
Oweekeno
Tsilhqot'in
Secwepemc
Kwakwaka'wakw
1 Homalco
and Klahoose
2 Sechelt
and Sliammon
3 Squamish
and Tseil-Waututh
4 Hul'qumni'num
St'at'imx
& Lil'wet'ul
Nlaka'pamux
Ktunaxa
Nuu'chah'nulth
K'omoks
Okanagan
Halq'emeylem
including Stó:lō, Musqueam,
and Tsawwassen
Straits
Salish

Figure 2 First Nations of the Northwest Coast

Archeological evidence indicates that the ancestors of contemporary First Nations have lived in the Americas for at least fourteen thousand years, with some researchers suggesting that human occupation may reach back even further.[1] On the Northwest Coast, the lifeways of First Nations peoples have been shaped by the abundant resources of salmon and cedar for at least three thousand years, permitting the development of a complex social organization and the occupation of semi-permanent villages.[2] A median estimate is that between 200,000 and 300,000 First Nations people lived in the region at the time of European contact, speaking thirty-four distinct languages.[3] The linguistic diversity of First Nations and the primacy of the local trading language, Chinook *wawa*, or jargon, would later both facilitate and complicate communication with colonists. Major ethnic-linguistic groups on or near the coast include the Tlingit, Nisga'a, Gitxsan, Ts'msyen, Haida, Haisla, Heiltsuk, Nuxalk, Oweekeno, Kwakwaka'wakw, Nuu-chah-nulth, Tsilhqot'in, St'at'imc, Straits Salish, and Nlaka'pamux.[4] The rainforests of the Northwest Coast were one of the most densely populated, non-agricultural parts of the world. In this book, the term "Northwest Coast" refers to the territory stretching from the southern tip of what is now Vancouver Island to what is now the boundary between northern British Columbia and Alaska.

Coastal First Nations societies were hierarchical, rank-oriented, and organized through bonds of marriage and kinship into networks of "multi-band or multi-village units."[5] Family groups moved throughout their territory for much of the year but, each winter, returned to large, permanent villages containing from two hundred to one thousand people.[6] Winter was also the season of the potlatch, a ceremonial feast of central cultural significance whose purpose was to validate meaningful events, such as a person's formal assumption of the role of chief, and always included the redistribution of wealth through gift-giving.[7] First Nations peoples on the Northwest Coast had extensive trading networks and violent conflict was not uncommon. War expeditions occurred primarily for the purpose of capturing slaves, who accounted for as much as 30 percent of the population in coastal villages.[8] As John Douglas Belshaw emphasizes, "The British Columbian coast was a cultural hothouse in which elaborate visual and performance arts (including architecture, engineering, dance, wood and stone, carving, and metalwork) could thrive with the support of a vital economic order."[9]

The archaeological record indicates that Polynesian settlement in New Zealand likely occurred in the thirteenth century CE.[10] Complicating this thesis, however, is evidence of the Polynesian rat's presence in Aotearoa from up to two thousand years before the present.[11] The original *tangata whenua* (people of the land) probably sailed from eastern Polynesia and first landed on the North Island (Te Ika a Maui – the fish of Maui) and then expanded to the South Island (Te Wai Pounamu – water [or river] of greenstone).[12] These first settlers were descended from Austronesians who had migrated across the Pacific Ocean from Southeast Asia some four thousand years before. While a great deal of mystery surrounds the questions of how many, when, and how the ancestors of Maori people arrived in New Zealand, it

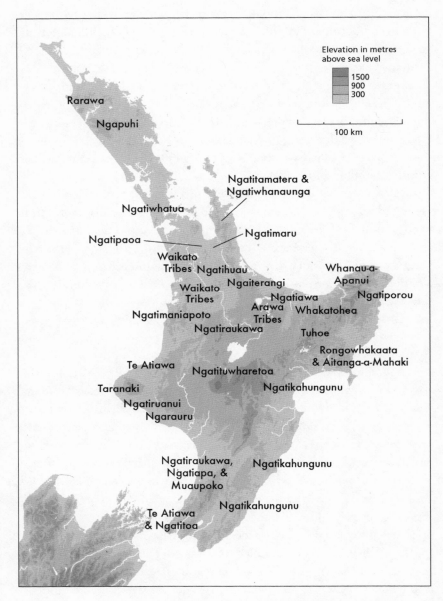

Figure 3 Indigenous peoples of Aotearoa. Compiled, with amendments, from a map drawn in the Defence Office, Wellington, 1869

appears that their settlement and subsistence patterns changed over time both as populations grew and as resources became scarcer. The *tangata whenua* inhabited a unique ecology in Polynesia: it was colder than they were used to and lacking any terrestrial mammals, but it was teeming with unique bird life. Living first as hunter-gatherers, the *tangata whenua* modified the environment by clearing swathes of land with fire and depleting sources of game, including Aotearoa's large flightless Moa. Historian Ethyll Anderson argues that, over time, Maori became more reliant on fish and shellfish and the cultivation of *kumara* (sweet potatoes) – one of the few Polynesian crops that could be adapted to cooler conditions.[13] By the eighteenth century, the majority of Maori lived on the northern part of the North Island inside the horticultural boundary, where farming was possible.

It is estimated that the population of Aotearoa was between eighty thousand and one hundred thousand when European newcomers first arrived.[14] The *tangata whenua* spoke a common language, *te reo Maori*, and were subdivided into four groups: *waka* (canoe), *iwi* (tribe), *hapu* (clan), and *whanau* (extended family). *Hapu* consisting of multiple *whanau* were the primary social and economic units of Maori society, with the average clan ranging from between forty and sixty people.[15] Of key significance to Maori culture were the concepts of *mana* and *tapu* (supernatural restrictions), which were personified in the authority of *rangatira*. Maori traced their descent through *whakapapa* (genealogy), which bound them to human ancestors, the gods, and the land itself. Chiefly authority was displayed through the acquisition and use of property and the distribution of resources in competitive displays with other *hapu*.[16] Alongside the importance of agricultural production, territorial stress encouraged warfare between *hapu* and the construction of defensive *pas* (fortifications) alongside settlements. The institution of slavery existed among Maori, as it did among First Nations of the Northwest Coast. In both Aotearoa and the Northwest Coast, the ability of Indigenous leaders to accumulate, display, and distribute resources played a pivotal role in shaping social hierarchies.

Contact and Maritime Trade

In the eighteenth century, both Aotearoa and the Northwest Coast were explored and claimed by a variety of British, French, Spanish, and Russian mariners.[17] The strategic and economic importance of these places encouraged imperial jockeying between European powers. France came close to consolidating its claim to Aotearoa, as did Spain to the Northwest Coast. On the ground, though, the most frequent visitors and first long-term residents were a polyglot variety of traders and whalers who came to exploit valuable local resources: timber, flax, fur seals, and whales in New Zealand, and otter skins, furs, and timber on the Northwest Coast. Yet, while Maori had a good deal more traffic with European newcomers, First Nations peoples appear to have suffered more grievously from Western diseases.

The Northwest Coast became a significant node in the West's global trade with China following the publication of news that sea otter skins purchased for a shilling's worth of trade goods by James Cook's crew in 1779 had garnered a return of ninety pounds per skin in Canton – a profit of 1,800 percent.[18] Soon afterwards, British, American, and Russian traders were all regularly cruising the Northwest Coast to trade with First Nations before travelling to China. This was the "Golden Round," a journey around the world, rife with both danger and the promise of vast profits. Initially, First Nations exchanged sea otter skins for iron goods, especially chisels, but this trade was rapidly superseded by demands for textiles and firearms. Historian James Gibson argues that, by the end of the eighteenth century, the Northwest Coast market was glutted with firearms, which were employed in warfare and as status symbols at potlatches. The peak years of the maritime fur trade occurred between 1792 and 1812, but it lasted until the 1840s, with maritime traders making at least 668 visits over this period.[19] Relations between traders and First Nations were often characterized by miscommunication, mutual suspicion, and violence.[20] Maritime traders did not usually return to the coast more than twice and were inclined to exploit First Nations peoples who, for their part, did not shy away from conflict.

Historians have tended to view the maritime fur trade as either destructive or enriching – to argue either that the arrival of European newcomers initiated the demise of Aboriginal cultural autonomy or that it launched a cultural fluorescence facilitated by increasing material wealth.[21] Neither view is satisfactory. Certainly, the infusion of European goods intensified potlatching and initially strengthened the positions of prominent chiefs who now had access to new goods.[22] Social hierarchies changed over time, too, with more First Nations people having access to European goods. Untitled individuals could then more easily gain social status by hosting potlatches, thereby threatening the primacy of hereditary leaders. A similar challenge to the social standing of Maori *rangatira* occurred in Aotearoa through the disruption of customs surrounding *tapu,* which had previously set Maori chiefs apart due to their sacred status.[23] Here we see in action Tony Ballantyne's argument that cross-cultural encounters between formerly unconnected peoples "have profound and often unexpected consequences that are both material and cosmological."[24] In both regions, increased attention to the acquisition of resources contributed to the intensification of warfare, and captured slaves were in demand for the role they could play in the processing of trade goods. Here we see how the social changes elicited by trade and contact were neither cultural disjunctures nor universally beneficial. Of more significance, and beyond the ken of either Indigenous peoples or European newcomers, was the introduction of Western diseases.

It is likely that, as early as the 1770s, Northwest Coast First Nations endured a smallpox epidemic that may have originated either via Aboriginal trading routes from Spanish Meso-America or via the 1775 expedition of Juan Francisco de la Bodega y Quadra.[25] If this first bout of smallpox was as severe as subsequent epidemics, Coast Salish peoples may have experienced initial mortality rates of 30 percent. Thus, even before the maritime fur trade became established on the Northwest Coast, the region's First Nations population had already been severely affected by a smallpox epidemic. Victoria's smallpox epidemic of 1862, which I consider in detail, was just one of a series of horrendous disease episodes. Maritime explorers and traders also introduced venereal disease, measles, malaria, influenza, dysentery, whooping cough, typhoid fever, typhus, and likely exacerbated the susceptibility of First Nations to tuberculosis.[26] Between the 1770s and 1835, it is possible that the Northwest Coast's First Nations population fell from 250,000 to 100,000.[27] This free-fall continued until the beginning of the twentieth century.

How did First Nations peoples respond in the face of such crises? Historian Keith Carlson, in his study of the Stó:lō people of the lower Fraser Valley, argues that scholars have generally ignored the social effects of epidemics in order to consider more quantifiable issues, such as when epidemics occurred and how many people died.[28] In contrast, Carlson suggests that, because First Nations peoples had a collective historical consciousness that provided precedents for dealing with similar cataclysmic events, the arrival of smallpox did not result in a sudden transformative break with precontact history and identity. As Carlson insists, "survivors relocated to build new tribal identities that would have been recognizable to their ancestors in form and substance because they were built upon existing social, economic, and storied foundations."[29] However, while recognizing that Aboriginal cultures provided a framework for cultural continuity, we should not diminish the hardships they suffered in this era. First Nations peoples in the mid-nineteenth century were still weathering an epidemiological crisis that had persisted for over a hundred years. As Cole Harris notes, one of the consequences of the demographic collapse of First Nations populations across this period was that, when Euro-Americans did arrive in substantial numbers, they encountered and appropriated a land that was much emptier than it had been a hundred years earlier.[30] And, adding insult to injury, settlers then cited declining Aboriginal populations as a pretext for seizing their land, wishfully predicting that all First Nations would be extinct in the near future.[31]

The history of European disease was different in Aotearoa. For example, malaria, bubonic plague, smallpox, yellow fever, and typhus did not reach Aotearoa in the precolonial period.[32] It is believed that New Zealand's great distance across maritime space functioned as an effective quarantine – those who were sick en route either died or got better before their arrival. At the same time, low population densities and the dispersal of Maori across Aotearoa ameliorated infection and transmission rates. While Maori did suffer terribly from diseases such as measles, tuberculosis, and influenza, their lethality may have been moderate rather than extremely high, with the most precipitous population decline occurring postcolonization. For example, in 1896 the estimated Maori population of forty-two thousand represented 42 percent of the estimated precontact total of 100,000, while in 1885, the First Nations population of twenty-eight thousand represented only 11 percent. Of course this is a fraught comparison. Assessments of Indigenous demographic decline are intrinsically connected to estimates of precontact populations, which are both speculative and politicized. Though in different ways, epidemic diseases were a trauma on both sides of the Pacific – one that informed and shaped the histories of colonization.

In place of smallpox, historians have associated Maori population loss since 1815 with an increase in the scale and intensity of inter-*iwi* warfare across Aotearoa during a series of conflicts that have become known as the Musket Wars.[33] According to James Belich, these wars were facilitated both by the use of firearms and by an agricultural revolution: the mass production of potatoes and pigs allowed *hapu* groups to accumulate the surplus food supplies necessary for long-range raids against both their customary foes and more distant *iwi*.[34] In these conflicts, Maori *hapu* who had attained firearms employed their military advantage to inflict bloody routs on their enemies, taking many slaves to labour in the production of goods for trading with Europeans. The Musket Wars ended when a rough parity in arms was reached across Aotearoa. As Philippa Mein Smith emphasizes, "the effects of the musket wars were horrendous," with thousands killed, wounded, or displaced.[35] It was amidst this war-torn landscape that British settlement occurred, sometimes on newly vacant territory whose original Maori inhabitants had been driven away and sometimes at the behest of Maori residents who sought the protection of British settlers. So when the Treaty of Waitangi was signed in 1840, the landscape of Maori society in Aotearoa was quite different from what it had been a hundred years before. As we see later, the trauma of the Musket Wars was long-lasting and influenced subsequent relations between Maori and British newcomers.

Missions and Indigenous Christianity

With the end of the Musket Wars in the 1830s, Maori across Aotearoa began to engage with Christianity in great numbers.[36] The spread of the Gospel coincided with the release of thousands of slaves by the Nga Puhi and Waikato *iwi*, many of whom had been in contact with British missionaries and had learned to read biblical scriptures translated into *te reo Maori*. The first mission station in Aotearoa was established in 1814 by Samuel Marsden, the Anglican chaplain of New South Wales. Over the following decades, missionaries from the Church Missionary Society, the Wesleyan Missionary Society, and the Roman Catholic Church followed suit, founding dozens of stations with several hundred staff members and their families by the 1830s. By the mid-1840s, these mission organizations claimed that the majority of Maori were regularly attending Christian services. This was an astounding reversal, from just a handful of Maori interested in Christianity in 1835 to the assertion, in 1845, that sixty-four thousand Maori were now nominal Maori Christians.[37]

The origins and meaning of Maori engagement with Christianity in the 1830s have been topics of considerable debate.[38] Not surprisingly, historians of the mid-twentieth century associated Maori conversion with "fatal impact," social disintegration, and the loss of *mana*, arguing that Maori had literally swapped cultures, exchanging their *kakahu* (flaxen cloaks) for woollen suits.[39] Later historians highlight both Maori agency and how Christian theology and biblical literacy resonated with the Maori worldview. At one extreme, this interpretive framework leads Belich to consider Maori engagement with Christianity as simply another forum for inter-*hapu* competition, devoid of spiritual meaning.[40] At the other extreme, Judith Binney's magisterial study of the prophet Te Kooti Arikirangi Te Turuki considers how both scripture and Maori spirituality were combined afresh in the cauldron of British colonialism.[41]

Several points must be emphasized. First, Maori engagement with Christianity in the 1830s was largely self-driven. Former slaves were the most effective evangelists as they had lost their *mana* and benefitted from alternative sources of prestige brought about by their allegiance to Christianity and biblical literacy.[42] Second, Maori indigenized Christianity in ways that sometimes offended and startled the British public. But this engagement also included the rejection of certain aspects of the Maori worldview. Third, Maori Christianity was of vital significance to humanitarian debates over Maori rights in the mid-nineteenth century and provides one of the most significant points of difference between New Zealand and Vancouver Island. As I discuss later, humanitarian commentators believed that Maori conversion to Christianity was intrinsically linked to the process of civilization and the assumption of the rights of full British subjects.

Faith in Christ brought tangible privileges. For example, Maori Christians were able to participate in the colonial courts from 1840 because they were able to swear an oath upon the Bible not to perjure themselves. And, as Shaunnagh Dorsett shows, Maori integration into New Zealand's settler society rendered uncontroversial the provision of legal rights to non-Christian Maori through the 1843 Unsworn Testimony Ordinance.[43] A similar provision of legal rights did not occur in the Australian colonies or in British Columbia until 1867.[44] Despite imperial legislation such as the Colonial Evidence Act, 1843, which allowed colonial legislatures to pass ordinances allowing for the unsworn testimony of Indigenous persons before the courts, First Nations people were denied the right to testify as witnesses because they were deemed without "knowledge of God and of any religious belief."[45] Here we see how assessments of Indigenous Christian conversion had political and legal relevance, which is perhaps why public critics of humanitarianism in mid-nineteenth century New Zealand sometimes doubted whether Maori were sincere Christians.

Protestant missions on the Northwest Coast were in their infancy in the mid-nineteenth century. The Hudson's Bay Company's first chaplain in the

Columbia District, Herbert Beaver, arrived in Fort Vancouver in 1836 but soon stirred controversy with his public criticism of fur traders and their marriage practices, known as *à la façon du pays* ("after the custom of the country").[46] He returned to England in 1839 after being publicly assaulted by Chief Factor John McLoughlin. The next HBC chaplain, Robert John Staines, reached Fort Victoria in 1849 and became embroiled in local infighting when he sided with settlers who were dissatisfied with the HBC's management of Vancouver Island. Staines left Victoria bearing two petitions that were critical of James Douglas, but he died en route to London when his ship sank in Juan de Fuca Strait. Finally, Edward Cridge began working as the Anglican chaplain of the HBC in Victoria in 1855.

The first CMS catechist, William Duncan, only arrived on the Northwest Coast in 1857, with Methodist missionaries reaching British Columbia in 1859 and Society for the Propagation of the Gospel missionaries arriving on Vancouver Island in 1860. This is not to say that First Nations along the Northwest Coast had not encountered Christianity earlier than this. There was a long history of Aboriginal engagement with Christianity through syncretic practices that occurred in tandem with the arrival of land-based fur traders at the end of the eighteenth century.[47] Oblate and Jesuit missionaries established themselves on the Northwest Coast in the 1840s, and, by the 1850s, Vancouver Island was an important centre for Roman Catholic missions.[48] However, while Roman Catholic clergy had influence among First Nations peoples, Aboriginal engagement with Roman Catholicism did not significantly affect most public debates regarding the rights of First Nations peoples. In fact, local newspaper editors in Victoria generally characterized First Nations peoples as heathen and uncivilized.

Early Settlement in New Zealand and Vancouver Island

Beginning in 1793, the North West Company established the land-based fur trade on the Northwest Coast. In 1821, it merged with the HBC, which considerably expanded the fur trade.[49] In the 1830s, the HBC was able to out-compete and drive away American maritime traders and gain a monopoly over the fur trade on the coast. The company then extended its operations from its base in Fort Vancouver across the Columbia District, which included present-day Oregon, Washington, and British Columbia. Instead of simply acquiring and shipping furs eastward along traditional trade routes, the Columbia District became a centre for agricultural production and for exporting fur, salmon, and lumber to Hawaii, then a supply depot for the Pacific whaling fleet. In the wake of the Oregon Treaty, 1846, the newly established post of Fort Victoria became the centre of HBC operations on the Northwest Coast and then, in 1849, became the capital of the colony of Vancouver Island.

In line with a fur trade economy, the British newcomer population across the Northwest Coast remained small. For example, there were only 774 Euro-Americans on Vancouver Island in 1855, two-thirds of whom were male.[50] Additional HBC posts were scattered along the coast and across the interior of what is now contemporary British Columbia, with supply links stretching to York Factory on Hudson Bay. These fur trade posts were forti- fied and well-armed but lightly occupied structures planted amidst much larger First Nations populations.[51] While there is an ongoing debate regard- ing the power dynamics between fur traders and their First Nations trading partners, it is fair to say that both groups were closely connected by both mercantile and intimate bonds.[52] After 1849, colonization on Vancouver Island did not modify this state of affairs as the HBC's officer class remained in control and the local economy continued to be dependent upon Aboriginal trade and labour. Victoria was a small company town, lacking even a local newspaper until 1858. It did not feature beyond the American newspapers of California and Oregon and the odd desultory comment by The Times's regular correspondent in San Francisco. It is not surprising, then, that, when an upstart press community became established in Victoria in the wake of the Fraser River gold rush, local press discourses were for- mulated primarily for a local audience. Like the region's gold rush society more generally, Vancouver Island and British Columbia simply lacked the transportation and communications infrastructure characteristic of more established and populous British colonies in the Pacific.

Early Pakeha (i.e., European) settlement in Aotearoa grew out of the sealing and shore-whaling industries in New South Wales. There were likely only about three hundred permanent or semi-permanent Pakeha residents in 1830, swelling to about two thousand by 1839.[53] These early settlements were usually closely connected with local Maori communities, upon which they were dependent for food, protection, labour, and intimate relations. Beginning in 1840, though, the newly founded colony of New Zealand grew rapidly. Indeed, the New Zealand Company transported nearly ten thousand settlers in the first few years of the 1840s. The fledgling villages of Wellington, Nelson, New Plymouth, and Auckland each had between one thousand

and four thousand people within the first two years of settlement.[54] And the settlers kept coming. New Zealand's European population grew from 26,707 in 1851 to 99,021 by 1861. By all accounts, by 1857 the number of Pakeha had surpassed the number of Maori. In contrast, Euro-Americans would not outnumber First Nations in the province of British Columbia until the end of the nineteenth century.

New Zealand was a colony on the make from 1840 onwards. Its economy was fuelled by growth as new immigrants brought capital that, in fledgling communities, stoked the market for local services.[55] Maori played a key role in this period, providing essential labour and selling foodstuffs to Pakeha.[56] In the 1850s, Maori farmers also benefitted from the trans-Tasman trade with Melbourne, exporting agricultural products to the booming, gold rush economy of Victoria. When this market collapsed in the mid-1850s, both Maori and Pakeha suffered. Pastoralism and speculation in real-estate were early sources of wealth in colonial New Zealand, which partly explains why the acquisition of Maori land was of such importance to a relatively small settler population. Local gold rushes were also significant boons to the colonial colony, enriching the province of Otago and the South Island with the infusion of thousands of prospectors and the investment of locally attained capital.[57] In this period, the North Island, especially the colony's capital of Auckland, looked with envy upon the South Island's prosperity, its own local gold rush on the Coromandel Peninsula having fizzled instead of catching fire.

From 1840, tensions between Maori and Pakeha were ongoing, exacerbated both by incidents of violence and warfare and by the exclusion of Maori from local government. While a small number of Maori landowners met the property-related franchise qualifications in the 1850s, the majority of Maori were denied input into settler governance. Events in New Zealand, were closely scrutinized in Great Britain, which was kept informed by both the voluminous correspondence of resident missionary humanitarians and the regular publication of local newspapers (which had sprung up in almost every settlement following their foundation in the 1840s). In this context, literacy and engagement with Christianity provided Maori with unregulated access to networks of colonial knowledge. In New Zealand, editors publicly acknowledged that Maori read their newspapers, and they adjusted their editorials accordingly; on Vancouver Island, however, editors ignored the significant mixed-raced and local Aboriginal population even though it was most certainly aware of the content of local newspapers. In New Zealand, unlike on Vancouver Island, spatial isolation and temporal dislocation were not barriers to settlers' perceptions of metropolitan surveillance.

Conclusion

The Indigenous societies of Aotearoa and the Northwest Coast were unique, as was their early contact with European newcomers. The settler societies that formed in colonial New Zealand and Vancouver Island were also unique. While both colonies began as sparsely settled entrepôts for European resource extraction, by the mid-nineteenth century New Zealand was a burgeoning settler colony while Vancouver Island remained on the edge of empire. The divergences intrinsic to these regions' experiences of British colonialism are what anchor this book and provide the context for my critical analysis. Significantly, in the mid-nineteenth century the landscape of Indigenous society in both regions was very different from what it had been a hundred years before, with Aboriginal populations being much reduced by both epidemic diseases and warfare. Settler anxieties around the presumed threat of Indigenous violence and debates over Indigenous rights played out differently in each locale, shaped both by humanitarian discourses and each colony's location within communications networks. So let us begin.

2
Violence and Eviction on Vancouver Island

"What will they say in England?" when it is known that an Indian population was fostered and encouraged round Victoria, until the small-pox was imported from San Francisco. Then, when the disease raged amongst them, when the unfortunate wretches were dying by scores, deserted by their own people, and left to perish in the midst of a Christian community that had (according to the Indian admirers' own showing) fattened off them for four years – then the humanizing influence of our civilized Government comes in – not to remedy the evil that it had brought about – not to become the Good Samaritan, and to endeavour to ameliorate the effects of the disease by medical exertion, but to drive these people away to death, and to disseminate the fell disease along the coast. To send with them the destruction perhaps of the whole Indian race in the British Possessions on the Pacific.

– Leonard McClure, *The Press*, 17 June 1862

IN 1862, LEONARD MCCLURE, the editor of *The Press*, castigated the administration of Vancouver Island for its treatment of local First Nations. That spring Aboriginal residents of Victoria had experienced an epidemic of smallpox that reputedly killed hundreds. At the height of this disaster, the local police commissioner Augustus Pemberton had mobilized both police and British naval forces to compel the city's First Nations residents

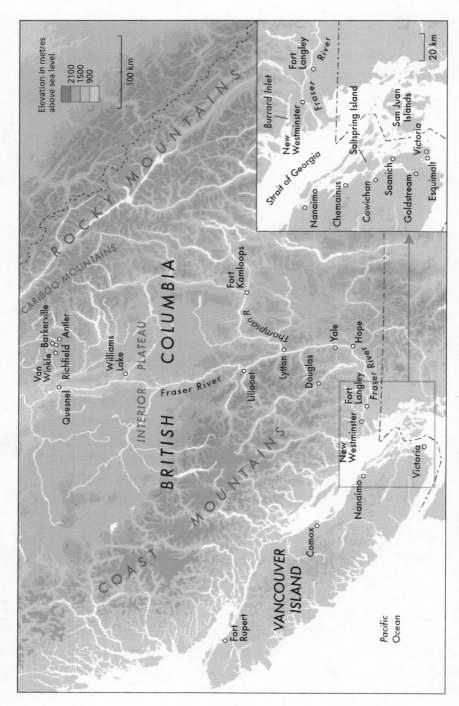

Figure 4 Colonial Vancouver Island and British Columbia

to leave. And McClure was correct: the effects of this eviction were deadly. Aboriginal people left their dead and dying strewn along the east coast of Vancouver Island as they fled northwards, taking the dreadful sickness with them to communities all along the Northwest Coast.[1]

But for McClure, this callous eviction was only the government's most recent blunder. Neglect had been the rule of the day. With alarming consequences, Aboriginal people had been allowed to run riot in Victoria without any interference from local authorities.

> For four years Victoria has suffered to an extent unknown in any civilized town in the universe from the residence of an Indian population. Time and again were the evils pointed out by the press, but no notice was taken of injunction or admonition ... How many men have been the victims of Indian assassination round about Victoria, we shall probably never know; but if we take those cases of murder that have been already substantiated in our law courts, the catalogue is the largest that ever disgraced, in comparison to the population, any civilized town. So familiarized, in fact, had the inhabitants become with Indian murders that the continued recurrence of the crime created but little excitement.[2]

Both Euro-American citizens and Aboriginal people had suffered grievously from this maladministration.

This outrage is ironic: just a few weeks earlier, McClure had praised the removal of local First Nations as a step that had been taken "none too soon."[3] And it was actually an editorial from another Victoria newspaper, the *British Colonist,* that had prompted Police Commissioner Pemberton to act.[4] Like every other newspaper editor since the establishment of the Victoria press in 1858, McClure had repeatedly called upon Governor James Douglas to remove the community's Aboriginal residents, emphasizing the unacceptable prevalence of Aboriginal violence and disorder. In 1862, they finally got their wish.

In this chapter, I consider the quest for the removal of First Nations peoples orchestrated by the Victoria press. I pay particular attention to how editors incited the anxiety of their readers through frequent narratives of Aboriginal violence in Victoria and on the Northwest Coast. The press intentionally and strategically emphasized First Nations antipathy towards the region's white residents in order to mobilize popular support for the confiscation of Aboriginal reserve land in Victoria and to eliminate

Aboriginal participation in the local economy. Editors in Victoria made use of rhetorical humanitarianism, but in a very different way than did editors in New Zealand. In order to assess the significance of the prevalence of violence and anxiety in Victoria press narratives, I explore the context in which they were produced. I do this by analyzing Governor Douglas's commentary on First Nations in his correspondence to the Colonial Office. My key question is: What do discourses of Aboriginal violence tell us about (1) the imagined audiences of editors in Victoria, (2) the attitudes of their perceived readers, and (3) Victoria's location within communications networks?

The Victoria Press

Victoria was a quiet community of around a thousand white and Aboriginal residents when the Fraser River gold rush began in 1858. News of the discovery of alluvial gold in the territory of New Caledonia prompted up to thirty thousand prospectors, predominantly from the United States, to flood the region.[5] Many passed through Victoria to reach the goldfields; many also stayed. Suddenly, when Victoria's Euro-American population spiked, the local economy transformed from being a regional centre for the Hudson's Bay Company fur trade into being the centre for the provision and maintenance of a gold rush economy in the newly formed colony of British Columbia. The initiation of a local press occurred in this context as experienced journalists and political opportunists travelled to Victoria to benefit from a booming new market for newspapers. Newly arrived prospectors and entrepreneurs constituted the readers of this nascent press, and information about the region's goldfields was its primary currency.

Nine newspapers emerged between 1858 and 1862, but only five survived for more than six months.[6] I consider four of the longest lived of these: the first *Victoria Gazette* (1858–59), the *British Colonist* (1858–1980), the second *Victoria Gazette* (1859–60), and *The Press* (1861–62). The first *Victoria Gazette* was established in June 1858 by James W. Towne, Henry C. Williston, and Columbus Bartlett, all professional journalists who came to Victoria with extensive experience in San Francisco, California.[7] These entrepreneurs imported a printing plant and sought to escape San Francisco's over-saturated press community, which had boomed following the California gold rush of 1849. Indeed, San Francisco had seen the emergence of 132 newspapers between 1846 and 1858.[8] Given the excitement in California regarding the

Fraser River gold rush, Towne, Williston, and Bartlett likely expected Victoria to be transformed just as had San Francisco, which had expanded from one thousand residents to twenty thousand between 1849 and 1850. These journalists were well positioned to exploit this new market and their connections to the press communities of the North American West Coast.

The manifesto of the first *Victoria Gazette* was educational. It was "devoted to the exposition of Facts in regard to the resources of the region in which it [was] located, the development of those capabilities, and the record of events" and was not intended to be "the organ of Opinions on any save the more practical questions of the moment."[9] The paper's American owners avowed political neutrality. This is not surprising, given the uneasy relations between Great Britain and the United States in the mid-nineteenth century. The Fraser River gold rush itself exacerbated the threat of hostile expansion with the arrival of so many American prospectors in the remote British wilderness.[10] But equally important, the first *Victoria Gazette*'s political neutrality was influenced by the newspaper's foundation in a new market. Towne, Williston, and Bartlett sought to define the first *Victoria Gazette* as non-partisan, considering political agitation to be "premature and unwise."[11] The intention was to capture the broadest readership possible in Victoria, wider British Columbia, and the United States.

In contrast, Amor De Cosmos initiated the *British Colonist* in December 1858 with a clear political agenda. De Cosmos was an aspiring politician and former Nova Scotian.[12] Prior to his arrival, he had worked in California as a photographer since 1853.[13] Originally named William Alexander Smith, De Cosmos had changed his name in California, supposedly to express his affection for the universe.[14] But this expansive love had distinct limitations as he detested Victoria's First Nations residents and, in his paper, fetishized the threat of Aboriginal violence.[15] In its first edition, De Cosmos identified the *British Colonist* as "an independent paper, the organ of no clique nor party – a true index of public opinion." But he embraced political controversy by denigrating the Douglas administration. It was "sordid; was exclusive and anti-British; and belonged to a past age."[16] Contrary to the disclaimer, De Cosmos established a paper dedicated to publicizing his partisan agenda.

In this manifesto for political "reform," De Cosmos drew upon the example set by Joseph Howe, a prominent Nova Scotian politician who had utilized his editorship of the *Nova Scotian* and *Morning Chronicle* to mobilize support for representative government in the British colony of Nova Scotia in the 1830s and 1840s.[17] According to historian Jean Barman, De Cosmos's attacks on Douglas's ties to the HBC as the "Family-Company-Compact" channelled the political language of Upper Canada, where the term "Family Compact" was associated with political autocracy.[18] There, too, as historian Jeffrey L. McNairn shows, the press had played a key role as the voice for the politically disenfranchised and as a medium for debate and critique.[19] As an advocate of the local reform party in Victoria, De Cosmos sought to remove the HBC's monopoly over colonial affairs by championing the interests of the community's newest residents and the implementation of responsible government. Marshalling the influence of a popular paper was a key tool in this political contest to win support for reform-minded candidates. De Cosmos's strident public dissent would have been familiar to many of the colony's new residents, who were used to the hurly burly of press and politics across the Anglo world.

This criticism did not go unnoticed in Victoria. Douglas attempted to shut down the *British Colonist* in April 1859 by instituting an archaic English statute that required editors to provide twelve hundred pounds as a surety for good behaviour.[20] The plan backfired, though, when De Cosmos raised the necessary funds at a public meeting.[21] De Cosmos had clearly hit a chord with some colonists, and he attempted to parlay this favourable publicity when he ran for election to Vancouver Island's Legislative Assembly in January 1860. De Cosmos lost this first election attempt as well as a by-election in August 1860, but he eventually achieved public office in 1863.[22] Upon election, De Cosmos resigned as editor of the *British Colonist*, selling his interest completely in 1866.[23]

Available records indicate that, by 1862, the *British Colonist* was Victoria's leading newspaper.[24] In that same year, Charles Forbes's guidebook to Vancouver Island reported that the circulation of the *British Colonist* had risen from two hundred newspapers in 1858 to four thousand for its weekly and daily editions in 1862. This is the only existing circulation figure available for the Victoria press prior to 1862, aside from De Cosmos's claim in 1860 that the *British Colonist*'s weekly circulation was in the thousands.[25] Because the colonial administration did not publish detailed statistics of the colony's postal records, it is impossible to infer the local press circulation from an analysis of how many newspapers local colonists sent and received.

Matching the figure of four thousand copies of the *British Colonist* published across six weekly editions in 1862 with Victoria's 1861 population of three thousand Euro-American colonists, it is possible to suggest that the

British Colonist published enough newspapers to ensure that 22 percent of colonists received a daily newspaper.[26] Though speculative, this basic measure indicates high local press saturation. Indeed, the baseline figure of 22 percent is artificially low because it neither delineates between adults and minors nor indicates how colonists may have bought newspapers as households rather than as individuals. Nor does it include the circulation figures of other papers. Placing the *British Colonist* in a comparative context, none of the New Zealand papers discussed in this book appears to have had a higher circulation-to-population ratio. We can imagine, too, that newspapers published in Victoria were circulated into the interior of British Columbia, where they were valuable commodities, functioning as a medium for the exchange of news between prospectors in the hinterland and communities across the anglophone world.

Additional evidence for the popularity of the *British Colonist* is provided by the shifting tenor of the Victoria press. As subsequent newspapers were established, they emulated the partisan political tone of the *British Colonist*. Indeed, even the first *Victoria Gazette* did not maintain its politically neutral format. Prior to its collapse in November 1859, the *Victoria Gazette*'s editorial manifesto had become more critical of Douglas and supported the United States during the San Juan Island controversy.[27] The first *Victoria Gazette* may have adopted this position to appeal to the numerous American residents of Victoria. In any case, with the failure of the first *Victoria Gazette*, subsequent editors clearly demarcated their political loyalties. In general, members of the Victoria press were divided over the Douglas administration: both incarnations of the *Victoria Gazette* were favourable towards Douglas, while the *British Colonist* and *The Press* were vociferous critics.

Perhaps the best example of the political tenor of the Victoria press is illustrated by the emergence of *The Press* in 1861. In late 1859, Edward Hammond King and Leonard McClure established both the *New Westminster Times* and the *Government Gazette*, entering an energetic local newspaper market that was already served by the first *Victoria Gazette* and the *British Colonist*. The *New Westminster Times* was initially published in Victoria but targeted a British Columbian audience, while the *Government Gazette* published information from Douglas's administration. In November 1859, the first *Victoria Gazette*'s American owners quit the colony, disgusted at the proliferation of three newspapers in a market large enough for only one. King and McClure then appropriated the first *Victoria Gazette*'s banner.[28] While operating the second *Victoria Gazette*, King and McClure had supported the Douglas administration and accused the *British Colonist* of harbouring sympathies for American expansion in the region.[29] Both King and McClure were from the United Kingdom and emphasized the British identity of Vancouver Island.[30] Early in 1860, McClure then purchased the *New Westminster Times* from King and relocated it to New Westminster. A year later, though, McClure shifted the *New Westminster Times* back to Victoria and renamed it *The Press*, with an editorial perspective critical of both the *British Colonist* and Douglas.

McClure's new critique of Douglas reflected his political ambitions and the general tenor of dissatisfaction in the region.[31] In New Westminster, McClure had been elected president of the local municipal council and became associated with a campaign to end Douglas's control of British Columbia.[32] Residents of British Columbia resented the fact that they lacked their own governor and that the Douglas administration favoured the interests of Vancouver Island. It seems that when McClure considered re-entry into the Victoria press in 1861, he judged that the best means to secure new readers was to emulate the *British Colonist*. Like De Cosmos, McClure had come to Victoria from California; however, unlike De Cosmos, McClure had worked as a journalist his entire adult life, apprenticing in Ireland before working in Australia and then California. McClure's political savvy is indicative of how editors of the Victoria press could pragmatically readjust their editorial perspectives over time.

The critical tone of the Victoria press reflected the failure of the Fraser River gold rush to meet expectations and the popular belief that Douglas had sabotaged the gold rush economy in order to protect the interests of the HBC. Clearly, both the *British Colonist* and *The Press* capitalized on and encouraged local dissatisfaction with the Douglas regime. What is less clear, though, is whether the sustainability of these newspapers stemmed from their profitability or whether De Cosmos and McClure were simply willing to operate at the margins of financial success in order to advance their political careers. For example, David W. Higgins, an editor and journalist who joined the staff of the *British Colonist* in 1860, retrospectively claimed that the paper was unprofitable until he reorganized its business practices.[33] Local readers may have enjoyed but not endorsed their controversial editorial manifestos. Douglas's political allies held the balance of power in Victoria, and they were aligned with the established interests of the local HBC elite. Certainly, the rise of De Cosmos to political office did not occur smoothly, illustrating that the popularity of the *British Colonist* was not exactly equivalent to substantial political capital. Douglas's public critics were vocal, but they were not yet politically influential.

Editors of the Victoria press disagreed about almost everything. This was to be expected in a press community operated by political rivals and business competitors. British contemporaries believed that the freedom of the press to voice dissent was intrinsic to British liberty and a vital means of combatting tyranny. Thus, newspaper editors defined their political manifestos in opposition to each other, and readers expected to encounter contrasting perspectives in the different members of a press community. Correspondingly, unanimity among editors was rare and merits attention. An issue upon which every editor agreed must either have had overwhelming public support or have benefitted the interests of each editor equally to overcome their bias towards dissention.

For example, every editor in Victoria championed the goldfields of British Columbia. This advocacy reflected the participation of newspapers in the gold rush economy. Locally, the purpose of providing useful information about the goldfields was to assist prospectors and to keep them in the region. At the same time, Victoria's editors directed their favourable reports towards the press communities of the west coast of the United States, where newspaper editors had written sceptical assessments of the British goldfields in order to convince locals not to seek their fortune in British Columbia.[34] Yet, in spite of these glowing accounts, the Fraser River goldfields experienced an exodus of miners in 1859 and 1860. Prospectors were driven away by the difficulties intrinsic to gold mining in the region – extreme environmental conditions, isolation, and the high cost of provisions. And as historian Daniel Marshall has detailed, miners were also scared off by the Fraser River War – a violent conflict that occurred between American gold rushers and local First Nations.[35] While, during the second Cariboo gold rush in 1861 and 1862, Victoria grew again with an influx of prospectors from across the British Empire, the community never rivalled the expansion experienced by San Francisco in 1849 during the California gold rush or by Melbourne in 1851 during the Victoria gold rush.[36]

Exuberant confidence oscillated with disappointment as Victoria experienced both seasonal changes in population and periodic economic depressions from 1858 to 1866. While the lack of extant circulation figures means that a quantitative assessment of the Victoria press is difficult, the failure of so many newspaper start-ups indicates that the boom-and-bust economy adversely affected local papers. Editors in Victoria were reliant on alternative sources of income, such as job-printing, and vied fiercely for the government's printing contracts.[37] Local newspapers appear to have operated at the razor's edge of sustainability, dependent on a finite number of local readers – a number that was not increasing quickly enough. Editorial perspectives, then, were shaped by this economic uncertainty. Journalists fought to capture a limited local readership and to support policies to spur the region's economic development and their own sustainability. And editors considered the appropriate administration of local First Nations to be central to these goals.

Victoria: The Aboriginal Entrepôt

Fort Victoria was established in 1843 by James Douglas when the HBC reorganized its trading posts on the Northwest Coast alongside the lead-up to the Oregon Treaty. The fort was located on the territory of local Lekwungen people, also known to settlers as "Songhees." Lekwungen people spoke the Lkungen dialect of Straits Salish, and their ancestral territories encompassed the southern tip of Vancouver Island.[38] They welcomed the creation of the HBC trading post and benefited from their strategic proximity to it. As historian John Lutz details, the Lekwungen people were Fort Victoria's most important trading partner, supplying the majority of its food provisions as well as labour for farming and construction.[39] The Lekwungen formally sold the territory occupied by Fort Victoria in 1850 and, at the same time, were guaranteed ownership of their village sites and fields. They continued to live alongside colonists on a reserve located across Victoria Harbour, opposite the fort, and worked extensively within the community. As historian Penelope Edmonds rightly asserts, Victoria has always been an Indigenous space.[40]

In 1853, Victoria became an even more significant Aboriginal entrepôt when local Lekwungen people held a potlatch that attracted First Nations participants from all along the Northwest Coast. These northern First Nations included Kwak'waka'wakw, Nuxalk, Heiltsuk, Haisla, Tsms'yen, Tlingit, and Haida peoples. They observed the wealth of the Lekwungen people and, on an annual basis, returned to Victoria in large numbers for trade and paid work, generally sojourning in the community over the summer months.[41] When the Fraser River gold rush occurred, Victoria's rapid growth also increased the economic opportunities of northern First Nations peoples, attracting more and more of them. For example, in 1855, an estimated two

Figure 5 Victoria from the Songhees Reserve, ca. 1865. Photograph (William Notman and Son), BC Archives, A-00296

thousand northern First Nations people congregated in Victoria, dwarfing the district's Euro-American population of 582 men, women, and children.[42] In 1860, up to four thousand northern First Nations people sojourned in Victoria, almost double the colonial population of two thousand.[43]

In 1851, James Douglas became the second governor of the Colony of Vancouver Island following the resignation of Richard Blanshard, a Colonial Office appointee. Blanshard had resigned when he found that his administration of the colony was being stymied by the HBC. Born in British Guiana in 1803, and of Scottish and West Indian heritage, Douglas had taken up employment in the Canadian fur trade at the age of sixteen and brought thirty years of experience with First Nations to his role as a colonial executive.[44] Like many fur trade officers in this era, Douglas was married to a Métis woman. Amelia Connolly Douglas was the daughter of the high-ranking fur trade officer William Connolly and Miyo Nipiy, a Cree woman. Members of the Victoria press believed that Douglas had been given the executive role because of his First Nations expertise. Like historian Adele Perry, I think Douglas was self-conscious about his atypical path to the colonial executive and judiciously protected his reputation as an Aboriginal expert. At the same time, however, almost every year between 1854 and 1860 Douglas drew the Colonial Office's attention to the discomfort and anxiety

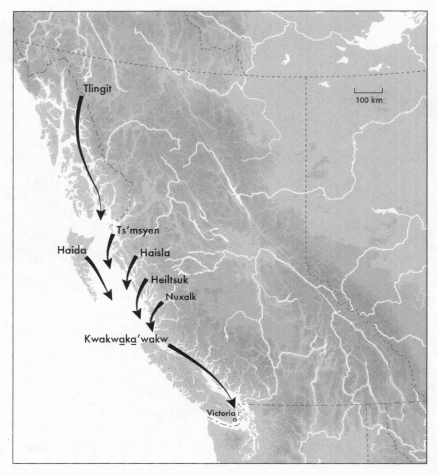

Figure 6 First Nations peoples travelling to Victoria

of local settlers regarding the presence of northern First Nations in the community.[45]

Two themes emerge in Douglas's correspondence. First, Douglas recognized that northern First Nations came to Victoria to participate in the local economy: they "executed a large proportion of the menial, agricultural, and shipping labour of the Colony."[46] John Lutz argues that, in this period, northern First Nations participated in modified traditional, or "moditional," economies through their seasonal migrations to Victoria. What this means is that northern First Nations took advantage of new economic opportunities in Victoria while continuing the raiding and slave-taking that had formerly motivated their coastal journeys.[47] The Fraser River gold rush further intensified these customary activities as Victoria's demand for female Aboriginal slaves increased. A large, transient, and homosocial community of prospectors created new trading roles for both northern First Nations and local Lekwungen people in the form of a burgeoning sex trade.[48]

As Jean Barman, Adele Perry, and Patrick A. Dunae show, the claims of middle-class settlers to respectability were tarnished by the pervasive mixing of Victoria's Aboriginal and white residents.[49] Similarly, sociologist Renisa Mawani describes this type of contact zone in Victoria as "a space of racial intermixture – a place where Europeans, aboriginal peoples, and racial migrants came into frequent contact."[50] The plurality of Victoria was itself a legacy of the fur trade. By their very nature, HBC communities were racially and ethnically diverse. The HBC maintained tight discipline in its forts through "divide-and-rule" labour practices, employing Hawaiian, Mohawk, Métis, Scottish, and Irish workers alongside each other, led by predominantly Scottish and English officers.[51] Many HBC staff, Douglas included, had Aboriginal or Métis spouses and were imbricated within networks of Aboriginal kin. Thus, ties of intermarriage, trade, and industry – bonds of both intimacy and economy – bound together Victoria's polyglot population. While a strict racial hierarchy defined the HBC regime and its often-punitive dealings, First Nations were accorded significant roles in this society. However, in the Victoria press, this lived engagement between Aboriginal and Euro-American residents only emerged in the form of narratives of social disorder. Editors of the Victoria press celebrated a particular form of middle-class Victorian sociability, which emphasized the maintenance of appropriate distance between classes and races. What we must remember is that this stark demarcation of the community into whites versus "Indians" was both fictive and part of a larger project to reform a community characterized by heterogeneity, miscegenation, and interracial encounters.[52]

The second theme that emerges in Douglas's correspondence with the Colonial Office concerns how he frequently characterized northern First Nations as a security threat and, almost every year between 1854 and 1862, took steps to remove the most "troublesome" of them from Victoria. According to Douglas, northern First Nations frightened local settlers: "Their presence inspired general terror and not without cause, as there is no restraining principle in their minds, and they have no scruples about committing acts of murder and rapine, whenever there is a prospect of escaping with impunity."[53] This insistence upon the absence of a "restraining principle" reflected a belief that Aboriginal people were irrational and embodied the characteristics of "savagery." According to this perspective, northern First Nations were incapable of acting in their own material interests by preserving peace in Victoria. It is no coincidence that Douglas described one precarious situation in 1856 as "a smouldering volcano, which at any moment may burst into fatal activity."[54] This description of northern First Nations as an impending natural disaster evokes their destructive and elemental nature. Above all, Douglas sought to avoid any outbreak of violence that might resemble the war between settlers and First Nations that had devastated the nearby Washington Territory in 1855–56. When northern First Nations were present, Douglas mobilized local British naval forces and organized a small militia, consisting mostly of local Métis men, to police Victoria and other outlying settlements on Vancouver Island. Douglas's correspondence reveals both his preoccupation with the presence of northern First Nations and his related efforts to maintain the community's security.

So when local editors demanded the removal of Aboriginal people from Victoria, they were spurring Douglas on to implement what, until then, had been a familiar defensive measure. However, Douglas notes in his correspondence that he was reluctant to force northern First Nations from Victoria when their increased numbers made eviction too dangerous.[55] But eviction meant one thing to Douglas and something else to the editors of the Victoria press. Douglas never supported complete racial segregation in Victoria; several editors, however, wanted to remove Victoria's Lekwungen residents along with visiting northern First Nations. These editors, who advocated a racialized urban space, wanted control over the valuable real estate taken up by the Lekwungen reserve. Douglas may have feared that the violence of northern First Nations might escalate and thus inadvertently destroy Victoria, but the more paranoid editors believed that Aboriginal people desired the destruction of the community and its white population. Here we see an implicit acknowledgment of Patrick Wolfe's observation that the settler colonial project was a zero-sum game intended to displace local First Nations.[56]

Aboriginal Eviction and Press Unanimity

At first glance, the Victoria press's unanimous support for racial segregation in Victoria appears consistent with Douglas's reports that local colonists experienced considerable anxiety related to the threat of violence from so-journing northern First Nations. One can rightly argue that local editors attempted to channel this anxiety as they sought to reorient the community towards white, middle-class respectability. However, Douglas never told the Colonial Office that local settlers desired the removal of all Aboriginal people from their community: his reports of settler anxiety were always linked to the disorder caused by northern First Nations. Our understanding of the unanimity of the Victoria press is complicated by the fact that Aboriginal eviction did not benefit all of the community's Euro-American residents. An 1861 letter to the editor of the *British Colonist* illustrates this point:

> We the undersigned storekeepers on Johnson street wish to inform you that our principal trade is with the Indian population, from whom we derive our subsistence, and that when you incite the government to drive the Indians away, you seek to deprive us of our livelihood, and of the means to pay our rent and taxes, to say nothing of our subscriptions to your news-paper, which is trying to ruin us. We feel neither willing nor able to discuss the usefulness or faults of their race, but we call your notice to the fact, that it would be far more worthy to organize some better means for Christianizing and improving them, than to drive them away merely to get rid of them; and that when you accuse them, for instance, of stealing, if you were to send away all those who are suspected of improbity, you would compel a great many others besides Indians to leave the country. At any rate we find them fair customers and good payers, whereas we have never seen you in any of our stores.[57]

This passage emphasizes how northern First Nations contributed signifi-cantly to the local economy, providing trade goods through handicraft production, cheap labour, and the reinvestment of earned capital. Nor was Aboriginal eviction palatable to the many colonists bound to local First Nations by intimate relations. Because public opinion was divided on this issue, editors were engaged in a contest to win over the hearts and minds of a majority of local colonists and decision makers.

The Victoria press's campaign for the removal of First Nations people from Victoria continued to increase, with demands for Aboriginal eviction appearing in forty-two editorials and articles between 1859 and 1862. As Edmonds shows, this campaign was imbued with the assumption that the colonial townscape was not the appropriate setting for Indigenous people.[58]

Most often, calls for racial segregation occurred amidst protests against unacceptable levels of Aboriginal crime, violence, and social disorder. Reports of Aboriginal violence were a staple of every edition of the local news. Alongside attention to the movement of First Nations in the region, the Victoria press chronicled incidents of Aboriginal violence occurring in and around Victoria, on the Northwest Coast of British Columbia, and across Puget Sound in Washington Territory. Aboriginal violence in Victoria itself varied in scale, from pitched gun battles with numerous fatalities and hundreds of participants to small-scale riots fought with knives and clubs. In this raucous atmosphere, the local police generally stayed on the sidelines.

Chronicling Aboriginal violence involving fatalities was a key element of editors' strategy to build support for racial segregation. Between 1858 and 1862, local editors called attention to the violent deaths of 248 persons in Victoria, Vancouver Island, and British Columbia. Aboriginal perpetrators were alleged to be responsible for 75 percent of these killings, including sixty murders in Victoria itself. In contrast, local editors detailed only eleven murders in this period that featured white victims and perpetrators. In this way, fatal violence came to be identified as an Aboriginal problem. This reportage also drew attention to the inadequacies of the Victoria Police Department and the local judiciary. Indeed, the local judiciary recorded only fifteen murder convictions in Victoria during this same period, indicating that 90 percent of incidents involving fatal violence reported to have occurred on Vancouver Island did not result in convictions. Proof of this level of violence implicitly critiques Douglas's reputation for managing relations with First Nations.

Of course, this leads to the question: Of what significance is this reportage of Aboriginal violence? The Victoria press's fixation on Aboriginal violence stands in stark contrast to the practice of press communities in New Zealand, a colony that had garnered a reputation for colonial warfare but that did not cover Maori violence in the same way that Victoria covered Aboriginal violence. It must be remembered that the reportage of First Nations-related fatal violence was never neutral. Through quantification, repetition, and editorial commentary, disconnected narratives of Aboriginal violence accrued symbolic meaning as tangible proof of First Nations antipathy towards white people. Journalists further amplified the force of their reportage by emphasizing their inability to fully assess the degree of Aboriginal violence occurring across the region. This self-awareness of the limits of colonial knowledge associated danger with both proximity to Aboriginal people and distance from sites of white occupation. Aboriginal eviction from urban space was seen as an answer to this problem.

It should go without saying that press reports of First Nations-related fatal violence cannot be taken at face value, especially given editors' tendency to exaggerate the threat of such violence. One of my recurring themes is how the staffing of mid-nineteenth-century newspapers affected their operations. Newspapers of this era featured small teams of printers and editors, and they lacked the investigative resources needed to test the accuracy of emerging news. Local news, then, was compiled, via informal communications networks, from regular correspondents and local traders who plied the Northwest Coast. These informants trafficked in rumour and hearsay, just as is described in the vignette that opens this book's Introduction. Indeed, the accuracy of the aforementioned records has not been verified, nor do the figures cited include the very few reports of fatal violence that were later determined to be false.

It is important to remember that this chapter is not a history of violence per se but, rather, an analysis of how editors of the Victoria press employed discourses of Aboriginal violence for a specific purpose. A history of violence per se would build on existing work regarding the prevalence of racialized violence against Aboriginal people perpetrated by Euro-Americans along the Fraser River gold diggings and the colonial administration's use not only of "gunboat diplomacy" but also judicial violence to coerce First Nations.[59] Such a study would also investigate the incidence of gendered violence against Aboriginal women in Victoria.[60] The Victoria press, however, did not depict the same public disapprobation towards these forms of violence (and their prevelance) as it did towards Aboriginal violence.

Along with narratives of Aboriginal violence, editors drew upon the reports of local Grand Juries to support demands for racial segregation. Victoria's Grand Juries were composed of eligible jurists who were chosen to sit on local court cases for quarterly sessions. One of their responsibilities was to prepare a report for Vancouver Island's chief justice, drawing attention to issues within the purview of Vancouver Island's judicial system. Periodically, these reports appeared in local newspapers. The scope of concerns identified by Grand Juries was broad. They frequently commented on the poor condition of the Victoria Gaol and also drew attention to Victoria's security and sanitation. This broad mandate may testify to that fact that, until 1862, Victoria lacked a municipal council that could offer a forum for discussing citizens' concerns.

Between 1859 and 1860, five out of seven Grand Jury reports complained about northern First Nations and recommended their eviction.[61] On 20 February 1860, for example, the Grand Jury foreman called attention to the community's Aboriginal residents:

> The Grand Jury beg to recommend that some vigorous action be speedily adopted with regard to the Indians in the neighbourhood of the town, the growing insecurity of the Esquimalt Road being daily manifested by attempts to molest passengers, which in some instances have resulted in grievous bodily harm. The frequent occurrence of strife and murder amongst the Indians calls for the adoption of immediate measures; the fact of such proceedings taking place in the vicinity of a civilized community reflecting but little credit upon the system pursued towards them.[62]

Subsequent Grand Jury reports, perhaps cognizant of Douglas's inability to remove northern First Nations from Victoria in 1860, recommended the confiscation of their firearms and the expansion of the Victoria Police Department, which was to be augmented with a military garrison. Editors called attention to these reports to provide independent confirmation of their own attention to the disorder that northern First Nations were causing in the community. Through this evocation of public support, editors purported to articulate the will of colonists.

Drawing on this extensive coverage of First Nations-related fatal violence, editors did not shy away from highlighting the threat of war.[63] This strategy stressed eviction as the best means of avoiding a large-scale conflict and stands as an excellent example of how editors attempted not only to chronicle but also to incite the anxiety of colonists in order to garner their support. In their efforts to build grassroots support to pressure Douglas to do something, Victoria editors stressed the risks of inaction. *The Press* expressed indignation on behalf of Victoria's Euro-American residents, noting on 27 December 1861: "We are all the time living over a mine that may at any instant explode and cause the most serious consequences."[64]

Yet the Victoria press attempted to highlight the spectre of a potential war without subverting notions of British racial and military superiority. This entailed identifying the risks colonists faced without admitting their vulnerability. Several editors struck this balance by citing the extermination of First Nations as the potential outcome of war.[65] An 1860 passage from the second *Victoria Gazette* illustrates this strategy:

Everybody must be fully convinced, by observation of the gradual increase of Indian depredations, that the leniency which has been exercised towards them hitherto, is of no avail, and if persisted in, will only succeed, by inspiring them with a false confidence, in rendering them still worse; until at length the day will come, when, perhaps for our very lives, we shall be forced to arms, with or without the consent of our Rulers; all the wild passions of our nature will be let loose, and we shall only feel a sense of security in the extermination of the tribes.[66]

In this passage, George E. Nias's rationale for imposing law and order is that the colonial administration's failure to respond to Aboriginal crime will instill local First Nations with a false confidence that will eventually precipitate an attack. While, in his allusion to "the wild passions of our nature," Nias hints at settler anxiety, he steadfastly affirms their ability to overcome First Nations. However, in highlighting both the prevalence of Aboriginal violence and the threat of war, the Victoria press provided a very dubious assessment of the community's future prospects.

In 1862, D.G.F. Macdonald capitalized on his experience as a surveyor in the region and published a guidebook to Vancouver Island and British Columbia that warns prospective immigrants to avoid the region because of the risk of Aboriginal violence. According to Macdonald, war was inevitable. However, his characterization of the threat that First Nations posed to settlers was unique. As I discuss in Chapter 7, the majority of guidebook authors took a different tack: they sought to allay fears of Indigenous violence and attempted to convince their readers to travel to the region. Macdonald's narrative is significant because he drew explicitly on the Victoria press. Indeed, he accurately describes the Victoria press as "literally teeming with records of the lawlessness of the people of these unhappy colonies."[67] The difference between Macdonald and local editors, however, was that the former predicted that, due to their superior numbers, First Nations might overwhelm colonists. Thus, Macdonald breached an unspoken covenant among public officials not to question the security of the colony.

Local reviews of Macdonald's book were harsh. The *British Colonist* described it as "the greatest collection of lies ever put together" and decried the possibility that metropolitan readers might take its claims at face value:

Here, no denial of such consummate falsehoods as it contains is necessary. But abroad, where this extract has found its way, it may be partially believed. That, however, is scarcely possible, as we observe that some of our English exchanges regard the picture as entirely overdrawn. It seems that McDonald has aimed at stuffing the British public with these lies simply with a view to damage this country, but has missed his aim by overdoing his design.[68]

This degree of hostility towards Macdonald is suggestive of the power of narratives of Indigenous violence in this era. De Cosmos attempted to downplay Macdonald's claims by accusing him of seeking to damage the country's reputation. However, local papers' pervasive coverage of Aboriginal violence clearly indicates the irony of De Cosmos's outrage. Editors in Victoria wrote about Aboriginal violence all the time and frequently highlighted the threat of war posed by local First Nations. These narratives had the potential to alienate those who resided abroad at the same time as they shaped the opinion of those at home in favour of racial segregation.

The way in which editors of the Victoria press drew attention to the threat of Aboriginal violence in their community suggests that they did not expect metropolitan newspaper readers to encounter their articles. In other words, local editorial perspectives were crafted for readers in Victoria, not for metropolitan Britons who might, upon reading narratives of First Nations violence, misinterpret them and avoid the colony. It must be remembered that postal connections between Vancouver Island and Great Britain were sporadic and that, because of this, editors in Victoria did not prepare special monthly editions for the British mail. Metropolitan papers did not feature regular extracts from the Victoria press in their coverage of the region. Interestingly, the majority of New Zealand editors handled the topic of Maori violence in a much more nuanced manner than Victorian editors handled the topic of First Nations violence, and this was precisely because of the New Zealanders' fears regarding metropolitan surveillance of colonial affairs.

An analysis of how Victorian editors used humanitarian discourses provides further circumstantial evidence of the isolation of the Victoria press. It is to this that I now turn.

Humanitarian Philosophy and Aboriginal Eviction

The first *Victoria Gazette,* the second *Victoria Gazette,* and the *British Colonist* all argued that the eviction of local First Nations people from Victoria would facilitate the process of their being civilized. According to these editors, the proximity of local First Nations to the vice of colonists impeded their social development.[69] As the editor of the *British Colonist* observed: "We see no ultimate course but the removal of these poor creatures from their present quarters. Humanity demands that efforts be made to civilize them, as well as restrain them from crime, and to do this, they must be placed in circumstances of less temptation and demoralization, than those which surround them at present."[70] According to this rationale, eviction was an element of the civilizing mission as it entailed relocating local First Nations to sites more amenable to their cultural transformation. This argument stresses the vulnerability of local First Nations, their potential for achieving a measure of British civilization, and the responsibility of the colonial administration to facilitate their improvement. Here, too, we see an example of historian Paige Raibmon's thesis that colonial observers viewed Aboriginal culture as static and unchanging.[71] Thus, removing First Nations people from the urban space of Victoria would facilitate their return to safer traditional subsistence activities far away from the dangers of modernity.

Clearly, this is an example of rhetorical humanitarianism as the Victoria press offered no pragmatic or systematic plan for Aboriginal improvement.[72] But the facile manner in which the Victoria press disguised its demands for segregation should not distract us from the implications of the humanitarian language of its argument. Why did editors feel compelled to articulate the benefits of eviction for First Nations rather than simply highlight the interests of the colonists?

In its quest for racial segregation, the Victoria press deployed a range of arguments, drawing on the beliefs and interests of several constituencies. Just as the reportage of Aboriginal violence was intended to unsettle readers, so the use of humanitarian philosophy attempted to elicit sympathy for First Nations. This humanitarian appeal reflects the belief that some colonists had an interest in the social welfare of local Aboriginal peoples and that a policy of racial segregation correlated with Douglas's mandate from the Colonial Office to use humanitarianism in his administering of local First Nations. After 1858, a group of like-minded evangelical humanitarians established the Indian Improvement Committee in Victoria. This organization included local churchpeople, British naval officers, and newly arrived missionaries who worked among the community's Aboriginal residents. This group had Douglas's ear and was influential in shaping his Indian policy (see Chapter 6).

Humanitarian philosophy also functioned as the language of political critique for both *The Press* and the *British Colonist*.[73] As this chapter's opening vignette illustrates, McClure accused Douglas of failing to meet the expectations of the Aborigines' Protection Society. De Cosmos echoes this sentiment:

> Are there magnates here who ape the philanthropy of the Aborigines' Society and the evangelism of Exeter Hall, and yet suffer such scenes to recur over and over again, in the broad day, causing Victoria harbor to be likened to the mythical gulf that divides Heaven and Hell? ... Occasionally an Englishman – we use the generic term – is heard to denounce the spirit of Indian extermination that characterizes Americans; but no where in that vast republic would such diabolical outrages as are here perpetrated be permitted for a day, let alone the year long. And yet we boast of British philanthropy to the Indian. Nonsense; we deceive ourselves, and do what we condemn in others.[74]

The implication is that Douglas had failed to protect local First Nations and had not lived up to his reputation as a superior manager of Aboriginal peoples. Humanitarian discourses were attractive because they offered a means of justifying eviction within an idealized framework, thereby affirming the press's role as an enlightened guide to colonists. In the same vein, in their characterizations of the community's black residents, editors deployed humanitarian discourses to celebrate Great Britain's abolitionist legacy.[75] This usage highlighted the superiority of Great Britain to the United States but did little to ameliorate the lived experiences of racism endured by black citizens in Victoria. The diverse application of humanitarian language reveals its usefulness in describing the colonial project in Victoria.

However, the Victoria press was very uneven in its assessments of the potential of First Nations. While *The Press* tended to defend the rights of First Nations peoples and repeatedly called upon Douglas to institute a more effective Indian policy, the *British Colonist* repeatedly stressed the inherent predisposition of First Nations to vice.[76] Indeed, while De Cosmos defended eviction as being in the best interests of local First Nations, he expressed little confidence in their potential:

> To engage in active and useful pursuits they will not, except some mere drudgery; and though they are possessed of "bone, muscle, energy and

intellect," their habits of indolence, roaming propensities, and natural repugnance for manual labor, together with a thievish disposition which appears to be an inherent characteristic of the Indian race, totally disqualifies them from ever becoming either useful or desirable citizens. The efforts of the last fifty years both in the Canadas and in the United States, where every exertion has been used to improve the social and moral condition of the native population, and redeem them from their wandering and idle habits, by the adoption of industrial pursuits, have proved a decided failure, so far, at least, as turning their "bone, muscle and intellect" to any useful or practical account, is concerned.[77]

This assessment drew upon the experiences of missionary humanitarians in North America. As historian C.L. Higham argues, in the first half of the nineteenth century Euro-American missionaries popularized their outreach by characterizing First Nations as "noble savages."[78] The idea of the noble savage, born out of the eighteenth-century Enlightenment as a tool for the critique European society, held that First Nations peoples shared a common origin with Europeans, had all the basic characteristics of humankind, and were amenable to the Gospel. As Higham explains, this idyllic vision of First Nations shifted to the image of "wretched Indians" over the early decades of the nineteenth century. This change had to do with the failure of missionaries to achieve widespread evangelization and the subsequent need to explain their lack of success.[79] Whereas the image of the noble savage highlights the positive qualities of First Nations and their similarities to Europeans, the image of the wretched Indian emphasizes both moral degradation and racial difference. The strategy of exaggerating the susceptibility of First Nations to European vice implicitly affirms the roles of missionaries as both physical and spiritual saviours.

Demands for eviction that emphasized the predisposition of local First Nations to vice employed the image of the wretched Indian to sanction urban segregation. Here we see another significant difference between how settlers in New Zealand and those on Vancouver Island assessed the cultural sophistication of Maori as opposed to First Nations. As we see in Chapters 3 and 5, public advocates of humanitarian philosophy in New Zealand celebrated Maori Christian practice and called for their greater integration into the colonial market as the best way to achieve continued advances in reforming them by civilizing them. Rhetorical humanitarians hoped to gain access to Maori land through the individualization of communally owned tribal property. On Vancouver Island, local First Nations were in the early stages of engaging with Christianity and they were already participating fully in the local colonial economy. However, editors of the Victoria press chose not to celebrate this employment and therefore offered no commentary on the benefits of Aboriginal trade, labour, and agricultural production. De Cosmos's description of "their habits of indolence, roaming propensities, and natural repugnance for manual labor" were not only lies that masked the actual working lives of local Aboriginal persons but also a form of myth-making regarding the "lazy Indian," the purpose of which was to support segregation. Here we see how racial discourses that influenced the creation of enduring stereotypes originated in conflicts over control of the colonial market.

This lack of consistency regarding the sophistication of First Nations suggests that editors did not believe that their indictments of local First Nations would negatively affect either their local standing or metropolitan perceptions of the colony. Again, this is in marked contrast to the consistent characterizations of Maori during the Taranaki War. The image of the wretched Indian appears to have had purchase in Victoria, perhaps as a consequence of the large number of North American settlers. Had Victorian editors conceptualized a metropolitan readership within their imagined audiences, it is possible that they would have been more consistent in characterizing local First Nations within an idealized humanitarian framework. That they felt no compunction to do so suggests both the isolated position of the Victoria press within imperial press networks and a unique variant of humanitarianism among Victoria's colonists.

Racial Segregation and a Sustainable Press

The unanimous support of editors for the racial segregation of Victoria is best understood as a quest to achieve a community organized for the sole benefit of its white residents. Not incidentally, the removal of First Nations people was linked to the establishment of a more sustainable press environment. The short-lived nature of many newspapers during this period is a tangible illustration of how local economic conditions affected the press. It is not surprising, then, that local editors were advocates of those particular forms of colonial development that would benefit their business concerns. This vision was exclusive, and it characterized Aboriginal workers as a problem rather than as a solution to the community's economic woes. For example, several editors associated local First Nations with a surplus of cheap labour.[80] The *British Colonist* reported that the common wage for Victoria colonists in 1861 was three dollars per day, with skilled workers receiving four to five dollars per day.[81] Aboriginal labourers, though, were apparently satisfied with fifty cents per day or twenty dollars per month.[82] Yet, instead of emphasizing the benefits of Aboriginal labour to people with capital, editors associated local First Nations with the depression of local wages. As the second *Victoria Gazette* explained in 1860:

> Among the many drawbacks from which our Colony suffers, is that of the superabundance of Indian labor, to the extent of almost entirely excluding the white working man, or unskilled labourer. That this is a serious evil, most persons, on reflection, will admit – but an apparent benefit is also mixed up with it, that many persons are deceived, and still more, influenced by actual business transactions – consider it an advantage ... We will admit that the Indians, male and female, spend a great deal of money among us, and spend it freely, that many traders among us realize very large profits from their dealings with the Indians – indeed it is stated that one street in our town is almost entirely supported by them. But where does this money come from – the Indians are not producers, fur and oil, to a comparatively limited extent, are almost their sole articles of barter. The money they spend, is all derived originally from the white man – for hewing wood and drawing water, carrying burthens, and all the course [*sic*] heavy work required by us – and some stealing not required – the small wages demanded by them, entirely underbids the white man; simply because the Indian requires inferior feeding, clothing and lodging.[83]

According to this rationale, local First Nations impeded local Euro-American colonists from gaining employment and a living wage. They also failed to contribute to community life. Indeed, this is the same critique that would be later mobilized against the Chinese residents of British Columbia. Eviction had a dual purpose: it would eliminate the community's social disorder and it would reform the labour market. By removing a class of labourers willing to work for less, local colonists and failed prospectors would be hired and wages would go up. This economic rationale also undergirded the efforts of the Victoria press in 1862, when local editors demanded the eviction of Victoria's Aboriginal population due to concerns over the contagion of smallpox. As *The Press* explained at the time: "The wholesale ejection of man, woman, and child, will effect, no doubt, a marked moral change in the state of the town; and further, as even those hitherto employed and permitted to remain are now imperatively told to depart, a new demand in the labour market will arise, which can but conduce to the permanent benefits of the colony."[84]

Editors of the Victoria press identified themselves as advocates of local Euro-Americans with limited means – failed prospectors and potential colonists who were struggling to survive in Victoria. These were the people who had initially flooded the region after 1858, and, as they left the depressed community, the market for local papers shrank. Not only did the presence of local First Nations impede Euro-American settlement but, most import-ant, editors and newspaper owners did not conceptualize local First Nations as interested consumers of the press or as being aware of their editorial manifestos. While press records do not allude to the existence of Aboriginal readers, one can be all but certain that local First Nations would have been aware of the press's content, given the long legacy of schooling in HBC communities on the Northwest Coast and the close ties between both Aborig-inal and Euro-American residents of Victoria. Certainly, the leader of the Lekwungen people – Chee-al-thuc, or King Freezy – was aware of efforts to achieve Victoria's racial segregation, and he complained about the pres-ence of northern First Nations in Victoria.[85] However, while Douglas did periodically order some northern First Nations people from Victoria between 1858 and 1862, he never gave in to editors' demands to remove all the com-munity's Aboriginal residents. Only in 1862, in the midst of smallpox, did something like this occur.

Smallpox and the Press, 1862

The smallpox epidemic that occurred in Victoria in 1862 was the fifth, if not the sixth, smallpox epidemic to occur on the Northwest Coast since the arrival of European newcomers in the late eighteenth century.[86] Robert Boyd argues that, in the first hundred years following European contact, the Aboriginal population of the Northwest Coast declined by 80 percent, or about 150,000 people, "largely [as a] result of mortality from introduced diseases."[87] Estimates of the total mortality rate in 1862 vary between fourteen thousand and twenty thousand Aboriginal people.[88] However, this high rate of Aboriginal mortality was avoidable. Smallpox was the best-known disease of the nineteenth century.[89] Effective vaccination technology developed by Edward Jenner at the end of the eighteenth century was in general use in Victoria, and several Euro-American missionaries successfully employed vaccination on the Northwest Coast.[90] But Victoria offered neither a comprehensive vaccination campaign nor a strict quarantine to protect local Aboriginal peoples.

The *British Colonist* reported the first case of smallpox on 19 March 1862, apparently brought by a steamer passenger from San Francisco.[91] Just over a week later, both the *British Colonist* and *The Press* called for local authorities to establish a quarantine and to take sanitary measures to impede contagion.[92] The *British Colonist* writer drew a connection between the risk of an epidemic and local First Nations:

> Imagine for a moment what a fearful calamity it would be, were the horde of Indians on the outskirts of town to take the disease. Their filthy habits would only perpetuate the evil; keep it alive in the community, sacrificing the lives of all classes. We have no wish to be an alarmist; but we believe there is danger, and great danger if the smallpox be allowed to spread through the neglect of the authorities.[93]

Here we see a clear recognition of the vulnerability of First Nations to smallpox and the related argument that this vulnerability posed a threat to local colonists. As Perry emphasizes, characterizations of the predisposition of First Nations to vice, poor hygiene, and unsanitary living conditions all fed the editors' anxiety regarding the susceptibility of Aboriginal persons to disease.

Transcripts from the local Legislative Assembly reveal that representatives discussed the topic of smallpox twice.[94] On 28 March 1862, the Legislative Assembly session opened with a message from Douglas that detailed his strong recommendation that four hundred pounds be designated to construct a building in which to isolate those infected with smallpox and thereby prevent the spread of disease.[95] In the following session, on 1 April 1862, this recommendation was debated and ultimately supported. Within the debate, though, Dr. John Sebastian Helmcken "deprecated the tone of the message, as creating unnecessary alarm, arguing that £400 was insufficient to build a hospital and that he did not believe in compelling patients to enter such an establishment."[96] Alternatively, a Mr. Burnaby suggested that a quarantine should be established within Victoria, but this recommendation was deemed too expensive. Of key importance to the representatives was that the liberty of colonists not be infringed. The topic was not raised again.

Even without a comprehensive smallpox strategy, Douglas and Helmcken did act to protect some local First Nations. Helmcken had lived in Victoria since 1850 and worked as a physician for the HBC. Thus, his blasé attitude in the Legislative Assembly is puzzling, as he must have experienced Victoria's earlier smallpox epidemic in 1852–53.[97] On 26 March 1862, Douglas summoned the principal leaders of the various First Nations living in proximity to Victoria and described the necessity of vaccination.[98] *The Press* reported that, on the following day, Helmcken vaccinated thirty Aboriginal persons, including the Lekwungen leader Chee-al-thuc and his family.[99] According to a newspaper report: "It was pretty hard at first to convince them of the benefit from this very simple operation, but after a while they were made to believe that the threatened sickness, the small-pox was far worse than their great enemy, the measles."[100]

A subsequent *British Colonist* article on 26 April 1862 said that Helmcken had vaccinated five hundred Aboriginal persons since smallpox had appeared.[101] It would seem that the majority of these were local Lekwungen as Helmcken's memoir records that he vaccinated most Lekwungen in 1862.[102] It is unlikely that many northern First Nations people were vaccinated. This conclusion is supported by the reminiscences of Reverend A.C. Garrett, a Society for the Propagation of the Gospel (SPG) missionary, who said that most Aboriginal persons in Victoria refused to be vaccinated.[103] Lekwungen people survived the 1862 smallpox epidemic with little loss of life, and it is possible that their amenability to vaccination stemmed from their prior experience with the procedure.[104]

Smallpox spread like wildfire in the absence of quarantine or preventative vaccination.[105] By the end of April 1862, local First Nations were experiencing considerable mortality, with possibly one thousand to twelve hundred Aboriginal persons dying from smallpox in Victoria.[106] In a letter to the editor of *The Press*, "A Father" attacked the colonial administration for allowing "the putrid bodies of the Indians who lately died with small-pox, to rot in the noon-day sun, without making the least effort to have them interred."[107] Local colonists were clearly privy to the devastation. On 26 April 1862, Reverend Garrett met with Police Commissioner Pemberton and attempted to enlist the Victoria Police Department to bury deceased Aboriginal victims of smallpox.[108] Pemberton refused. According to Garrett's account of smallpox's "fearful ravages," 10 percent of local Ts'msyen had already died or were "hopelessly ill."[109] While failing to garner assistance, Garrett's report galvanized the press.

On 28 April 1862, both the *British Colonist* and *The Press* called on the colonial administration to remove Victoria's Aboriginal population as a safety measure to protect colonists.[110] It was argued that Aboriginal access to Victoria threatened all colonists.[111] The *British Colonist* also castigated Pemberton for refusing to evict northern First Nations simply because Douglas was not in Victoria to authorize doing so.[112] Then, that same day, Pemberton gave local Ts'msyen people twenty-four hours to leave Victoria. This was clearly a direct response to the press as Pemberton was hypersensitive to public criticism. To Douglas's chagrin, in 1858 Pemberton had publicly disputed an attack by the *British Colonist* and, in 1861, had privately contested an attack by *The Press*.[113] On 30 April 1862, the Victoria Police Department evicted local Ts'msyen, burning down their village under the gun sights of a British warship that had been requisitioned to support the action.[114] On the same day, local Lekwungen voluntarily left Victoria to a self-imposed quarantine on nearby Discovery Island.[115] In addition, Pemberton ordered all Aboriginal persons not living in Victoria inside colonists' homes to relocate to the Lekwungen reserve across Victoria Harbour.[116] Later, Pemberton instituted a certificate system that allowed only the Aboriginal spouses and employees of Euro-Americans to stay in Victoria.[117]

Further evictions of northern First Nations then occurred on 12 May 1862, and all the Aboriginal homes on the reserve were burned to the ground on 13 May 1862.[118] Between mid-May and June, Victoria police officers, supported by a British gunboat, twice more evicted northern First Nations from camps located close to Victoria – at Esquimalt, Ogden Point, and Cadboro Bay.[119] These police actions effectively spread smallpox all along the Northwest Coast as refugees sought the shelter of their former homes. The tragedy of 1862 was twofold: (1) limited efforts were made to aid sick and dying northern First Nations people in Victoria and (2) editors demanded their eviction knowing full well what effect this would have on First Nations across the region. This may not have been an act of premeditated genocide, but certainly both McClure and De Cosmos shared responsibility for this disaster.[120]

Conclusion

> How the mighty have fallen! Four short years ago, numbering their braves
> by thousands, they were the scourge and terror of the coast; today, broken-
> spirited and effeminate, with scarce a corporal's guard of warriors remain-
> ing alive, they are proceeding northward bearing with them the seeds of
> a loathsome disease that will take root and bring a plentiful crop of ruin
> and destruction to the friends who have remained at home.[121]

As this opening passage acknowledges, the eviction of northern First Nations
people from Victoria in 1862 marked the end of an era. While northern
First Nations never ceased visiting the community, they did so in much
reduced numbers. While newspaper editors still occasionally demanded
that local Lekwungen people be evicted from their valuable reserve, there
was no longer any reason to demand that northern First Nations be removed
or barred from participating in the local economy.[122]

The forced removal of First Nations people from Victoria was not a new
practice in 1862; rather, it was the customary strategy employed by Douglas
and his lieutenants to mitigate the threat of violence by sojourning northern
First Nations. However, in the midst of smallpox, eviction occurred on a
more comprehensive scale than ever before and more closely resembled what
the Victoria press had campaigned for all along. For over five years, editors
had reported First Nations-related fatal violence to emphasize the threat of
an outbreak of war between colonists and First Nations peoples. At the same
time, editors argued that First Nations peoples would benefit from being
relocated far from the vice of local colonists. These appeals fell upon deaf
ears until a moment of crisis in 1862, when the threat of contagion prompted
Pemberton to take action. And, while many northern First Nations people
were sick when they were forced to leave, Pemberton continued to treat
them as military threats. Eviction was a coercive act, implemented with
both police and naval forces.

Discourses of Aboriginal social disorder and violence were central to the
press's campaign for eviction. Yet, in these discourses of Aboriginal violence, editors did not draw on examples of Indigenous violence from other
regions of the British Empire. The Indian Rebellion, for example, did not
provide a framework or a justification for editors' concerns regarding the
threat of war posed by local First Nations. I consider this in more detail in
Chapter 4, when I discuss the Victoria press's support for the recognition

of Aboriginal title and examine the repercussions of continued Aboriginal violence on the Northwest Coast as well as news about the Maori war in New Zealand after 1862.

Likewise, there is no evidence that editors conceptualized metropolitan Britons within their community of imagined readers. Local newspapers were located within wider circuits of information transmission as editors paid attention to and published international news, especially that providing information about the region. But they did so as passive recipients rather than as active agents forwarding local news that they knew would be of interest in the metropolis. Evidence for this conclusion may be found in the fact that the editors of the Victoria press did not reflect upon a metropolitan audience and were inconsistent in their characterizations of First Nations. Unlike New Zealand's newspapers, Vancouver Island's newspapers did not articulate any anxiety regarding metropolitan misinterpretations of their editorial perspectives. Local imperatives, particularly the drive to reorient the community for the sole benefit of its Euro-American residents, are what influenced editorial characterizations of First Nations. And, as we see in Chapter 4, this pursuit of the local settler project could also prompt editors to champion the property rights of Aboriginal people.

3
New Zealand's Humanitarian Extremes

A RUMOUR REACHED New Plymouth, Taranaki, on 21 April 1860 that terrified local colonists. Brought from Auckland by ship, the news warned of the suspension of British military operations in Taranaki. Apparently, the Anglican bishop of New Zealand, George Augustus Selwyn, had convinced Governor Thomas Gore Browne of the Taranaki War's injustice. This was an about-face. Just a month before, Colonel Charles Gold had followed Browne's orders and attacked the *pa* (Maori fortification) of Wiremu Kingi Te Rangitake to quash the resistance of some members of the Te Ati Awa *iwi* to the sale of the Waitara Block to the Crown. When Garland Woon, the owner and editor of the *Taranaki Herald*, learned of the rumour, he published a second edition immediately, as the weekly paper had just gone to press.

According to Woon, the rumour was "ABSOLUTELY INCREDIBLE," if true a "PUBLIC CALAMITY."[1] Woon urged colonists to "be tranquil." But according to Jane Maria Atkinson, a prominent New Plymouth colonist and sister of Native Secretary C.W. Richmond, the rumour "threw the place into ... the depths of despondency ... that the Gov was completely converted to Bishop Selwyn's views and that a most ignominious peace would be concluded."[2] Fortunately for the worried colonists, the rumour was untrue. Nevertheless, its initial credibility indicates the degree to which colonists feared both Selwyn's influence and the possibility that Browne might weaken his commitment to enforce the Waitara purchase. Given the overwhelming support for the Taranaki War in New Plymouth, one would expect the

Figure 7 Colonial New Zealand

Taranaki Herald to have then published a fierce anti-humanitarian diatribe against Selwyn. Yet this did not occur.

Following the panic, the *Taranaki Herald* published a series of articles that critiqued Selwyn's opposition but that did so by justifying the Taranaki War as the best means of civilizing Maori.[3] Alongside the objection that Selwyn favoured Maori interests over those of colonists, the *Taranaki Herald* charged that the bid of Selwyn and other "ultra-missionaries" to "arrest the rapid decline of the Maori race" through isolation was "fraught with disaster."[4] Drawing on a stadial understanding of European historical development, the *Taranaki Herald* writer emphasized that the antecedents of the "Old World" had not progressed in isolation, nor would Maori become civilized without "toil, and struggle, and subjection." Here the *Herald* stresses the benefits of British hegemony. The successful prosecution of the Taranaki War would once and for all achieve British dominance, thereby compelling Maori to embrace all aspects of British culture.

> It is because we cannot help regarding the Maori race as fellow-men, because some of them are closer to us even than that word implies, that we would desire to see, without a day's useless delay, the British flag on every pa through the islands; British steamships in every creek, – British towns from north to south, and let us add churches where the English tongue is heard, near every stream, lake, and hill, of this beautiful land.[5]

This was a secular vision of Maori civilization couched in the language of rhetorical humanitarianism. But why did the editor of the *Taranaki Herald* emphasize the benefits of the Taranaki War for Maori rather than for colonists?

Although a culture of anonymity was central to mid-nineteenth-century journalism, it is possible to identify the author of these articles: James Crowe Richmond, a prominent New Plymouth colonist and member of the local Provincial Council.[6] In correspondence with his wife, Maria Richmond, on 12 May 1860, James Crowe explained: "[I wrote] some long winded articles in the *Herald* of the 5th and preceding week on the Bishop ... I feel great regret at my inability to do justice to our case, for we need help from the English press if our present losses do not issue in a satisfactory arrangement."[7] He commented separately to his brother, the Native secretary: "We feel intense anxiety about the issue of the missionary efforts ... I do not wish to revile them but they have sadly wronged their clients and their countrymen."[8]

Richmond's correspondence reveals both the degree of his anxiety regarding the threat of Selwyn's criticism of the Taranaki War and his hope that his own articles might influence the "English press." Richmond's vision for civilizing Maori was crafted as a counterpoint to Selwyn's position. His intention was to enlist the support of a metropolitan audience by evidencing the concern of colonists for Maori welfare. Richmond's comments reveal the centrality of humanitarian discourses to competing interpretations of the Taranaki War and show how even a provincial newspaper like the *Taranaki Herald* was thought to have resonance in Great Britain.

This chapter examines two significant newspapers from 1855 to 1862: New Plymouth's *Taranaki Herald* and the Crown's bilingual publication *Te Karere Maori*, or the *Maori Messenger*. Sited at the epicentre of the Taranaki War, the *Taranaki Herald* provided authoritative first-hand accounts of the conflict that shaped subsequent understandings of it across New Zealand, Australia, and Great Britain. It defined the Taranaki War as a defence of Maori rights and championed the secular administration of Maori. *Te Karere Maori* functions as a natural counterpoint to the *Taranaki Herald* by articulating the Crown's vision of settler relations with Maori. *Te Karere Maori* was crafted for a Maori audience and employed the language of Christian brotherhood to persuade Maori readers to transform their culture through the process of racial amalgamation. Humanitarian racial discourses were central to both newspapers but for very different reasons and with very different imagined audiences. The first part of this chapter follows the evolution of the *Taranaki Herald*'s wartime manifesto from before the Taranaki War to its end, while the second part examines *Te Karere Maori*'s prewar editorial manifesto and its interpretation of the origins of the Taranaki War.

Taranaki: "The Sore Place of the Colony"

It was no surprise when war broke out in Taranaki. Henry Sewell, a member of the New Zealand House of Representatives, described the province as literally "the sore place of the Colony."[9] Taranaki had been marred by contention between settlers and Maori since New Zealand's inception. These tensions originated, in part, from the long-lasting effects of the inter-*iwi* Musket Wars of the 1830s. As discussed in Chapter 1, following Cook's voyages in the Pacific at the end of the eighteenth century, New Zealand had become a station for European and American whalers. These maritime visitors carried on a vigorous trade in muskets, transforming what had been

Figure 8 New Plymouth, ca. 1860. Tinted lithograph (John Gully, 1819?-88), Alexander Turnbull Library, Wellington, NZ, B-051-015

localized inter-*iwi* conflicts into large-scale wars that ranged across both the North Island and the South Island of New Zealand. The Taranaki region was particularly devastated. In the 1820s and early 1830s, successive invasions by Waikato Maori from the central North Island displaced most of the local Te Ati Awa population and subsequently complicated the New Zealand Company's attempts to purchase land in 1840.[10] Indeed, the NZC agent Colonel William Wakefield controversially purchased vast territories in Taranaki from multiple sellers, including from the Waikato Maori who had driven the Te Ati Awa people from their homes.

In 1844, New Zealand's second governor, Robert Fitzroy, stoked the anger of local settlers when he concurred with George Clarke Sr., the chief protector of Aborigines, that the NZC had not negotiated with the rightful Maori landowners in Taranaki. Here Fitzroy overturned the ruling of Commissioner William Spain, who had recognized the NZC's claims. In the end, colonists lost access to sixty thousand acres of Maori land, including the highly sought after Waitara district, where settlers had originally wished to establish themselves. This legacy of violence, displacement, and controversy haunted settler relations with Maori and then, in 1860–61, framed debates over the Taranaki War's legitimacy.

So during the 1850s, while other North Island provinces like Auckland and Wellington purchased hundreds of thousands of acres of Maori territory, no similar large-scale land sales occurred in Taranaki.[11] Colonists in New Plymouth felt hemmed in. Their bitterness stemmed from their belief that the majority of Maori territory had been laid to waste, left unused and unsold, for selfish reasons.[12] Historian Hazel Petrie also argues that settlers in New Plymouth were jealous of the agricultural successes of Te Ati Awa people at Waitara.[13] At the same time, settlers endured periodic episodes of Maori violence following the return of local Te Ati Awa to their customary territories in the late 1840s. These disagreements over a series of land sales with settlers pitted rival Te Ati Awa *hapu* groups against each other. Worth recognizing here is the fact that Maori *hapu* and *iwi* held the rights, or *mana*, of the land collectively. Individual Maori could receive, use, and pass on land rights as an inheritance, but these rights were subject to collective authority. Land sales to the Crown, then, depended upon the difficult task of achieving the consensus of Maori kin groups. During Te Ati Awa conflicts, and especially in 1858, colonists appealed to Browne for military intervention.[14] These requests were not supported. As Browne remarked to C.W. Richmond in 1858, "the people at Taranaki appear to think we have the power and means of protecting them which we really do not possess."[15] During this period, British sovereignty did not extend beyond the town limits of the many scattered British communities.[16]

In March 1859, though, Browne shifted away from non-engagement. Meeting first with Taranaki Maori leaders on 8 March, Browne addressed the issues of local crime and land sales. Regarding Maori crime, Browne stated that he was "determined that the peace of the settlers should no longer be disturbed by evil-doers."[17] Turning to the topic of land, Browne encouraged his Maori listeners to sell their surplus lands, stating that "he would never consent to buy land without an undisputed title. He would not permit any one to interfere in the sale of land, unless he owned part of it." In response, Te Teira Manuka, a local leader of the Puke Kowhatu *hapu* of Te Ati Awa, offered to sell his lands at Waitara. However, another, more pre-eminent, Te Ati Awa leader named Wiremu Kingi Te Rangitake stated: "Listen, Governor. Notwithstanding Teira's offer I will not permit the sale of Waitara to the Pakeha. Waitara is in my hands, I will not give it up." Te Rangitake was a leader of great influence and authority who had previously supported the Crown but who was committed to maintaining control over the customary territory of the Te Ati Awa *iwi*. Following this statement, Te Rangitake abruptly walked out of the public meeting with his followers, leaving Browne to tentatively accept Te Teira's offer pending an investigation.

Browne immediately recognized the significance of Te Teira's offer. In a despatch to the duke of Newcastle on 29 March 1859, he described the situation in detail, remarking that there seemed to be little doubt regarding Te Teira's right to Waitara and that he was committed to defend the land purchase in the face of likely violent opposition because "any recognition of such a power as that assumed by William King [Te Rangitake] would ... be unjust to both races, because it would be the means of keeping millions of acres waste and out of cultivation."[18] As Te Rangitake continued his opposition over the course of 1859 and early 1860, the stage was set for a confrontation defined by Browne's perceived defence of the rights of both colonists and Maori.

The *Taranaki Herald*

James Richmond trusted that the *Taranaki Herald* could shape views of the Taranaki War abroad. This faith took for granted the existence of a communications infrastructure that would transport newspapers from New Zealand across the British Empire and that British readers were keenly interested in the colony's affairs. Not only did ship captains carry newspaper packets from port to port but British citizens also sent volumes of newspapers across the Empire via a cheap postal service. As the Introduction's opening vignette shows, there was significant public interest in narratives of colonial violence in the mid-nineteenth century. Following the outbreak of the Taranaki War, newspaper accounts of the conflict were republished across the anglophone world. Through its provision of in-depth coverage and on-the-scene commentary, the *Taranaki Herald* was the most influential voice in shaping public debate over the Taranaki conflict.

Founded in 1852 by Garland Woon, the *Taranaki Herald* was New Plymouth's first paper and was published weekly. Like other New Zealand communities, as it grew New Plymouth garnered additional newspapers, each of which articulated opposing political perspectives. Charles Brown and Richard Pheney initiated New Plymouth's second paper, the *Taranaki News*, in 1857 when the *Taranaki Herald* switched its political allegiance from Superintendent Charles Brown to his electoral challenger, George Cutfield. Brown had been the incumbent during the 1857 election for Taranaki superintendent, and he was subsequently defeated by Cutfield. Pheney, the editor of the *Taranaki Herald* at the time of its political about-face, was dismissed for his protest over the editorial change. According to J.S. Tullett, the operations of the *Taranaki News* were plagued with difficulties.[19] The *Taranaki Herald* was the more popular of the two papers. This is corroborated by the fact that newspapers across New Zealand, the Australian colonies, and Great Britain carried more extracts from the *Taranaki Herald* than they did from the *Taranaki News*.

One of my central premises is that colonial newspapers were popular forums for the exchange of ideas and information and that they captured cross-class interest. Available records of newspaper circulation provide evidence of the popularity of the *Taranaki Herald*. In 1862, it published five hundred copies of its weekly edition, or one newspaper for every two colonists over the age of eighteen.[20] The paper's prewar circulation was likely very similar as Taranaki's population of European descent was slightly larger prior to the war: 2,650 colonists in 1858 versus 2,211 in 1862.[21] This being the case, in 1858, the *Taranaki Herald* would have published one newspaper for every 2.5 colonists eighteen years of age and over, which is to say that it would have had a circulation rate of 40 percent.[22] Another way to measure the *Taranaki Herald*'s saturation is to compare its circulation rate to the number of households in Taranaki (newspapers were most likely consumed by family units rather than by individuals). According to this measure, the *Taranaki Herald* published sufficient copies for 74 percent of households in Taranaki.[23] Cumulatively, these measures attest to the *Taranaki Herald*'s ready availability in New Plymouth and suggest that its consumption was not limited to a small elite readership. Of course, this assessment does not include the circulation of the *Taranaki News*, which indicates that, in combination, New Plymouth's two papers saturated the available market.

The circulation of the *Taranaki Herald* increased to one thousand copies per week following the outbreak of violence, buoyed by the influx of several thousand British troops and the market for war news abroad.[24] Postal records illustrate this demand. In 1860, New Plymouth's post office despatched roughly double the number of newspapers that it had the previous year: 21,549 in 1860 versus 10,720 in 1859.[25] In 1860 alone, 8,070 newspapers were mailed to Great Britain, 2,789 to the Australian colonies, and 10,529 to other parts of New Zealand.[26] This increased transmission continued in 1862 but fell away slightly with the end of the Taranaki War.[27] Given the fact that the *Taranaki Herald*'s wartime articles dominated the coverage of the Taranaki War in New Zealand and Australian newspapers, it seems likely that a larger percentage of newspapers despatched from New Plymouth were editions of the *Taranaki Herald* rather than the *Taranaki News*. If the *Taranaki Herald* published fifty-two thousand newspapers in 1860, it is possible that up to 38 percent of its production was forwarded to non-local readers.[28] Not only were thousands of copies of the paper sent directly to Great Britain, but the reach of the *Taranaki Herald* was amplified as newspapers across New Zealand and the anglophone world reproduced its editorial manifesto in toto.

British Sovereignty and Maori Rights

The central tenets of the *Taranaki Herald*'s wartime manifesto originated during the long delay between Te Teira's offer to sell the Waitara Block in March 1859 and the outbreak of war in early 1860. During this period, the *Taranaki Herald* published a series of leading articles urging Thomas Gore Browne to complete the purchase of the Waitara Block.[29] These articles reveal an evolving interpretation of the Waitara purchase's importance as frustration built in New Plymouth. The *Taranaki Herald*'s first article, published in September 1859, noted that five months had passed with nothing being accomplished and that a critical opportunity was being lost.[30] Again in October 1859, the *Taranaki Herald* reiterated that the Crown's procrastination was dangerous.[31] However, for the first time, the *Taranaki Herald* also addressed the topic of Maori opposition, commenting: "The opposition in the present instance is influenced by factious motives alone, not from any legitimate claim to the land which they have dared the Governor to pay for, and their opposition can only become dangerous from the extraordinary delay that is taking place."[32] By 3 December 1859, the *Taranaki Herald*'s description of this opposition's significance had escalated:

> The question then was not one of mere local interest – the purchase of
> a few hundred acres of land in a district from which the settlers were
> unrighteously expelled by a former Governor, but was to be judged of by

the influence it promised to exercise on our future relations with the Natives throughout the island. As such it was watched by them far and near, and even emissaries of Potatau were busily engaged in it.[33]

Here the editor of the *Taranaki Herald* is alluding to Potatau Te Whero-whero, the monarch of the Kingitanga, who was said to be closely observing events in Taranaki. The Kingitanga was a Maori political movement that had elected its own king in 1858 as a symbol of its commitment to end land sales with the Crown and to implement an alternative code of laws. The Kingitanga was centred in the Waikato region just south of Auckland and northeast of Taranaki. Prior to the Taranaki War, colonists in New Zealand were divided over whether the Kingitanga represented a threat to British sovereignty or whether it was a well-intentioned attempt by Maori to implement a form of self-government that the Crown had failed to provide.[34] From 1858, Browne had chosen not to confront the Kingitanga directly, hoping that it would dissipate over time.[35] The *Taranaki Herald* called attention to the Kingitanga's interest in the Waitara purchase to elicit the concern of colonists across New Zealand who were alarmed by the movement's growing influence.[36] While the *Taranaki Herald* did not accuse Te Rangitake of being an agent of the Kingitanga, this allusion associated the Waitara purchase with a worrying trend – the increasing opposition of Maori to land sales across the North Island. This strategy also sought to weaken Browne's ability to renege on his pledge to support land sales in Taranaki. Interestingly, when the Taranaki War began, in his correspondence with the Colonial Office Browne also linked Te Rangitake's resistance with the Kingitanga. Did Browne imitate the *Taranaki Herald* or was it the other way round?

Certainly, the Crown's non-interference during local Maori inter-*iwi* conflicts of the late 1850s provided the context for the *Herald*'s campaign. Prior to the Waitara purchase, New Plymouth colonists had rightly perceived that the Crown's local non-interference had stemmed from the fear of "the old bugbear of Native war."[37] Indeed, the British had fought a war on the North Island in 1845–46 against several Ngapuhi *hapu* that had featured several battlefield defeats for the British military. In this period Taranaki colonists believed that their province had been sacrificed to maintain peace across New Zealand. What we must recognize, too, is that the *Taranaki Herald*'s evolving characterization of the Waitara purchase's importance occurred alongside the growing realization among local colonists that armed conflict would result if the Crown enforced the Waitara purchase.[38] While the initiation of the Taranaki War surprised many across New Zealand, colonists in New Plymouth had spent the preceding months in defensive preparations, which, in turn, escalated already troubled relations with local Maori by giving the impression that colonists desired war.[39] In a way they did, believing that the sharp use of British military force would achieve their aims.

So well before British rockets and artillery bombarded Te Rangitake's Te Kohia *pa* on 17 March 1860, the *Taranaki Herald* had associated the Waitara purchase with the issue of British sovereignty throughout New Zealand. Editorials published just prior to the initiation of hostilities were repeatedly emphatic. On 18 February 1860, the *Taranaki Herald* proclaimed: "The natives do not claim the land in question, but they deny the right or power of the owners to dispose of it. They, in fact, assume sovereignty over the land!"[40] Again Woon wrote in the following week's editorial on 25 February 1860: "The completion of the purchase of a comparatively small portion of land at Waitara opens up the question of the Queen's sovereignty over the colony, the opponents of the sale denying, in fact, not only this, but the right to pre-emption, both of which are secured to Her Majesty by the treaty of Waitangi."[41] Te Rangitake was symbolically defying Queen Victoria and breaching the Treaty of Waitangi. He could not be ignored.

The irony of this argument, of course, is that many colonists in New Plymouth despised the Treaty of Waitangi and resented how the recognition of Maori ownership to all the territory of New Zealand in 1840 had thwarted the NZC. The emphasis on British sovereignty and Maori rights veiled local colonists' long-standing desire to secure Waitara and appealed to an audience ignorant of the actual situation in Taranaki. The language of sovereignty was also attractive because it affirmed Browne's original pledge to protect the rights of local Maori, thereby aligning editorial sentiment with official policy, and justified the use of military force against Maori "rebels." The *Taranaki Herald* was well aware of both Browne's humanitarian pledges and his instructions from the Colonial Office to govern New Zealand in a manner that respected the rights of both colonists and Maori as British subjects. Indeed, as we see in Chapter 6, the evangelical humanitarian critics who assailed Browne's policy during the Taranaki War had formerly been his greatest allies. Browne saw through this rhetorical humanitarianism, though, stating that, in New Plymouth: "The settlers and their newspapers are determined to get up a war if they can."[42] Yes, yes they were. But, as we see in both Chapter 5 and Chapter 7, the *Taranaki Herald* was surprisingly effective in shaping initial understandings of the Taranaki War in the nearby community of Auckland, the Australian colonies, and Great Britain. The paper's provision of local knowledge carried weight in a press environment that lacked an adequate interpretive context, and its justification of the Taranaki War as a defence of Maori rights seemed honourable. This editorial manifesto might have carried the day had the war ended quickly.

Instead, New Plymouth colonists experienced the Taranaki War as a prolonged series of disasters.[43] Following the initiation of hostilities, local colonists spent the war confined to New Plymouth under a state of siege.[44] Between March 1860 and April 1861, settlers witnessed the devastation of outlying homes and fields.[45] Worse yet, the British military never achieved a decisive victory.[46] In early 1861, the Taranaki War sputtered to a close with a ceasefire negotiated by Native Secretary Donald McLean and Kingitanga leader Wiremu Tamihana Tarapipipi Te Waharoa. It may be that Browne supported the ceasefire because of his anxiety over Auckland's safety.[47] In March 1861, McLean had warned Browne that the majority of North Island Maori were in "a state of disaffection" and that the Kingitanga was actively planning an assault on Auckland.[48] Indeed, historian James Belich argues that the Taranaki War's conclusion in a military stalemate constituted a British defeat. Even if this assessment is too strong, it is certainly true that colonists had expected better.[49] The British military's inability to achieve a quick and decisive victory was extremely disheartening.

Thus, throughout the war, the *Taranaki Herald* responded to repeated crises. An analysis of its wartime manifesto reveals a constant tension, with the Crown's policies being continually debated and the *Taranaki Herald*'s own limited endorsement of humanitarian racial discourses being stretched to its limits. One such crisis occurred at the end of April 1860, when Browne suspended military operations in Taranaki pending the results of a conference of Maori leaders held at Kohimarama, near Auckland, in July 1860. The intention of the conference was to gather the support of influential Maori *rangatira*, thereby isolating Te Rangitake and preventing the outbreak of a general war.[50] But the *Taranaki Herald* attacked the very notion "that an assembly of semi-savages should furnish by their deliberations a key to our difficulty. New Zealand chiefs have but very rudimentary notions of political and social organization ... Utterly ignorant of history, how should they help us to meet a condition of things quite out of their experience."[51] Explicitly, this critique claimed that the primitive state of Maori culture, and even a lack of history, rendered Maori leaders incapable of facilitating any resolution in Taranaki. But what warranted this attack?

Here it is important to highlight the anxiety underlying this position. The editor of the *Taranaki Herald* feared a hidden motive behind the conference at Kohimarama: "To return to the July meeting, it is not possible to disguise the fear, that the interpretation of its object above suggested, is not the true one."[52] Colonists in New Plymouth worried that Browne might utilize the conference to negotiate with Te Rangitake through a third party. This possibility evoked the danger of Browne assuming a pattern of Maori administration that had characterized former governor Sir George Grey's "undignified, short-sighted, deceitful system."[53] To the *Taranaki Herald*, Grey had appeased Maori to maintain peace, purchasing loyalty without establishing British sovereignty. We can interpret the *Taranaki Herald*'s assessment of Maori cultural inferiority in light of its broader goal of discrediting any chance at peace making. However, as I show in the following section on *Te Karere Maori*, this attack on Maori cultural sophistication was grounded in the same stadial worldview endorsed by many humanitarians.

In a sense, then, the defeat of British forces at Puketakauere *pa* on 27 June 1860 was a mixed blessing for supporters of the war effort.[54] The battle invigorated Maori insurgents and reaffirmed the need for the force of British arms. Certainly the *Taranaki Herald* asserted that, in light of the defeat, the Kohimarama conference would "prove worse than useless."[55] In New Plymouth, though, the *Taranaki News* reacted to the British loss by libelling Maori as "cruel, untameable, and false."[56] In response, the *Taranaki Herald* commented on both the growing "Maori-phobia" in New Plymouth and the implications of this antagonistic editorial: "A writer so plainly delirious might be left to run his muck, if it concerned only individuals, but a whole race is here libelled, and the settlers at large become implicated in the libel unless it is promptly disavowed." In explicit contrast, the *Taranaki Herald* emphasized that settler perceptions of Maori were essentially positive: "Who has not found the Maoris almost universally docile and obedient laborers? Who has not found them just and honest trades-men?" The real issue that Maori faced was their stubborn refusal to accept the subordination necessary to allow themselves to be civilized: "Civilisation requires subordination, and a collision ensures; but civilisation will never designedly, or with passionate recklessness, 'sweep away every savage from her path.'" Again, the *Taranaki Herald* linked the pursuit of the Taranaki War with its vision of Maori potential. What settlers needed to remember, above all, was that: "To conquer a peace, not a land covered with corpses, is the aim of the good warrior. Let not us who are engaged in this miserable warfare, be guilty of the black sin of quoting 'God and Nature' to lash our passions, always too easily excited; or stimulate indiscriminate suspicions and hate by falsehood and exaggeration."[57]

The *Taranaki Herald*'s swift rebuke of the *Taranaki News* illustrates the careful crafting of its own racial characterizations of Maori. Quite simply, a public "racial libel" besmirched the integrity of all colonists. This is not to say that the *Taranaki Herald* did not advocate harsh measures for rebel Maori. Several times the *Herald* argued that the large-scale confiscation of territory was a suitable punishment for Maori rebellion.[58] Indeed, this form of punishment would later be implemented in 1864 against Waikato Maori. The *Taranaki Herald* was particularly harsh regarding the repercussions for Ngati Ruanui and Taranaki Maori, two *iwi* that had allied themselves with Te Ati Awa and had allegedly murdered civilian colonists without cause.[59] And when peace was reached between the Crown and Te Ati Awa in early 1861, the editor of the *Taranaki Herald* was deeply disappointed by Browne's failure to impose more onerous reparations on Maori combatants.[60] For the *Taranaki Herald*, the war was a "collision between the races" in the sense that it pitted Maori against settlers and represented a critical moment in New Zealand's colonial history. But its characterizations of Maori were defined by cultural difference rather than racial antagonism. The *Taranaki Herald* did not denigrate the Maori race or utilize racial slurs, such as the epithet "nigger," which was in common use among prominent Taranaki colonists.[61] In this way, the editor asserted the righteousness of the Crown's cause.

It is particularly striking that the 1857 Indian Rebellion did not resonate in the *Taranaki Herald* during the Taranaki War. The Indian Rebellion was a global media event, and its narratives were reported across the British Empire and the United States.[62] This is attested to by the fact that 47 percent of the *Taranaki Herald*'s editions between 1857 and 1859 featured extracted articles detailing the events of the Indian Rebellion. No similar event garnered the same publicity during this period. Historian Jill Bender shows how narratives of the Indian Rebellion spread fear and distrust of Indigenous peoples across the British Empire.[63] Certainly, the Indian Rebellion's parallels were not lost on either the *Taranaki Herald*'s editor or local colonists.[64] In February 1858, in the midst of Maori violence and governmental non-interference, the editor of the *Taranaki Herald* raised the spectre of the Indian Rebellion to highlight the threat faced by colonists:

It may be needless, but with the vast and unsuspected Indian rebellion before our eyes, it cannot be out of place to entreat our readers to obey the call to arms promptly. The immediate danger may pass over, and we may in pity be vouch-safed peace by the tribes who deride our authority and power, but we shall continue to be victims to fear and apprehensions discreditable to our race and origin so long as we neglect those means which of themselves command respect, and, if need be, can enforce it.[65]

Here the writer exhorts settlers to volunteer with the local militia, equating local Maori to rebel sepoys in India. What is fascinating, though, is that the *Taranaki Herald* never again invoked the Indian Rebellion – neither during the extended build-up to the war's initiation in 1859 nor during the Taranaki War itself.

But local colonists did. According to William Marjouram, a sergeant in the Royal Artillery stationed in Taranaki, in February 1860 settler anxiety was exacerbated by a belief that the racial atrocities that had defined the Indian Rebellion's ferocity were going to be replicated in Taranaki:

But we are not without a few amongst us who, with despair in their countenances, anticipate the horrors of Cawnpore, and believe that the natives are planning a second Indian revolt. Some foolish person has stated that there is an intention to murder secretly all the white people in Taranaki; and so easily are the fears of some people worked upon, that many believe in the rumour.[66]

Marjouram believed these rumours were groundless. He held Maori in esteem, remarking: "You may safely trust it [i.e., a colonist's child] with any native in New Zealand; they would take as much care of it as you would yourself."[67]

The *Taranaki Herald*'s silence regarding the Indian Rebellion's parallels to the Taranaki War was intentional rather than accidental. Narratives of the Indian Rebellion that had featured in the *Taranaki Herald* from 1857 to 1859 stressed both the savagery of Indian mutineers and the subsequent right-eousness of British vengeance. Alongside descriptions of sepoys' indecent assaults on and massacres of British women and children, the press narrated the execution of thousands of mutineers. No quarter was given, either by mutineers or by the British. It was this racial ferocity, explicit in narratives of the Indian Rebellion, that rendered comparisons unacceptable. Settler relations with Maori in Taranaki were fraught, and any comparison with the Indian Rebellion would only have alienated the colonists' Maori allies, who also paid close attention to the paper's content. Moreover, drawing on the Indian Rebellion's parallels would have contradicted the *Taranaki Herald*'s humanitarian characterization of the Taranaki War. This argument coincides with our knowledge that the *Taranaki Herald* was preoccupied with impressing a metropolitan audience and avoiding the taint of a racial libel.

The self-censorship of the *Taranaki Herald* comes clearly into view when we compare it with the third member of New Plymouth's press, the *Taranaki Punch*. Begun on 31 October 1860 and lasting until 7 August 1861, the *Taranaki Punch* emerged as a wartime paper that documented the experience of local settlers: it parodied the disasters of the Taranaki War in starkly racist illustrations and in verses that referred to Maori as "niggers," "savages," and "murdering wretches."[68] Maori insurgents, British military incompetence, and treasonous missionary humanitarians were all topics of derision. Believed to have been authored by the artist Henry Freer Rawson, the *Taranaki Punch* was published and advertised by the *Taranaki Herald*'s office.[69] Woon's close affiliation with this newspaper prompts several questions. Why did he decry the racial antagonism of the *Taranaki News* but tacitly endorse the *Taranaki Punch*'s racist manifesto? What does the tonal disparity between the *Taranaki Punch* and the *Taranaki Herald* reveal about public opinion in New Plymouth and the purpose of the *Taranaki Herald*'s manifesto?

Audience mattered, and the *Taranaki Punch* had a limited reach. Only the *Taranaki Herald* and *Nelson Examiner* advertised the newspaper, and it merited commentary only in these newspapers and the *Lyttelton Times*.[70] The communities of New Plymouth, Nelson, and Lyttelton all had close ties due to their participation in the systematic colonization schemes implemented by the NZC and the Canterbury Association. The more significant press communities of Auckland and Wellington did not comment on the *Taranaki Punch*, nor does it appear to have resonated in Australian and metropolitan newspapers. But, as the *Lyttelton Times* noted, the *Taranaki Punch* was valuable because "much of the secret history of the campaign [was] disclosed in its facetious sketches and paragraphs."[71] We can draw several conclusions from this commentary. The *Taranaki Punch* accurately reflected colonists' fraught relations with Maori and evangelical humanitarians, satirizing, as it did, the rhetoric of reforming Indigenous peoples by civilizing them. But this crude, hateful, and racist manifesto was only acceptable for local readers.

GOVERNMENT HOUSE COLLOQUY.

B——r S——n.—I admit, your Excellency, that these misguided natives (acting, no doubt, under European influence) have opposed your arms, and have unfortunately, and probably in self-defence shot a few people who foolishly strayed too far from the town, and also made some mistakes respecting the rights of property, but, after all, they are but semi-barbarians, and it is your duty to ——

G——e B——z.—Of course ; I understand ! Let them return to their homes in peace ; withdraw my troops, and throw the settlers on Maori protection ; eh !

B——r S——n.—Precisely so ! with the addition of paying them for the disputed land and the expenses they have been put to during the war.

G——B——p I'll see them d——d first !

[Printed for the Proprietor, at the " Herald " Printing Office, and sold at Mr. Black's, Devon street, New Plymouth, New Zealand.]

Figure 9 "Government House Colloquy," *Taranaki Punch*, 13 March 1861. Puke Ariki, New Plymouth, NZ, ARC2002-538

Indeed, in the *Taranaki Punch*'s edition of 27 February 1861, the *Taranaki Herald* itself assumed symbolic importance. In a cartoon entitled "Government House Colloquy," Bishop Selwyn is portrayed in conversation, attempting to persuade Thomas Gore Browne to withdraw British troops from Taranaki, return the disputed land, and compensate Maori insurgents for their troubles. Behind Selwyn looms a demoniacal Maori shadow. Browne's cartoon character replies: "I'll see them d – d first."[72] I draw attention to this cartoon because of the symbolic props the artist utilizes to highlight the differences between both men's perspectives. The cartoonist depicts Bishop Selwyn holding a copy of *Te Karere Maori*, and below Browne is an edition of the *Taranaki Herald*. Rawson used these two newspapers to symbolize two competing visions for New Zealand and Maori. The *Taranaki Herald* represented settler interests, the fight for British hegemony, and a secular discourse of civilization for Maori, while *Te Karere Maori* embodied Selwyn's misguided idea that settlers needed to be protected from a menacing and evil Maori force. The irony of this cartoon, of course, is that *Te Karere Maori* was published by the government, and its humanitarian manifesto was authorized by Browne.

Te Karere Maori

Te Karere Maori, or the *Maori Messenger*, was a bilingual newspaper published in both *te reo Maori* and English by the Native Department between 1849 and 1863.[73] Its eclectic content included local and international news, government legislation, editorials, announcements of land sales, letters to the editor, and market prices for commodities. The paper aimed "to increase the wealth and encourage the industry of the native people of New Zealand" by encouraging Maori participation in the colonial free market economy through entrepreneurship, wage labour, and the individualization of collectively owned property.[74] In this way, *Te Karere Maori* sought to convince its readers to refashion themselves by putting aside all aspects of their customary culture.[75]

Central to this manifesto was the argument that England's own history offered a template for Maori development. Just as the Anglo-Saxon progenitors of the British Empire were products of racial amalgamation, so, too, it was believed, a similarly desirable process was occurring in New Zealand.[76] Historical narratives, then, functioned as guides for cultural development as well as a means to illustrate the divine attributes of the British Empire and, by extension, the colonial project in New Zealand. An analysis of *Te Karere Maori* offers a way of gauging the distinctiveness of the *Taranaki Herald*'s humanitarian vision for reforming Maori through civilizing them. Moreover, *Te Karere Maori*'s editorial manifesto suggests how Maori were integrated into networks of colonial knowledge in the mid-nineteenth century. Indeed, *Te Karere Maori*'s characterization of the British Empire's providential role in the world sought to correct misinformation prevalent among Maori during this period. This story of rumour and response provides further evidence that the *Taranaki Herald*'s silence regarding the Indian Rebellion's parallels the Taranaki War was not accidental.

In 1849, following his arrival in the colony, Governor George Grey initiated *Te Karere Maori* in order to communicate more effectively with Maori. The paper ceased publication in 1854 with his departure and was then revived with the arrival of Governor Thomas Gore Browne in 1855. Published first as a monthly newspaper, *Te Karere Maori* became a bi-monthly publication in May 1857. Its circulation in 1855 was one thousand copies per monthly edition, but this later fell to five hundred per edition.[77] Given the Crown's 1858 estimate of there being 30,132 Maori over the age of fourteen, a circulation of five hundred newspapers would have equalled one copy per sixty Maori.[78]

This level of circulation was much lower than that of other leading New Zealand papers, and colonists recognized this as an impediment to the paper's effectiveness.[79] In 1859, the editor of Auckland's leading newspaper, the *New Zealander*, noted that the Maori press was "by far the most efficient means" for the Crown to educate Maori but that it published only a single copy for every three hundred Maori readers.[80] However, a combination of factors facilitated the broad circulation of this newspaper, including: high rates of Maori literacy in the mid-1850s, the oral transmission of newspapers within Maori communities, and Maori receptivity to Maori-language publications.[81] Indeed, in 1859, Arthur S. Thompson reported in *The Story of New Zealand* that one-half of adult Maori could read *te reo Maori* and that one-third could both read and write.[82] The Native Department distributed copies of *Te Karere Maori* to prominent Maori *rangatira*, government officials, and missionaries who then shared the newspaper with their communities. *Te Karere Maori*, then, represented an affordable and relatively efficient means for both Grey and Browne to disseminate information to Maori.

The importance of this paper only increased following the outbreak of the Taranaki War in 1860. Memoranda detail that the Native Department increased *Te Karere Maori*'s circulation to one thousand copies per edition following the war's outbreak.[83] This increased circulation appears to have continued throughout the hostilities.[84] Also during the war, the Native Department published the extensive proceedings of the Kohimarama conference, which featured detailed reportage of many Maori leaders' speeches of support for Governor Browne.[85] This was a significant expenditure, and it illustrates the importance that Native Secretary McLean placed in the paper to rally support for the Crown.

Te Karere Maori was also closely integrated into New Zealand's settler press. Not only did colonial editors pay attention to its content as an indicator of the Crown's policy towards Maori, but, from 1849 to 1860, it was also edited by David Burn, a member of the Auckland press.[86] Recently, historian Ross Harvey investigated the principal role that Burn played in the creation of the *Te Karere Maori* throughout the 1850s.[87] Burn worked alongside C.O. Davis, *Te Karere Maori's* Maori language editor, until Davis's departure in 1857.[88] During his editorship, Burn came into conflict with *Te Karere Maori's* translators and constantly challenged attempts to reduce his salary.[89] Burn's correspondence with the Native secretary shows how the Native Department attempted to publish *Te Karere Maori* with the utmost economy, leaving much of the paper's organization up to Burn, who was considered "almost the exclusive writer of the Maori Messenger."[90]

Te Karere Maori, like other colonial papers across the British Empire, provided its readers with both commercial and editorial content. Burn's diaries detail the key role he played in shaping both *Te Karere Maori's* commercial stories and many leading articles. At the same time, though, Burn worked as a journalist and editor at several Auckland newspapers, including the *Southern Cross*, the *New Zealander*, and the *Auckland Weekly Register*.[91] These close ties were no doubt strengthened by the fact that W.C. Wilson, the controller of both the *New Zealander* and the *Auckland Weekly Register*, often printed *Te Karere Maori*. Burn's significant involvement in the Auckland press made him keenly aware of local papers' coverage of international news and likely influenced *Te Karere Maori's* commentary on events within the British Empire. At the same time, Burn brought to *Te Karere Maori* the range of skills that he employed in other Auckland newspapers. *Te Karere Maori* constantly featured commercial information, including market prices and shipping news, and, according to Burn, this was its most popular content.[92]

This chapter is based solely on *Te Karere Maori's* English text. As Lachy Paterson argues, *Te Karere Maori's* parallel Maori and English texts did not always share the same meanings.[93] Indeed, Paterson suggests that Maori readers most likely ignored the English text, which was probably crafted primarily for settlers, Crown administrators, and members of the Colonial Office.[94] On the surface, though, both English and Maori texts were expected to provide similar meanings. While it is difficult to measure the impact of this paper among its Maori readers, an interpretation of *Te Karere*

Maori's English text offers valuable insights into the Native Department's vision for Maori.

Te Karere Maori and the History of England

According to *Te Karere Maori*, history could not be equated with Maori tradition. Maori myth might "amuse the fancy," but it could not "inform the understanding."[95] The value of history lay in its reliability, its recitation of "the actions of men who have really existed, and [it] affords us an opportunity of acquainting ourselves with the manners and customs of former times."[96] This interpretive framework privileges print culture and associates Maori orality with barbarism and a timeless prehistoric chaos. Not only had the British brought the *Word*, but they had brought *time* as well. *Te Karere Maori* employed historical narratives to illustrate "how other nations that have been in a state of barbarism have progressed in civilization and improvement."[97] By introducing readers to models of Western temporality and cultural development, *Te Karere Maori* purported to introduce Maori into history itself. *Te Karere Maori*'s contrast between English history and Maori tradition articulated the same logic employed by the *Taranaki Herald* to argue that Maori *rangatira* who attended the Kohimarama conference would find it impossible to resolve the Taranaki War because they had no historical referents with which to contextualize the conflict. Both interpretive frameworks assumed that an oral Maori culture existed within an eternal present.

Te Karere Maori's articles on English history expounded a stadial theory of human development. These narratives of the making of the British nation were intended to naturalize the cultural disjunctions that Maori were experiencing as a consequence of colonization, especially those that entailed replacing some aspects of their culture. The importance of these editorials is evidenced by the fact that Governor Browne himself authored several chapters on the history of England.[98] *Te Karere Maori*'s historical articles also explicitly drew upon a Judeo-Christian worldview. In series such as "Geography, or the World We Live in," "Letters on History," and "History of the World," *Te Karere Maori* describes the world's biblical origins, its ancient civilizations, European exploration and colonization, and the cultural differences between and among foreign nations. These narratives stress the authenticity and continuity of biblical narratives and highlight cultural differences in descriptions of pagan religiosity. This interpretive framework characterized the Bible as a history text whose claims to reliability were increasingly corroborated by new archaeological and historical research from the Middle East. Explicitly, these narratives increased Maori readers' general knowledge of the world. At the same time, *Te Karere Maori* established a seamless timeline from the biblical age of the patriarchs through to the rise of the British Empire. This was an anglo-centric vision of world history in which divine agency was clearly discerned and the British Empire was an agent of providence.

England's history received particular attention, its being perceived as an archetype of how to reform Aboriginal peoples by civilizing them and as an example of God's continued work in the world. *Te Karere Maori* explained the process by which the modern English nation had been formed, focusing particularly on its legacy of racial amalgamation. Series of articles such as "The Early History of England," "The Ancestors of the Pakeha," and "The People of England" describe how England was transformed by successive invasions. First, pagan Celts were conquered by the Roman Empire. Eventually, Christianized Celts were invaded by Saxons, then by Danes, and finally by Normans. Moreover, each successive invading force melded with the preceding one to create a whole that was greater than the sum of its parts:

> But even out of all this tyranny and misery the God who orders all made good come forth. The conquerors learnt from the men they had subdued many good laws and customs which before had been unknown to them, and the English never would have been the men they are had they not the Nooman [sic] courage and the Norman higher power of mind been added to the Saxon temper which did not rise enough above the pains and pleasures enjoyed by beasts as well as men.[99]

As this passage makes clear, the editor emphasized how these conquests and the related work of racial amalgamation were part of God's plan.

Christianity and *Te Karere Maori*

Christianity functioned as a bridge for the writers of *Te Karere Maori* as they sought to normalize British colonialism, exploit Maori openness to innovation, and correct what they perceived to be deviations from orthodoxy. This strategy built upon Maori readers' familiarity with the Bible and the theme of the members of the nation of Israel as God's chosen people.

Drawing on the theology of divine providence, readers were invited to recognize the British Empire as God's agent in the world and, by extension, the divine inspiration for the British colonial project in New Zealand. Here we see the centrality and significance of Christianity to *Te Karere Maori* and its attempts to engage Maori readers.

While, prior to the Taranaki War, the majority of Maori had relatively little direct contact with the colonial government's administrative apparatus, large numbers of them were affiliated with both Protestant and Roman Catholic denominations. Indeed, as Chapter 1 illustrates, much had changed within Maori communities since the arrival of European newcomers. According to Lyndsay Head, "the arrival of Europeans in the early nineteenth century destroyed the intellectual and moral coherence of existing Maori political culture, which was based on the spiritual and temporal authority of chiefs."[100] Maori Christian conversion, then, entailed a shift from belief in the primacy of customary *tapu* (supernatural restrictions) to the primacy of a Christian deity. It is important to recognize that both Maori customary spirituality and European forms of Christianity were unstable formations that Maori encountered through a syncretic interface of both knowledge systems.[101] It is also important to remember Gauri Viswanathan's insight that "conversion is not necessarily a mode of assimilation to a predetermined reality, identity, or system of thought.[102] Rather, in New Zealand, conversion was a dynamic and dialogical process shaped by both the "ideal system to which the convert aspire[d]" and her/his pre-existing worldview.[103]

Maori cultural perspectives informed their Christian practice: Maori did not simply set aside certain cultural practices (such as cannibalism, polygamy, and *moko* [tattooing]) upon conversion. Rather, conversion entailed dynamic discontinuities between the social organization of pre-Christian Maori culture and its subsequent Christian incarnation.[104] Recognizing agency entails acknowledging that Maori utilized Christian practice to reject certain aspects of their cultural worldview in their pursuit of modernity. What troubled colonists, though, was that Maori engagement with Christianity also resulted in novel interpretations and practice, which, like the Kingitanga, drew upon scriptural authority to resist the Crown. Kingitanga leaders such as Wiremu Tamihana Tarapipipi Te Waharoa likened the experience of Maori to the experience of the people of Israel, illustrating how biblical narratives could inspire unexpected interpretive meanings far beyond those that British missionaries had intended when they translated the Bible into *te reo Maori*.[105]

It is clear that the writers of *Te Karere Maori* took it for granted that Maori were receptive to cultural innovation. They based this belief on the fact that many Maori were sincere Christians who, through conversion, had willingly rejected certain aspects of their customary culture. Maori letters to the editor published in *Te Karere Maori* touch on this enthusiasm for aspects of modernity. While the interpretation of Maori correspondence is fraught, given that questions pertaining to translation, motivation, and representational quality must be considered, it is fascinating to see that Maori correspondents often readily accepted that their conversion to Christianity entailed the rejection of certain parts of their former culture.[106] In the mid-nineteenth century, Maori society was in flux, and Indigenous forms of Christianity played a significant role in this.

It is worth noting that the explicit religiosity of *Te Karere Maori* led historian Alan Ward to dismiss the paper as "tawdry" and historian Keith Sinclair to consider it as "a hotchpotch of sloppy piety, dull moralizing, and condescending didacticism."[107] But this view that *Te Karere Maori*'s fervent Christian themes were unattractive to Maori readers tells us more about the anti-religious, modernist bias of these historians than it does about the interests of Maori readers. In their comments, both Ward and Sinclair reiterate the more extreme denunciations of the paper that appeared in the colonial New Zealand press in the mid-nineteenth century.[108] Then public critics of *Te Karere Maori*, like the editor of the *Taranaki Herald*, had asserted that that paper's religious themes were misdirected because Maori were not really Christians. Indeed, Maori Christianity was itself a subject of controversy. From New Zealand's foundation in 1840, both British settlers and missionaries had fought over the shape of local colonialism. In these debates, the conversion and Christian faith experience of Maori believers was deployed as a rationale for their being protected by the Crown. The language of Christian brotherhood employed by *Te Karere Maori* signified a particular, and hotly contested, humanitarian worldview.

Racial Amalgamation

Te Karere Maori asserted that British settlement in New Zealand had initiated a process of racial amalgamation. However, this promised vision of a Maori future had complex meanings. For example, narratives of English history showed that racial amalgamation was a messy and lengthy process, involving coercion, violence, invasion, and the coupling of many peoples.

But *Te Karere Maori* made no mention of how a process of racial fusion would tie Maori to colonists through intermarriage. As both Damon Salesa and Angela Wanhalla show, by the mid-nineteenth century New Zealand had a significant half-caste population, itself a legacy of intermarriage and partnership between European newcomers and Maori.[109] However, encouraging further racial mixing was not considered respectable and did not garner any attention; rather, *Te Karere Maori* depicted racial amalgamation as the transformation of customary Maori cultural practices, with emphasis on the reformation of the Maori body (both corporeal and politic), through personal hygiene, individual land tenure, English law, and education. As Salesa illustrates, the origins of the Crown's policy of racial amalgamation lay in the pre-settlement prospectus of the NZC, which outlined plans to avoid the separation of the races in New Zealand by placing Maori reserves alongside colonists' settlements and maintaining the social order of Maori through special land grants to Maori *rangatira*.[110] According to Salesa, the NZC's humanitarian mandate has not been taken seriously because it failed so spectacularly: the reality of Maori-settler relations never matched the naiveté of NZC propaganda.[111] At the same time, however, during the 1840s and 1850s, the humanitarian policy of racial amalgamation as imagined by the NZC became enshrined as a policy objective of both the Colonial Office and colonial executives in New Zealand. Articulated most clearly in *Te Karere Maori*, the policy of racial amalgamation was transformed into the merger of two cultural systems, with the weaker Maori being subsumed within the stronger Anglo-Saxon. This bias against Maori culture reflected a particular humanitarian worldview – that Maori were capable of becoming civilized but would only be properly civilized when they were no longer Maori.

However, while the policy of racial amalgamation was rather vague, *Te Karere Maori* was quick to note the differences between England's historical experiences and those of New Zealand: "The difference is very great between the robbers of those days who seized what pleased them, and the settlers of the time we live in, who pay for the land they live on, and are willing to share with those amongst whom they dwell the advantages of their laws and civilization."[112] In other words, British settlers were not invaders. As Chief Justice William Martin argues in his leading article "The Laws and Customs of the Pakeha," England's prosperity and its divine mission drew upon the Christian faith. Formerly, England had been like New Zealand, "in a state of ignorance"; however, "after the introduction and establishment of

Christianity it began to rise; for God is mindful of the people who are mindful of Him."[113] In this way, *Te Karere Maori* utilized England's history of invasion to stress the beneficial conditions under which Maori had encountered the British. As Martin emphasizes, the historic relationship between Maori and the British Empire was founded on integrity. Great Britain had been *invited* to colonize New Zealand by Maori and, in doing so, was an agent of God's blessing. By embracing Christianity, Maori had embarked upon the same path as the ancient English. Great Britain could easily have invaded New Zealand.[114] In its historical narratives and appeals to Maori to embrace racial amalgamation, *Te Karere Maori* offered an idealized view of the past and an undefined vision of the future. But these narratives broke down amid the uncertainties of mid-nineteenth-century news.

News, Anxiety, and Maori Rebellion

> From time to time we hear of reports being in circulation amongst them the tendency of which is to disturb the friendly relations subsisting between the two races and to impair the confidence which the Maori people have hitherto placed in the Government. A vague and indistinct suspicion of some imaginary harm intended them by their Pakeha neighbours is entertained by some of the less intelligent and well-informed, suggested probably in the first instance by the mischievous and disaffected.[115]

Written in 1859 in a period of growing tension, the author of the above passage explicitly seeks to allay Maori anxiety. This passage reminds us that the historical narratives and interpretations offered by *Te Karere Maori* were articulated against public discourses that insisted that the British intended to harm Maori. The 1850s was the beginning of what Belich refers to as "swamping," whereby the population of immigrant colonists grew rapidly while the population of Maori declined.[116] This phenomenon was widely recognized by both Maori and Pakeha.[117] At the same time, while the early 1850s had featured strong Maori participation in an export-oriented agricultural economy, which had supplied the Australian goldfields with foodstuffs, this market collapsed in the mid-1850s, causing considerable harm to Maori agriculturalists.[118] During the Taranaki War, too, rumours abounded that the Crown intended to enslave all Maori and to steal their land.[119]

It appears that *Te Karere Maori*'s narratives of English history may also have played a role in fomenting anxiety. For example, Hugh Carleton, the editor of the Auckland newspaper the *Southern Cross*, noted on 17 May 1859 what he considered to be the ingenious way in which Maori had adapted British knowledge.[120] Carleton referred to how local Maori objected to the construction of a road from Auckland to Ahuriri based upon the logic that the Roman Empire's successful invasion of Britain had occurred through road building. Paterson provides a similar anecdote from F.D. Fenton, the resident magistrate for Waikato, collected on 29 July 1859, which details Maori opposition to road construction based upon a Roman precedent.[121] Neither Carleton nor Fenton linked this use of English history to the content of *Te Karere Maori*, despite the fact that several editorials detailing the Roman invasion of England were published in this paper in 1857.[122] This use of English history evidences a dynamic engagement with *Te Karere Maori*. Waikato Maori accepted that the experience of the ancient Celts paralleled their own, but they were not reassured. And, indeed, these leading articles inspired strategic resistance.

The links between rumour and editorial content suggest that *Te Karere Maori*'s expositions of world history may have been more purposeful than is readily apparent. Not surprisingly, *Te Karere Maori* interpreted international events within celebratory anglo-centric narratives. For example, in June 1855, *Te Karere Maori* published two leading articles concerning the Crimean War.[123] These pieces detailed the moral justification of Great Britain's partnership with Turkey and France against a Russian oppressor, characterizing the war as a defence of human liberty, and they also stressed how the numerically inferior British and French forces had defeated their Russian foes. At first glance, these articles are unremarkable pieces of propaganda. However, comments by Henry Sewell shed light on their actual purpose. Sewell was a prominent Canterbury colonist and member of the House of Representatives. In 1855, he recorded in his diary that relations between colonists and Maori were dire, exacerbated not only by inter-*iwi* violence in the province of Taranaki but also by visiting American whalers. Apparently, these American whalers were "preaching sedition all through the Colony, persuading the Natives that Russia has destroyed all our fleets and armies, and that the Troops are about to be recalled. Then they say – Hand over New Zealand to America, she will protect your Land Rights."[124]

Governor Browne echoed Sewell's concern, and he complained to the Colonial Office: "The American whalers who are very numerous in our ports take every opportunity to aggravate this [i.e., Maori] discontent."[125] These comments cast *Te Karere Maori*'s exposition of British military successes in the Crimea in a different light. Their celebratory tone can be interpreted as an attempt to counteract rumours of British imperial weakness. This example has a couple of connotations. First, Sewell's and Browne's concerns illustrate a significant degree of anxiety over the thought that misinformation about the British Empire might adversely affect local relations with Maori. Second, these fears reveal how Maori were integrated into unregulated networks of information transmission that included sites where anti-British rhetoric flourished. Not only could Maori misinterpret the news but they could also be deceived by enemy propaganda.

Like its response to the Crimean War, *Te Karere Maori*'s response to the Indian Rebellion was inspired by misinformation and sought to influence Maori understandings of the conflict. In early 1858, Browne wrote to Henry Labouchere at the Colonial Office complaining that *Te Karere Maori*'s former editor, C.O. Davis, had printed accounts of the Indian Rebellion in a Maori language paper (*Te Waka o Te Iwi*) and that this might incite insurrection.[126] *Te Karere Maori* subsequently published a series of articles on the Indian Rebellion in 1858 and 1859.[127] As Tony Ballantyne notes, these articles detailed the rebellion's origins and emphasized "the swift reassertion of British authority."[128] These narratives also stressed that the Indian Rebellion had been initiated by "traitorous" Indian sepoys who had betrayed the British by perpetrating "diabolical cruelties ... upon the helpless and un-offending women and children who fell into the hands of the rebels."[129] Explicitly, *Te Karere Maori* observed that, while Maori readers were probably aware of the Indian Rebellion, their "imperfect information" would not allow them to "form very distinct or correct notions on the subject." These leading articles sought to remedy this deficit by elaborating how Great Britain's war in India was just, was fought only in self-defence, and was warranted by the atrocities committed by Indian rebels.

Te Karere Maori's description of the Indian Rebellion was paired with a historical article detailing the development of Great Britain's presence in India. According to the writer of this article, English troops had not con-quered India through numerical superiority; rather, British hegemony had occurred over an extended period, facilitated by Indian leaders' partnerships with the English, who "soon found that the religion of the Christians made them act very differently from any of the Idolatrous Sovereigns who had hitherto ruled over their Country."[130] England's presence in India had been facilitated by its integrity and by its non-interference in Indian society. But a hundred years of excellent treatment of Indian soldiers had been rewarded with betrayal. Here, too, a historical narrative contextualizes a contemporary event within an anglo-centric frame, emphasizing the British Empire's providential role.

Te Karere Maori devoted considerable attention to the Indian Rebellion for several reasons. First, the Indian Rebellion was the most significant news story in 1857 and 1858, and it garnered a vast amount of coverage in New Zealand papers, information that was accessible to Maori. Second, the antagonistic racial language employed in metropolitan descriptions of the Indian Rebellion as a war of the races undermined the Natives Department's characterization of the British Empire's providential role in the world. Local papers in New Zealand reproduced in detail narratives of the summary executions of rebel sepoys and arguments that Delhi should be annihilated in the same manner as Sodom and Gomorrah. The custom of publishing extended metropolitan coverage of the Indian Rebellion reproduced the language of racial warfare, along with a vengeful and antagonistic portrait of British and Indian relations. As we also saw with the *Taranaki Herald*'s editorial manifesto, the discourses surrounding the Indian Rebellion were too fraught with racial antagonism to be employed in New Zealand, which had its own deepening racial crises.

Te Karere Maori and the Taranaki War

The editor of *Te Karere Maori* did not characterize the Taranaki War as a dispute between Maori and colonists over land; rather, he characterized it as a conflict between Maori over the merits and obligations of British colonization. This theme was subsequently expanded in an editorial, "The Maori of the Past and the Maori of the Present," which accuses the Te Ati Awa insurgents of seeking to return to the values of the precolonial era:

> In former times gross darkness pervaded the land. The Maori was a savage
> – superstitious, cruel, bloodthirsty. "Blood for blood" was his only law.
> Every man's hand was against his neighbour, and his neighbour's hand
> against him. Wars and rumours of war convulsed the people. No tribe
> was exempt. The aggressor of to-day was besieged of to-morrow – the
> tyrant of one time was the oppressed of another. The thick veil of hea-
> thenism clung around the minds of men, and the service of the Evil
> One prevailed. The Maori of the past was little better than the beast of
> the field.[131]

As the writer emphasizes, the benefits of British colonization were great, and Maori would be extremely regretful if the British abandoned New Zealand. *Te Karere Maori*'s harsh assessment of precolonial Maori society was no different from the *Taranaki Herald*'s assessment. In addition to this particular interpretation of the Waitara purchase, *Te Karere Maori* attempted to persuade its readers of the validity of the Crown's actions in Taranaki by depicting both Te Rangitake's lack of a valid claim to Waitara and his role in initiating the war. Moreover, *Te Karere Maori* buttressed its argument by publishing letters from prominent Maori correspondents who were critical of Te Rangitake's actions.[132]

Later, when the Kingitanga became actively involved in the Taranaki War, *Te Karere Maori* characterized the Maori King as being "a root of dissention" within New Zealand.[133] Utilizing scripture, *Te Karere Maori* compared Maori support of the Kingitanga to the people of Israel's unwise clamouring for a king. And, citing English history, *Te Karere Maori* argued that when England had multiple kings there was bloodshed until such time as only one king was acknowledged. This editorial manifesto emphasized the Crown's neutrality while, at the same time, criticizing the Kingitanga as embodying a form of cultural regression. The choice was clear: loyalty to the Crown represented material prosperity and Christian orthodoxy; allegiance to the Kingitanga represented cultural regression and heresy.

Conclusion

Both the *Taranaki Herald* and *Te Karere Maori* were small newspapers with wide influence. The Native Department maximized *Te Karere Maori*'s effective reach by distributing copies to prominent Maori leaders and missionary humanitarians, trusting in the orality of Maori culture to disseminate its editorial manifestos. As the example of opposition to road building in the Waikato district illustrates, Maori readers responded dynamically to the content of this newspaper. Indeed, the Kingitanga held the power of the press in such esteem that several of its members established their own newspaper, *Te Hokioi o Niu Tireni e Rere Atu Na*, which operated from 1862 to 1863. In contrast, the *Taranaki Herald* took advantage of the mechanics of mid-nineteenth-century press transmission and the widespread interest in colonial violence across the British world. Forms of argument were what mattered in a model of news transmission that lacked an adequate local context. Racially inclusive language had the potential to impress metropolitan

Britons who were unaware of colonists' actual relations with their Indigenous neighbours. The *Taranaki Herald*'s metropolitan focus was defined by settler perceptions of Great Britain as a site of political influence – a place where decisions with profound implications for New Zealand were made within the Colonial Office and Houses of Parliament by politicians and bureaucrats who were influenced by a popular press. As we see in subsequent chapters, though, the *Taranaki Herald*'s interpretive monopoly did not outlast the Taranaki War.

Both the *Taranaki Herald* and *Te Karere Maori* strategically deployed humanitarian racial discourses. This humanitarian language presented British colonialism within an idealized frame and stressed Maori potential. Highlighting the Waitara purchase's implications for British sovereignty fit this paradigm; drawing attention to the bitterness of settlers, their land hunger, and racial antagonism did not. In this same vein, the *Taranaki Herald* argued that the British armed forces represented a vital tool for manifesting British supremacy and achieving the necessary subordination and preservation of Maori. The Taranaki War was a force for good, and settlers were the premier agents of a secular form of reforming Maori by civilizing them. This descriptive strategy sought to mitigate accusations that the Taranaki War was a "settlers' war."

In contrast, Christianity functioned as a central trope for *Te Karere Maori*, uniting Maori and the Crown in a form of spiritual and cultural brotherhood. *Te Karere Maori* took for granted Maori openness to cultural innovation and sought to downplay Maori anxiety by offering narratives of English history as guides for cultural development. *Te Karere Maori*'s expository narratives on the Crimean War and the Indian Rebellion are powerful examples of the paper's lack of monopoly over the knowledge of its readers. Indeed, Maori integration into colonial information networks was believed to have prolonged the Taranaki War as Maori leaders (like Wiremu Tamihana Tarapipipi Te Waharoa) were understood to be aware of the level of opposition to the conflict and were content to wait for the British Parliament to intervene on their behalf.[134]

Accurately characterizing the level of racial violence in the British Empire or the antagonism of colonists towards Maori was not expedient for either of these newspapers. In a discussion of the origins of Maori distrust of British colonization, Native Secretary McLean emphasized the repercussions of colonists' violent epithets and taunts such as: "bloody Maori," "black nigger," and "treacherous savage."[135] To this assessment, we can add reports of

British racial violence that Maori encountered from a variety of sources, including the settler press. Were discourses of racial antagonism more normative than the humanitarian discourses of brotherhood in colonial New Zealand? This question is difficult to answer. What is clear, however, is that neither *Te Karere Maori* nor the *Taranaki Herald* accurately reflected settler relations with Maori. The *Taranaki Punch* could snidely deride Maori for comic effect, but other papers could not risk alienating their broad audiences.

4

Aboriginal Title and the Victoria Press

As to the superiority of the Indian title over every other, no person who is not an atheist can logically deny the Almighty for some wise purpose placed the Indians in the regions they inhabit, generally with an abundance of fruit, game and fish to subsist on, to all of which they have an almighty good title. But the best mode of arriving at a just appreciation of our relative position to the Indians is to change places with them. Let us suppose white men were occupying their places and we theirs, we should not consider that we had too much land, and that it were necessary for the good of society, that a race superior to ourselves (which the Americans are as pioneers) should come (really for speculative purposes) but under the pretext of converting the howling wilderness into smiling farms and homes of civilization. The conduct of such men would not be one jot more unjust towards us than ours is towards the unfortunate aborigines.

– *Victoria Daily Chronicle*, 6 May 1863

IN 1863, THE *Victoria Daily Chronicle*'s regular contributor, "Monitor," penned a vindication of the property title of First Nations. This was the first in a series of extended articles written between 1863 and 1866 that called attention to the injustices experienced by local Aboriginal peoples on Vancouver Island.[1] Allegedly, "Monitor" was Charles Bedford Young, a local merchant and politician who was closely allied with James E. McMillan and David W. Higgins, the operators of the *Victoria Daily Chronicle*.[2]

Young's first article on Indian policy was written in the midst of a crisis. That spring several murders had occurred on the Gulf Islands off the east coast of Vancouver Island. Three Euro-American settlers had been murdered in two separate incidents, and then a shootout had occurred between a naval gunboat and the alleged perpetrators. This prompted Governor James Douglas to mobilize all available naval forces to track down the Cowichan suspects, and, eventually, seven Aboriginal men were hanged in Victoria for their roles in these events.[3] But, according to Young, the responsibility for this spilled blood lay in the "culpable negligence" of the colonial administration for its failure to honour its pledge to pay the Cowichan for their land. In consequence, settlers were in grave danger – "seated as it were on a powder magazine."[4]

In one way, Young's attention to the property title of First Nations was not unique. From the initiation of the Victoria press, almost every editor had called upon the colonial administration to pay Aboriginal peoples for their land. This public support for Aboriginal title lasted roughly until the colonies of Vancouver Island and British Columbia were merged in 1866. What makes Young's manifesto different, however, is his characterization of the superior nature of Aboriginal title. Young's key point is that First Nations peoples derived their title "from divine right and therefore have an Almighty good title."[5] Young asserts that God had placed Aboriginal people in the region for a purpose. This invocation of history draws upon the seventeenth-century notion "that nature was imprinted with the divine" rather than the nineteenth-century notion that Indigenous territory was idle until transformed by settlement.[6] According to the seventeenth-century belief, when settlers usurped Aboriginal territory they were thwarting God's will. This was a powerful indictment of the prevalent belief that the transformative work of British settlement fulfilled the biblical injunction in Genesis 1:28 – "Be fruitful and multiply, replenish the earth, and subdue it" – in a manner that Indigenous peoples did not.[7]

Indeed, the timelessness of Aboriginal history had a certain nobility. Like the editor of *Te Karere Maori* in New Zealand, Young drew upon a stadial theory of history that interpreted the achievement of civilization as a process that, across the world, had occurred over time and unevenly. But, whereas the editor of *Te Karere Maori* saw divine agency in the rise of England, Young saw the early English as "pirates and marauders" and the codification of English property rights as amoral. English monarchs had plundered and robbed lands from their subjects, with a particular notion

of property gaining respectability over time. In this way, Young cast asper-
sions on the superiority of English civilization and the rule of law. According
to his reckoning, the political sovereignty garnered by the British Empire
from the Spanish and from the United States to the Northwest Coast could
never supersede the God-given rights of First Nations.

In essence, Young offered a theological justification of Indigenous title
that was underpinned by the threat of violence. This was not a legal treatise.
It did not clarify the nature of Aboriginal *dominium* (ownership rights); it
did not draw on existing precedents from the British Empire or the United
States. Yet, while Young provided the strongest evangelical humanitarian
voice for Aboriginal rights, many of the editors of the Victoria press agreed
in principle that the colonial administration had an obligation to pay for
Aboriginal land. And they, too, favoured moral rather than legal arguments:
the claims of Aboriginal peoples were *equitable*, and when the colonial
administration failed to compensate First Nations this represented *a breach
of faith*. These public discourses were anchored in English notions of "natural
justice" as well as in the perceived moral code of local First Nations. But
these endorsements were not static.

This chapter examines the contingent nature of public support for the
recognition of Aboriginal title on Vancouver Island and in British Columbia.
It establishes a strong correlation between editor-politicians' support for
the land rights of First Nations and press reportage of Aboriginal violence.
It considers the influence of reported news of Maori violence in New
Zealand and then tracks the decline of public support for Aboriginal title
by the time Vancouver Island and British Columbia were merged in 1866.
This analysis reveals a progression of assumptions – from the belief that
paying for Aboriginal land is inevitable, to the belief that Vancouver Island's
colonial administration's breach of faith with First Nations had elicited
violence, to the conclusion that Aboriginal reserve lands should be diminished in order to facilitate settlement. "Monitor" called the system of Indian
policy on Vancouver Island "a mockery of religion, morality, and common
honesty."[8] This argument was strong when editors feared the consequences
of their sins.

Buying Land on Vancouver Island, 1849–66

In the early 1850s, James Douglas followed the instructions of both the Colonial Office and the Hudson's Bay Company to secure land for settlement

through fourteen treaties: twelve with the Coast Salish peoples of southern Vancouver Island and two with the Kwakwaka'wakw peoples at the north-eastern end of the island.[9] In this way, Douglas gained control over a small area around settlement communities, leaving Aboriginal title to the vast majority of Vancouver Island unextinguished. In framing these treaties, Douglas drew upon a copy of the *Kemp Deed* (a New Zealand Company conveyance document prepared for transferring land title from Maori) provided by HBC secretary Archibald Barclay in 1850. The "Douglas Treaties" were boilerplate agreements, signifying the transfer of land ownership to the colonial administration and featuring the X's of Aboriginal signatories. In exchange, Aboriginal participants received payment in trade goods, the demarcation of their sites of settlement and cultivation as reserves, and recognition of their hunting and fishing privileges.

As both historian Hamar Foster and archivist Raymond Frogner argue, considerable ambiguity surrounds the Douglas Treaties because Douglas never defined the nature of Aboriginal title and his actions are best described as ad hoc.[10] For example, Douglas's practice was to garner Aboriginal signatures on blank documents and then add the text of the treaty at a later date. So there were always two parallel treaties – the oral agreement to which Aboriginal participants agreed to in pen and the separate written text affixed to the treaty document. Negotiations were also made difficult by the absence of a mutually comprehensible language as Chinook *wawa*, or jargon, lacked the vocabulary necessary for land sales. Indeed, oral testimony suggests that Aboriginal participants were not always aware of the implications of the treaties or, indeed, that they were selling their land at all.[11] As Frogner argues in his investigation of the North Saanich Treaty, 1852, Aboriginal signatures may have symbolized the mutual agreement of two parties but the treaty itself was a "legal fiction" – "a modernist device designed to reconcile and articulate in measured textual detail, the social, geographic, and legal spaces necessary to build the colonial settlement project."[12]

In treaty making, Douglas responded to the push and pull of both local and metropolitan demands – the imperative to maintain friendly relations with local First Nations and the Colonial Office's legal requirement to recognize tribal dominium.[13] Certainly Douglas himself characterized his treaty-making practice as the fulfillment of Aboriginal demands. Writing to the Colonial Office in 1861 to request funds to extinguish Aboriginal title on additional territory, Douglas explained his actions as follows:

As the native Indian population of Vancouver Island have distinct ideas of property in land, and mutually recognise their several exclusive possessory rights in certain Districts, they would not fail to regard the occupation of such portions of the Colony by white settlers, unless with the full consent of the proprietary Tribes, as national wrongs ... Knowing their feelings on that subject, I made it a practice up to the Year 1859, to purchase the Native rights in the land, in every case, prior to the settlement of any District.[14]

In this despatch Douglas explains that his inability to continue buying land stems from a lack of funds following the HBC's loss of control over Vancouver Island. Of course, Douglas was rather disingenuous in this message as he had in fact made his last official treaty in 1854 rather than in 1859 and never made another. Before his retirement in 1864, Douglas stopped paying for land and acknowledged Aboriginal title only through the creation of reserves that included Aboriginal sites of habitation and occupation.

Understanding Douglas's moving away from the purchase of Aboriginal land has been a significant problem for historians of colonial British Columbia. Robin Fisher accepts that Douglas ceased purchasing Aboriginal territory because he lacked funds, while Paul Tennant argues that money was not an issue and that Douglas came to favour the creation of reserves because they represented the best means of creating self-reliant Aboriginal communities. Cole Harris believes that both Fisher and Tennant are correct and that the ever-pragmatic Douglas probably turned to the creation of reserves out of both fiscal prudence and a belief in their merit.[15] Foster argues that the decision of Douglas to cease treaty making was influenced by a controversial 1853 ruling of the Oregon Supreme Court, which argued that there was no obligation to extinguish Aboriginal title because Oregon was not technically "Indian Country."[16] Vancouver Island's ruling elite had close ties to the authors of this precedent-setting law and may have followed its lead, arguing that historic European claims to the region had extinguished Aboriginal sovereignty. Remaining largely unaddressed in these debates are the implications of Chris Arnett's work on Douglas's last attempt at treaty making with the Cowichan First Nation in 1862 and why the Victoria press provided strong support for the recognition of Aboriginal title until 1866.[17]

When editors of the Victoria press referred to the issue of Aboriginal title, they did so primarily in reference to the Cowichan district located northwest of Victoria. Already in 1856 Douglas had recognized the suitability of this region for settlement, remarking in a despatch that he "greatly admired the beauty and fertility of the Cowegin valley, which contains probably not less than 200,000 acres of arable land."[18] The Cowichan First Nation had originally offered to sell part of its territory in 1850, but Douglas had demurred because there was no demand for the land at that time.[19] The situation changed in 1858, when the Fraser River gold rush brought an influx of potential settlers.

Vancouver Island never had a shortage of unoccupied land. What it did lack, however, was land that was readily adaptable to agriculture. Just as Douglas had been drawn to establish Fort Victoria on the meadowlands created by local Lekwungen people for the cultivation of camas roots, so the Cowichan district became the focus for settlement because of the success of Cowichan potato farmers.[20] Hence, the problem for settlers was that the most desirable land proximal to Victoria was already owned, occupied, and cultivated by an estimated six thousand Aboriginal residents.[21] In 1859, Douglas elaborated on the tension in the region when he told the Colonial Office how his survey of the Cowichan Valley had caused "much excitement" as Cowichan people assumed "that their lands [were] to be immediately sold and occupied by white settlers, an impression which it [was] difficult to remove and that [gave] rise to much contention amongst themselves about the disposal of their lands."[22] In this despatch, Douglas also noted that the Cowichan were divided into two factions: one favouring the sale of their lands, the other being opposed to it.[23]

Some limited settlement by Euro-Americans occurred in the district in 1859, but local Aboriginal residents met it with resistance and demands for compensation. In March 1860, Douglas requested that the Legislative Assembly allocate funds to extinguish Aboriginal title through purchase.[24] At the same time, though, Douglas officially opened the Cowichan district to settlement without the permission of its Aboriginal owners.[25] The ensuing uncertainty prompted colonists who had paid initial installments for Cowichan land to petition Douglas to compensate local First Nations. In reply, Colonial Secretary William A.G. Young promised that initial settler payments would be employed to extinguish Aboriginal title.[26] Many were too afraid to occupy their purchased lots without this measure.

Then, in August 1862, Douglas led a party of nearly one hundred settlers aboard a British gunboat into the Cowichan Valley. The participation of the British navy in this expedition sent a not so subtle message to local First Nations: the Crown would uphold the property claims of the new settlers with force. This incident of "gunboat diplomacy" is an example of Cole Harris's broad assertion that the threat of violence backed by the British military provided a crucial backdrop to the dispossession of First Nations in the region.[27] As the *British Colonist* also reported, the majority of Cowichan residents were away at their summer fishing camps when this party arrived. Reportedly, Douglas then negotiated a deal that included the creation of a designated reserve and a promise that compensation would be paid in the form of blankets later in the year. However, this land payment never occurred,[28] and no official treaty text chronicled the oral pledges. It is possible that Douglas intended to ratify the oral agreement at a later date, a practice not dissimilar to what occurred during the creation of the earlier Douglas Treaties. According to Colonial Secretary Young's 1866 memorandum to the new governor, Frederick Seymour, Douglas had recanted on his promise to pay the Cowichan people for their lands as a punishment for their participation in the murders of three Euro-Americans in 1863.[29]

But the promise of compensation lived on in public memory. Those who corresponded with the Victoria press from the Cowichan district and other settler communities regularly commented on the demeanour of local First Nations and the question they frequently encountered from their Aboriginal neighbours: "When are you going to pay us for our land?"[30] The tension between settlers and First Nations in the Cowichan district was further exacerbated by competition for land resources and conflicts over animal husbandry practices. Settlers supplemented their income by raising pigs and cattle for markets in Victoria, and they allowed this livestock to range freely across the district and to devastate unfenced Aboriginal potato fields. Likewise, many settlers complained that Aboriginal persons deliberately disregarded their property boundaries. The colonial administration's 1862 breach of faith with the Cowichan people assumed symbolic importance.

Aboriginal Title in the Victoria Press

Why is not the Indian title to Cowitchen extinguished at once? This is repeated over and over again, and yet no response is heard from the government. It may require judicious management, but it has to be done. The country expects it without delay. We want farmers, – and the best way to get them is to open the lands of Cowitchen to actual settlers by extinguishing the Indian title.[31]

From 1859 to 1866, leading editors of the Victoria press campaigned for the recognition of Aboriginal title.[32] This support for the rights of Aboriginal peoples occurred in spite of the general racial antagonism of editors and their quest to bring segregation to Victoria.[33] Understanding how and why editors simultaneously sought both to diminish and to acknowledge Aboriginal rights is central to this chapter. Just as editors drew upon anxiety and the threat of Aboriginal violence in their efforts to evict First Nations from Victoria, so the threat of Aboriginal violence came to be a pivotal element of their characterizations of support for Aboriginal title. The era between 1858 and 1866 can be separated into three distinct periods: (1) from 1859 to 1862, editors called upon Douglas to open the Cowichan district to settlement; (2) from 1863 to 1864, in the context of increased levels of reported Aboriginal violence on Vancouver Island and the Northwest Coast, editors chastised Douglas for breaking his promises to the Cowichan people; and (3) from 1865 to 1866, editors' support for Aboriginal title diminished at the same time as Cowichan settlers petitioned to reduce the size of the Aboriginal reserve in the Cowichan Valley.

The context for editors' support for the recognition of Aboriginal title was of course the mixed fortunes of the local gold rush economy and the imperative to retain failed prospectors in the region by providing them with land for settlement. This was the same motivation that spurred editors to demand the racial segregation of Victoria to ensure that failed prospectors might find employment. From 1859 to 1862, editors of the Victoria press demanded to know the colonial administration's intentions. When would the Cowichan district be opened to settlement? When would Cowichan people receive payment for their land? Why were the initial installments paid by settlers not used to purchase Aboriginal title? These same questions were being asked in Vancouver Island's Legislative Assembly, and it is useful to look at an overview of the political context from 1858 to 1866.

Indian policy was the domain of the colonial executive, and the issue of Aboriginal title was primarily debated within the Legislative Assembly in response to Douglas's requests for funds in the annual Colonial Estimates. Always, the most important question was: Where would the funds to extinguish Aboriginal title be found? Certainly, members of the Legislative Assembly had mixed feelings on the topic. Some, like George Foster, considered the idea of extinguishing Aboriginal title to be absurd: "it has never been done by any government, nor has it ever been done by an English colony."[34] In contrast, the long-time HBC officer William Fraser Tolmie stated: "[I] did not say they had any title; but that it was necessary to extinguish their claims, to avoid a war."[35] John Coles spoke for many: "The Indians have a right to be paid for their lands, but the Home Government must do it."[36] In 1860, the Legislative Assembly rejected Douglas's request for two thousand pounds to extinguish Aboriginal title and instead, in 1861, petitioned the Colonial Office to cover this cost. When the Colonial Office refused in 1862, the Legislative Assembly then voted for funds to extinguish Aboriginal title in 1862, 1863, and 1864. But Douglas never spent this money.

The period leading up to the unification of Vancouver Island and British Columbia in 1866 was marked by political turmoil. Vancouver Island especially faced a series of crises. Victoria's economy was oriented towards the provisioning and entertainment of prospectors on the mainland. Local merchants depended upon the continued success of the goldfields of the interior of British Columbia, but the excitement of the Cariboo gold rush in 1862 was not sustained. At the same time, in 1864, the Colonial Office responded to complaints from the residents of British Columbia and replaced Governor Douglas with two separate governors – Arthur Kennedy on Vancouver Island and Frederick Seymour in British Columbia. Rightly so, members of Vancouver Island's Legislative Assembly viewed this change with chagrin because Victoria had benefitted from Douglas's control over both colonies. Indeed, Douglas had designated Victoria as a free port while merchants on the mainland were forced to pay tariffs on imports. As Robert L. Smith notes, the replacement of Douglas marked the end of Victoria's preferential status and precipitated an acrimonious political showdown.[37]

Kennedy and the members of the Legislative Assembly clashed from the moment he arrived in the colony until his departure in 1866.[38] Local dissatisfaction with Vancouver Island's loss of control over British Columbia exacerbated conflict over the transfer of control over the Civil List. The deal put forward first by Douglas in 1864, and subsequently by Kennedy following his arrival, offered the Legislative Assembly control over the colony's revenues in exchange for guaranteeing the salaries of the colony's administrative officers. Control over the Civil List provided an enhanced form of responsible government alongside increased responsibility. Local politicians rejected this offer for several reasons, though. First, members of the Legislative Assembly did not believe that the income from the sale of public lands, which was the primary source of the colony's income, was adequate to cover expenditures, including the cost related to the extinguishment of

Aboriginal title.[39] Second, acceptance of the Civil List was also tied to the formal transfer of control over Crown Lands from the HBC to the Legislative Assembly. By rejecting the Civil List, local politicians sought to force the Colonial Office to give them control over valuable real-estate within Victoria and surrounding districts that had been recognized as the property of the HBC in 1862. Kennedy never overcame the political impasse that he had stepped into, leaving the Colonial Office and commenting that Douglas's administration had seen "a great deal of mismanagement and erroneous judgement."[40] In response, the Colonial Office merged Vancouver Island into British Columbia in 1866 under less than favourable terms to the residents of Victoria, the city losing its status as both a free port and a colonial capital.

The issue of Aboriginal title was not a legislative priority in this era of political rancour. And we know very little about Kennedy's views as he wrote almost nothing about the land rights of First Nations peoples in his correspondence to the Colonial Office. Once, early in his tenure, he outlined several principles necessary for dealing with First Nations, including: "They must be secured in possession of their lands, and prohibited from alienating them except for a fair consideration, and through the intervention of the Government."[41] In several public meetings with Aboriginal people on Vancouver Island, Kennedy stated: "I will see that you are unmolested in the lands you occupy, and that they shall not be taken from you or encroached upon, unless by equitable agreement between the Government and the chiefs of the tribes to whom they belong."[42] No doubt these pledges were intended to allay the persistent complaints of First Nations peoples regarding the abuse of their rights and confiscation of their lands. But Kennedy never designated funds within the colonial estimates for 1865 and 1866 to extinguish Aboriginal title. According to Colonial Secretary Young in 1866, the Cowichan First Nation considered Kennedy to "speak fair" but believed his words were *kultus wawa* – worthless.[43] From 1858 on, the issue of Aboriginal title appears to have been bound up in the impasse over the transfer of control over Crown Lands from the HBC to the Legislative Assembly. Perhaps Kennedy was waiting to gain control over his recalcitrant assembly before initiating a controversial land policy. The public records do not say.

In 1865, when funds for Aboriginal land claims did not reappear in the budget, Speaker of the House John Helmcken remarked: "The Speaker did not see any sum set aside for purchasing Indian titles. The natives had been promised, year after year, that they would be compensated for the lands taken from them. The faith of the country ought to be kept, whether to an Indian or any one else ... Indian wars had always occurred in consequence of this very land question."[44] Helmcken articulated the most vocal support for the recognition of Aboriginal title in the Legislative Assembly, and his feelings appear to have been linked to the belief that "the natives should be treated as rational human beings. [He did not agree] that they should be removed or packed up in small places." So, editors' attention to Aboriginal title did not occur either in response to extensive debates in the Legislative Assembly or to clear policy directives from Douglas or Kennedy; rather, it occurred in response to a lack of political activity and as a catalyst for action.

For example, in April 1860, Leonard McClure's second *Victoria Gazette* published a leading article supporting the recognition of Aboriginal title. In his rationale for this measure, McClure acknowledged the historic purchases of Aboriginal territories that Douglas had made in the early 1850s, touched on the legality of Aboriginal title, and emphasized the financial benefits of purchasing rather than appropriating Aboriginal territories. McClure also addressed the inability of colonists to remain in the Cowichan district due to Aboriginal resistance to their incursions on un-extinguished territory. McClure's comments on the issue of Aboriginal title are worth quoting in full:

> We are well aware that there are *civilized nations* which consider the aborigines not to have any title to their wild domain, and try to bring arguments from sacred and legal works to prove the assertion correct; but those arguments appear so far-fetched, strained, and warped, that the idea is forced upon us of an attempt to conceal the fact, that our only title to the Indian inheritance exists in our being the *more powerful*, an argument usually very convincing, and the one by which nations hold their own. But however much the "title" may be disputed, it is and has been usual to subsidize the Indian upon taking possession of his patrimony, and thus while denying a right *de jure* admitting it *de facto*.[45]

Notice how McClure identifies the contested nature of Aboriginal title but focuses on the practical rather than the legal implications of paying for land. The costs associated with purchasing Aboriginal title were minimal in comparison to what they might be should a war follow the coercive appropriation of Aboriginal lands. Looming over McClure's reflections was the war that had occurred in the Washington Territory between local First Nations and American colonists only a few years earlier:

> We need not enlarge upon the horrors of such a war; the records of one in the neighboring Territory are so painfully engraved in the memory of many of us as to render it unnecessary. Economy, then invites the Indian title to be extinguished; custom calls for it. The retention of the confidence of the Indian, and to give him a proper sense of our justice requires it, the prevention of hostilities demand it, and colonists wishing to settle earnestly pray for it.[46]

This editorial reveals how the Douglas Treaties lived on in public memory and how the threat of a war with Aboriginal peoples came to be connected with non-payment for Aboriginal land. McClure closed this editorial with the statement: *"Prevention is better than cure."*[47]

Almost two years on, though, the issue of First Nations title within the Cowichan district remained unresolved. In 1862, in *The Press*, McClure again addressed the issue. This time, McClure commented on the duke of Newcastle's refusal to finance the purchase of Aboriginal title on Vancouver Island.[48] Douglas had forwarded a petition from the Legislative Assembly in March 1861, calling on the Colonial Office to subsidize the extinguishment of Aboriginal title.[49] In this petition representatives called attention to the danger colonists faced in occupying unextinguished Aboriginal territories and argued that the onus was on the Imperial government to fund local land purchases.[50] McClure himself held that it was inappropriate for the Colonial Office to expect the Legislative Assembly to fund the purchase of Aboriginal title when the HBC had not yet released control over Crown lands.[51] Entirely missing from this editorial is the argument that the Colonial Office's refusal to fund the purchase of Aboriginal title implied that the Legislative Assembly was no longer obligated to recognize Aboriginal title. Between 1860 and 1862 McClure's attitude towards Aboriginal title did not change substantially. Certainly he did not equivocate as did De Cosmos in the *British Colonist*.

Between 1859 and 1862, in the *British Colonist* Amor De Cosmos also campaigned for the colonial administration to resolve local First Nations title. Initially, De Cosmos simply demanded that Douglas take measures to purchase Aboriginal title in the Cowichan district.[52] In August 1860, he articulated the rationale for this demand:

What therefore is expected is the speedy extinction of this title. We call it the title though lawyers may quibble about an Indian title, and say there is no such thing. But still we hold that they possess an equitable title, disguise it in legal lore as you please, and that it is our policy to respect that title, which may be vested in the government now at a trifling expense compared with its value in the future.[53]

Like McClure, De Cosmos referenced contemporary debates regarding the legal existence of Aboriginal title and affirmed local First Nations possession of an "equitable" but legally undefined title.[54] By March 1861, though, De Cosmos's attitude had shifted. Referencing the ongoing debate between the Legislative Assembly and the Colonial Office over whose responsibility it was to subsidize the recognition of Aboriginal title, De Cosmos linked the support of colonists with Victoria's history of Aboriginal violence. According to De Cosmos:

> For months and years the Indians on the Reserve cut each other's throats every day, attacked pedestrians, fired into town; and we were told: "Don't arrest them, or we will have an Indian war." We did arrest them; hung one of them and now they are all as quiet as mice. We were then frightened by a bugbear. On the land question we are frightened by another: "Pay the Indians for the land or we'll have an Indian war." We don't believe it. We hold it to be our best policy to pay them, to avoid even the possibility of a war.[55]

Here, De Cosmos makes an explicit link between public support for the recognition of Aboriginal title and settler anxiety. Citing the recent successful imposition of law and order among northern First Nations, De Cosmos suggests that the fears of colonists are groundless, demarcating his now conditional support for the recognition of Aboriginal title. If the necessary funds could not be procured, then local First Nations should be settled on reserves and punished severely if they trespassed on the lands of colonists. As De Cosmos notes: "We are willing to take this course, provided we *cannot* buy out the title."

Later in 1862, De Cosmos celebrated Douglas's efforts to establish a treaty with the Cowichan First Nation. As previously mentioned, in August 1862 Douglas had pledged to Cowichan people that they would receive compensation for their territory in the form of blankets paid to each person in the coming autumn.[56] When this payment failed to occur, in December 1862 De Cosmos condemned the colonial administration:

> The Indians have a right to be paid for their lands. If the Government [has] made any agreement with them they should in honor fulfil it; if not, it is high time that they should come to a fair and definite arrangement and have it carried out to the letter. They will thus avoid the troubles that the question has given rise to in the Territories of the United States.[57]

This last attempt at treaty making on Vancouver Island was abandoned and, subsequently, has not received a great deal of attention, even though this event transforms our understanding of Douglas.[58] Douglas's attempt to purchase First Nations territory in 1862 indicates that he was not intrinsically opposed to land purchases when the risk of violence threatened, just as it had when he pursued the earlier treaties. Indeed, we can date Douglas's final shift away from treaty making to 1863. Ultimately, however, we do not know why Douglas did not fulfill his promise to the Cowichan.

This comparison of the editorial perspectives of McClure and De Cosmos between 1858 and 1862 reveals that their support for Aboriginal title was informed primarily by two important assumptions: first, that both the Douglas Treaties of the 1850s and the American land purchases in Washington Territory were established precedents that compelled the colonial administration to pay for Aboriginal land in the Cowichan district; second, that both the resistance of Cowichan people to settler incursions and the dreadful example of warfare in Washington Territory indicated that violence would occur if the Cowichan First Nation was not paid for its land.[59] Notice, though, that neither editor dwelled on Aboriginal conceptions of land ownership, the legal definition of Aboriginal dominium, or how the original European acquisition of sovereignty to the region had affected Aboriginal land claims. In these arguments, editors essentially echoed the sentiments articulated by members of the Legislative Assembly in their 1861 petition to the Colonial Office:

> That the Indians, well aware of the compensation heretofore given for lands, appropriated for colonization, in the earlier settled districts of Vancouver Island, as well as in the neighbouring territory of Washington, strenuously oppose the occupation by settlers of lands still deemed their own. No attempts of the kind could be persisted in, without endangering

the peace of the Country, for these Indians, though otherwise well disposed and friendly, would become hostile if their supposed rights as regards land were systematically violated.[60]

Interestingly, neither the Legislative Assembly nor the editors of the Victoria press ever cited other British colonial precedents, such as New Zealand's Treaty of Waitangi or British North America's Royal Proclamation, in their arguments in support of the recognition of Aboriginal title. The emphasis remained almost entirely local and focused on the *supposed* rights of local Aboriginal peoples – rights that editors and politicians did not necessarily believe were real but that they felt compelled to endorse. This obfuscation of British imperial practice is suggestive of at least two possibilities. First, it suggests that editors were not aware of or did not consider other historical precedents to be relevant or legally binding with regard to their own situation. Certainly Jane Samson makes the case that there was general ignorance in Victoria regarding imperial statutes that pertained to Indigenous rights. For example, local administrators were not aware of the existence of the Colonial Evidence Act, 1843, which allowed the local Legislative Assembly to pass an ordinance allowing for unsworn Aboriginal testimony.[61] Second, it suggests that editors understood that Douglas was empowered to take the most appropriate actions necessary and that metropolitan critics were not closely monitoring local events. The support of both editors and politicians for the recognition of Aboriginal title was grounded in the need to open the Cowichan district to settlement and, thereby, to spur colonial development. This support was meant to ensure that Victoria's economic development would continue apace and, with it, the press's readership. While McClure's advocacy, in particular, was framed within a humanitarian paradigm, De Cosmos's advocacy was explicitly contingent.

Aboriginal Violence and Land Title, 1863–64

Victoria reportedly became quieter following the expulsion of northern First Nations people in 1862. While northern First Nations never ceased visiting the community, they did so in much reduced numbers in subsequent years.[62] Correspondingly, the large-scale Aboriginal disorder characteristic of the period before 1862 no longer occurred on the edge of town. This change was writ large in the Victoria press's coverage of fatal violence within the community. Between 1858 and 1862, local journalists identified sixty incidents of fatal violence involving Aboriginal perpetrators; however, Aboriginals were reported to have participated in only eight incidents of fatal violence in Victoria between 1863 and 1866. And this was not an effect of a more efficient Victoria Police Force as, at this time, the organization's membership had been gutted amid scandal and economic retrenchment. While newspaper editors still occasionally demanded that local Lekwungen people be evicted from their valuable reserve, there was no longer cause to demand that northern First Nations people be removed from the community or that they be barred from participating in the local economy. In 1862, smallpox and eviction really did mark the end of an era.

But while the residents of Victoria experienced new feelings of security, this local tranquility did not extend into the interior of Vancouver Island or along the Northwest Coast of British Columbia. Indeed, in both 1863 and 1864, some editors in both colonies feared the outbreak of a general war with First Nations. Three episodes garnered considerable press attention. As previously mentioned, in 1863 a series of murders attributed to Cowichan persons occurred on the Gulf Islands off the east coast of Vancouver Island. Chris Arnett, in his study of these events, suggests that these attacks may have been motivated by Aboriginal anger related to Euro-American trespasses on unextinguished territory. In response, Governor Douglas enlisted local British naval forces to carry out several punitive expeditions to capture the Aboriginal perpetrators. A pitched battle followed between the British gunboat *Forward* and the residents of the Lamalcha village on Kuper Island, resulting in the death of one seaman.

Then, on 29 and 30 April 1864, fourteen Euro-American road workers were killed by Tsilhqot'in warriors in a night-time raid. These men had been building a trail from Bute Inlet on the Northwest Coast to Alexandria in the interior, a scheme pursued by the Victoria businessman Alfred Waddington to secure a shorter route to the Cariboo gold mines. John Lutz suggests that the Tsilhqot'in attack may have been motivated by the belief that Waddington's construction party had introduced smallpox to the region. Smallpox did devastate Tsilhqot'in communities in 1862 and, indeed, it did coincide with the arrival of road builders. Subsequent to the initial attack at Bute Inlet, the Tsilhqot'in warriors, led by Klatsassin, then ambushed a pack train, killing four people, including three Euro-Americans. In response, the newly arrived Governor Seymour organized a local militia force from

New Westminster to capture those responsible. This party was eventually able to secure seven Tsilhqot'in prisoners when Klatsassin was tricked into entering the militia camp under the pretense of brokering a truce and was then arrested on the spot. Ultimately, six Tsilhquo'tin men were tried, condemned, and hanged for their participation in the events at Bute Inlet.[63]

In late 1864, the British navy engaged in several cruises up the west coast of Vancouver Island to capture Aboriginal persons accused of murdering the crew of the Euro-American trading vessel the *Kingfisher* and the killing of the Indian Agent William Banfield. This police action culminated in the bombardment of nine Aboriginal villages at Clayoquot Sound, the reported deaths of at least fifteen Aboriginal persons, and the wounding of many more. Official reports that the expedition had successfully intimidated First Nations may have been exaggerated, but they still fit within a broader pattern of increasing racial violence on the Northwest Coast. As Samson argues, the efforts of the British navy to combat "piracy" were part of Kennedy's efforts to prove to local First Nations that he was "a sterner man than Douglas" and to extend in real terms the writ of British law and order along the west coast of Vancouver Island.[64] Security operations like these were linked to a larger process of redefining Indigenous peoples as legal subjects.[65] As in New Zealand, though, so in Vancouver Island and British Columbia: British hegemony was urban in character and mobile across the hinterland, shifting along the coast with the movement of warships.

Alongside these specific incidents, both Vancouver Island and British Columbia underwent a significant general increase in fatal violence. Indeed, the Victoria press reported that, in 1863 and 1864 on Vancouver Island, along the Northwest Coast, and in the interior of British Columbia, a total of eighty-eight Euro-American persons were killed by Aboriginal violence as compared to sixteen in the previous two years. This led the editor of the *Evening Express* to conjecture: "Possibly we are slumbering unconsciously on the edge of a volcano, which sooner or later will break out into an explosion of bloodshed and flame from one end of the Island to the other."[66]

In this context, all of the members of the Victoria press commented extensively on the topic of Aboriginal violence, and many of their editorials identified the colonial administration's non-payment for land as a cause. For example, in 1863, regarding the murders in Cowichan, the editor of the *Evening Express* noted: "The settlers are told that the principle cause of this difficulty arises from the Government having broken its promises in regard to the payment for the land, and the belief in general that until they are paid the settlers can have no feeling of security."[67] Likewise, regarding the violence at Bute Inlet, the editor of the *British Colonist* stated:

> However much we regret the occurrence of this horrible slaughter of unoffending men, we are by no means amazed at the growing insecurity of the white man's life amongst the northern savages. What between the reckless indifference to Indian life, amounting to inhumanity, of one portion of our population, and the maudlin sympathy, amounting to the encouragement of crime, of another, the Indian is actually forced into disregarding the law. When we add to these mischievous extremes, the notorious bad faith of our own Government with the Indian tribes, the great wonder is that a general warfare with the savages has not broken out long ago ... We all know how the Government has dealt with the Cowichan Indians, and how its bad faith, in that instance, has only been equalled by its indisposition to punish Indian criminals in others.[68]

In the context of this violence, members of the Victoria press supported the purchase of Aboriginal lands alongside the inauguration of a systematic "Indian policy." The term "Indian policy" represented an overarching set of concerns that included not only the issue of Aboriginal title but also the demand that the colonial administration establish an official department to oversee First Nations. This proposed system contrasted with Douglas's practice of dealing with First Nations personally or through agents such as Police Commissioner Augustus Pemberton and local missionary humanitarians such as William Duncan or A.C. Garrett. What local editors objected to was the fact that, not counting occasional moments of crisis, First Nations were left alone. Alongside the breach of trust regarding non-payment for Aboriginal land, Aboriginal violence was understood to be caused by alcohol abuse, Aboriginal people being perceived to be incapable of controlling themselves while intoxicated. In this case, the colonial administration itself was to blame for failing to clamp down on lawless Euro-Americans who both carried out the illicit whisky trade with First Nations and mistreated their customers, thereby causing resentment and violence.

The Victoria press stressed the understandable nature of Aboriginal thinking. Editors put forward a list of reasons for Aboriginal violence, of which the colonial administration's breach of trust regarding First Nations land rights was but one. A balance needed to be restored to settlers and First Nations of the region, and paying for Aboriginal land was part of the cost of peaceful colonization. As the editor of the *Vancouver Island Times* stated in 1865:

> The press of Victoria has, so far as we can recollect, consistently done its duty in urging the consideration of the Indian title to lands question upon the representatives of the people. The settlement of the Cowichan districts, which took place under the auspices of the then Attorney General in the summer of 1862, was upon the distinct understanding that these titles were to be extinguished ... So long as the Indians are led to believe that their lands have been unfairly and deceitfully taken from them, our settlers will never be safe, and the Government is inflicting a double wrong, a great one on the Indians, but a monstrous injustice upon those who have been induced to take up land in the fallacious hope of perfect security.[69]

The great majority of commentary in the Victoria press regarding Aboriginal title was reactive. In this way, the press's campaign for the recognition of Aboriginal title was very similar to its efforts to achieve the racial segregation of Victoria. Editors during this period did not dwell on the legal nature of Aboriginal land rights but, rather, encouraged the colonial administration to pay for land in order to avoid the escalation of racial conflict and the occurrence of more serious violence. However, in 1865 and 1866 reported incidents of deaths due to Aboriginal violence declined, with only thirty-three incidents of fatal violence attributed to Aboriginal perpetrators in this period, including the murders of six Euro-Americans. As reported Aboriginal violence declined, so, too, did the explicit rationale for editors' support of Aboriginal land rights.

To see this pragmatic shift in editorial opinion in action, it is useful to consider the views of John Robson, editor of New Westminster's leading paper, the *British Columbian*, and a prominent rhetorical humanitarian. Robson arrived in British Columbia in 1859, working initially as a prospector. He quickly joined a citizen group in New Westminster that sought to remove Douglas from the colony's executive. These reformers purchased the *New Westminster Times* from Leonard McClure, renaming it the *British Columbian*, with Robson as its editor. Along with political reform, Robson was deeply interested in Indian policy. He was likely influenced by his sibling, Ebenezar Robson, a Methodist missionary from New Westminster who worked extensively with local Coast Salish peoples.

From its initiation in February 1861, the *British Columbian* supported the removal of First Nations people from New Westminster, arguing that their social disorder and unsanitary habits were a detriment to the settler community.[70] Regarding the question of Aboriginal title, in June 1862 Robson expressed support for the creation of designated reserves.[71] British Columbia had no legacy of compensating First Nations peoples for their territories prior to settlement, and Robson did not identify the Douglas Treaties as relevant precedents for British Columbia. Besides agreeing with urban segregation, Robson was against providing the full rights of British citizenship to Aboriginal persons. For example, he deprecated reports that Aboriginal persons would be able to pre-empt Crown lands in the same manner as Euro-American settlers. Robson insisted that First Nations peoples would dominate the whole colony if they were allowed to locate wherever they pleased, adding: "no white colonists would be likely to settle with their families in a country where they would be liable to have Indians for neighbors on every side."[72] Of course, Douglas believed that Aboriginal persons should have the ability to establish themselves as independent settlers.

Between 1863 and 1864, however, Robson wrote a series of editorials regarding "Our Relations with the Indians" in which he identified the "sacred duty" of the colonial executive to formulate an Indian policy. In June 1863, Robson stated: "The Government should at once purchase, at a reasonable price, all the just and proper claims of the Indians to the lands of the Colony – at least those parts of it which are being settled. There should, however, be ample reserves surveyed in the most suitable localities, including, wherever practicable, the lands already under cultivation by the Indians."[73] As Robson emphasized in July 1864 in the context of the violence at Bute Inlet: "They are the original 'lords of the soil,' and a treaty must be made with them before we can hope to have a good understanding. What land they want would be comparatively a trifle; but it must be laid out with proper regard to their views and desires."[74] Like his peers in Victoria, Robson associated Aboriginal violence with the issue of land claims.

Between 1865 and 1866 Robson's viewpoint changed. Arguments in favour of the creation of treaties and payment for Aboriginal title disappeared. Instead, Robson began to support the shrinking of existing Aboriginal reserves, which he now deemed too large. Prior to his retirement in 1864, Douglas had created a number of First Nations reserves in the BC interior, authorizing surveyors to mark them out according to the boundaries requested by their Aboriginal residents. In December 1866, Robson argued that, in spite of his supposed dedication to the rights of First Nations: "But these rights we do not conceive to be to hold large tracts of valuable agricultural and pastoral land which they do not use, and cannot use."[75] According to Robson, the appropriation of Aboriginal land followed the natural order of things as uncivilized First Nations receded in the face of colonization. From 1863 to 1866, Robson's rhetorical humanitarianism, his emphasis on the rights of First Nations and the obligations of settlers, shifted from explicit support for Aboriginal title to a finely delineated advocacy of those Aboriginal rights that did not impede Euro-American settlement. What influenced this transformation of Robson's perspective? It appears that, as the threat of Aboriginal violence declined, so, too, did his editorial support for Aboriginal land rights. Later, of course, Robson would play an influential role in local politics as an elected representative in the colonial Legislative Council of British Columbia, in the provincial assembly, and, eventually, as premier.

In the Victoria press we can see the same pattern in 1865–66. The last editorial calling for the recognition of Aboriginal title appeared in the *Vancouver Island Times* in 1865. Then the terms of debate shifted from demands that the Cowichan First Nation receive compensation to requests that the Cowichan reserve, which had been established in 1862, should be diminished. In 1865, David Higgins, in the *Victoria Daily Chronicle*, suggested that the colonial administration could fund its Indian policy through the sale of the majority of the Cowichan reserve, which was not used by its Aboriginal inhabitants.[76] Petitions in favour of this appropriation subsequently appeared in the Legislative Assembly and sparked a lively debate in the letters to the editors printed in the Victoria press. Editors were largely silent regarding this campaign to downsize existing Aboriginal reserves, but they no longer publicly supported Aboriginal title. So how do we understand this swift reversal in editorial policy? And what external factors may have influenced public discourses?

The War in New Zealand and the Victoria Press

The scenes lately enacted in the colony of New Zealand should be matter of profound reflection to the inhabitants of his colony, similarly situated as it is in many respects. In that once attractive and prosperous, but now unhappy and distracted land we find the most bloody and protracted war being hotly and determinedly waged, and with no appearance as yet, of coming to an amicable termination. The causes of this unfortunate struggle, which has paralyzed the growth and prosperity of the colony, are in no way different from the difficulties which have arisen or may at any moment occur in our own case. Disputes about lands, interference by whites with the fishing and hunting privileges of the natives, and most of all that potent worker of mischief, whiskey, are causes which in all times and countries, have brought civilized and savage races into hostile conflict.[77]

Editor-politicians in the Victoria press do not appear to have supported Aboriginal title in response to any pressure from, or perceived surveillance by, metropolitan humanitarians. In contrast to the close attention paid to the treatment of Maori in New Zealand, there was very little metropolitan press coverage related to the welfare of First Nations peoples on Vancouver Island and in British Columbia. The Aborigines' Protection Society sporadically lobbied the Colonial Office regarding the treatment of First Nations in the region, but this advocacy did not generate a great deal of publicity.[78] The lack of metropolitan attention was the product of several factors. The absence of established communications networks tying Vancouver Island to Great Britain meant that local scandals involving First Nations stayed largely out of sight. And this was not accidental: authors who wrote about the region for a metropolitan audience intentionally avoided commenting on how the local Aboriginal population complicated settlement (see Chapter 7).

Yet, at the same time that editors in Victoria were discussing the merits and nature of Aboriginal title in isolation, metropolitan commentators were musing over the rights of Maori in New Zealand. Of course, this extensive metropolitan coverage of the New Zealand Wars was transmitted across the Empire and was of considerable interest to editors in Victoria, who identified parallels with their own situation on Vancouver Island. As the editor in the opening passage of this section emphasized, the causes of strife in New Zealand were "in no way different from the difficulties which have arisen or at any moment may occur in our own case."[79] What is interesting about these reflections is the degree to which editors drew contradictory lessons from the New Zealand Wars. For example, the editor of the *Vancouver Island Times* argued that the origins of the New Zealand Wars lay with settlers – "the great mistake that the British settlers make is in treating such a noble race as savages and interfering with their undoubted rights to the soil which they occupy."[80] In contrast, the *Victoria Daily Chronicle* blamed the "ill-timed and impudent interference of the missionaries in the quarrel."[81] Both editors identified lessons from the situation in New Zealand for the implementation of Indian policy on Vancouver Island, but there was no consensus regarding the New Zealand Wars' local significance.

The range of interpretations of the New Zealand Wars in the Victoria press contains several points. First, we can see that Vancouver Island received a great deal of news about the situation in New Zealand, including many interpretations of the conflict. Second, local editors endorsed interpretations of the conflict in New Zealand that aligned with their own particular vision of Indian policy on Vancouver Island. In this way, narratives of the New Zealand Wars were applicable to each editor's agenda – be it the recognition of Aboriginal title or the state's increased use of coercive military violence.

Worth noting is that editors of the Victoria press never commented on the relevance of the Treaty of Waitangi, nor did they cite the Royal Proclamation of 1763 as a precedent for the acknowledgment of Aboriginal title in British North America. The only editor to reference the Treaty of Waitangi was Robson in the *British Columbian*. He characterized the treaty as "unjust" and "fraudulent" because it had been established in the name of all Maori but featured only a limited number of Maori signatures (i.e., those of the *rangatira*).[82] According to Robson, the Treaty of Waitangi was the cause of all the subsequent conflict in the colony. Like other editors, Robson did not dwell on the exact legal nature of Indigenous title in his discussion of the treaty but, instead, focused on how it stood as an example that negotiations with Indigenous peoples should be conducted in good faith if future violence were to be avoided. Neither Robson nor any other editor commented on one of the central questions of the Taranaki War: What was the nature of Maori property rights prior to British colonization and how did the treaty preserve Maori custom? As we see in Chapter 6, rival definitions of Maori sovereignty were absolutely central to the discourses about the Taranaki War that emerged from New Zealand, but they were also the subject that was least well understood overseas. They elicited no commentary in the Victoria press.

Treaty making has been understood as a process whereby claims to Aboriginal title and sovereignty are extinguished through the affirmation of national sovereignty, often in exchange for compensation and the recognition of Aboriginal rights. From this perspective, First Nations polities function as equal partners in a negotiating process with the Crown. However, this is not the way that editors of the Victoria press characterized Aboriginal title or First Nations peoples. They did not look to treaty making in New Zealand for a legal precedent, just as they did not look to the non-recognition of Indigenous land title in the Australian colonies. The New Zealand Wars were relevant because Maori and settlers were fighting over land, and, to Victoria's editors, it appeared to be a conflict similar to what might occur on Vancouver Island. Editors' lack of commentary on the legal nature of Aboriginal rights suggests several points. First, it is unlikely that editors of the Victoria press believed that First Nations had legitimate legal rights to, or sovereignty over, their territory. Second, they presumably took it for granted that British sovereignty in the region had been achieved through negotiations first with Spain and then with the United States rather than with its First Nations inhabitants. This view would explain Monitor's attempt to prove how the "almighty good title" of First Nations superseded the territorial claims that Great Britain had garnered from Spain. From the early days of the Douglas Treaties in the 1850s until the merger of Vancouver Island with British Columbia in 1866, it had never mattered what Aboriginal title meant as Aboriginal sovereignty had always been denied.

Conclusion

For a brief time, roughly corresponding with Vancouver Island's existence as a British colony, Victoria editors supported the notion of paying First Nations for their land. During this ephemeral moment, it was taken for granted that First Nations peoples had rights to extensive tracts of land and that they would be paid a nominal amount for the transfer of ownership. This assumption had important local precedents. Douglas had paid local First Nations peoples for their lands in the 1850s, the local colonial administration suggested that it would pay for Aboriginal land in the 1860s, and First Nations peoples continued to demand that treaty making occur prior to Euro-American settlement. When Douglas and then Kennedy failed to pay the Cowichan First Nation for its lands, they deviated from the established custom and broke faith with both First Nations and local settlers. Of course, the threat of Aboriginal violence was central to editors' demands that the colonial administration take action and pay for Aboriginal territory. The examples of nearby Washington Territory and faraway New Zealand provided evidence that duplicitous land dealings resulted in wars. But nothing happened. Slowly but surely expectations changed, until finally Joseph Trutch rewrote the historical narrative entirely.

On 24 June 1869, W. Sebright Green, a local solicitor in Victoria and one-time editor of the *British Colonist,* fired a broadside at the colonial administration of British Columbia in a letter to the Aborigines' Protection Society that was published in the society's newspaper, the *Colonial Intelligencer.*[83] Green implored the society to nominate a local agent to protect First Nations peoples, alluding to how colonial executives had not implemented an appropriate "Indian policy" during his seven years' residence in the region. According to Green, local First Nations were unprotected. They were again left to die in droves when smallpox reappeared in Victoria in 1868. In particular, Green called attention to the pledge made in 1862 to the Cowichan people, who had been promised payment for their lands when the district was thrown open to settlement: "They have *never* been paid for their land, their reserve has *not* been kept intact, and *no sort* of protection has been extended to them." First Nations peoples were being denied their basic rights as British subjects – protection under the rule of law and compensation for confiscated property.

Green's incendiary letter prompted Earl Granville at the Colonial Office to request a reply to these charges from Anthony Musgrave, the governor of British Columbia. In turn, Musgrave forwarded a response from Trutch, then the commissioner of lands and works and surveyor general.[84] In an extended letter, Trutch refuted Green's allegations as "entirely inconsistent with the facts" and provided a detailed history of Indian policy in the region. This document elaborated a seldom officially discussed subject – the historic treatment of Aboriginal land rights on Vancouver Island and then in British Columbia. As Trutch explained: "The title of the Indians in the fee of the public lands, or of any portion thereof, has never been acknowledged by Government, but, on the contrary, is distinctly denied."

Of course, Douglas had made a series of fourteen small land purchases on Vancouver Island in the early 1850s and had continued to reference the property title of First Nations up until 1861. Trutch had lived in British Columbia from 1858 and on the west coast of the United States from 1849, working as an engineer and surveyor before achieving a government appointment.[85] He must have known about the Douglas Treaties. Yet he gamely explained how this series of agreements and payments in goods were "made for the purpose of securing friendly relations between those Indians and the settlement of Victoria ... and certainly not in acknowledgement of any general title of the Indians to the lands they occupy." In this way, Trutch erased the inconsistencies between Douglas's early purchases of land and his own allocation of small reserves for First Nations and denied the crux of Green's complaint: that Cowichan peoples had legitimate claims to compensation for lost territory. By this time, the editors of the Victoria press no longer supported the principle of Aboriginal title and certainly did not draw attention to the early 1860s, when they had acknowledged the property rights of First Nations peoples.

So how firm was support for Aboriginal title? Not firm at all it would seem. Throughout the mid-nineteenth century both colonial executives such as Douglas and Kennedy and members of the Legislative Assembly delayed dealing with the issue of Aboriginal land rights. In the context of political inertia over the transfer of Crown land from the HBC to the Legislative Assembly, the issue of Aboriginal land rights was raised most frequently in the context of the threat of Aboriginal violence. As perceptions of this threat declined in 1865–66, the terms of the debate shifted from the issue of payment to the reorganization of Aboriginal reserves. Ostensibly, settlers wanted access to high-value land. Of course there had never been a shortage of land on Vancouver Island or in British Columbia, but reserve lands often featured territory that was most readily adapted to cultivation for the simple reason that it was, or already had been, utilized for that purpose by First Nations. The appropriation of reserve land, then, not only served the purpose of settlers but also aligned with the ambitions of local evangelical humanitarians to limit the independence of First Nations and to encourage their assimilation into settler society. Small reserves often did not provide First Nations with sufficient resources to maintain their custom-ary subsistence activities, forcing Aboriginal people to labour within the settler economy.[86] The prevalent voice of humanitarianism from the 1860s on, and the one articulated by Trutch in his defence of local Indian policy, characterized First Nations as legal minors and wards of the state. This view of Aboriginal rights was more compatible with the allocation of reserves controlled by the Crown than with the recognition of Aboriginal title to the great majority of Vancouver Island and British Columbia.

For a brief time public voices in Victoria and New Westminster argued in favour of the recognition of Aboriginal title in order to facilitate colonial expansion. Editors drew on notions of "natural justice" and the obligation to treat First Nations fairly – notions that were anchored in the perceived moral codes of both Euro-Americans and First Nations. But the weight of this moral argument shifted alongside the perceived ability of Aboriginal persons to coerce settlers. By 1866, Monitor remained the only voice of conscience in the Victoria press. Later, many of the editor-politicians who had supported Aboriginal title during the colonial era became the political leaders of the province of British Columbia, in which capacity they engaged in the ongoing denial of Aboriginal land rights. Of course, the Aboriginal advocates of land rights were never silenced but, rather, continued to pursue redress along all the political and legal avenues at their disposal.[87] And this struggle continues today.

5

The Auckland Press at War

In Auckland, the influential entrepreneur J.C. Firth organized a public meeting to rally support for the Taranaki War.[1] The "Monster Meeting" was planned for 19 May 1860 in front of the court house on Queen Street. In the publicity for the rally, Firth stressed that local colonists had to strengthen the "hands of His Excellency ... [and] set the question in its true light before the people of England."[2] Here Firth is referring to the opposition to Governor Thomas Gore Browne's use of the military to enforce the Waitara purchase just a month before. The demands of missionaries for "peace, and at almost any price," had to be refuted because their "mistaken philanthropy" emboldened Maori rebels. Times had changed, too, and missionaries could not expect to garner support in England: "Our country-men have learned a terrible lesson in the Indian Rebellion, and they are not likely to stand by, and see another holocaust of victims sacrificed on the ladder of mistaken philanthropy." Britons at home needed to know: "The Colonists, almost to a man, have endorsed the policy of the Governor in this war throughout ... They only desire the opportunity to express that approval publicly."

Twelve speakers addressed a large crowd at the Monster Meeting.[3] Discussion centred on four resolutions expressing support for Browne, but not every speaker celebrated the meeting's purpose. J.T. Boylan, a member of Auckland's Provincial Council, complained: "The effect of that meeting would be that the war would go home as the people's war ... and it would be made use of at home as a great argument in Parliament when the question of expense was raised." Then Captain Hale stated that he, too, "had considerable doubts as to the wisdom of holding the meeting" as metropolitan Britons might misinterpret the Taranaki conflict as a "settlers' war." Outraged by this dissent, Firth stressed that he "had not intended to come forward and address the meeting ... but, still from what had taken place, he felt he ought to do so" because of Boylan's attempt to "cover the whole affair with ridicule." Firth then reiterated that Anglican clerics were to blame for the outbreak of the Taranaki War and were inappropriately seeking to censure Browne. When Hugh Carleton, the editor of the *Southern Cross*, challenged Firth to identify the target of his insinuations, he named the prominent Anglican bishop of New Zealand, George Augustus Selwyn, whom he accused of having "more sympathy for one brown man than ten white ones."

Selwyn had both "influential friends at home" and "private channels of communication." The implication was that Selwyn was abusing his privileged connections to policy makers such as William Gladstone, then the chancellor of the exchequer. Moreover, colonists lacked the means to counter Selwyn's influence. Spurred on by Carleton's objection, Firth then castigated the Auckland press: "If the press had come forward and done its duty, and there had been no white faced men to rule it, they might have counteracted that influence ... Had it done so, there would have been no occasion for this meeting." Instead, the *New Zealander* and *Southern Cross* had remained silent, either because of fear or because of intimate connection with local clergy. Here Firth alludes to the well known fact that Carleton was the brother-in-law of Archdeacon Octavius Hadfield, one of the most vocal critics of the Taranaki War and the son-in-law of Henry Williams, another prominent Church Missionary Society missionary.

In the next edition of the *Southern Cross*, Carleton defended the integrity of Bishop Selwyn and repeated his complaints against the Monster Meeting:

> The effect of the meeting, both upon the Natives, and upon our English friends at home, will be most prejudicial ... We know that it was asked among them [i.e., the Maori present at the meeting], whether Europeans were really desirous of extirpating the race. As to our friends at home, the meeting will have the effect ... in persuading them to believe, – namely that the settlers were inimical to the Natives, and that the interests of the Natives were cared for by the Government alone.[4]

Carleton also challenged the significance of the Monster Meeting in this editorial. He downplayed the number of colonists reported to be in attendance and asserted that those present had not supported the meeting's resolutions.[5] In contrast to Firth, Carleton, in his characterization of the meeting, sought to downplay the colonists' enthusiasm for the war.

None of the speakers at the Monster Meeting criticized the Taranaki War, but they vehemently disagreed about the merits of expressing support for it. Public men like Boylan, Hale, and Carleton were worried that the British Parliament might refuse to pay for a war that had been initiated by settlers. This concern related to a prevalent stereotype – that colonists were opposed to Maori welfare and eager to use military force to their advantage. Carleton also expressed concern over alienating local Maori. As Firth's comments illustrate as well, Auckland's press was understood to be central to the representation of colonial public opinion in Great Britain. And Firth was right: local editors did not transparently reflect public opinion.

In this chapter, I explore how editors of the Auckland press crafted their responses to the Taranaki War for multiple imagined audiences. I begin by exploring Auckland's political and press formation during the 1850s, showing how debates over Maori policy dominated. Paying attention to the mechanics of news transmission, I then elaborate upon why New Zealand's most significant newspapers endorsed the *Taranaki Herald*'s characterization of the war's significance and affirmed the humanitarian paradigm of Maori civilizing reform found in *Te Karere Maori*. I pay particular attention to how the anxiety associated with both metropolitan and Maori surveillance encouraged the use of humanitarian themes. I divide this chapter into four sections, the first two describing the organization of the Auckland press and its prewar editorial manifestos, the last two describing the response of the Auckland press to the Taranaki War.

The Inclusive Auckland Press

Auckland was New Zealand's capital and its most populous province in the mid-nineteenth century. Its press community had been established almost immediately following British colonization with the foundation of the *New Zealand Herald and Auckland Gazette* in 1841. Four newspapers dominated by the late 1850s: the *Southern Cross* (1843), the *New Zealander* (1845), the *Auckland Examiner* (1856), and the *Auckland Weekly Register* (1857). These

Figure 10 Auckland, 1857. Tinted lithograph (Patrick Joseph Hogan, 1804–78), Alexander Turnbull Library, Wellington, NZ, A-109-044

were political and commercial institutions. John Williamson, Auckland's provincial superintendent and the leader of the Constitutional Party, owned the *New Zealander* and the *Auckland Weekly Register* with his business partner William Wilson.[6] William Brown and John Logan Campbell, both former superintendents of Auckland and leaders of the Progress Party, owned and operated the *Southern Cross*.[7] As previously mentioned, the editor of this paper was Hugh Carleton, a long-time member of the House of Representatives and political strategist for the Progress Party.[8] The *Auckland Examiner* was not affiliated with a political party, but its owner and editor, Charles Southwell, did have political ambitions. A notorious atheist and demagogue, Southwell had stood for election to Auckland's Provincial Council in 1857 and lost.[9] Along with these newspapers, Auckland also featured the emergence and decline of several short-lived papers during the 1850s and early 1860s.[10] This instability is evidenced by the fact that both the *Auckland Examiner* and the *Auckland Weekly Register* collapsed in 1860. By circulation, the *New Zealander* was the most popular paper, followed by the *Southern Cross*, the *Auckland Weekly Register*, and the *Auckland Examiner*.[11]

The Auckland press was New Zealand's most influential press community, with 30 percent of newspapers posted from New Zealand's nine provinces originating in Auckland. Looking at this data in detail, in 1860, Auckland's European population of 23,732 received and despatched 311,206 newspapers versus 248,342 letters.[12] Clearly, newspapers constituted the bulk of posted material. More significantly, though, this exchange was dominated by traffic between New Zealand and Great Britain. Colonists actively forwarded more newspapers across the British Empire, and particularly back to Great Britain, than they received.[13] Records do not detail posted content, but it is likely that local newspapers comprised the bulk of the 42,392 newspapers that Auckland colonists forwarded to Great Britain in 1860. Just as there is evidence of an increased circulation of newspapers in New Plymouth during the Taranaki War, so postal records indicate a significant rise in the number of newspapers sent from Auckland during the conflict.[14] In 1860, colonists despatched 23 percent more newspapers than in 1859; in 1861, 43 percent more newspapers were despatched than in 1859. This increase correlates with the duration of the Taranaki War as Auckland's population only grew by 11 percent between 1859 and 1861, and the number of newspapers despatched from Auckland dropped in 1862 with the end of the war.[15] Obviously, Auckland's press community was caught up in the coverage of the war.

Three points need to be emphasized regarding the significance of the Auckland press: (1) existing circulation records reveal that newspapers saturated the press market;[16] (2) newspapers were focal points for public life in colonial New Zealand; and (3), because of the colony's inclusive political culture, local editor-politicians were motivated to appeal to broad audiences. Turning first to press circulation, records from 1857 indicate that the *Auckland Weekly Register* sold fifteen hundred copies a week, that the *New Zealander* sold one thousand copies of each of its bi-weekly editions, and that the *Trumpeter and Universal Advertiser* published four hundred copies.[17] We can also incorporate the subscription rate of the weekly *Southern Cross* from November 1856, which featured 361 subscribers.[18] If we compare these circulation figures with the province of Auckland's European population, the *Auckland Weekly Register* may have reached 16 percent of adult colonists, the *New Zealander* 11 percent, the *Trumpeter and Universal Advertiser* 4 percent, and the *Southern Cross* about 4 percent.[19] In combination, then, the Auckland press may have published enough newspapers for 35 percent of adult colonists in 1858.

However, given the lack of infrastructure in Auckland during this period, the province's urban population of 3,705 settlers may have constituted the press's primary readership. If so, the combined production of 3,261 newspapers per edition would have been sufficient for 88 percent of urban colonists. At the same time, however, this measure of circulation does not address patterns of newspaper consumption. Newspapers may have been purchased by individuals but consumed by families or other social units. An alternative measure of press saturation involves matching newspaper production to the number of buildings in Auckland Province, interpreting dwellings as potential household units. Matching newspaper circulation from 1857 to building statistics from 1858 indicates that there was sufficient newspaper production for 79 percent of "households" in Auckland Province to have received a newspaper.[20] Considering Auckland city alone, 2.7 newspapers were published for every potential "household" in the city. Like New Plymouth, the press community of Auckland published sufficient newspapers to reach the majority of colonists.

These measures of press saturation are imperfect, though, because existing circulation figures are both incomplete and lacking in clarity. For example, it is not clear whether circulation figures are indicative of the subscription lists of newspapers, their average print runs, or sales of monthly summaries. For example, the historian Ross Harvey cites the *Auckland Examiner*'s circulation in 1861 at five hundred copies.[21] This figure originates in comments made in the *Auckland Examiner* and may refer to the paper's total print run rather than its subscription list.[22] It also does not appear likely that the *Auckland Weekly Register*'s circulation of fifteen hundred represented its subscriber list, given that its editor, David Burn, recorded in his diary that the newspaper had two hundred subscribers shortly after its initiation.[23]

The correspondence between the owners of the *Southern Cross*, Brown and Campbell, in 1860–61 sheds light on the paper's publishing activity and the attempts to save it from financial decline. In it, Brown reveals how the subscription rate of the *Southern Cross* fell by 25 percent from 361 in November 1856 to 271 in 1860.[24] However, the *Southern Cross* did not just reach 271 colonists: Brown also recorded that it sold twelve hundred copies of its monthly summary in September 1860.[25] This information reveals how Auckland colonists consumed local papers. Monthly summaries were special extended editions, featuring concise reports of local news and events. They were crafted for metropolitan readers and published just prior to the mail's despatch. Every Auckland paper published monthly summaries. Given the ability of the *Southern Cross* to sell twelve hundred copies of its monthly summary, it is clear that these comprehensive special editions were more attractive to local colonists than were the regular editions of the newspapers. Monthly summaries probably comprised both the bulk of local newspapers forwarded to Great Britain and the source of the majority of the colonial news published by metropolitan papers.

The publication rates of Auckland papers were not static but, rather, matched popular demand. Printers published enough papers for both subscribers and casual readers, publishing possibly three to four times the number of monthly summaries as regular editions. This was a cyclical market, oriented around the regularly scheduled transmission of the mail to other New Zealand provinces, the Australian colonies, and Great Britain. Moreover, postal records provide evidence that existing circulation records underestimate the actual production of the press. For example, in 1860, Auckland colonists despatched an average of 3,420 newspapers per week through the mail.[26] This sum equals 75 percent of the Auckland press's estimated total weekly production.[27] So, did colonists forward three-quarters of the Auckland press's production elsewhere each week or are existing circulation figures both incomplete and too low? I favour the latter view.

Colonists in the mid-nineteenth century also encountered newspapers in public settings such as reading rooms, libraries, public houses, and voluntary associations. J.E. Traue provides evidence for this phenomenon in his observation that settlers in New Zealand founded 263 libraries between 1840 and 1874.[28] Over this period, New Zealand achieved the highest density of libraries to population ratio ever reached by any country or state in the world. Traue attributes the proliferation of libraries in New Zealand to a European reading revolution in the eighteenth century, which established reading as a popular leisure activity across all classes.[29]

The popularity of the Auckland Mechanics' Institute illustrates this culture of reading.[30] The Auckland Mechanics' Institute originated in the 1840s with a mandate to educate working men in scientific and technical principles and to provide a site at which men from diverse political, religious, and social backgrounds could meet on equal terms. This organization had an average of 351 members between 1857 and 1864.[31] Of particular interest, too, is how the Mechanics' Institute created a reading room in 1857 that was intended to be an alternative to public houses.[32] Both the Mechanics' Institute and the Auckland Young Men's Christian Association stocked their reading rooms with both local and British newspapers, including copies of the *Auckland Weekly Register*, the *Auckland Examiner*, the *Southern Cross*, and the *New Zealander*.[33] The popularity of the Mechanics' Institute's reading room indicates that Auckland's colonists often encountered newspapers in public settings, where local editorial perspectives provided the focus for discussion and debate.[34] It seems likely, then, that many Auckland settlers did not require a newspaper subscription to engage with the local press. Further, the Mechanics' Institute's sale of old newspapers indicates that New Zealand's spatial isolation extended the longevity of newspapers. Newspapers in the mid-nineteenth century were not of ephemeral value.

Earlier, I noted how the controllers of Auckland papers were almost all members of the political establishment. Their editorial manifestos thus reflected a preoccupation with debating, popularizing, and critiquing political discourses. Editors also articulated populist editorial manifestos because working-class men had voting rights and participated in political discourses.[35] For example, 75 percent of adult men in Auckland qualified as electors in 1861, and voting rates in elections were high.[36] In 1855, voters cast up to 90 percent of eligible electoral votes; in 1861, again possibly 90 percent of eligible electors cast their vote.[37] It is important, then, to describe the organization of Auckland's political establishment and its relationship to the press. Of course, it must be kept in mind that the task of making connections between editors' political manifestos and the accuracy of their representations of public opinion is fraught with difficulty: newspapers tell us most about their creators and their perception of the public then they do about actual public opinion.

New Zealand gained responsible government with the Constitution Act, 1852, based on a Canadian template authored by Lord Henry George Grey and implemented by Governor George Grey in 1853–54.[38] The colonial government featured a two-tiered structure consisting of both provincial councils and a general assembly. While the General Assembly featured law-making powers and the prerogative to supersede provincial legislation, provincial councils had control over revenues from land sales, immigration, and public works.[39] The business of shaping colonization on the ground largely occurred in the provincial councils. In consequence, struggles between Auckland's rival Constitutional Party and Progress Party occurred at both levels of government. According to historian Russell Stone, Auckland was the most "highly politicized community in the colony" throughout the 1850s.[40] Auckland's upper class comprised the membership of both the Progress Party and the Constitutional Party. Yet the two parties differed markedly in their appeal. The Progress Party, as personified by Carleton's

Southern Cross, appealed to merchant capitalists and monied professionals.[41] The Constitutional Party, personified by Williamson, an Irishman and a Wesleyan Christian, was Liberal in its political orientation and, in the *New Zealander*, a champion of both the "small man" and the Maori.[42]

In 1860, Constitutionalists controlled Auckland's Provincial Council and had done so since 1856. The early 1850s had featured fierce political rivalry. With the introduction of responsible government in 1853, Brown's Progress Party had lost the first superintendency election to R.H. Wynyard, the candidate endorsed by Governor Grey.[43] In 1855, though, the Progress Party's popularity culminated in the election of first William Brown and then John Logan Campbell to Auckland's superintendency. But this success proved to be short-lived. In July 1855, Brown resigned due to family concerns; Campbell, his successor, resigned in September 1856 in protest over the political partisanship of his own party.[44] The subsequent election victory of John Williamson to Auckland's superintendency signalled the ascendency of the Constitutional Party. From 1856 on, with both Brown and Campbell in Great Britain, the Progress Party lacked a popular leader to challenge Williamson. While Carleton was an important political strategist, his elitist personality rendered him unfit for popular leadership.[45]

Auckland's political volatility was matched by economic instability. Rapid changes in the nascent economy affected the popularity of both the Progress and Constitutionalist parties.[46] For example, the successes of the Progress Party in the early 1850s occurred while the Victoria gold rush provided a buoyant market for Auckland's agricultural exports.[47] Not coincidentally, the Constitutional Party's victory in 1856 coincided not only with factional infighting within the Progress Party but also with the collapse of Victoria's market for agricultural exports, which initiated an economic depression in Auckland. Indeed, it appears that the Constitutional Party's success from 1856 to 1862 stemmed from both Williamson's populist appeal to Auckland's yeomanry and his successful implementation of an assisted emigration scheme, which compensated immigrants' transportation expenses through the provision of free land grants.[48] Williamson's "Forty Acre" system attracted thousands of new colonists to Auckland and was the envy of colonial boosters on Vancouver Island.[49] And it was this infusion of new colonists and their capital that stimulated the economy by enlarging the local market. Here we see a prescient example of James Belich's argument that the growth of Anglo settler communities across the nineteenth century was driven by "the massive importation of goods, money, and people; the attraction, supply, support, and housing of immigrants; the process of making farms and towns; and the rapid creation of infrastructure, notably transport infrastructure."[50]

Just as Williamson had consolidated his political ascendency by empowering Auckland's working and middle classes, so the *New Zealander* and the *Auckland Weekly Register* explicitly targeted Auckland's working class as their intended audience.[51] Indeed, it appears that the *New Zealander*'s pre-eminence in the late 1850s and early 1860s related to its broad appeal.[52] Certainly, Southwell believed that the *New Zealander* had a low-brow manifesto: "The *New Zealander* is not the newspaper of a people, but of an 'uneducated' faction. It is in part the property of our Superintendent. It aims at a twofold monopoly – monopoly commercial, and monopoly political. It hopes to scare away opposition by systematic vilification of opponents ... It panders to popular ignorance that it may profit by popular vice."[53] While the *Southern Cross* was more elitist than its Constitutionalist competitors, it, too, attempted to win over working-class colonists and newly arrived immigrants through its 1859–60 campaign to prove that Williamson's Forty Acre system had failed to provide newly arrived immigrants with useful farmland.[54] The community's newspaper controllers could not afford to alienate working-class colonists.

Prewar Editorial Manifestos

In December 1856, Charles Southwell defined the *Auckland Examiner* as an independent voice: "An organ untrammelled by party ties, while thoroughly imbued with the sentiment that our Colony is ripe for radical change in the administration of our affairs, an independent voice within Auckland's press, unaffiliated with either the Constitutionalist or Progress parties."[55] This political independence became manifest in the newspaper's advocacy for Auckland's separation from New Zealand's other provinces.[56] Southwell also revelled in the "blackguard" reputation he received for political mud raking. As historian John Stenhouse argues, Southwell's atheism and experience in Great Britain as an outspoken opponent of the Christian establishment deeply influenced the *Auckland Examiner*'s manifesto.[57] While Southwell's notoriety as a Freethinker followed him to Australasia, he concealed his atheism while working for the *Auckland Examiner*. Yet anti-clericalism pervaded the *Auckland Examiner:* it was made manifest in the newspaper's opposition to the participation of Christian denominations

in public education and in a scientifically inspired and Manichean interpretation of Maori racial difference.[58]

Hostility to the Maori policy proposed by Browne and the Native
Department was a central concern of the *Auckland Examiner*. Browne,
or "Governor Wait-a-bit," was "small-minded" and a "dupe of flatterers"
who utilized their undue influence to benefit from land speculations.[59]
These bitter attacks did not go unnoticed. When Southwell died, Harriet
Louisa Browne, the spouse of Governor Thomas Gore Browne, recorded in
her diary that the *Auckland Examiner* had "done Gore more harm than
anything else at New Zealand."[60] But Southwell levelled his most bitter
diatribes at the influence accrued by missionary humanitarians.[61] Southwell
described missionaries as "Humanity-mongers" and as "the curse of the
Colony." As far as he was concerned, their evangelism had harmed Maori:

> Formerly, that character if savage was sincere, if ignorant was generous,
> if superstitious was earnest and self-sacrificing. Now, the Maori in dupli-
> city, in sensualism, in impudence, in talent for bargaining, in eagerness
> for profit, is a match for the European ... Religion sits loosely upon him.
> He will oblige you by taking it off or putting it on for a few blankets or
> figs of tobacco. Whether he change his faith, fall to nose-rubbing with
> some other savage no less "heddicated" than himself, he invariably justifies
> the thing by a Maori version of *Cos I likes it*.[62]

Here Southwell claims that Maori Christianity was an artifice: actual civilization included "Good food, good clothing, good dwellings."[63] These were
secular measures that ascribed no significance to spiritual transformation.
Christian conversion had accomplished almost nothing: "Boshee is still
three parts animal; and, though much preached at, cannot be preached out
of Pigdom."

In Southwell's comparison of Maori "Boshee" to Caribbean "Quashee,"
we hear echoes of Thomas Carlyle's 1849 attack on former black slaves in
Great Britain in his *Occasional Discourse on the Negro Question*.[64] Carlyle
condemned the fruits of emancipation, accusing freed Caribbean slaves of
sloth and defending the principles of English overseership. He did not think
that former black slaves were capable of becoming civilized but, rather, that
they were an inferior race. By invoking Carlyle, Southwell condemned the
entire humanitarian project, dismissing both Maori racial capability and

the work of missionary humanitarians. In this way, Southwell rejected the Crown's policy of encouraging Maori racial amalgamation. Indeed, Southwell's racial antagonism appears to be an exemplar of the growing popularity of antagonistic racial discourses in the mid-nineteenth century. So how popular was the *Auckland Examiner*?

Drawing on the work of Peter Mandler, it is important to reflect on the *Auckland Examiner*'s "throw" – that is, "the conditions not only of its production but also of its distribution and reception" in Auckland.[65] Southwell obviously believed that his independent voice and stringent critique of colonial policy would draw readers to his paper. But Patrick Day argues that, over its four-year existence, the *Auckland Examiner* never captured public support.[66] As we see later, Auckland colonists did acknowledge the significance of the *Auckland Examiner*, but this recognition stemmed from their anxiety that, in Great Britain, it might be interpreted as representative of local public opinion. The *Auckland Examiner*'s iconoclasm, as expressed in its racialized editorial manifesto, did not capture widespread support. A central question is: Why did other Auckland press editors not imitate Southwell's racial vitriol?

Commentary on Maori policy was also central to both the *New Zealander* and the *Southern Cross*, but these papers articulated very different viewpoints than did the *Examiner*. Real estate functioned as a significant commodity in Auckland's colonial economy. Thus, the most important political issue in Auckland prior to the outbreak of the Taranaki War concerned the management of provincial Waste Lands.[67] In 1859, members of the Progress Party had initiated a campaign to eliminate the Crown's monopoly over the purchase of lands from Maori. The Treaty of Waitangi had enshrined the Crown's pre-emption right in 1840, and it had been in force except for a brief period during the tenure of Governor Robert Fitzroy in 1844. Advocates of "Direct Purchase" argued that the Crown and, by extension, Williamson had failed to secure an adequate quality of land for agriculturalists.[68]

Recent scholarship suggests that the Direct Purchase Movement's origins lay not in a lack of available land but in its poor quality. Indeed, Vaughan Wood and colleagues argue that the Progress Party sought access to lands in the Maori-controlled Waikato region south of Auckland because of its suitability for pastoral agriculture, a lucrative export-oriented business practice.[69] Available lands north of Auckland city suffered the ill-effects of a warm and wet climate, a lack of soil nutrition, and the high costs intrinsic to transforming treed bushland into seeded grassland.[70] Conversely, Waikato's grasslands were readily adaptable to pastoral agriculture and appeared to be lying in waste. As a result, the "land hunger" of Auckland pastoralists had serious repercussions for political policy and has been wrongly downplayed as a causative factor in the wars of the 1860s.[71] The difference between the rival political parties lay in their intended beneficiaries: the Progress Party sought to aid local capitalists' pursuit of a pastoral economy similar to that of the South Island, while the Constitutional Party sought to advance the interests of small-scale agriculturalists who were focused on wheat production.[72]

In 1859, then, Hugh Carleton published a series of articles demanding the removal of the Crown's monopoly over land purchases from Maori. What is most intriguing about this campaign is that Carleton highlighted the benefits of Direct Purchase for Maori rather than for colonists. He linked the privatization of Maori property rights with the cessation of their slide towards racial extinction and depicted it as a way of reinvigorating their efforts towards cultural reform. While both the *Auckland Examiner* and the *Southern Cross* supported the Direct Purchase Movement and criticized the Native Department's administration of Maori, their basic premises differed markedly.[73] Perhaps most significantly, Carleton lauded the evangelism of missionaries among Maori. Christian conversion had benefited Maori, yet they remained in perilous danger of racial extinction. While a belief that imperialism facilitated Indigenous extinction was common in the mid-nineteenth century, Carleton's concerns were directly affected by F.D. Fenton's 1858 census of Maori, which had revealed an alarming population decline. Carleton deployed Fenton's study to argue that Maori were occupying a dangerous cultural middle ground. Maori were susceptible to physical decline because their adoption of European customs had occurred only on a piecemeal basis. Interestingly, Carleton did not hold Browne responsible for the failed administration of Maori. The Native Department itself, whose "bigoted dread of innovation" and "sluggish fear of an energetic movement," represented the most serious impediment to continued Maori progress.[74]

For Carleton, the emergence of the Kingitanga in Waikato represented the most blatant example of the Native Department's failure. In the Auckland press, the Kingitanga was interpreted as an expression of Maori nationality with clear implications for British sovereignty.[75] As we see later, when the Taranaki War began Auckland's colonial population became apprehensive that the Kingitanga might support Te Rangitake by attacking Auckland, a fear exacerbated by the proximity of Kingitanga territory, which was located just south of Auckland in the Waikato region. Carleton asserted that, in the absence of British law and order, the Kingitanga had filled a political vacuum. The antidote lay in the reorganization of Maori property rights:

> The existing difference of system, in regard to property, is in fact the great gulf which remains fixed between the two races: until that be bridged across, a radical change in the condition of the natives is hopeless. Amelioration of their condition, we admit, is possible, even without the measure proposed; but the raising them to an absolute equality with Europeans (which none desire more heartily than ourselves, though none, perhaps, more seriously doubt the possibility) is not to be dreamed of until the two races become of one accord as to the rights and tenure of property.[76]

Here Carleton endorses both a stadial view of human development and the political philosophy of Edmund Burke, which holds that civilization, industry, and liberty grow out of property rights.[77] Direct Purchase promised to integrate Maori into the colonial economy; land sales would provide Maori with capital, which might in turn be invested in individualized titles from the Crown. By exchanging communal property rights for individual land tenure, Maori would be inculcated with the principles of a liberal economy – something that was seen as crucial to their ability to exercise their full rights as British subjects.[78] Here we must remember that individual property rights were also intrinsically tied to the franchise and representation through local government. These rights were part and parcel of Carleton's promised benefits for Maori.

That Carleton highlighted Maori cultural reform rather than the interests of Auckland pastoralists illustrates the salience of humanitarian racial discourses. It seems clear that Carleton's editorial strategy constituted a form of rhetorical humanitarianism, whereby the pursuit of Maori land was subsumed within an idealized narrative. However, given Carleton's persistent advocacy of reforming Maori by civilizing them, it is perhaps more appropriate to describe him as a sincere *incorporationist* humanitarian, whose emphasis on the benefits of a liberal economy differentiated him from other evangelical humanitarians. Carleton's editorial strategy reveals the perceived values of his imagined audience – that policy makers were humanitarians and that any change to Maori policy had to conform to humanitarian principles. Carleton's peers, however, doubted his sincerity.

In contrast, the *New Zealander* and the *Auckland Weekly Register* focused on the promotion of Williamson's political policy, celebrated Auckland's economic performance, and attacked Williamson's political enemies.[79] Editorials related to the Native Department and Maori cultural improvement occurred in reaction to the *Southern Cross*'s missives.[80] The *New Zealander* and the *Auckland Weekly Register* never referenced the *Auckland Examiner* directly. One might assume that Southwell and Carleton were more interested in Maori cultural reform than Williamson and Wilson. That, however, would not be correct. Both the *New Zealander* and the *Auckland Weekly Register* chose not to comment extensively on the colonial government's administration of Maori because Williamson implicitly supported the Native Department. Criticism was unnecessary. However, an important difference between the *New Zealander* and the *Auckland Weekly Register* was that the latter was much more direct in its criticism. The *Auckland Weekly Register* stressed Carleton's elitism, his apparent disdain for New Zealand, and his lack of experience to comment accurately on Maori.[81] Carleton, and, by extension, the *Southern Cross*, did not represent the interests of working-class colonists.

In response to the Direct Purchase campaign, the editor of the *New Zealander* critiqued both the *Southern Cross*'s assessment of Auckland's economic condition and the purported benefits of Direct Purchase for Maori. According to this view, Auckland was glutted with 500,000 acres of unsold Crown lands, a testament to the Native Department's successful purchase of five times more land from Maori than had occurred during Fitzroy's era of purchasing freedom.[82] And the title to Maori lands obtained by the Crown was secure. Instead of Direct Purchase being a "high pressure engine of civilisation," the *New Zealander* argued that the new measure would cause Maori to "live in idleness and debauchery, by means of the money derived from sale of their lands."[83] Two divergent policies were at stake:

> There are two several styles of what is called "Native Policy," each of which finds supporters in this Province just now: the one, distinguished as the Progress, the other as the Obstructive – "Policy." The most prominent points in the respective schemes for the amelioration of the condition of the Maori race are the following. The progressive philanthropists appear to think that a plentiful supply of arms and ammunition, and the concession to Natives of the right to sell their lands directly to whomsoever they

choose, are essential conditions for Maori improvement. The obstructive philanthropists are weak enough to rely wholly upon the efficacy of religious teaching, upon the establishment of schools, upon the promotion of useful knowledge, the introduction of the European system of agriculture, the encouragement of industry and fixity of residence, the adoption of better clothing, the building of better houses, the use of more wholesome food, and lastly, though not least in importance, the establishment of Courts of Justice and the gradual introduction of the use of such of our English laws as may be found suitable or necessary to the wants and social condition of the Native race.[84]

The *New Zealander* championed the transformation of Maori through the trinity of Christianity, education, and participation in the colonial market. These were all tenets of *Te Karere Maori*'s manifesto for racial amalgamation (see Chapter 3). According to Williamson, though, Maori were not mature enough to participate in a free real-estate market, Carleton and the Direct Purchase advocates were "land jobbers" and "expectant sharks."[85] Direct Purchase would benefit only a few land speculators and would reverse Auckland's progress – points with which Browne concurred.[86] In 1859, Carleton's Direct Purchase Movement failed to garner either Browne's endorsement or general support among colonists. In a published response, Browne denied that "the Native Land Purchase Department ha[d] failed in its endeavour to procure land sufficient both in quality and quantity for the wants of the European population of the Province."[87] In private correspondence, Browne accused Carleton of "reckless" behaviour.[88]

The primary difference between Carleton and Williamson lay in their assessment of the best strategy for civilizing Maori. Carleton promoted deregulation and the power of the free market in the form of measures that would have also benefitted local capitalists. Williamson defended the role of the Crown as a neutral third party, supporting the idea that Maori needed to be protected from settlers. Not coincidentally, Williamson's support for the continued limitation of Maori rights also kept the price of their land low. Here we see how both major political parties and three out of four members of the Auckland press endorsed humanitarian themes. It is not surprising, then, that the Auckland press, with the exception of the *Auckland Examiner*, continued working within this established framework during the Taranaki War.

An Evolving Response to the Taranaki War

The *Auckland Examiner* exploited the outbreak of the Taranaki War to castigate its favourite targets. In a series of letters entitled "Native Policy and Native Humbug Exposed," Southwell blamed Browne, the Native Department, and New Zealand's evangelical humanitarians for the war.[89] Browne was weak and had too much affection for Maori, while the Native Department and missionaries had corrupted them out of self-interest: "The official schemer and the clerical self-seeker have combined to spoil him. They have demanded such sort of justice for him as would secure power for themselves. They have converted 'amiable savages' into dangerous rebels."[90] Southwell's racial antagonism touched a nerve and achieved international notoriety. But the *Auckland Examiner*'s response to the war was actually very brief. The paper ceased publication on 25 July 1860, apparently the result of the failure of its subscribers to support it. Almost two weeks later Southwell died of pulmonary tuberculosis.[91] The collapse of the *Auckland Examiner* occurred precisely when its iconoclastic response to the Taranaki War contrasted most sharply with that of its peers.

In contrast, the *Southern Cross* and the *New Zealander* used a humanitarian paradigm to justify the Taranaki War. Both newspapers supported Browne, arguing that he had been compelled to defend the rights of Maori land sellers to dispose freely of their property against the illegal resistance of a Maori land league; the strength of the Waitara purchase rested in its having been initiated by a Maori seller.[92] Also, editors of the *New Zealander* and the *Southern Cross* associated Te Rangitake's resistance to the Waitara purchase with the Kingitanga's defiance of the Crown.[93] The Waitara purchase and, by connection, the Taranaki War were not local issues; rather, they had implications for British sovereignty over all of New Zealand.[94] Both the *New Zealander* and the *Southern Cross* interpreted the conflict at Waitara as a crucial moment when Maori rights as British subjects were being challenged. As the *New Zealander* emphasized, the Waitara purchase represented an opportunity to free Taranaki Maori from "a tyranny which had become intolerable, and the European settlers from an obstruction which barred the acquisition of land."[95] This unified response essentially reiterated the *Taranaki Herald*'s characterization of the war's origins and significance.[96] This was no accident. Auckland papers regularly carried material taken from the New Plymouth press, and these articles shaped their coverage. Most important, neither the *New Zealander* nor the *Southern Cross* interpreted the outbreak of the Taranaki War as indicative that humanitarian policies were untenable or that the conflict signalled the inability of Maori to achieve cultural reform.

⸱ Yet, while the *Southern Cross* and the *New Zealander* voiced similar editorial responses at the beginning of the Taranaki War, they soon diverged. Throughout the Taranaki War the *New Zealander* maintained its support for Browne. In contrast, between May and September 1860, the *Southern Cross* shifted from doubt to outright suspicion and finally to outspoken criticism of the Waitara purchase.[97] By 7 September 1860, Carleton remarked:

> None, saving a few of the *desperate intelligentsia* – gladiatorial partisans, venture to affirm any longer that the vendors at the Waitara had a clear title to the whole of the six hundred acres in dispute. No one affirms any longer that Taylor is a higher chief than King; he is long since, in spite of tinkered pedigrees, set down as a "nobody" ... It is no longer maintained that the Governor acted up to his expressed intention, – namely, of never purchasing a piece of land the title to which was in dispute – an expression in which we once placed implicit confidence, directing our course accordingly, – for his Excellency has chosen out for enforced purchase the very piece of land, which, perhaps, of all others in New Zealand was overlaid with the greatest complication of disputes.[98]

Carleton's shifting opinion mirrored the emergence of public opposition to Browne's war policy. Indeed, his about-face paralleled that of several papers in Wellington and his ally William Fox, the leader of the opposition to Edward William Stafford's ruling ministry in New Zealand's House of Representatives.[99] Both Carleton and Fox were influenced by evangelical humanitarians such as Archdeacon Octavius Hadfield as well as by High Church men like Bishop George Augustus Selwyn and former chief justice William Martin, who argued that Browne and members of the Native Department had failed to thoroughly investigate Te Rangitake's claim to Waitara. They also argued that the initiation of hostilities in Taranaki had been ill-considered and illegal. These commentators acknowledged metropolitan authority over New Zealand by publishing their critiques of Browne's policies in pamphlets that were forwarded to Great Britain to contest the legitimacy of the Taranaki War (see Chapter 6).

Carleton justified his initial endorsement of the Waitara purchase by explaining that he had placed implicit trust in the reports from Taranaki but had not been able to investigate the merits of Te Rangitake's claims himself.[100] This justification suggests that even editors in New Zealand had difficulty gauging the accuracy of news from other provincial centres. In this period, most newspapers operated with small staffs of editors and printers and did not have dedicated investigative journalists. To determine the context of a given news story, editors depended upon competing members of a press community to provide contrasting perspectives and, thus, a full portrait of a given narrative. However, in the case of the Taranaki War, the unity of opinion in New Plymouth corroborated the war's justification. Both New Plymouth papers and the Crown explained the relevance of the Waitara purchase to British sovereignty in similar terms, creating a *dominant* interpretation. There were dissenting voices to this narrative in Taranaki – Wiremu Kingi Te Rangitake and his Te Ati Awa followers likely read New Plymouth papers too and knew how they dissembled. But local editors were not inclined to report their perspectives in the same way that they published the letters of their Maori allies. Both the unity of opinion from Taranaki and its relative isolation created a distinct time lag between initial reports and the emergence of public opposition in neighbouring press communities.

One of my key points is that editorial manifestos were shaped by both the structure of press communities and their operating in an environment that lacked an adequate interpretive context. In the absence of any way to verify non-local stories, editors endorsed perspectives that corresponded closely to their own. Now we can see how the *Taranaki Herald*'s manifesto had been tailored to affirm the pre-existing humanitarian tone of the Auckland press and how it exploited earlier expressions of anxiety regarding the threat of the Kingitanga. Supporting the war effort in Taranaki also conformed to the commitment of both the *New Zealander* and the *Southern Cross* to stabilizing the relations of settlers with Maori and encouraging land sales. At the same time, a sense of inertia impeded the likelihood of editors changing their viewpoints when contradictory information became available. News transmission between New Zealand and Great Britain featured an even more significant information time lag and inertia regarding "commitment," and this militated against editors reversing their initial conclusions (see Chapter 7). No doubt, Carleton's familial ties to Archdeacon Octavius Hadfield and other members of the Anglican establishment led him to take their opposition to the war seriously and then to execute an about-face despite the embarrassment of having to admit his error. Intimate ties do seem to have influenced the press.

The *Southern Cross*'s opposition to the Taranaki War was brief. In 1860, Campbell had returned to New Zealand from Europe with a mandate to reorganize or dispose of the *Southern Cross*. It appears that Campbell held Carleton responsible for the newspaper's poor financial performance.[101] This concern over the *Southern Cross*'s profitability indicates that the newspaper was never just a tool for political advocacy; rather, Brown's belief in the *Southern Cross*'s value as a "great source of power" pertained to his and Campbell's business concerns. Political and commercial interests were intrinsically connected within the Auckland press. So in November 1860, Carleton officially severed his association with the *Southern Cross*, and its editorial manifesto once again turned to supporting Browne's war policy.[102] The writer of *Chapman's Almanac* for 1861 noted that Carleton had been terminated because of his growing opposition to the war.[103] Campbell's motivation for shifting the *Southern Cross* towards supporting the Taranaki War may be interpreted in several interconnected ways. By supporting the Taranaki War, the *Southern Cross* realigned itself with the ruling Stafford Ministry, Campbell's political allies.[104] At the same time, supporting the war effort benefitted Brown's and Campbell's business interests, which profited from the British military's expanded garrison in Auckland.[105] Interestingly, it appears that Brown agreed with Carleton regarding the injustice of the Waitara purchase, but Carleton appears to have refused to remain as an editor of the *Southern Cross* if he was granted only limited autonomy.[106]

The Taranaki War ended in March 1861 – as unfavourably for colonists as it had been when it had begun. The British military had been unable to decisively defeat Maori combatants, and colonists expressed indignation when the terms of a negotiated settlement reached Auckland.[107] By contrast, the Auckland press responded positively to the cessation of hostilities. However, editors had their own reasons for this. During the period between the end of hostilities in Taranaki in March 1861 and the announcement of Browne's being replaced by New Zealand's former governor, George Grey, at the end of July 1861, it appeared that Browne might attack the Kingitanga in Waikato. Thus, the *Southern Cross* endorsed peace in Taranaki in the context of Browne's ability to confront the Kingitanga, which it identified as the real enemy of British sovereignty in New Zealand.[108] Again, it is important to note that this message was framed in humanitarian terms. Just as the Auckland press had minimized settler antagonism towards Maori at the beginning of the war, so the *Southern Cross* argued that its encouragement of a confrontation with the Kingitanga represented an effort by settlers to avert attempts by some Maori to arrest the progress they had made towards becoming civilized by, instead, regressively asserting their Maori nationality.[109] In contrast, the *New Zealander* welcomed peacemaking in Taranaki and the announcement of George Grey's governorship as the best means of achieving a negotiated resolution with the Kingitanga.[110]

Mediating Influences on Editorial Perspectives

The opening vignette of the chapter elaborates Firth's claim that the Indian Rebellion offered settlers a "terrible lesson."[111] This rhetorical shorthand warned settlers of the dangers of maladministration and heralded a new era of race relations predicated upon coercive strength rather than philanthropy. Like the evidence of settler anxiety in New Plymouth (see Chapter 3), this statement reveals how the Indian Rebellion influenced some Auckland settlers to view the conflict as a "war of the races."[112] Just like the *Taranaki Herald*, though, the majority of editors in Auckland did not draw parallels between what was happening in Auckland and the Indian Rebellion. This disparity between settler perceptions of the Indian Rebellion's resonance and the pregnant silence of the press is suggestive. In fact, the Auckland press's response to the Taranaki War was significantly affected by local settler anxiety regarding the surveillance of both metropolitan Britons and local Maori.

Well before the outbreak of war in Taranaki in 1859, Southwell had identified the threat posed by the Kingitanga:

> King Potatou is not the unambitious peaceful sort of personage that he has been represented. Not only do his subjects avow their determination "to have their own again," and "wash the island" of Pakehas, but he, King Potatou himself, coolly talks of commencing his undivided dominion by levying an import duty at all New Zealand ports where the Native is larger than the European population. Should King Potatou attempt the fulfilment of his threat – war is inevitable – war to the knife. Our rulers will then wake up, rub their eyes, and do – something. India is the battlefield of races. British statesmen were long ago told that their Indian system could not last; that to eternal smash it must go; that Europeans and

Hindoos were to each other alien in language, alien in blood, alien in religion, alien in everything. Still British statesmen persisted. They could not be persuaded that they stood on extremest verge of a precipice, and might with truth be likened to children torch-flourishing in a powder magazine. They believed in Sepoys, just as Governor Browne believes in Maories.[113]

According to Southwell, Browne was blind to how the Kingitanga's defiance paralleled that of rebel sepoys in India. When the Taranaki War began, Southwell continued to define the conflict in stark, racialized terms: "Natives are in open rebellion. War has commenced, and blood has been shed. The rebels bid us defiance. They have added crime to crime – cold dastardly murder to open undisguised treason. They assert for their race supremacy. Not even equality will satisfy them. To be supreme is their ambition."[114] Note Southwell's definition of the Taranaki War as a battle for "racial supremacy." For Southwell there was no difference between Maori combatants in Taranaki and Auckland's own Maori population: conflict with both was inevitable. Nor was Southwell apprehensive that his editorials would incite local Maori to violence in Auckland: he asserted that the Taranaki War stemmed from the false flattery of Maori.[115] Notice that Southwell did not deny the existence of a Maori audience for his paper but, instead, defended the authenticity of his threatening language. In contrast, both the *Southern Cross* and the *New Zealander* carefully identified the tribal affiliations of Maori combatants during the Taranaki War, avoiding blanket denunciations. The *Auckland Examiner*'s forceful racial antagonism and use of the Indian Rebellion as a symbolic warning renders the *Southern Cross*'s and the *New Zealander*'s alternative editorial responses to the Taranaki War even more notable.

The *Southern Cross* and the *New Zealander* did not characterize the Taranaki War in the same way as did the *Auckland Examiner*, in part due to the interplay between editors' political and commercial imperatives and their diverse imagined communities of readers. This audience included an Auckland colonial readership, a local Maori readership, and a metropolitan readership. In this context, the editors' challenge was threefold: (1) to popularize their own partisan agendas, (2) to appear to be broadly representative of public opinion, and (3) to avoid alienating either Maori or metropolitan readers. We can imagine, then, that editors in Auckland were wary of the Indian Rebellion's association with racial conflict, and their decision not to employ this symbolic power was deliberate. But why not highlight the Indian Rebellion's parallels as a means of garnering metropolitan support?

Throughout the Taranaki War, Auckland colonists feared an attack on their community and constantly asked the question: "What will the Waikatos do?"[116] This anxiety was not groundless. Browne and other members of the colonial administration took the threat of the Kingitanga seriously, redirecting and maintaining British troops in Auckland to the detriment of the campaign in Taranaki.[117] Indeed, Browne's informant in Waikato territory, the CMS missionary John Morgan, warned of Kingitanga plans to attack Auckland.[118] The settler politician Henry Sewell asserted that settler fears were exaggerated but at the same time stressed that Waikato Maori could muster between four and five thousand fighting men and represented a "formidable enemy."[119] Sewell also felt that anxiety in Auckland was not confined to the "common people." The implication was that Auckland's sophisticated upper classes, even those with keen knowledge of Maori, shared this fear. The many references to the threat of Kingitanga violence in Auckland newspapers suggests that local colonists experienced a heightened sense of danger that the war in Taranaki might spread to Auckland. No doubt adding to settler anxiety in Auckland was the fact that some Waikato Maori affiliated with the Kingitanga did fight alongside Te Ati Awa in Taranaki.

While the *Auckland Examiner* ignored the threat of Maori violence almost completely, both the *Southern Cross* and the *New Zealander* published a series of editorials on the topic, with the former providing more coverage than the latter.[120] This following passage exemplifies the general tone of the *Southern Cross*:

> It appears that there are some few in the town who are apprehensive of a native attack upon Auckland. They must remain so, for such are not likely to be talked out of apprehension. For our own part, we agree with the Governor's dictum (if he did say it, for we have heard it contradicted), that we are as safe in Auckland as in London, or rather more so, for there is less chance of having one's pocket picked.[121]

Both the *Southern Cross* and the *New Zealander* assessed the fears of colonists as "groundless apprehensions."[122] Neither paper utilized this anxiety to spur on the Taranaki War or to encourage Browne to attack the Kingitanga; rather, both newspapers walked a fine line between obfuscating the threat of Maori violence and recognizing it. In the *New Zealander*'s more limited response, its editor attacked the *Southern Cross* for its role in both exacerbating and causing settler anxiety, alleging that Carleton's 1859 Direct Purchase campaign had antagonized local Maori.[123] The *New Zealander* also argued that the identification of the threat of Maori violence was positive in the sense that it spurred colonists to take practical steps towards their own defence.[124] But, at the same time, the *New Zealander* warned colonists that their defensive preparations might spur Maori to violence. Here we see how editors sought to alleviate settler concerns without dwelling on their cause in any depth.

One editorial strategy was to use a patronizing tone when acknowledging the fears of settlers, to associate anxiety with "effeminate" behaviours (e.g., gossip and hysteria), indicative of values contrary to "manliness" and the presses provision of "facts." This editorial tone indicates that settler anxiety transgressed both normative Victorian masculinity and racial discourses of British superiority. Furthermore, acknowledging the degree of settler anxiety in Auckland was potentially destabilizing, and this helps us to understand why editors attempted to couch their recognition of genuine threats in disarming language. The controversy surrounding anxiety and the frequency of its mention in the press suggests that editors and, by extension, colonists in Auckland were very frightened during the war. The *New Zealander* and the *Southern Cross* sought to mitigate local racial tensions and to avoid further racial violence by discouraging violent rhetoric. A point also worth emphasizing is that this strategy targeted both local and metropolitan readers. This is most clearly demonstrated by an analysis of responses to the *Auckland Examiner*'s racial vitriol.

On 21 April 1860, the *Auckland Examiner* published an article entitled "Blood for Blood." In it, Southwell condemns the possibility that Browne might end the Taranaki War by despatching Native Secretary Donald McLean on a peacemaking mission.[125] This was the same rumour that had caused consternation in New Plymouth. Regarding a "potentially dishonourable peace," Southwell asks his readers: "Does the government mean to brave public opinion?" Offering his own terms for peace, he states: "Let this community stand forward and demand, as the first basis for peace, the head of Wiremu Kingi – demand it in the name of the British blood that has been shed – the blood of innocent settlers and their helpless offspring." Southwell closes his article by highlighting the local implications of the Taranaki War, stressing how vindictive Maori in Auckland threatened the community with destruction. All Maori were suspect.

Southwell's racial vitriol did not go unnoticed. The *Southern Cross* responded a few days later on 24 April 1860:

> A series of fiery articles or letters – the distinction is immaterial, is appearing in that journal, which, although in ordinary times they would be harmless enough, are at present, to our knowledge, productive of great evil. Their tendency is to exasperate the ill feeling which is unhappily springing up between Natives and Europeans, – to run the natives down, and, indirectly, to menace them with extermination. We presume that our co-temporary is as well acquainted as ourselves with the fact that whatever appears in the Auckland newspapers concerning the native race, is regularly translated to them ... There is a further consideration involved. We take this occasion to express our belief that if a few homesteads were fired by the natives, and the inmates murdered, all efforts in this province, to restrain the numerous and well armed European population would be ineffectual, – that a war of races – that is to say, of extermination, would be the ultimate result. It would be, for the first time, colour against colour.[126]

Carleton's key point is that colonial editors had a responsibility to avoid antagonizing their Maori audience. This response reminds us that Maori engaged with the colonial press and that Carleton included a Maori audience in his imagined community of readers.[127] Here, too, we see why *Te Karere Maori* acted to mediate Maori engagement with colonial knowledge. Carleton's criticism of the *Auckland Examiner* acknowledged the symbolic power of newspapers for Maori; his anxiety illustrates a belief in the potential of Maori, like colonists, to interpret an editorial manifesto as a manifestation of public opinion.[128] Thus, it seems likely that the *Southern Cross* and the *New Zealander* also muted their characterizations of settler anxiety in Auckland and their patriotic fervour regarding the Taranaki War in order to avoid offending local Maori. Further, by characterizing support for the Taranaki War within a humanitarian framework, these newspapers replicated the Crown's endorsement of racial amalgamation. As my analysis of *Te Karere Maori* shows, the Crown expressed its relationship with Maori in humanitarian language that emphasized both the Christian underpinnings of the British state and Maori conversion to Christianity.

However, the notoriety of "Blood for Blood" did not end here. Browne forwarded it to the Colonial Office, commenting that newspapers like the *Auckland Examiner* were "engendering such a crop of passions as [would] make the maintenance of peace exceedingly difficult."[129] The *Auckland Examiner* article reappeared in July 1860 in a House of Lords debate over the duke of Newcastle's proposed New Zealand Bill.[130] There Lord Granville attributed Browne's peacemaking difficulties to colonists' demand for "Blood for Blood."[131] Colonists well understood that Granville had quoted from the *Auckland Examiner* to accuse them of obstructing peacemaking efforts.

In October 1860, in New Zealand's House of Representatives, the opposition leader William Fox criticized Browne for forwarding "Blood for Blood" to the Colonial Office. As Fox remarked: "He should have thought that his high sense of duty would have prevented him from selecting one trumpery newspaper, and sending it home as a true representation of the feelings and sentiments of the people of the colony ... Instead of the sentiment of the colonists at large, it was only the sentiment of one single individual in the colony."[132] While members of the House of Representatives disagreed regarding Browne's culpability, it was evident to all that the appropriate context for reading "Blood for Blood" did not exist in Great Britain. Fox did not doubt that an editorial from the colonial press might be interpreted in Great Britain as a representation of public opinion. This is not to say that Fox was not well aware of how editorial perspectives trumpeted the commercial and political imperatives of newspaper owners and editors; rather, he simply took it for granted that, across the British world, the press was commonly accepted as an index of public opinion. This representational value gave newspapers symbolic power. Colonial political leaders were outraged that Browne had chosen a particularly unpopular and subversive newspaper to characterize colonists. Metropolitan Britons did not know about the *Auckland Examiner*'s reputation as "a rascally paper of the lowest kind."[133] Browne's despatch had never claimed that the *Auckland Examiner* was representative of colonial public opinion: he did not have to because Lord Granville took it for granted.

The humanitarian justifications of the Taranaki War on the part of the *Southern Cross* and the *New Zealander*, their characterizations of public sympathy for Maori, the alleviation of settler anxiety, and the articulation of humanitarian dissent were crafted to shape metropolitan public opinion and policy. Bridging this divide was especially important for the *Southern Cross*. As advocates of New Zealand's responsible government, Carleton,

Campbell, and Brown were sensitive to accusations of bias against Maori. For example, the *Southern Cross*'s quest for Direct Purchase depended upon convincing both local and metropolitan policy makers that colonists had Maori interests at heart. In this light, both the *Southern Cross*'s and the *New Zealander*'s editorial perspectives on the Taranaki War employed selective reportage, through their obfuscation of both colonists' antagonistic attitudes towards Maori and anxiety related to Maori violence. The reality of racial antagonism in Auckland did not garner press attention.

Interestingly, the efforts of both the New Zealand press and humanitarian dissenters to shape interpretations of the Taranaki War in Great Britain have merited little attention from contemporary historians. No doubt, the Colonial Office's reluctance to interfere in New Zealand's colonial affairs in the late 1850s and 1860s has contributed to this lack of interest. But the Auckland press's sensitivity to metropolitan public opinion was significant: local editors feared the ramifications of metropolitan interference and sought to head off any negative fallout from the war. The anxiety of editors had tangible effects. Humanitarian discourses were politically relevant in Auckland because of the diversity of the imagined audiences, but they were also, to a degree, populist. To conclude that, by 1861, colonists had simply embraced antagonistic racial discourses towards Maori is not borne out by an examination of the Auckland press and it certainly does not capture the multiple uses of humanitarian language.

Conclusion

The leading papers of Auckland presented the Taranaki War within a humanitarian framework that stressed the benefits of the British war effort for both Maori and colonists. This interpretation mirrors the *Taranaki Herald* at the beginning of the war and corresponds to the prewar manifestos of Auckland's newspapers. Now we see the context for the *Taranaki Herald*'s editorial strategy: its characterizations of both the Waitara purchase and the Taranaki War conformed to prevalent attitudes towards Maori both in Auckland and in other New Zealand centres. In an environment lacking adequate interpretive context, the *Taranaki Herald*'s editorial manifesto appealed to Auckland editors because it matched their pre-existing views. Indeed, only Carleton's *Southern Cross* chose to contradict its early impressions of the conflict, and this was because of Carleton's close ties to opponents of the war. During the war, colonial editors were influenced by anxiety related to the surveillance of both metropolitan Britons and local Maori. This anxiety led to editors downplaying both the level of colonists' racial antagonism towards Maori and their anxiety regarding the threat posed by nearby Kingitanga. By seeking not to offend, the Auckland press chose not to be transparent in its reflection of public opinion. As the *New Zealander* observed in April 1861: "Out of doors, amongst ourselves, there is a senseless clamour for violence, which might be mistaken for an expression of exuberant courage, if it were not attended by circumstances which, in this moment of public danger, illustrate the truth of the adage that 'fear is always cruel.'"[134]

Racial antagonism in mid-nineteenth century New Zealand was fuelled by a disconcerting reality: Maori still owned three-quarters of the North Island and had a great capacity for resistance.[135] However, as I show, this racial antagonism was not yet publicly acceptable. In the shadow of the Indian Rebellion, most editors avoided articulating racial discourses that might exacerbate the threat of Maori violence and alienate metropolitan onlookers. Instead, they strategically deployed humanitarian racial discourses to prove that the successful prosecution of the Taranaki War was compatible with Maori cultural reform and to emphasize that colonists had the best interests of Maori at heart. The *Auckland Examiner*'s collapse during the Taranaki War and colonists' subsequent criticism of its editorial manifesto is testament to the unpopularity of racial vitriol.

I take seriously the consequences of both the Auckland press's integration into networks of imperial information transmission and the effects of editors' perceptions of their locations within these networks. This analytical framework enables me to show how perceptions of metropolitan control overshadowed colonial affairs. Even if the Colonial Office and metropolitan politicians did not decisively intervene in New Zealand in the 1860s, this does not negate the fact that colonists acted as though Great Britain was a site with political power over colonial affairs. And this viewpoint was neither paranoid nor imaginary; rather, it was grounded in the structure and the power of British communications networks, which transmitted news via thousands of newspapers from Auckland to Great Britain each year. In what follows, I build upon this analysis by focusing on the role of prominent humanitarians in New Zealand and the mechanics of press transmission between New Zealand, the Australian colonies, and Great Britain.

6

Colonial Humanitarians?

As Thomas Gore Browne sailed from New Zealand in October 1861, he reflected on two and a half years of disappointment.[1] His pursuit of the Waitara purchase had started a war, and that war had ended with an unsatisfactory peace. Then his allies in the House of Representatives were defeated in July 1861, forcing him to work with William Fox, one of his sharpest critics. But perhaps most disappointing, the Colonial Office recalled him just as he was about to challenge the Kingitanga.[2] In the fallout of the Taranaki War, Browne had identified the Kingitanga as the most important threat to British colonization and he had been mobilizing British forces for a confrontation.[3]

Bitter confusion marred his recall. When Browne received a forwarded telegram message – "New Zealand Governor reappointed" – on Friday, 26 July 1861, he had celebrated the vindication of his wartime administration.[4] But the actual arrival of the mail packet by sail on late Monday afternoon, 29 July 1861, brought a rude surprise. George Grey, not Browne, had been reappointed. Harriet Louisa Browne recorded in her diary that the news left Browne "humiliated and dispirited," considering his replacement to be "a humiliating concession to the Maories."[5] Both of Auckland's most prominent newspapers, the *New Zealander* and the *Southern Cross*, welcomed Grey, confident of his ability to reconcile Maori to the Crown.[6] But in Browne's mind, Grey's previous successes had stemmed more from generous financial resources and a lack of political opposition than from his personal charisma.[7] In contrast, Browne had always been stymied by New Zealand's colonial government. The popular perception of Grey's superiority was deeply frustrating.

Yet Browne did not lament the Waitara purchase in his reflections aboard ship: he reaffirmed the justice of his opposition to Wiremu Kingi Te Rangitake. What Browne regretted was the error of not ordering a commission of inquiry that, he believed, would have "disarmed many opponents."[8] Browne also rued his former pride. He had mistakenly believed that he could end "Maori difficulties by a vigorous and decisive act." The Waitara purchase had represented an opportunity to substantiate the authority of the Crown over Maori and equitably meet the demands of settler lobbyists for more land in New Plymouth. However, Browne concluded, "I was not supported." The war had not been lost on the battlefield but through his failure to win approval for his policy.

I suspect that Browne most regretted that his former allies had become his fiercest critics. Indeed, opposition to the Taranaki War had emerged almost immediately from prominent Anglicans, including Bishop George Augustus Selwyn, Archdeacon Hadfield, the bishop of Wellington Charles Abraham, and the former chief justice of New Zealand Sir William Martin. These were the very men Browne had earlier relied upon to frame his Maori policy. In 1855, they had advised him to maintain control over the Native Department, and he had listened. They were cultural intermediaries, valued for both their knowledge and their influence. Indeed, vocal critics like Hadfield and Selwyn had close ties to Te Rangitake and other rebel Te Ati Awa through their shared membership in the Anglican Church. They believed Te Rangitake was justified in his opposition to the Waitara purchase and that Browne had acted rashly. Following the initiation of the Taranaki War, these men drew upon their considerable influence in local and metropolitan networks to criticize Browne.

Bitterness among former friends and allies pervades the pamphlets, correspondence, and diaries published by Browne and his Anglican critics. It is not controversial to argue that New Zealand's political and clerical elites were divided over the Waitara purchase and the Taranaki War. However, the arguments of both the critics and the supporters of Browne were more similar than has been previously recognized. Perceptions of metropolitan surveillance, networks of imperial communication, and an obligation to administrate Maori with justice encouraged both sides to frame their positions within similar humanitarian paradigms. In turn, both sides stressed the significance of Maori treaty rights, and both sides differed in their assessments of Maori cultural sophistication. I begin with an examination of Browne's connections with his Anglican opponents and then offer a brief analysis of the pamphlet war that occurred in tandem with the conflict in Taranaki.

In this chapter I explore a crucial divergence. Missionary humanitarians were not as well established on Vancouver Island as were their counterparts in New Zealand, nor did they share the same connections within metropolitan networks of influence in their critique of local policy. The crucial similarity between both colonies during this period was that colonial executives in both regions self-identified as liberal humanitarians and felt compelled to protect and facilitate reforming vulnerable Indigenous populations by civilizing them. In particular, I analyze the partnership of Governor James Douglas with William Duncan, a CMS lay-missionary. In the perilous summer of 1860, Douglas worked with Duncan to defuse tensions with the northern Aboriginal peoples in Victoria and authorized him to implement a plan for their better administration. This relationship, as reflected in Douglas's despatches to the Colonial Office, Duncan's diary, and the press, reveals the local utility of humanitarian missionaries to colonists in Victoria.

Thomas Gore Browne's Taranaki War

Thomas Gore Browne is the least well known of New Zealand's colonial executives and is best remembered for his errors of judgment. He was appointed the fourth governor of New Zealand in 1855 when he was forty-eight years old. He was a former career soldier with service in India and had previously governed St. Helena following his marriage to Harriet Louisa in 1851. As a military man with a bias against representative government, Browne fits the mould of the type of governor commonly employed across the British Empire by the Colonial Office in this period.[9] This section draws on the wartime diaries and correspondence of Browne and Harriet Louisa.

Harriet Louisa's two diaries from 1860 and 1861 are especially valuable previously ignored sources. Harriet Louisa wrote almost exclusively about New Zealand's political milieu. She was a consummate lobbyist who utilized her public persona to advance Browne's career. I believe that, like Charlotte Macdonald's analysis of Sarah Selwyn (the spouse of Bishop George Selwyn), Harriet Louisa's diaries present "a working example of the dynamics of connection by which the imperial world came to be constituted in and across diverse spaces and communities, via patronage, social and personal networks as well as systems of governance."[10] Harriet Louisa's diaries reveal how colonial politicking occurred outside the Legislative Assembly's chambers, facilitated by sociability and hospitality, amid networks cultivated by both men and women. Given the official exclusionary nature of mid-nineteenth-century politics, it is also not surprising that Harriet Louisa's enthusiasm for politicking was tempered with anxiety regarding the impropriety of her activism – championing Browne's perspective was "dangerous."[11]

During the first five years of his administration, Browne faced the challenge of implementing New Zealand's Constitution Act, 1852. As mentioned earlier, Browne had reserved control over Maori policy in 1855. This decision to limit the General Assembly's powers reflected Browne's perception of many colonial legislators: "[They] know as little of the New Zealanders as they do of the Japanese ... talk rubbish on the subject and what is more, refuse or grudge the smallest support."[12] In turn, stymied colonial ministries refused to designate funds for Maori policy, arguing that colonists should not pay for an administration over which they had no control. In aligning himself with local humanitarians, Browne continued the legacy established by former governors Robert Fitzroy and George Grey, who had also balanced Maori interests against the demands of an expansionist settler society.[13] This reliance on Anglican clerics and missionaries reflected the esteem in which they were held in Maori society and the significant Maori membership in Christian denominations.[14] Browne never became proficient in the Maori language or an expert in Maori culture, as did Grey, but he was committed to govern Maori with a humanitarian ethos.

As Browne described in private correspondence to the duke of Newcastle, the break with Martin and other Anglican critics was made all the more difficult by the fact that he had always "endeavoured to work with and through them."[15] The legislation that Browne supported belies this point. In 1860, legislation to create an independent Native council that would manage Maori affairs in coordination with the governor and New Zealand's Representative Assembly came before both the imperial and colonial legislatures. Browne had drafted the proposed imperial bill with the help of Martin, Selwyn, and Attorney General William Swainson and intended to staff the Native Council with Maori experts such as Martin.[16] The legislation was introduced to the British Parliament at the worst moment, though, and attracted fierce criticism amidst the Taranaki debacle. Critics in both Great Britain and New Zealand blamed Browne for the initiation of the Taranaki

War in order to decry the colonial government's lack of control over the Native Department.[17] The furor left the Brownes alienated from everyone: "All the world is against us. The Bishop party on account of the war and the Assembly on account of Gore's referring a scheme for the management of the natives to be passed by the imperial government."[18] Browne was too closely associated with his former allies, and their published opposition represented a significant threat.

Indeed, on 25 January 1861, Browne made a rare public statement in the *New Zealand Gazette*. Emphasizing the power of "opinion," Browne criticized the press's opposition to the Taranaki War. While recognizing the right "of every British subject to discuss, criticize, and censure the acts of Government," Browne argued that the wartime environment rendered "the unrestrained use of such a right" as "dangerous to the community."[19] Here Browne acknowledged the implications of Maori access to colonial print culture. We know that Maori engagement led several local editors to rebuke the use of antagonistic racial language that might incite racial violence (see Chapter 4).[20] But, according to Browne, the danger lay in the relative lack of Maori cultural sophistication: Maori were incapable of discerning between the free right of colonists to express dissent and the illegal military resistance of insurgents. In its opposition, the press itself had become an agent of Maori rebellion. The editor of the *Southern Cross*, however, interpreted Browne's demand as a sign of weakness: "It would lead lookers-on to believe that His Excellency fears discussion, and apprehends that his position is not tenable in the eyes of the world."[21]

While the *New Zealand Gazette* proclamation addressed the press generally, Browne also had this message personally delivered to Sir William Martin.[22] In late 1860, Martin published *The Taranaki Question*.[23] This 152-page pamphlet provided a comprehensive description of Maori customary land tenure; it also disputed the legality of the Waitara purchase and Browne's rationale for initiating the Taranaki War. Martin had sent the pamphlet to political representatives in both New Zealand and Great Britain,[24] and, according to rumour, selected extracts had been translated and distributed among Maori.[25] When the *New Zealand Gazette* article appeared, Martin was just about to publish another pamphlet. This second publication rebutted the pamphlets of C.W. Richmond and Francis Dillon Bell, Browne's allies in the Stafford Ministry, who had published their own replies to Martin's thesis.[26]

Browne's effort to gag Martin reflected his anxiety over the possibility that published opposition might have harmful repercussions. However, while the *New Zealand Gazette* article highlighted the local role of the press, Browne's correspondence reveals his concerns over Martin's metropolitan audience. The day after learning about Martin's pamphlet on 3 December 1860, Browne sent a voluminous message to the Colonial Office.[27] He described this despatch as follows:

> I send home by this Mail a lengthy report on the Tribal title to land among the N.Z. natives and on the native Chief W.K.'s claim to interfere at the Waitara. I have been so bitterly attacked by the Episcopal party in this Colony and they have sent home so many gross misstatements on the subject that I am anxious to have this report laid before Parliament as being the only way in which I can answer such attacks.[28]

Browne's despatch drew upon the previously published opinions of his Anglican critics and attacked the crux of Martin's pamphlet by attempting to prove that there were "no fixed rules" to guide the government in its negotiations for Maori land.[29]

In private correspondence, though, Browne complained that Martin had allowed a month to elapse before alerting him of his pamphlet's existence and its having been despatched to Great Britain.[30] New Zealand's geographic isolation meant that *The Taranaki Question* reached Great Britain significantly ahead of Browne's hastily written reply. This head start gave Martin's pamphlet a vital monopoly. As has been mentioned, the ability to communicate first and to shape the initial perspectives of readers in a trans-imperial debate gave one a significant advantage. And, as Browne's private correspondence reveals, he believed that his responsibility to remain officially neutral stymied his ability to respond effectively. Unlike the personal attacks launched by Brown's more outspoken critics, Martin's measured refutation amounted both to a breach between personal friends and to damning opposition from a figure esteemed in both New Zealand and Great Britain. Worst of all, Browne had previously written to the Colonial Office describing Martin as a man who "may always be trusted to give information on native affairs."[31]

Browne fought back in two ways. When his Anglican opponents requested that he forward letters describing their opposition to his policy to the Colonial Office, Browne always despatched them in tandem with letters of support from members of the Stafford Ministry.[32] Second, he frequently deployed memorials of settler support as representations of public opinion, implicitly critiquing the lack of public support for his opponents.[33] Similarly, when Maori from the community of Otaki in Wellington Province requested that Browne forward a petition to the Colonial Office demanding his recall and censuring his actions in Taranaki, he challenged its authenticity, forwarding evidence that suggested Hadfield had secretly authored this petition.[34]

However, Browne's private correspondence reveals a deep distrust of the very evidence he cited. Writing privately to Chichester Fortescue of the Colonial Office in November 1860, he stated: "Public opinion in a Colony can never be depended on for a moment."[35] Indeed, Browne associated the enthusiasm of colonists with his hope that he might reverse the humanitarian tenets that had marked his administration of Maori: "Public meetings have been held and addresses have been showered upon me, but very many of those who have piqued them entertain hopes and expectations which will certainly be disappointed, for I have no intention of reversing the policy I have so steadily adhered to."[36] Browne took seriously his role as "a guardian and Trustee for the native race."[37] He had no intention of favouring colonists over Maori. I suggest that Browne felt compelled to call attention to colonists' supportive memorials as manifestations of colonial public opinion because he feared the metropolitan influence of his Anglican opponents. Despatches to the Colonial Office were public documents, and they represented one of the few respectable tools at his disposal with which he could justify his actions. As Harriet Louisa remarked in March 1861, she, too, felt compelled to take an "active part" in promoting Browne's perspective as "there [was] no one else to put things in their true light."[38] For this purpose, Harriet Louisa penned her own pamphlet supporting Browne.[39]

The Anglican clergy's partnership with Fox in the General Assembly made the rupture with Browne all the more difficult. According to Browne, prior to the Taranaki War, Anglican clerics had perceived the members of Fox's party as their "bitterest opponents."[40] For this reason, the Brownes interpreted the clerics' alliance with Fox as expedient and unprincipled. But this bitterness was mirrored by their Anglican opponents, and nothing illustrates this better than the pamphlet entitled *Extracts of Letters from New Zealand on the War Question*. Through the publication of "private" correspondence, the spouses of prominent Anglican clerics detailed the turmoil caused by the Taranaki War. Like Harriet Browne in her own pamphlet, Sarah Selwyn, Mary Martin, and Caroline Abraham broke gendered conventions regarding political activism by publicly lambasting Browne.[41] What roiled Mary Martin the most was that Browne had pledged "himself to a course of action before he consulted the oldest and most independent men here."[42] Caroline Abraham repeated this theme:

> One feels that the Governor has been led into a much wider and deeper question than he was aware of when he made his declaration, and when he still more foolishly resolved to stick to it, because he had made it; and one cannot help feeling that he was wrong in never seeking information at least, if not counsel, of those best qualified to give it. One feels sorry for him – for he has not intended to do the wrong, or to make the mischief which follows on it; but we must blame him too, for the responsibility of going to war is a heavy one, and he might have known more if he had sought it.[43]

This pamphlet stresses that New Zealand's Anglican clerics had been caught off guard and that they felt betrayed by their supposed apprentice. It gained power not simply because it was circulated among influential persons "back home" but because it articulated an emotional and intimate portrait of Browne's incompetence, strengthened by the moral witness of these proper Victorian women.[44] Honourable gentlemen could not openly write like this.

Throughout the Taranaki War, the Brownes feared the censure of the Colonial Office via the arrival of the English mail, experienced heartache due to the hostile local press, and paid close attention to the danger of a potential Maori attack on Auckland by Kingitanga forces.[45] They, too, suffered bitterness because of the disruption of their former close relations with local Anglican humanitarians. Before the war, Charles Southwell's *Auckland Examiner* had accused Browne of favouring both missionaries and Maori.[46] He had been right. Browne wished that his critics would have acted as John Morgan did. Morgan was one of the few CMS missionaries to support Browne's war policy and provided important intelligence regarding the movement of Kingitanga forces during the Taranaki War.[47] Yet the very commitment to Maori that attracted Anglican clerics to Browne also guided their opposition to him. So if Browne and his former Anglican allies shared a commitment to Maori welfare, what pulled them apart?

The Taranaki Pamphlet War

Frederick Alonzo Carrington referred to the Treaty of Waitangi, New Zealand's founding document, as the "incubus of New Zealand."[48] His 1860 pamphlet also alleged that the Crown's recognition of Maori ownership over unoccupied "wastelands" breached God's commandment to transform the earth.[49] Carrington had been the Plymouth Company's chief surveyor in the 1840s, and his hostility to Maori treaty rights represented the opinion of many colonists in New Zealand.[50] However, during the Taranaki War neither Browne's critics nor his defenders articulated a disregard for the Treaty of Waitangi or an antagonistic attitude towards Maori. It was simply too impolitic to do so. In order to understand this, it is necessary to consider the humanitarian themes espoused by the fifteen pamphlets that emerged from both opponents and proponents of the Waitara purchase.

These wartime pamphlets were crafted in the context of both parliamentary and press debates related to the Waitara purchase and the Taranaki War. This trans-imperial dialogue occurred across time and space as reams of war reportage were transmitted to Great Britain, resonating in influential metropolitan papers and the Houses of Parliament. Pamphleteers also crafted their narratives in reference to one another, even while varying in tone and focus. Archdeacon Hadfield, the author of three pamphlets, provided the harshest personal attacks on Browne.[51] Pursuing his own political manifesto, Fox stressed the necessity of transferring control over the Native Department to the Legislative Assembly.[52] Martin provided the most comprehensive explanation of Maori property rights, drawing on his tenure as the colony's chief justice.[53] Conversely, Browne's political allies – F.D. Bell, C.W. Richmond, and F. Whitaker – challenged the accuracy of Martin's general principles regarding Maori land tenure.[54] Both James Busby and George Clarke Sr. debated Martin's interpretation of the Treaty of Waitangi and the nature of Maori rights.[55]

The Waitara purchase brought to a boil long-simmering disputes that had divided New Zealand's settler society from its inception. At their heart, these were debates over the nature of Maori customary rights. Indeed, the pamphleteers were caught up in describing the Maori world as it had been before colonization and the implications of treaty making in 1840. These debates over Maori precolonial life were very different from debates over Aboriginal title on Vancouver Island, where commentators paid almost no attention to the nature of Aboriginal land tenure. In short, the New Zealand pamphleteers disagreed on the chiefly stature of Te Rangitake versus Te Teira Manuka, the repercussions of the 1830 invasion of Taranaki by Waikato Maori during the Musket Wars, the correctness of Governor Fitzroy's disqualification of the NZC's original land purchases in Taranaki, and the exact nature of Maori chiefly rights preserved by the Treaty of Waitangi.

Browne's opponents asserted that Te Rangitake was the paramount *rangatira* of the Te Ati Awa *iwi* and that the Treaty of Waitangi sanctioned his right to veto the Waitara purchase on behalf of his *iwi*.[56] Related to this argument was the belief that the Te Ati Awa *iwi* did not lose its claims to Taranaki after the invasion by Waikato Maori because the latter had never occupied the region, a prerequisite for Maori claims to territory according to the right of conquest, or *take raupatu*. For this reason, Fitzroy was correct to disallow the NZC's land purchase because the company's payment to Waikato Maori for land in Taranaki had no meaning. Thus, when Martin summarized the Taranaki War as "a land quarrel," he explicitly attacked Browne's contention that it represented a defence of British sovereignty.[57] The Waitara purchase was a dispute over legal rights and obligations, and the use of military force was a gross overreaction. Browne erred by pursuing a land sale with an individual Maori landowner who lacked the right to dispose of communally owned property. This was an attempt to circumvent the customary authority of Maori *rangatira* and a breach of the Treaty of Waitangi.[58]

Browne's allies argued that the Waitara purchase followed the precedent set by all other land sales in New Zealand, whereby the Crown undertook negotiations with only the rightful owners of Maori territories – in this case Te Teira and his *hapu*. This was not a new policy.[59] Further, Browne's allies argued that the historic territorial rights of the Te Ati Awa *iwi* had been disrupted by the invasion of Waikato Maori in 1830. This made the NZC's purchases of land in Taranaki valid, and they were appropriately recognized by Commissioner William Spain before Fitzroy wrongly disallowed them.[60] According to this rationale, Te Rangitake had no substantial proprietary interest in the Waitara block and the Treaty of Waitangi did not recognize the chiefly veto that he could have employed as paramount chief of Te Ati Awa.[61] Browne's opposition to Te Rangitake represented a defence of both British sovereignty and the chiefly authority of Te Teira over Te Rangitake, whose opposition on behalf of a land league was seen as illegal.

The only point that this summary makes clear is that these debates were multifaceted, complicated, and completely centred on defining the nature of Maori rights. As Chapter 7 shows, these public discourses left metropolitan commentators utterly confused. Cutting through the rhetoric, historian Michael Belgrave argues that Browne did act with considerable naiveté. Prior to the confrontation with Te Rangitake, the Crown had been judicious in its land-purchasing policy, avoiding disputed land where possession could not be guaranteed or where violence might occur.[62] The Waitara purchase amounted to a new policy because it established a ready context for conflict. At the same time, though, Belgrave challenges the assumptions that underscored both opposition and support for the Waitara purchase. According to him, Browne's critics over-simplified their definitions of Maori customary title, overstating the constitutional and political autonomy of Maori tribes. Indeed, both opponents and proponents of the Waitara purchase "understated the complexity of relationships between *rangatira*, tribal communities and the land in order to argue that rights could be alienated and Maori absorbed into a civilized European world."[63] All the pamphlet writers exercised a misplaced certainty in assessing Maori cultural practice, failing to recognize how colonialism had both consolidated and transformed it. Each of the agents involved in the Waitara purchase – Browne, Te Teira, and Te Rangitake – was attempting something innovative by testing the limits of his respective authority.[64]

Harriet Louisa believed that Browne's opponents were more successful than his allies in winning the public relations battle over the Taranaki War.[65] This trend continued across the twentieth century.[66] For example, *The Taranaki Report* is unequivocal in its criticism of Browne.[67] This document was commissioned by the Waitangi Tribunal in 1996 to assess the Crown's breaches of the Treaty of Waitangi and closely assesses Browne's motivations for initiating the Waitara purchase and the origins of the Taranaki War. It argues that Browne's pursuit of the Waitara purchase represented an attempt to undercut Maori chiefly authority through a new land-purchasing policy that recognized only individualized Maori title.[68] Indeed, the report writers argue that New Plymouth colonists had convinced Browne to discard his former recognition of Maori communal property rights.

But important evidence calls into question this theory of Browne's duplicity. In 1857, Browne had criticized the land hunger of settlers:

> The demand for land is not only wicked but obscure. It is a breach of the 10th Commandment and it is absurd because there are five millions of acres (in round numbers) open for selection in this Island and no one knows how many in the middle island. Any individual however who, in his wanderings, sees "a Naboth's vineyard" thinks he ought to be allowed to stove Naboth and go in and possess it. If the people of the land should resent such a proceeding he would call upon his "corrupt and imbecile Gov." to protect him and chastise the barbarians. The cry for land is

however not the less popular because it is unreasonable and many are honest men joined in it from pure ignorance.[69]

Browne describes settlers as coveting the "Naboth's vineyard," an allusion to the Old Testament narrative of the king of Israel's theft of land from his subject, Naboth, through subterfuge and murder. This biblical text came to symbolize the Waitara purchase in Great Britain. Previously, we saw how, in 1859, Browne repudiated a campaign in Auckland to individualize Maori title. At that time Browne opposed Hugh Carleton's Direct Purchase campaign, which sought to remove the Crown's monopoly over land purchases from Maori. Browne saw through Carleton's rhetorical humanitarianism, emphasizing his reticence to risk impoverishing Maori by subjecting them to land speculators.[70] All evidence suggests that Browne's support for the Waitara purchase stemmed from his belief that Te Rangitake had no proprietary interest in the Waitara block and that Te Teira represented the interests of his own *hapu* – information that had been provided to him by the Crown's agents in Taranaki.[71]

This argument is supported by Harriet Louisa's description of a meeting on 24 July 1860 between Browne, Chief Land Commissioner Donald McLean, and members of Edward William Stafford's ministry.[72] At this meeting Browne anxiously questioned McLean as to whether Te Rangitake had a valid claim to Waitara, and he was less than impressed with McLean's equivocal replies. Remember that this was over a year after the whole controversy had begun. These were not the actions of a confident cabal; rather, they reflected Browne's anxiety that "things looked fishy."[73] Browne placed too much trust in his subordinates, and his use of military force was both pre-emptive and unjust. However, *The Taranaki Report*'s lumping of Browne with land-hungry New Plymouth colonists does not acknowledge the imperatives that framed his actions.

We are not looking at a conspiracy: Browne was comfortable with the use of force as a punitive strategy for establishing British authority over Maori.[74] The legal historian Damen Ward's recent study of Browne's proposed Native Offenders Bill, which was unsuccessfully put forward in 1856 and 1860, illustrates this point.[75] Through this legislation, Browne proposed a carrot-and-stick approach to Maori policy, which would have allowed the Crown to punish Maori by banning any communication or commerce within an outlawed district. Browne's critics considered this bill to be an example of "European 'despotism' rather than British constitutional traditions" because it infringed upon the liberty of friend and foe alike.[76] Through the Waitara purchase, Browne believed that, because he occupied the moral and legal high ground, he could intimidate Te Rangitake into acquiescing to the Crown. This rash action was informed by Browne's humanitarian worldview, which coloured his knowledge of Maori culture and his assessment of Te Rangitake's character.

Returning to the frames of reference that defined the views of both opponents and proponents of the Waitara purchase, most pamphleteers articulated their fidelity to the Treaty of Waitangi but differed in their assessments of Maori custom.[77] For Martin, Te Rangitake's objection to the Waitara purchase originated in the treaty's preservation of both Maori communal property rights and the customary rights of Maori chiefs.

> The Treaty of Waitangi carefully reserved to the Natives all then existing rights of property. It recognised the existence of Tribes and Chiefs, and dealt with them as such. It assured to them "full, exclusive and undisturbed possession of their lands and other properties which they may collectively or individually possess, so long as it is their pleasure to retain the same." This Tribal right is clearly a right of property, and it is expressly recognised and protected by the Treaty of Waitangi. That Treaty neither enlarged nor restricted the then existing rights of property. It simply left them as they were. At that time, the alleged right of an individual member of a Tribe to alienate a portion of the land of Tribe was wholly unknown.[78]

According to Martin, the Treaty of Waitangi enfolded Maori customary law into the British legal landscape. In a vein familiar to contemporary historical interpretation of the treaty, Martin defended the tribal right of Maori chiefs through both (1) a precise definition of the treaty's parallel English and Maori meanings and (2) an analysis of the actual implications of the British recognition of Maori leadership.[79] In so doing, Martin codified a system of Maori laws. This interpretation, though, assumes that a clear hierarchy of Maori leadership existed in Taranaki and denies that customary practices had changed since 1840. In defending Maori treaty rights, Martin established that both an English and a Maori code of laws were in operation in New Zealand.[80] In this way, he continued in the same vein as his first pamphlet, which, in 1847, was written in opposition to Lord Grey's proposal to rescind British recognition of Maori ownership over supposed Waste Lands in New Zealand.[81]

James Busby, however, argued that Martin's arguments were inventions – "Sir. W. Martin ascribes to the natives rights which they never possessed, and claims for them privileges to which they have not a shadow of title."[82] According to Busby, pre-European Maori custom regarding land ownership was undeveloped and had evolved through interactions with Europeans: "In New Zealand, law had no existence."[83] There had been only one law before Europeans – "that of the strong arm."[84] As Lindsey MacDonald observes, here Busby invokes Lockean political philosophy to conclude that Maori had been living in a "state of nature" without law or property rights prior to European contact.[85] To Busby, then, Te Rangitake's actions represented a reassertion of pre-treaty Maori custom – the coercion of one *rangatira* by another through force.[86]

Just as Busby responded to Martin, so, too, did an infuriated George Clarke Sr. respond to Busby. Clarke observed that no one would have paid any attention to Busby had he not claimed that his knowledge of New Zealand history was superior to Martin's.[87] Busby asserted his expertise on the basis of his long-time residence in New Zealand (since 1833), his experience as the official British resident until 1840, and his purported role in drafting the Treaty of Waitangi. Clarke, who had worked as a CMS missionary in New Zealand since 1824 and as the chief protector of the Aborigines (1840–49), took umbrage, writing that Busby did not have expert knowledge of *te reo Maori* and had not travelled the length and breadth of New Zealand (as had Martin). Most emphatically, though, Clarke attacked Busby's characterization of Maori precolonial culture as being an anarchic blank slate: "It is beyond dispute that the natives had rights; that no one but Mr. Busby has ever questioned those rights, and that had not the British government acknowledged the rights of the aboriginal inhabitants of the soil, the Treaty of Waitangi would never have been agreed to."[88] Here Clarke characterized Maori as partners in the creation of British New Zealand and emphasized how the content of the treaty reflected Maori understandings of their rights. As Clarke remarked sarcastically, Busby was more than aware that if he had attempted to claim a Maori resource prior to the Treaty of Waitangi, "he would very soon have been taught to acknowledge their rights; however unwilling to take a lesson." Busby was "in error on every point in which he oppose[ed] Sir William Martin's statements and views."[89]

Yet Busby's pamphlet was significant. He represented a knowledgeable interlocutor of the Treaty of Waitangi to whom Browne could turn following his break with Martin. Indeed, Browne endorsed Busby's opinions so strongly that he offered to pay for his pamphlet's publication.[90] We can see this reliance on Busby in Browne's detailed summary of Maori land tenure for the Colonial Office and in the pamphlet that his brother, Harold Browne, compiled in Great Britain from published sources provided by Browne. Harold Browne's assessment of Maori precolonial society owed much to Busby:

> All notions of property among savages are lax and vague: among Englishmen they are singularly exact. An inexperienced Englishman is therefore peculiarly unfitted to deal with Maori rights. If, for instance, he learns that individual title, title of an individual proprietor, is seldom, if ever, recognized in New Zealand, he may readily conclude that there is a definite recognition of tribal title, that the title is vested in a tribe, not in a single owner. If he hears of a chief exercising a power of veto over the sale of lands, he falls back on notions of feudal superiority and seigniorial rights. But the truth is, that such definite principles are principles which have grown up with our European civilization, and that they do not belong to the peculiarly wild condition of society, in which New Zealand was forty years ago.[91]

In this passage Harold Browne emphasizes the "wild condition" of precontact Maori society, arguing that Maori customs of land tenure had developed in tandem with colonization, making it misleading to characterize Maori land ownership with referents from English history. Maori were not proto-English; therefore, apparent precedents from English history could not be relied on to interpret Maori custom. Indeed, utilizing examples from English history to provide parallels to Maori communal land tenure is exactly the strategy that Martin employed to contextualize Te Rangitake's claim to Waitara on behalf of Te Ati Awa. Both Browne and his brother believed that "the Maories had no law, but the law of the strongest."[92] This view accorded little merit to Maori society.

Here we see how divergent assessments of Maori precolonial sophistication constituted the most significant difference between Browne and his Anglican opponents. While Martin defined a clear system of Maori property rights, Browne and his supporters doubted whether such a system could have existed. It is safe to conclude that Browne shared a monogenist worldview with his Anglican opponents, which accorded spiritual equality to

Maori and Britons alike: everyone, regardless of race, was going to either heaven or to hell. But the big tent of mid-nineteenth-century humanitarianism left much room for debate concerning the cultural sophistication of Indigenous peoples. At one extreme, some humanitarians rejected all aspects of Maori culture, advocating their complete assimilation; at the other, some humanitarians recognized positive Maori cultural attributes and believed that the best features of Maori could be maintained.

Clarke was correct in saying that Busby's knowledge of Maori was not the equal of Martin's. Neither was Browne's. Browne's Anglican critics tended to have more experience with Maori people and, correspondingly, more esteem for certain aspects of Maori culture. Browne never had the same respect for Maori *rangatira* as did his evangelical humanitarian allies, and his subsequent endorsement of Busby reflected his own particular stadial view of Maori cultural development, which accorded much merit to acts of cultural transformation but little merit to Maori cultural practices that did not parallel alleged English precedents. As historian Mark Hickford shows, both Browne and Te Rangitake felt slighted by the failure of each to acknowledge the rightful authority of the other, and the resulting miscommunication contributed to start of the Taranaki War.[93] It is not controversial to say that Browne did not take Te Rangitake seriously or recognize the complexity of the Maori worldview. However, what we must also understand is that Browne's assessment of Maori cultural inferiority shaped his perceptions of Maori vulnerability and empowered his own executive mandate. Browne believed that the Waitara purchase represented his responsibility to *protect* Maori. The Taranaki War began *because* of Browne's particular variant of humanitarianism – not in spite of it.

Douglas and Duncan in Victoria

William Duncan travelled to Victoria in the spring of 1860 from his CMS mission station at Fort Simpson, British Columbia. Bishop George Hills, the newly arrived head of the local Anglican diocese, had asked Duncan to minister to Victoria's unsettled Aboriginal population. At the time, Duncan was sick, probably from overwork;[94] however, he did not rest while in Victoria. Over the course of May to August, he proved indispensable to Governor Douglas, acting as a mediator between colonists and northern Aboriginal peoples during several threatening incidents. Indeed, Douglas found Duncan so useful that he tried to convince him to stay in Victoria.[95]

In this section, I examine Duncan's relationship with Douglas, their shared vision for the administration of northern First Nations in Victoria, and the subsequent failure of their plans.

Duncan was the first CMS missionary on the Northwest Coast.[96] He arrived in June 1857 to establish a ministry among the Ts'msyen people at Fort Simpson, an isolated HBC trading post. This plan was the brainchild of James Charles Prevost, a captain in the British navy and a sincere Christian.[97] In the course of Prevost's service on the Northwest Coast he became impressed with the Ts'msyen people and had approached the CMS to establish a mission station at Fort Simpson while in Great Britain in 1856. The CMS demurred, citing a lack of money, but encouraged Prevost to publish an article in its newspaper, the *Church Missionary Intelligencer*, requesting funds for this service opportunity. In his article, Prevost drew attention to the "intelligent character" and "manly bearing" of the Ts'msyen people and highlighted their similarities to Maori: "Persons who are acquainted both with this people and with the New Zealanders, are of opinion that the former are mentally and physically equal, if not superior, to the latter; and that, were like measures taken to convert and civilize them, they would be attended by similarly happy results."[98]

Like other British naval officers stationed on the Northwest Coast, Prevost gauged First Nations peoples according to an index in which Maori figured prominently as a racial and cultural benchmark. Here, too, Prevost drew upon his readers' knowledge of the large-scale conversion of Maori to Christianity to suggest that, with an evangelical investment, the Ts'msyen would respond to the gospel in a similar fashion. The appeal netted five hundred pounds, and the CMS promptly took advantage of Prevost's offer of free passage, despatching Duncan aboard the HMS *Satellite* to British Columbia.[99] Though prompted by Prevost's personal faith and subsidized by metropolitan philanthropy, the establishment of Duncan's mission depended upon the institutional support of both the British navy and Vancouver Island's colonial administration: missions depended upon empire.

When Duncan first reached Victoria, Douglas had tried to convince him to establish his mission there, citing the dangers of Fort Simpson.[100] Regarding this obstruction, the biographer Peter Murray suggests that Douglas sought to protect the HBC's trading monopoly from interference.[101] It is probably more likely, as historian Jean Usher (Friesen) argues, that Douglas believed that Duncan would have been of more benefit to the colonial administration in Victoria.[102] This argument makes sense in light of the reported Aboriginal social disorder in Victoria. But Prevost and Duncan were adamant, eventually convincing Douglas of their commitment to Fort Simpson.[103] Prevost's insistence likely hinged on the belief that mission work would occur more easily in a community isolated from the immorality of colonists.[104] From 1857 to 1860, then, Duncan lived at Fort Simpson, during which time he became fluent in the Ts'msyen language and established a school that, by 1860, was attended by two hundred Ts'msyen pupils.[105]

Duncan is most famous for the establishment of Metlakatla, a model industrial village organized according to a Christian ethos and located close to the contemporary community of Lax Kw'alaams, or Port Simpson, on the Northwest Coast of British Columbia. The purpose of Metlakatla was to separate Ts'msyen Christians from their former community. Founded by Duncan and fifty Ts'msyen converts in 1862, Metlakatla grew rapidly amidst the 1862 smallpox epidemic.[106] While neighbouring Fort Simpson Ts'msyen suffered a horrendous mortality rate, all but five of the vaccinated residents of Metlakatla survived.[107] Susan Neylan suggests that Duncan's ability to protect Metlakatla's residents from smallpox gained him a reputation as a figure of significant spiritual authority.[108] Between 1862 and 1887, Duncan dominated this community. But his refusal to accept ordination and related tension with the local Anglican hierarchy eventually soured his relationship with the CMS. When the CMS cut its ties with Duncan, he relocated to nearby Alaska along with most of the Ts'msyen residents of Metlakatla. There he founded New Metlakatla, where he lived until his death in 1906.

The extremes of Duncan's life – his formation of a utopian community, authoritarianism, defence of Aboriginal land rights, bitter split with the CMS, relocation to the United States, and sheer longevity across the nine-teenth century have elicited considerable attention. The first guidebook writers of the mid-nineteenth century praised Duncan "as a man of ten thousand" and celebrated his transformation of both the material and spirit-ual worlds of Ts'msyen converts.[109] In Duncan's own lifetime enthusiastic admirers penned hagiographical biographies.[110] More recently, Peter Murray and Adele Perry provide more balanced portraits of Duncan's character.[111] Alternatively, Jean Usher, Clarence Bolt, and Susan Neylan utilize the study of Duncan's mission as an analytical frame within which to assess the con-nections between Ts'msyen agency and their conversion to Christianity. These writers interrogate the heroic portraits of Duncan and also identify the syncretic aspects of Ts'msyen Christian practice, especially how Duncan operated within a Ts'msyen worldview.[112] These historians, especially Neylan, define the missionary enterprise as an act of colonialism that exploits the unequal power relations between Aboriginal peoples and colonists.[113] This insight is a useful reminder that Duncan's influence among Ts'msyen people stemmed, in part, from his access to British economic and political power.

Duncan's work at Fort Simpson had reverberated in Victoria before his return. Soon after Bishop Hills reached Victoria in January 1860, he encountered former Ts'msyen students of Duncan who demonstrated both their ability to read and write in English and their enthusiasm for Christian services.[114] Hills was impressed. He recorded in his diary that Duncan had "a great influence" among Ts'msyen people.[115] Similarly, in a despatch to the Colonial Office in February 1860, Douglas praised Duncan as "an exemplary and truly worthy gentleman" who "ha[d] acquired the Native language, and succeeded in winning the confidence and attachment of the Natives."[116] Clearly, Duncan's peers believed that he had achieved remarkable success in just three years. While unfiltered sources of Aboriginal opinion of Duncan are limited, his ability to successfully mediate relations with northern Aboriginal peoples in Victoria illustrates his social standing. This assertion is supported by an anecdote reported by Richard Charles Mayne, a British naval officer stationed in Victoria. Mayne recounted meeting northern Aboriginal leaders who expressed their desire that a teacher like Duncan be sent to their communities.[117] According to Mayne, these Aboriginal persons were jealous of their Ts'msyen neighbours and could not comprehend why the British had not favoured them in a similar fashion. Mayne's anecdote indicates that Aboriginal people viewed Duncan as an official agent of the Crown. This assumption is not surprising, given the public recognition and support Duncan received from the colonial administration and the British navy.

Duncan began working among northern Aboriginal peoples immediately upon arriving in Victoria on 28 May 1860. At this time, Douglas was away visiting British Columbia. Duncan's initial activities included preaching, teaching, and admonishing northern First Nations to cease alcohol consumption and fighting among themselves.[118] In this way, Duncan sought to end the disruptive behaviour of northern First Nations. Here we see how his efforts at social reform aimed at results that would please local colonists. Though Duncan's journal provides no detail regarding who directed his initial activities, it seems likely that his priorities reflected the concerns of local evangelical humanitarians.[119] The centrality of admonishment to Duncan's engagement with northern Aboriginal peoples can be seen in the biblical texts he utilized. In general, Duncan preached from texts that describe God's wrath with regard to the unrepentant.[120] He put forward a gospel of fear that encouraged northern Aboriginal peoples to quit their defiance to God. But this emphasis on judgment may have also reflected a belief that northern Aboriginal peoples were already experiencing God's wrath – that their demographic and moral decline originated in their continued heathenism. Duncan's biblical preferences reveal an uncompromising demeanour: his influence was not associated with appeasement.

Douglas met with Duncan shortly after his return to Victoria in June 1860. At this meeting, Duncan presented a plan "for the bettering of the condition of the Indian tribes in 15 propositions."[121] Duncan's "Memorandum – With a view to improving the Condition of the Indians at Victoria" proposed to organize Victoria's sojourning northern Aboriginal population into discrete, self-policing, and self-sufficient tribal communities, with monies to be collected from taxes on both individual Aboriginal persons and their homes.[122] As Usher illustrates, the tenets of this plan would provide the basis for the organization of Metlakatla in 1862.[123] Even though Duncan penned the memorandum's fifteen propositions, they seem to reflect the consensus of other evangelical humanitarians in Victoria. The diary of Bishop Hills to 6 April 1860 details how, in conversation with police commissioner Augustus Pemberton and Reverend Edward Cridge, it was decided that the frequency of Aboriginal "disturbances" demanded some form of "police regulations": "All the families should be registered, should be taxed a small annual amount, order should be maintained, houses should be placed so that sanitary measures could be observed, a superintendent, native police, an Institution under a clergyman, a school under a teacher, an orphanage [and] a hospital."[124] These proposed regulations mirrored Duncan's, hinting that his later proposal was drafted with their input. In these recommendations for social reform, we see how a confluence of interests united local missionary humanitarians to Victoria's colonial administration – Aboriginal social disorder in Victoria was both a problem of security and a spiritual concern. Indeed, Hills's discussions with concerned colonists led to the initiation of the Indian Improvement Committee in 1860, which immediately raised funds and built a school for local Aboriginal peoples.[125]

When Duncan met with Douglas on 21 June 1860, he learned of his intention to evict northern First Nations from Victoria. However, after Duncan presented his plan, Douglas immediately changed his mind. As we have seen, 1860 was one of the few years between 1854 and 1862 when the eviction of sojourning northern First Nations did not occur. Now we see the direct role Duncan played in Douglas's decision making. In his journal, Duncan described his astonishment at Douglas's impulsive reversal.[126] Douglas's endorsement of Duncan's plan can be found in two sources. Writing to the Colonial Office on 7 July 1860, Douglas first described the scene in Victoria to which he had returned: the aggregation of two thousand northern Aboriginals whose abuse of alcohol led to "scenes of riot, disorder, and outrage, disgraceful to a civilized Country" and threatened to erupt into open warfare.[127] After noting that it was not prudent to evict northern First Nations as doing so might lead to "collision and bloodshed," Douglas described the tenets of Duncan's plan.[128] While he did not reference Duncan's authorship, he mentioned his invaluable aid: "Mr Duncan, whose labours as a Missionary at Fort Simpson, I have already had the honor of bringing to the notice of your Grace, has cheerfully placed himself at my disposal in carrying out the before mentioned arrangements, and has been of the utmost assistance to me."[129]

In August 1860, Douglas again reiterated Duncan's plan. This time he responded to the local British commander-in-chief, Rear Admiral R.L. Baynes, who had counselled him that northern Aboriginal peoples should not be allowed to remain in Victoria. Douglas explained:

> 5. To remove the Indians from Victoria is another desideratum not easy of attainment, so that permanent good would result. Coercive measures would but be productive of greater evils in other parts of the British Possessions, more exposed and less protected than Victoria. 6. I have given much anxious thought to the subject, and am of opinion that the only really effective means of permanently remedying the evil, is to improve the social condition of the Indians, at the same time maintaining every proof of physical superiority, an impression which it is of the utmost consequence the Savage should be deeply imbued with.[130]

Again, Douglas closed this letter with a reference to Duncan: "Mr. Duncan will take up residence amongst them, and I confidently hope we may by degrees overcome many of their barbarous and demoralizing habits."[131]

This correspondence is striking both for Douglas's enthusiasm and for his claiming credit for the innovative plan for Aboriginal administration. Writing to the Colonial Office, Douglas stated: "I have long cherished the hope of being able to organize the Indian Tribes into Communities." To

Baynes, he stated: "I have given much anxious thought to the subject."[132] This may have been true. Douglas might have long envisioned implementing a plan for the better administration of Victoria's Aboriginal population. But his letters display no originality; they simply reiterate the key tenets of Duncan's plan – the reorganization of northern Aboriginal tribes into separate communities, the creation of an Aboriginal police force, and the use of taxation to make the plan financially self-sufficient.[133] If Douglas had an authentic vision for the reform of Victoria's Aboriginal community, he did not share it.

The way in which Douglas expressed his enthusiasm for reforming local Aboriginal peoples by civilizing them suggests that he believed these sentiments would impress the Colonial Office. Certainly, this humanitarian persona was not a new one. Adele Perry shows how, from the late 1830s, Douglas peppered his official correspondence with liberal humanitarian sentiments that expressed his desire to get First Nations to stop practising slavery.[134] But, as Perry also reveals, Douglas was always shrewd and pragmatic: he favoured "exert[ing] ... moral influence alone" rather than conducting an active campaign to expunge Aboriginal slavery, which might have proven disruptive to HBC business and elicited hostility from Aboriginal people.[135] Like Governor George Grey in New Zealand, there was considerable dissonance between Douglas's pledges and his actions.

The first step towards the implementation of Duncan's plan involved his communicating his intentions to the different northern First Nations assembled at Victoria.[136] At these meetings, Duncan acted as an interpreter for Douglas, who did not speak Ts'msyen. Later, when addressing Haida, Duncan spoke in Ts'msyen and an Aboriginal interpreter then relayed his speech in Haida.[137] Here we see how Douglas authorized Duncan to act on his behalf at these meetings. Duncan's second step involved his organizing the relocation of northern Aboriginal peoples to separate camps according to tribal affiliations. Several events complicated matters, though. On 29 June 1860, Douglas employed British naval forces to surround the local Haida camp in order to capture the Aboriginal persons responsible for firing on a schooner named *Royal Charlie*.[138] Then, on 2 July 1860, Victoria police shot and killed two Haida leaders – Captain John and his brother – when the men drew knives while being held in the jail.[139] Their imprisonment and the raid on the Haida camp were part of a broader plan to better police local northern Aboriginal peoples. The police department's departure from its customary policy of non-interference threatened to escalate into a larger outbreak of violence.

Duncan's journal reveals the fear and confusion experienced by northern First Nations who witnessed the use of British military force in Victoria. During the crises of 29 June and 2 July 1860, Duncan mediated relations between northern Aboriginal peoples and the Crown by assuring them of the latter's benign intentions.[140] Regarding the *Royal Charlie* incident, Duncan stated: "I stayed among the Tsimshean Indians to pacify them. They felt greatly alarmed at seeing the red jackets near."[141] Again, with regard to the deaths of Captain John and his brother, Duncan emphasized in his journal that "the event ha[d] caused great stir among Indians and whites" and that he had accompanied Commissioner Pemberton to the Haida camp.[142] In addition, during Duncan's time in Victoria he also helped local police to arrest a Ts'msyen murderer and worked as a translator during court cases involving northern Aboriginal persons.[143] Duncan's close work with Pemberton during these perilous moments illustrates his utility to the police and the judiciary.

Regarding this period, Mayne states in his guidebook that Duncan had been "of much value in keeping these Northern Indians in order."[144] Later, when the CMS published Duncan's journal in 1871, its editor quoted from Duncan's correspondence, in which he describes his role more boldly: "Had I not come, most probably the Indians would have been driven away from Victoria, and that might have led to a quarrel, then a war, then we should have had a repetition of the misery and trouble the Americans have experienced in their western territories."[145] Retrospectively, Duncan identified his ability to convince Douglas not to evict northern Aboriginal peoples as a significant factor contributing to the avoidance of war. Certainly, in Douglas's discussion of his new plan for Aboriginal administration, he, too, argued that the number of northern Aboriginal people in Victoria rendered eviction too dangerous. It is also important to recognize that it was Duncan's knowledge of the Ts'msyen language that facilitated his influence among northern Aboriginal peoples. This point is obvious but worth emphasizing: Duncan broke convention when, as an agent of the Crown, he utilized the Ts'msyen language in Victoria.

Douglas's common practice was to communicate with northern Aboriginal peoples through Chinook *wawa*, an Aboriginal trading language that utilized some English and French vocabulary and that was a staple of fur trade culture on the Northwest Coast.[146] As John Lutz argues, "Chinook jargon was the language of exchange and the workplace, of the 'middle ground' between Aboriginal people and immigrants" on the Northwest Coast.[147] As has been mentioned, Chinook *wawa* was the language of treaty making on Vancouver Island; however, it was also "a language of approximate meaning," characterized by "deliberate ambiguity."[148] Lutz argues that Chinook *wawa* is an example of Bakhtin's notion of dialogism (i.e., the idea that "all deliberate communication takes the intended recipient into account"), and he stresses the miscommunication that characterized both cross-cultural dialogue in the nineteenth century and ongoing Aboriginal and non-Aboriginal relations.[149] It appears that Duncan's facility in Ts'msyen set him apart from many missionaries. As Usher argues, Duncan's acquisition of the Ts'msyen language reflected the ethos of CMS secretary Henry Venn, who encouraged missionaries to learn and employ Indigenous languages.[150] Indeed, Duncan's decision to employ Ts'msyen rather than Chinook *wawa* differentiated him from the Society for the Propagation of the Gospel missionaries who later became established in Victoria.[151]

Both Douglas and local northern Aboriginal peoples found Duncan useful because his language skills facilitated more effective communication. This linguistic situation complicated the Crown's relationship with local Aboriginal peoples and differentiated Vancouver Island from New Zealand, where *te reo Maori* was both the single language of use and was spoken by many colonists. The repercussions of poor communication are evident, too, in the Haida's dissatisfaction with Duncan's inability to speak their language, leaving them unsure of the Crown's intentions.[152] As Duncan's experience in Victoria illustrates, with regard to his ability to reform Victoria's Aboriginal community, he had the personal influence and skills to do so as well as Douglas's trust, which was also necessary.

When Duncan left on 19 August 1860 to accompany the new CMS missionaries, Lewen Street and Mary Wild Tugwell, to Fort Simpson, he intended to return to Victoria.[153] Duncan's journal reveals his considerable uncertainty regarding his permanent relocation to Victoria and his desire to be in several other deserving communities.[154] Part of Duncan's concern related to a lack of financial support. He noted in his journal that Victoria's Indian Improvement Committee was unwilling to contribute financially to the initiation of a CMS mission in Victoria.[155] He does not indicate that Douglas offered any financial incentive for him to remain in Victoria. In retrospect, we know that Duncan had difficulty working with other missionaries, especially those who had authority over him.[156] From 1860, Victoria had seen the arrival of seven Anglican missionaries belonging to the SPG.[157] It seems plausible that Duncan's reluctance to remain in Victoria may be associated with the fact that he would have been under the control of Bishop Hills and would have to interact with other higher-ranked missionaries. Whatever the reason, Duncan did not return to Victoria after arriving at Fort Simpson with the Tugwells. Later, he expressed satisfaction when he learned that the SPG missionary A.C. Garrett would assume his former role in Victoria, ministering to the community's Aboriginal population. Writing to Douglas, he remarked: "The good and welcome news, so opportune, greatly relieved my mind. I felt again free to remain where I am and to pursue my usual course of duties among the Tsimshean Indians."[158]

So what happened to the plan for the reorganization of Victoria's northern Aboriginal population? Very little it seems. Duncan had accomplished only two of the plan's fifteen goals before his departure: the separation of local tribes into distinct encampments and the registration of local Aboriginal peoples. Taxes had not been raised, an Aboriginal police force and "general overseer" had not been appointed, and an Aboriginal jail and church had not been built. In the spring of 1861, Victoria again experienced Aboriginal violence, the severity of which prompted Garrett to write to Douglas personally, calling attention to the "Riot and Bloodshed among the Indians" that had occurred on the previous Sunday night, noting: "a scene similar to that of last Sunday is enacted *every* Sunday, only on a smaller scale, and with less fatal consequences."[159] On 4 April 1860, a riot had broken out in Victoria's Aboriginal encampment and resulted in the death of Tom Handywood, a mixed-race man.[160] Garrett called upon the Victoria police force to patrol the local Aboriginal encampment and preserve the peace. In his letter, Garrett, ever ready to defend his character, prompted police commissioner Pemberton to also write to Douglas, telling him that he did not have sufficient officers to comply.[161]

Duncan followed the situation in Victoria closely. Indeed, he responded to the *British Colonist*'s 20 April 1861 demand for the eviction of northern Aboriginal peoples. In a letter to the editor, Duncan argued that the proposed eviction would initiate conflict between Aboriginal peoples and colonists, punish Aboriginal peoples indiscriminately, and violate their rights as British subjects. The scheme was "contrary to the laws of humanity, and inconsistent with the spirit of true religion."[162] In addition, Duncan stated that: "It cannot be argued that we have tried to bring the Indians into a state of law and order and have so far failed." His organizational system had not been implemented:

> You no doubt will remember that a large assembly of Indian chiefs were brought together last summer before the Governor at the Government House, when a number of "salutary regulations" (I quote the *Colonist*'s words) were propounded to them. Only let us have those regulations put in force, and the driving policy will not be further called for. Let the Governor simply carry out what he has pledged himself to do, and what the Indians have been led to expect from his hands, and all will be well.[163]

As Duncan's letter reveals, he concluded that the reoccurrence of Aboriginal violence in 1861 stemmed from Douglas's failure to implement his (i.e., Duncan's) system of administration.

When he wrote his letter on 4 July 1861, Duncan was not aware that Douglas had responded to Garrett's earlier criticism by authorizing Pemberton to initiate an Aboriginal police force that was to be funded by a tax on local Aboriginal peoples.[164] As Douglas made clear, it was Pemberton's responsibility to organize this force and he was free to initiate any system of management that occurred to him.[165] The *British Colonist* recorded that Douglas convened a meeting with local Aboriginal leaders for this purpose on 19 July 1861.[166] Speaking at times in English, French, and Chinook *wawa*, Douglas chastised the assembled Aboriginal leaders for their "bad" conduct and then empowered them to arrest Aboriginal criminals.[167] While there may have been Aboriginal persons who were familiar with English, and Euro-Americans who were familiar with First Nations languages, Chinook *wawa* was the official medium for cross-cultural exchange in this era – including in court, whenever Aboriginal people appeared as witnesses or defendants. Initially, the *British Colonist* praised the new Aboriginal police force, but problems soon became apparent when a reportedly intoxicated Aboriginal police officer attempted to arrest another Aboriginal man and colonists assaulted another Aboriginal officer.[168] By 14 August 1861, in the Legislative Assembly, William Fraser Tolmie described the Aboriginal police force as "a failure."[169]

On 2 September 1861, Aboriginal violence again occurred between Haida and Tlingit persons, prompting Pemberton to request permission from Douglas to employ local British military forces to enact their eviction.[170] On 4 September 1861, a detachment of police officers supported by a British naval gunboat compelled the Tlingit and Haida to leave Victoria and then demolished their homes.[171] Garrett responded to these evictions by writing a letter to *The Press* in which he attacked "the new and terrible policy of driving the Indians from our midst."[172] The central points of Garrett's critique was that Pemberton had not communicated his intentions prior to the police action, that northern Aboriginal peoples were therefore unprepared to winter on the Northwest Coast, and that local First Nations were perfectly prepared "to pay one dollar per house per month to be allowed to remain." Here Garrett referenced Duncan's original plan to create an Aboriginal police force supported by taxes raised from local Aboriginal peoples. As Garrett noted, earlier efforts to initiate an Aboriginal police force had amounted to giving a few batons to Aboriginal persons: "The idea of expecting untaught savages, to jump intuitively into such a love for English law, as to risk their heads perpetually to gain nothing, but a probable reprimand for exceeding their duty, seems so entirely without the bounds of reason, that one wonders how it could ever have been entertained."[173]

Again, Pemberton took offence at Garrett's published attack, writing another letter to Douglas defending his conduct.[174] In particular, Pemberton decried Garrett's argument that eviction constituted a new policy. On that point he was correct. Regarding the previous initiation of an Aboriginal police force, Pemberton emphasized that it had "interfered and [was] resisted," resulting in the "old state of things" being revived.[175] What is particularly striking about Pemberton's defence is that he attacked Garrett for refusing to assume responsibility for collecting taxes from northern Aboriginal peoples. Douglas had empowered Pemberton to create an Aboriginal police force to be administrated in any way he chose. Evidently, Pemberton never carried out this duty: taxes were not gathered and the Aboriginal police were not paid. But it seems that part of Pemberton's inaction related to Garrett's refusal to accept the role of tax collector to the northern Aboriginal peoples to whom he already ministered. Garrett, it seems, had been unwilling to act as an unpaid agent of the Crown. Thus Duncan's plan never came to pass. And, as we know, the 1862 smallpox epidemic resulted in the complete eviction of northern First Nations from Victoria.

Several observations can be made upon considering this sequence of events. Douglas found Duncan useful because there was a congruence between his own desire to resolve Victoria's social disorder and Duncan's skill set: the ability to speak Ts'msyen, to establish connections with northern First Nations, and a passion for evangelizing and reforming Aboriginal peoples by civilizing them. In moments when violence threatened, Duncan's ability to gather intelligence and to communicate effectively with northern Aboriginal peoples was invaluable. Best of all, he cost nothing. Douglas's keeping Duncan in Victoria represented an economic strategy subsidized by the CMS. One can appreciate Douglas's affinity for Duncan and other missionary humanitarians when one remembers that missionaries expected Christian conversion to transform all aspects of northern Aboriginal peoples' lifestyles and cultures – spiritual and material. It is no surprise that, as its first official act, Victoria's Indian Improvement Committee built a school for local Aboriginal peoples.[176] Education and evangelization were synonymous activities, intended to create productive and orderly British subjects through the transformation of Aboriginal children. This project connected missionary humanitarians to colonists. As we can see, Duncan's efforts in Victoria depended upon his willingness to act as an informal partner of the Crown, and his diary reveals how he enjoyed the acclaim associated with this role. However, in the face of Garrett's unwillingness to assume an informal role for the Crown, the reorganization of local Aboriginal peoples floundered.

Douglas's failure to implement Duncan's plan illustrates both his perception of the Colonial Office's attitude towards Aboriginal cultural reform and his lack of commitment to the project. Nothing occurred to regulate northern Aboriginal peoples' communities after Duncan left. As Douglas's correspondence reveals, he only empowered Pemberton to initiate an Aboriginal police force in response to Garrett's criticism. Even then, Douglas provided no oversight to ensure that Pemberton actually established a sustainable Aboriginal police force, even though sustainability had been the hallmark of Duncan's plan. His plan had been designed with Vancouver Island's limited resources in mind, the intention being to employ Aboriginal persons in positions of responsibility, thereby minimizing the need for an additional administrative level. Yet Douglas did not appoint anyone to oversee Duncan's plan. It is in the context of this apparent disinterest that we must interpret Douglas's remarks to the Colonial Office regarding his own passion for Aboriginal cultural reform. Douglas's endorsement of a humanitarian discourse reflected both his perception of the Colonial Office's expectations and an opportunistic attempt to take credit for Duncan's initiatives. Douglas did a good job of miming a humanitarian theme, but his enthusiasm existed only on the written page, much like his commitment to paying for Aboriginal land.

Colonists' unsettled relations with Aboriginal peoples in Victoria created an environment in which missionary humanitarians like Duncan could achieve acclaim. Several Victoria editors praised Duncan's efforts. As the second *Victoria Gazette* exclaimed:

> The Rev. Mr. Duncan has rendered most important services at this time, from his knowledge of the Indian character and language, and from the confidence the Tshimshean tribes repose in him, they have remainined [sic] quiet when they might possibly have glven [sic] much trouble. Mr. Duncan is a man of very firm and decided character, and if an Indian Agent is to be appointed, he must surely attract the attention of the Executive.[177]

Indeed, even the *British Colonist* praised Duncan.[178] This is noteworthy because throughout 1860–61 De Cosmos engaged in an editorial campaign against both Bishop Hills and Douglas's intention to subsidize the Anglican diocese with a grant of Crown land.[179] The *British Colonist* drew clear distinctions between the beneficial work of missionary humanitarians among local First Nations peoples and its criticism of the colonial administration's preferential treatment of the Anglican Church.

However, this public support was fickle. From 1863 to 1866, Duncan briefly served as a justice of the peace, acting aggressively to clamp down on the illegal sale of alcohol to local First Nations on the Northwest Coast. His official tenure ended in controversy when he employed Aboriginal police officers to arrest Euro-American suspects and handed out what were thought to be excessive punishments. As Clarence Bolt argues, attitudes further shifted against Duncan in the 1870s and 1880s, when he became associated with advocacy for Aboriginal land claims.[180] The attempts of Ts'msyen people to gain recognition of their customary territories were not taken seriously and were attributed to missionary meddling. While occurring later than in New Zealand, this shift to hostility marked a familiar trajectory: on Vancouver Island missionary humanitarians were initially lauded for their ability to reduce the social disruption caused by Aboriginal peoples but were then castigated for their supposed malevolent (i.e., settler-unfriendly) manipulation of Aboriginal rights. In both cases, it was the special relationships of missionary humanitarians to Aboriginal peoples that either led to their acclaim or elicited their castigation.

Conclusion

Both Browne and Douglas emphasized to the Colonial Office their duty to protect vulnerable Indigenous peoples. This imperative led both Browne and Douglas to partner with missionary humanitarians because of the latter's special knowledge and influence. Both executives also appear to have endorsed the central aim of missionaries – the religious conversion of Indigenous peoples. Indigenous Christianity was a vehicle for reforming Aboriginal peoples by civilizing them, and it came with benefits for the colonial project. In the face of under-funded bureaucracies, missionary humanitarians offered accurate intelligence and were able to implement policy gratis. When Indigenous violence threatened, as it did in both colonies, missionary humanitarians became even more influential and controversial through their role as cultural intermediaries.

Prior to the Taranaki War, Browne had relied upon the advice of missionary humanitarians. Indeed, he attempted to consolidate this relationship formally through the creation of a Native council. Thus, when Anglican clerics opposed his policy during the Taranaki War, he was criticized by the very persons whom he had previously recommended to the Colonial Office. The opposition posed by evangelical humanitarians threatened Browne because these people had both a reputation for integrity and expert knowledge of Maori culture. To combat their opposition, he was forced to defend himself by invoking settler public opinion, which even he did not trust. Browne's actions vis-à-vis the Waitara purchase were those of a self-proclaimed evangelical humanitarian.

Further, in the Taranaki pamphlet war we see how both proponents and opponents of the Waitara purchase accepted similar foundational truths. Almost all writers took the Treaty of Waitangi's legal significance to be non-negotiable – but not its meaning. Pamphlet writers disagreed in their assessments of Maori cultural sophistication and the related nature of Maori land tenure. This diversity of opinion corresponded to the subjectivity of humanitarian racial discourses. Any colonist, on the basis of his or her assumed superior cultural status, could comment on how to reform Maori by civilizing them. In general, Anglican humanitarians like Martin and Hadfield, who had lived alongside Maori and spoke their language, had greater esteem for Maori culture than either Browne or Busby. These divergent perspectives had profound implications.

The situation on Vancouver Island in the late 1850s and early 1860s was more akin to that in New Zealand in an earlier period, prior to the widespread Maori adoption of Christianity. The investigation of Duncan's sojourn in Victoria clearly reveals the utility of missionary humanitarians. Duncan's ability to communicate effectively with northern Aboriginal peoples in Victoria during escalating tensions facilitated the maintenance of peaceful relations. Duncan was happy to work with Douglas, seeing the reorganization of Victoria's Aboriginal community as parallel to his goals in Fort Simpson. The migration and, in Duncan's mind, the dissolution of Ts'msyen people in Victoria could only be remedied by reform. While Duncan and Douglas shared certain interests, their successful implementation depended solely upon Duncan. Here we see the fragility of humanitarian initiatives: their realization depended upon financial investment and the sincerity of their agents. Douglas lauded the initiation of a humanitarian system for Aboriginal administration, anticipating that the Colonial Office would credit him with its implementation. However, when Duncan did not return to Victoria the rhetorical nature of Douglas's humanitarianism became apparent. As Chapter 7 illustrates, the ability of Browne and Douglas to manage metropolitan perceptions of their humanitarian initiatives depended upon the location of their respective colonies within the imperial networks of information transmission.

7
The Imperial Press

What a pity that there should be so vexatious and deadly a war in so desirable a colony. What a warning to the Imperial Government to strike terror among the aborigines of British Columbia at once ere they become more troublesome, if not dangerous, to the European population.[1]

– D.G.F. Macdonald, *British Columbia and Vancouver Island*

D.G.F. MACDONALD's 1862 guidebook did not describe British Columbia and Vancouver Island favourably. The climate was too severe, the region lacked agricultural potential and opportunities for emigrant labourers, and only men with significant capital could benefit from the rich goldfields.[2] Most important, though, Macdonald cautioned prospective emigrants that "the new arrival is waited for by the crafty bloodthirsty and implacable savage, who never throws away a chance, never exposes himself to the weapon of an enemy, nor misses an opportunity of slaughter and revenge."[3] A "war of extermination" loomed. In contrast, he suggested that Australia, the Cape Colony, Upper Canada, Lower Canada, and even New Zealand were more attractive destinations.[4]

Macdonald's narrative is unique. While several gold prospectors published accounts of their misfortune in British Columbia, only Macdonald highlighted the threat of Aboriginal violence as a deterrent to emigration.[5] In contrast, the threat of Aboriginal violence barely registered in Donald Fraser's extended correspondence for *The Times*, which was Great Britain's most influential source of news regarding British Columbia and Vancouver Island. As mentioned in Chapter 2, editors in Victoria rejected Macdonald's guidebook precisely because of its allusions to the threat of Aboriginal violence. Macdonald's text has been interpreted as an act of recrimination that reflects his own disappointing experience as a surveyor in the region.[6]

Certainly, Macdonald vents his spleen in *British Columbia and Vancouver Island* and in his subsequent lectures in Great Britain, which framed him as an expert on British Columbia.[7] His guidebook is relevant, though, because it illuminates the uneven transmission of information across the British Empire and how colonial news resonated with a metropolitan audience. When Macdonald published his guidebook in 1862, debates over the Taranaki War figured prominently in Great Britain and coloured his rejection of Vancouver Island and British Columbia. The Taranaki War offered a salutary lesson for Macdonald: British Columbia's colonial administration should pre-emptively strike local First Nations in order to avoid a similar conflict.[8] This conclusion followed upon an extended extract from William Swainson's *New Zealand and Its Colonization*, which details the successful integration of Maori into New Zealand's economy during the 1850s.[9] The Taranaki War revealed how this so-called civilizing of Maori had not been an impediment to the outbreak of violence. Again, citing a 13 March 1862 House of Commons speech by John Roebuck regarding New Zealand in the aftermath of the Taranaki War, Macdonald argued that Great Britain should quit equating colonization with humanitarianism.[10] Humanitarianism was just a waste of time.

Macdonald's comments illustrate the fundamental unity of the Victorian imperial world (whereby insights from one colony could be redeployed in debates about other colonial situations) and the contested relationship between British colonialism and humanitarianism during this period. He drew parallels between the situation in Victoria and the Taranaki War to enhance his authoritative voice and to situate British Columbia and Vancouver Island within an over-arching British imperial perspective. But what is also fascinating about Macdonald's assessment of the threat of Aboriginal violence is that he drew extensively on the Victoria press.[11] Macdonald did not exaggerate when he remarked:

The public Journal of Victoria is literally teeming with records of the lawlessness of the people of these unhappy colonies. In a single copy of the paper referred to, the following unparalleled black list is given – black, indeed, considering the scanty population: one murder, two attempts at murder, three cases of burglary, four of theft, one of stabbing, one of indecency, and numerous other minor offences.[12]

Macdonald cited the content of the Victoria press to support his warnings pertaining to the threat of Aboriginal violence. He knew that metropolitan readers were sensitive to descriptions of Indigenous violence, and such information might convince prospective emigrants to reconsider settling in a troubled colony. But, in offering this negative assessment, Macdonald broke the rules of guidebook writing. And he did so by alluding to news from the Victoria press that had not received a great deal of attention in Great Britain.

In this chapter, I compare the imperial press's coverage of New Zealand and Vancouver Island and chart the resonance of colonial narratives in Great Britain. For New Zealand, I investigate not only prominent metropolitan newspapers but also the Australian press. The Australian press is important because news from New Zealand was frequently transmitted to Great Britain via Australian papers, and metropolitan newspapers showcased Australian interpretations of the Taranaki conflict. For Vancouver Island, I examine characterizations of the region found in *The Times* and guidebooks as well as in newspapers from California. In the mid-nineteenth century, British and American newspapers were integrated into what James Belich terms an "Anglo-world."[13] Californian perspectives on Vancouver Island illustrate the regional resonance of news emerging from Victoria.

Metropolitan Perspectives on the Taranaki War

The Taranaki War elicited a lively exchange between colonial and metropolitan journalists, shaped both by a transmission lag of several months and by the influence of several well placed lobbyists. Between 1860 and 1862, editors in New Zealand reproduced metropolitan articles that commented on the Taranaki War, publishing, in turn, their own responses to these metropolitan interpretations of developments on the New Zealand frontier.[14] To be clear, I do not provide a quantitative assessment of metropolitan perspectives on the Taranaki War; rather, I chart the key interconnections and divergences between the coverage of the war in several significant metropolitan newspapers and their colonial counterparts. I focus particularly on *The Times* and the *Saturday Review*, the newspapers that received the most attention in New Zealand.

Before describing British reactions to the Taranaki War, it is useful to comment briefly on New Zealand journalists' perceptions of the metropolitan press in order to establish the context for colonial interest in metropolitan perspectives. Editors in New Zealand paid close attention to the metropolitan press because of its symbolic status and political power within British culture (see Chapters 3 and 5). Describing the significance of the metropolitan press, the editor of the *Southern Cross* remarked: "The opinions of the fourth estate in that mother country, which still rules our destinies with an imperial sway, are not to be lightly regarded: our private fortunes and the future of the country of our adoption may depend on the impressions created by them in the minds of our imperial legislators."[15] Here the writer acknowledges the connections between the metropolitan press and British political discourses and their implications for colonial affairs. New Zealand in the late 1850s and early 1860s still lay in the shadow of British imperial control. Colonial editors crafted their editorial perspectives in the context of this political reality, defining the war in terms of British sovereignty in order to stress the legitimacy of the Crown's defence of both Maori and settler rights. This line of argument reflects anxiety rather than confidence concerning support for the colonial project in Great Britain. In this effort to shape metropolitan opinion, we see evidence of Alan Lester's and Simon Potter's broad conclusion that colonial editors took advantage of the complex networks of communication that tied Great Britain to its settler colonies to advocate their political interests in the metropolitan press.[16] However, at the same time, editors in New Zealand understood that their relationship to the metropolitan press was not straightforward. British newspapers did not just regurgitate colonial perspectives according to the mechanics of cut-and-past journalism. Editors engaged with emerging colonial news according to their own political, economic, and personal agendas.[17] It was by no means clear to colonists, then, how the metropolitan press would respond to the Taranaki War.

The grave attention paid by New Zealand colonists to the metropolitan press reflected the social and cultural significance of newspapers. By 1860, newspapers in Great Britain had assumed a position of cultural and political importance, even as they were continuing to undergo rapid economic expansion.[18] For example, the official history of *The Times* argues that this newspaper's power "to stimulate, to anticipate, and on occasion to organize public opinion had by 1850 been recognized for a full generation in official circles at home and abroad."[19] The repeal of the "Taxes on Knowledge" through the Newspaper Stamp Act, 1855, and the elimination of duties on newspapers in 1861 facilitated the expansion of the press by decreasing the cost of newspapers.[20] Writing in 1887, the journalist and historian Henry Richard Fox Bourne described this period as featuring "years of stupendous change in the conditions of journalism."[21] The deregulation of the British press over the first half of the nineteenth century reflected an increasing consensus among legislators that the press's propagation of knowledge was beneficial rather than harmful (i.e., a cause of social discord).[22] In real terms, eliminating the Newspaper Stamp Act facilitated the initiation of hundreds of new newspapers across Great Britain and enabled a larger proportion of Britons to afford them.[23] James Grant observed in 1871 that the annual circulation of the British press increased fourteenfold between 1831 and 1864, from 38,648,314 newspapers to 546,059,400.[24] Indeed, the circulation of *The Times* increased from five thousand copies per edition in 1803 to sixty thousand copies per edition in 1860.[25] This increased production was facilitated by both innovation in printing technology and the removal of duties.[26] In 1857, following the repeal of the Newspaper Stamp Act, *The Times* installed a Hoe Ten-Feeder steam-powered press that could print twenty thousand sheets an hour, printed one side at a time.[27] The New Zealand press's close attention to *The Times* corresponded to the belief that the latter was the "Monarch of the Press."[28]

At the same time, though, colonial editors recognized the paradoxical nature of metropolitan newspapers. *The Times* was "an index to public opinion" even though its editorial perspectives were crafted by individual writers who reflected a narrow set of interests.[29] As the *Taranaki Herald* noted in 1861, the practice of anonymous journalism lent a "corporate style" to prominent metropolitan newspapers, giving a writer an authority "exaggerated beyond what belongs to his arguments or character."[30] This dichotomy between a healthy respect for the social power of the metropolitan press, on the one hand, and insider knowledge of the mechanics underlying editorial perspectives, on the other, is best understood in the context of James Carey's theory of communication as ritual.[31] Rather than simply transmitting information, newspapers and their editorial perspectives were believed to embody collective identities. It was this social and political meaning that inscribed newspapers with significance and attached increased symbolism to news narratives. Thus, editors in New Zealand paid heed to metropolitan perspectives because of the latter's imagined power both to represent and to influence public opinion across the British Empire.

The Times and the Taranaki War

In the early 1860s, *The Times* was owned by John Walter and edited by John Thadeus Delane.[32] According to historian Geoffrey Hamilton, *The Times* advocated a Liberal political perspective under Delane's editorship, which, in order to maintain the paper's independence, was intentionally not too closely associated with any particular ruling ministry. The official history of *The Times* argues that Delane supported Lord Palmerston's ministry in the late 1850s and early 1860s and that newspaper benefited from this close relationship through Palmerston's provision of information to Delane.[33] Also according to *The Times*'s official history, 1855 marked the zenith of its dominance within the British press. With the repeal of the Newspaper Stamp Act both provincial and metropolitan newspapers were able to make inroads into *The Times*'s market share.[34] The New Zealand press's attention to *The Times* reflected its endorsement of that paper's dominance in Great Britain, a position that it no longer had an iron grip upon when the Taranaki War erupted. In what follows I build on the work of both A.J. Harrop and James Belich, whose studies of the New Zealand wars reflect on the significance of *The Times*.[35]

The Times published thirty-seven articles and editorials on Native policy in New Zealand during and just after the Taranaki War. Its first article appeared on 13 June 1860, almost three months after the conflict had begun on 17 March. Ironically, the news of war in New Zealand coincided with the release of a report from a House of Commons committee on the military defences of British colonies. This report criticized New Zealand's lack of financial support for its own defences.[36] Initially, *The Times* characterized the Taranaki War as a Maori insurrection, precipitated by Wiremu Kingi Te Rangitake's illegal resistance to the Waitara purchase and his denial of British sovereignty.[37] This editorial position mirrored the initial response of the New Zealand press generally and reiterated specifically the *Taranaki Herald*'s original manifesto. The initial commentary of *The Times* also described the lack of cooperation between Taranaki volunteers and regular British military forces.[38] Again, this attention to British military incompetence echoed news from New Zealand. These reports prompted *The Times* to suggest that the Taranaki War might be best fought by a volunteer force alone, with the provision of sufficient arms by the imperial government.[39] This endorsement of Taranaki's volunteer militia not only reflected an engagement with emerging editorial perspectives from New Zealand but also resonated with debates over colonial self-sufficiency then current in Great Britain. According to this view, New Zealand's achievement of responsible government carried with it increased responsibilities for self-defence. This sort of praise for the volunteer militia made colonists nervous as it hinted at a lack of support for imperial troops in the region.[40]

The Times first reported on the controversy related to the justification for the Taranaki War on 10 October 1860 through the publication of a letter from William Fox, the opposition leader in New Zealand's General Assembly. Fox's letter, originally sent to the *Wanganui Chronicle* on 27 April 1860, justified his decision not to endorse a memorial of support for Browne because of the uncertainty surrounding the Waitara purchase.[41] Just over a month later, on 14 November 1860, *The Times* featured an article by its Melbourne correspondent from the Australian colony of Victoria who maintained that debates within New Zealand's General Assembly revealed that "a belief [was] gaining ground that the war [was] unjust; that Governor Browne ha[d] committed a great error."[42] Describing a speech by Dr. Isaac Featherston in the General Assembly alleging that Browne's war policy was "unanswerable," the correspondent contended that the Taranaki War was illegal. In this edition *The Times* offered a counterpoint to the Melbourne correspondent in the form of "Another Correspondent" from Sydney in New South Wales, who criticized the dissent of "Episcopal missionaries" (who were against the war) and supported Browne's war policy. Subsequently, however, the Melbourne correspondent's viewpoint dominated *The Times*'s coverage of the war. Remember, these correspondents from the Australian colonies remained anonymous, just like the paper's editorial staff.

The comments of the Melbourne correspondent sparked a flurry of letters to the editor. Harold Browne, a professor of divinity at the University of Cambridge and the brother of Governor Thomas Gore Browne, exclaimed: "The statements [of the Melbourne correspondent], if uncontradicted, must be most injurious to the Governor."[43] Harold defended his brother by declaring the latter's "most anxious care" for Maori, and he took this opportunity to accuse Thomas's other vociferous critic, Archdeacon Octavius Hadfield, of intemperate conduct. Harold's indictment of Hadfield then elicited a reply from Colonel Charles Hadfield of the Royal Marines, Octavius Hadfield's brother in Great Britain, which, in turn, prompted further replies from Harold Browne.[44] This exchange reveals that metropolitan readers with ties to New Zealand paid close attention to *The Times* and attempted to further influence readers through their letters to the editor. Thus, letters to the editor functioned as a medium for both public debate and metropolitan commentary regarding the news emerging from New Zealand. Throughout the Taranaki War, *The Times* featured correspondence from both colonists in New Zealand and former New Zealand residents living in Great Britain regarding its interpretation of the war (including Octavius Hadfield, who accused *The Times* of refusing to publish his correspondence).[45]

What is most surprising about *The Times*'s coverage of the Taranaki War is the degree to which it was shaped by the controversy over the war's justification. Here we must recognize that *The Times* did not publish a large number of original articles from New Zealand's press. Indeed, it is difficult to ascertain the degree to which *The Times* drew upon reportage from New Zealand papers or to determine which specific colonial newspapers its editor favoured. In addition, New Zealand editors did not comment on *The Times*'s sources. It was *The Times*'s Melbourne correspondent who provided the paper with its most vocal and frequent Antipodean editorial viewpoint. And he persistently criticized Browne and his justification for the conflict.[46]

We know from Browne's wartime diary that the Melbourne correspondent was in fact Henry Samuel Chapman.[47] In 1860, Chapman was an elected representative of the Legislative Council in Victoria, Australia. But between 1843 and 1852, he had served as a judge in New Zealand's Supreme Court.[48] Harriet Browne's wartime diary also reveals that Fox and his political allies in Wellington had enlisted Chapman in their efforts to oppose Browne.[49] While there is little information available regarding Chapman's employment by *The Times*, his biographers detail both his suitability for this role and his political sympathies.[50] Both K.R. Miller and Peter Spiller emphasize Chapman's experience as a politically radical journalist in Lower Canada and England from the 1820s until the early 1840s.[51] While Miller notes Chapman's close ties with members of Wellington's political establishment, Spiller details his respect for Chief Justice William Martin, his former colleague in New Zealand's Supreme Court.[52] Recent scholarship suggests that *The Times* drew upon foreign correspondents who were integrated into colonial social and political elites.[53] Both Chapman's earlier career as a metropolitan journalist and his connections to political networks in New Zealand positioned him well for this role. His close ties to Fox, Featherston, and Martin, all opponents of Browne during the Taranaki War, predisposed him to champion their perspectives. His ability to draw on these connections helped him shape the editorial perspective of *The Times* from its initial support for colonists to its opposition to a war policy.

Following Chapman's initial description of the controversy over the Waitara purchase, the editor of *The Times* stressed his own inability to judge the merits of the conflict. Ultimately, *The Times* side-stepped the question of the war's justification and criticized Bishop George Selwyn's argument that British colonization had occurred in New Zealand to benefit Maori. As the writer notes:

> We again confess our inability to decide upon the merits of the particular question, but we have no such hesitation on the question of general policy. We say distinctly that the native-ascendency theory cannot be upheld. If the interests of the rival populations cannot be reconciled, those of the natives must give way. The result, whether consistent with justice or not, is simply inevitable.[54]

According to the editorialist, his continued support for colonists affirmed "the laws of nature" and the presumed future extinction of local Indigenous peoples in the region.[55] At face value, this endorsement of settler rights could be interpreted as an affirmation of the dominance of antagonistic racial discourses. However, it is worth remembering that *The Times* had never supported a humanitarian agenda during the abolitionist era and had traditionally favoured the interests of settlers.[56] *The Times*'s general endorsement of the natural rights of settlers implicitly reflected the contentious nature of the Taranaki War. Unjust or not, *The Times* asserted that Great Britain's colonial projects were for the benefit of settlers, not Indigenous peoples. However, the weakness of this argument helps to explain why, in 1861, *The Times* began criticizing New Zealand colonists.

Over the course of 1860–61, *The Times* increasingly expressed dissatisfaction over the British military's inability to defeat Maori combatants:

> Nothing can be more extraordinary than the comparative or temporary success with which the natives have resisted the power of the Government. We know of no parallel to this story even in the comprehensive annals of

our own colonial contests. Naked savages who still commence a campaign with a war dance, and who ought to be as helpless before our artillery and rifles as the cannibals before Robinson Crusoe's fowling piece, are bound to profit by all the resources of military science and to hold their own against some of the best troops in the world.[57]

Here the writer asks: How could an amateur force of Maori insurgents successfully resist the British military? To metropolitan eyes it appeared as though the British faced a plethora of Maori enemies rather than just Te Rangitake in Taranaki.[58] Interestingly, *The Times*'s flip-flop regarding the maintenance of imperial troops in New Zealand occurred after the news that peace had been achieved in Taranaki and stemmed, in part, from the slow rate at which news was transmitted from New Zealand to Great Britain.

Again, it was Chapman who instigated the controversy. In an article published on 16 August 1861, Chapman argued that Browne had shifted his attention to the Kingitanga of Central Waikato and was about to initiate a second war, which would be "disastrous, protracted, and costly."[59] In response, *The Times* proclaimed: "We are again at war. We should be deceiving ourselves if we supposed that hostilities in New Zealand were merely imminent. We may feel perfectly assured that they have already begun."[60] Of war in Waikato, the writer asserted: "But in the present case we are making war with even less prospect of advantage and greater certainty of injury and disgrace than usually attends that most wicked and wasteful of all waste and wickedness." The possibility of a second and even more protracted war in New Zealand functioned as a tipping point. *The Times* criticized the increasing build-up of imperial troops in New Zealand, claiming that expanding British military forces to seven thousand troops from the original garrison of 800 troops amounted to exile for the soldiers involved and starved Great Britain of its own defence simply to "exterminate the Maories of New Zealand."[61]

This about-face did not occur because of a reappraisal of Maori rights; rather, it reflected a pragmatic assessment of the British military's performance during the Taranaki War, its poor prospects in a second, more general, war, and the significant cost of lengthy conflicts – all issues of metropolitan concern. But from this point, *The Times* critiqued the morality of colonists in language that indicated sympathy for Indigenous peoples, highlighting the mis-use of metropolitan resources to benefit settler interests. As this illustrates, *The Times*'s commitment to New Zealand settlers was rather superficial. However, Browne's confrontational posture towards Waikato Kingitanga in 1861 did not result in the outbreak of a general war, as Chapman had feared. Great Britain's temporal and spatial dislocation from New Zealand contributed to this interpretive leap. This reminds us that metropolitan commentators sometimes made predictions based on assumptions because their knowledge of colonial affairs was perpetually out of date. At the end of 1861, Chapman's final report for *The Times* argued that the change in New Zealand's government from William Stafford's to William Fox's ministry, and the replacement of Thomas Gore Browne by George Grey, signalled both settler rejection of Browne's war policy and a chance for peace.[62] Chapman's assessment confirms what we have learned regarding the public relations victory of Anglican humanitarians at the end of the Taranaki War (see Chapter 6). Following this change in administration, any attention *The Times* paid to New Zealand lapsed until war again broke out in 1863.

One of the most intriguing aspects of *The Times*'s response to the Taranaki War concerns the degree to which it drew upon the Australian press. For example, 40 percent of *The Times*'s articles and editorials on the Taranaki War originated from Australian sources.[63] In comparison, only 16 percent of its war articles stemmed from identified New Zealand sources.[64] Possibly this Australian filter reflects the fact that *The Times* had more established connections within the Australian press than with the New Zealand press. Certainly the Australian colonies transmitted a larger flow of news to Great Britain than did New Zealand. For example, colonists in New South Wales alone posted 2,516,366 newspapers in 1861 in comparison to 797,915 despatched from New Zealand post offices in 1861.[65] In addition, Australia also enjoyed a faster transmission of news to Great Britain than did the more isolated New Zealand. The *Sydney Morning Herald*'s editorial response to the Taranaki War was the most cited Australian response in both *The Times* and the New Zealand press.

The *Sydney Morning Herald* featured at least thirty-five editorials on the Taranaki War and 115 articles extracted from the New Zealand newspapers, all of which I examined. In brief, throughout the Taranaki War the *Sydney Morning Herald* supported the argument that the conflict was a contest over British sovereignty. However, it appears as though metropolitan debates over colonial defence influenced the *Sydney Morning Herald*'s unwavering support for New Zealand colonists. Thus, the newspaper's solidarity with New Zealand colonists can be understood, in part, as a way of ensuring continued imperial support for the maintenance of British defences in Australia. An analysis of the Australian press's coverage of the Taranaki War confirms my argument that Auckland's and New Plymouth's newspapers were the most important representatives of New Zealand's press during this period as it was their articles that were most commonly extracted by Australian newspapers. My analysis of the *Sydney Morning Herald* also illustrates that, in the early 1860s, metropolitan Britons would have encountered narratives of the Taranaki War in both Australian and New Zealand newspapers.

The *Saturday Review*

A.J.B. Beresford Hope founded the *Saturday Review* in 1855 with the express purpose of challenging the dominance of *The Times*. It was edited by John Douglas Cook and, by 1858, had a circulation of five thousand copies per edition.[66] According to historian Barbara Quinn Schmidt, the *Saturday Review* was "an organ of moderate conservatism" and, by 1863, was Great Britain's leading weekly newspaper.[67] The *Taranaki Herald* characterized *The Times* and the *Saturday Review* as "the two leading papers of their classes"; likewise, the *Southern Cross* described both papers as the "two leading journals in England."[68] Though colonists would have encountered a large variety of papers from the press communities of the United Kingdom, iconic newspapers like *The Times* and the *Saturday Review* were believed to be the most significant.

The *Saturday Review* published thirteen extended editorials on the topic of New Zealand during and just after the Taranaki War. Its first article appeared on 25 August 1860.[69] This commentary occurred in the context of the duke of Newcastle's withdrawal of the New Zealand Bill from the British House of Commons. Writing in support of this aborted legislation, the *Saturday Review* argued that the bill's purpose had been to regulate the sale of Maori land through the appointment of a council to advise the General Assembly and governor. The Taranaki War's occurrence symbolized the need for additional metropolitan legislation to constrain British settlers. Maori needed protection because colonists coveted their land in spite of the Treaty of Waitangi's guarantees.

Thus, the *Saturday Review* interpreted the Waitara purchase as an act of confiscation – one that Browne had been "browbeaten" into committing by colonists who were "storming for more land."[70] Comparing the Waitara purchase to the Old Testament narrative of King Ahab's theft of Naboth's vineyard, the *Saturday Review* writer made it clear that the Taranaki War had both a financial and a moral cost. The conflict tainted Great Britain's reputation in the eyes of the "civilized world." Here we have an example of James Heartfield's argument that humanitarian critiques of settler colonialism were inscribed with class conflict as this elitist writer clearly considered lowbrow settlers to be incapable of self-governance.[71] Curiously, coveting Naboth's vineyard was the same biblical metaphor that Browne had employed to describe the "land hunger" of settlers and that Wiremu Tamihana Tarapipipi Te Waharoa had employed to describe Browne's actions at Waitara. Tarapipipi's speeches were widely reported in New Zealand's press, and it seems plausible that the *Saturday Review* writer drew upon Tarapipipi's rebuke of Browne.[72] This biblical narrative represented a potent metaphor, indicting the Christian beliefs of colonists.

In a subsequent editorial, the *Saturday Review* writer observed that it was impossible to form a decisive opinion regarding the Waitara purchase, given the conflicting testimony coming out of New Zealand.[73] Regardless of this, the writer concluded that Browne had been wrong to pursue the Waitara purchase, especially given his foreknowledge that there would be resistance to it. Browne's actions were a striking example of "the 'nigger despising' temper – the bane of our colonial policy": "He has dealt with a Maori as he never would have dared to deal with an Englishman, and ... he has plunged us into a costly and perilous quarrel to uphold a paltry claim which, be it good or bad, has been advanced, prosecuted, and carried out with very little regard for the most obvious principles of justice."[74] The implication is that Browne had ignored the rights of Maori as British subjects.

Throughout the Taranaki War and into 1861–62, the *Saturday Review* castigated both Browne and New Zealand colonists for their racial prejudice. In explicit contrast to Harold Browne's defence of his brother's policy, the *Saturday Review* writer argued that the Treaty of Waitangi granted Maori the legal right to establish land-leagues and to refuse land sales to colonists.[75] In this argument, the *Saturday Review* emphasized the legal equality between Maori and colonists, paying less attention to the divergent cultural status of Maori than did rhetorical humanitarians in New Zealand. Worth noting, though, is that the *Saturday Review*'s criticism did not amount to a denial that Great Britain should support the colonial war effort or that New Zealand colonists should bear the cost of their defence alone.[76] Indeed, the *Saturday Review* writer acknowledged that, so long as British colonies had no input into imperial foreign policy, it was Great Britain's responsibility to subsidize colonial defences. The Taranaki War represented a failure in imperial administration. The Colonial Office should never have appointed Thomas Gore Browne: its bid to save money had resulted in a failure to attract a talented administrator and cost the Empire more in the long run.[77] This editorial manifesto advocated an interventionist role for the imperial government in New Zealand, arguing that a skilful governor was needed to balance race relations.

The *Saturday Review*'s distrust of New Zealand colonists is best illustrated by its scathing indictment of colonists as the advocates of a "damned-nigger principle."[78] This accusation drew parallels between New Zealand and the repression of Indigenous peoples in the United States and the Dutch colonial empire in Africa and South East Asia. Here the *Saturday Review* articulated precisely the sort of response that some settlers had sought to avoid when they objected to expressions of public support for Browne and the Taranaki War. Indeed, the *Saturday Review* accused the colonial press, along with the General Assembly and ruling ministry, of pushing Browne into war.[79] Clearly, the *Saturday Review* was not convinced that the Taranaki War was about defending British sovereignty and Maori rights, nor did it think that Browne's actions had been motivated by a regard for Maori rights. Indeed, it was extremely sceptical of rhetorical humanitarianism.

The editorial viewpoint of the *Saturday Review* may have originated with Charles Jasper Selwyn, the brother of George Augustus Selwyn, then the bishop of New Zealand and a firm opponent of Browne's war policy. Writing to C.W. Richmond in 1861, R.H. Hutton noted that the *Saturday Review* was connected, through Charles Selwyn, to the bishop of New Zealand.[80] This connection seems plausible given that, in 1860, Charles Selwyn was the member of Parliament for Cambridge University, an institution from which the *Saturday Review* frequently drew its commentators.[81] In the House of Commons, Selwyn had played a leading role in attacking Browne's justification for the Waitara purchase and the Taranaki War.[82] Like Chapman's role with *The Times*, Charles Selwyn's role with the *Saturday Review* exemplifies how, for their constituencies, lobbyists with connections to networks of colonists exerted influence over metropolitan papers.

However, in spite of this evidence of Selwyn's influence over the *Saturday Review*, we must recognize this paper's ambivalence regarding the arguments of dissenting New Zealand clerics who opposed the war. The *Saturday Review* writer concluded that colonial ecclesiastics had attached a damaging stigma to those who opposed the Taranaki War.[83] For example, the writer argued that Bishop Selwyn had sabotaged his defence of Maori rights through the outlandish claim that British colonization in New Zealand had originally occurred for the primary benefit of Maori rather than for colonists. Clearly, this evangelical humanitarian vision of the British Empire's purpose was naive. These comments echoed the New Zealand press's criticism of Selwyn and show that Anglican humanitarians' protests against the war were not accepted at face value in Great Britain. The *Saturday Review* positioned itself as a critic of both rhetorical and evangelical humanitarian discourses.

Not surprisingly, the critical perspective of the *Saturday Review* received significant attention in New Zealand. In February 1861, both the *Taranaki Herald* and the *Southern Cross* downplayed the paper's negative characterization of New Zealand colonists, emphasizing that its editorial manifesto was always formulated in opposition to *The Times*.[84] According to this argument, because *The Times* supported the war effort, the *Saturday Review* did not and, hence, was not to be taken seriously. This dismissal was impossible, though, when, in 1861, *The Times* became critical of New Zealand colonists. Describing the combined attack of both papers, the *Southern Cross* stated: "It appears to be the high and mighty pleasure of the leaders of public opinion in the mother country to endeavour, as much as lies in their power, to lower the character of the settlers of New Zealand in the eyes of the world."[85] In response, the editor of the *Southern Cross* argued that the metropolitan press's attack on the garrison of British troops in New Zealand stemmed entirely from its cost to Great Britain. The affection of the metropolitan press for Maori was entirely feigned: "The spirit of that part of the English press from which we have been quoting is unmistakable. They care as little for the native race as they do for their fellow-countrymen here, and judging by their arguments, would not deign to notice New Zealand if the natives were being exterminated without any expense to the mother country."[86] *The Times*'s and the *Saturday Review*'s criticism of colonists was very disappointing and, in this case, prompted the editor of the *Southern Cross* to discredit the integrity of the metropolitan press.

The Times and *Saturday Review* did not meet colonial expectations. These newspapers paid close attention to the Taranaki War but did not simply regurgitate colonial editorial manifestos. For example, the *Taranaki Herald*'s interpretation of the Taranaki War was not long accepted by *The Times*. What cannot be denied, though, is that metropolitan responses to the Taranaki

War were formulated through dialogue. The editorial manifestos of the New Zealand press were transmitted to Great Britain and functioned as important sources of colonial knowledge in parliamentary and press debates.[87] Great Britain did not receive one, straightforward account of events in New Zealand; rather, multiple conflicting interpretations of the Taranaki War were transmitted from New Zealand both by members of the colonial press and by individual proponents/opponents of the war, all of which were affected by a contextual vacuum and significant temporal dislocation. In this context, lobbyists like Chapman and Selwyn played a critical role in shaping metropolitan responses, and it would appear that in Great Britain, over time, opponents of the Taranaki War achieved more success than did its proponents. While the Colonial Office did not officially censure Browne, his recall had much to do with the fact that the duke of Newcastle accepted the arguments of evangelical humanitarians who were supported by Under-Secretary Sir Frederick Rogers.[88] Though cause and effect is not clear-cut, it would appear that the significant controversy elicited within both colonial and metropolitan press coverage of the Taranaki War influenced and directed the Colonial Office's endorsement of George Grey as Thomas Gore Browne's successor. In 1861, Grey was seen as a proven colonial administrator who had restored the Crown's relations with Maori during his tenure in New Zealand from 1845 to 1853. The attention the New Zealand press paid to both *The Times* and the *Saturday Review* is best understood in light of the iconic status of both newspapers and to the desire of colonial editors to contest oppositional metropolitan discourses. While members of New Zealand's press had no illusions that their editorial manifestos would resonate in Great Britain in the same manner as did metropolitan newspapers in New Zealand, they still engaged with the metropolitan press. Indeed, they had little choice, as the press was one of the few mediums through which colonists could attempt to influence metropolitan policy.

Metropolitan Perspectives on Vancouver Island

Metropolitan Britons encountered war news from New Zealand via a large variety of public and private sources, but an analysis of metropolitan coverage of Vancouver Island does not reveal the same phenomenon. For example, it does not appear that metropolitan papers paid close attention to newspapers from Victoria. While Macdonald's books mention his personal access to Victoria papers, they provide no indication of the extent, depth, or speed of the flow of newspaper reportage from Victoria to the United Kingdom. Unlike with regard to New Zealand, there are no data regarding the number of newspapers forwarded from Victoria to Great Britain. Editors in Victoria did not publish monthly summaries for a metropolitan market, nor did they appear to have crafted their editorial manifestos for metropolitan readers. They paid close attention to metropolitan characterizations of their region, but they did not pander to metropolitan sensibilities. Vancouver Island and British Columbia were not well integrated into wider British press networks.

Yet, in the late 1850s and early 1860s, Great Britain featured a good deal of news about Vancouver Island and British Columbia. The Fraser River and Cariboo gold rushes and the San Juan Island crisis were significant news events. Indeed, the BC gold rushes occurred in the context of a series of large gold rushes in the United States and Australia that had energized British migration across the anglophone world from 1849 on. Indeed, it may have been this lack of press connection between Great Britain and British Columbia that prompted so many authors to write guidebooks about the region. In comparison, the Otago gold rush of 1861 attracted thousands of prospectors to the South Island of New Zealand but did not elicit a similar corpus of guidebooks, likely because interested readers could find relevant information in the established press communities of New Zealand and the Australian colonies. Significantly, too, much of the information published in *The Times* and numerous guidebooks originated from writers who had personal experience of the region. These writers often commented on local First Nations, but they did so in ways that did not detract from their positive characterizations of the region. In this section, I examine metropolitan characterizations of Vancouver Island and British Columbia in the context of the Victoria press's negative characterizations of First Nations, utilizing a brief analysis of California's press to highlight the regional coverage of narratives of Aboriginal violence.

Donald Fraser's fifty articles for *The Times* are the most important source of metropolitan news regarding colonial Vancouver Island and British Columbia. The majority of these articles, published between May 1858 and August 1866, were written in Victoria and subsequently became source texts for the authors of metropolitan guidebooks.[89] Fraser wrote extended narratives, averaging three full columns of broadsheet at five thousand words per article, or about 250,000 words over eight years. It is probably not possible to exaggerate their importance in popularizing British Columbia's goldfields. Certainly, mid-nineteenth-century chroniclers believed that Fraser had persuaded thousands of Britons from across the Empire to travel to the region, especially during the Cariboo gold rush.[90] According to the Victoria resident and guidebook writer Matthew Macfie: "The letters of the 'Times' correspondent, published in 1862, excited great attention, and in that year several thousands were induced to visit the country from England, Canada, Australia, and New Zealand."[91]

Of course, these articles also resonated across the British Empire, as evidenced by the *British Colonist*'s coverage of the arrival of several shiploads of prospectors to Victoria from New Zealand in May 1862 who testified to the "considerable excitement" in New Zealand regarding the gold rush in British Columbia.[92] The *British Colonist* reported that these miners had left the goldfields of Otago because of that region's lack of timber and that they had cancelled their plans to winter in Australia when they had learned of the Cariboo goldfields from "London papers."[93] In 1861 and 1862, in an attempt to dissuade prospectors from leaving Otago, Dunedin's *Otago Daily Times* published both an example of Fraser's correspondence and a series of articles condemning the prospects of the Cariboo goldfields.[94] These narratives underline the important role that metropolitan newspapers played in shaping the mobility of miners. That so many Britons travelled thousands of kilometres to a relatively unknown and isolated destination because of something they read in *The Times* is a testament not only to the implicit trust readers had in the factuality of the press but also to the prevalence of gold rush discourses, which led readers to associate gold rushes in British Columbia with those in California and Victoria.

As with the majority of the mid-nineteenth-century journalists discussed in this book, very little is known about Donald Fraser, aside from the details that emerge from his public life. He was a veteran newspaper correspondent from Inverness, Scotland.[95] It is possible that Fraser's employment by *The Times* originated in his childhood connection with John Cameron Macdonald, a journalist for that paper in the 1840s who later became its manager. Fraser had originally travelled to California in 1849 as a special correspondent for *The Times*. From 1849 to 1858, he penned at least sixty-five despatches from San Francisco chronicling the California gold rush for British readers. When he learned of the Fraser River gold rush in the spring of 1858, he followed in the wake of thousands of Californian prospectors and travelled to Victoria to chronicle it. In general, Fraser described the BC goldfields in glowing terms. It is also well known that Fraser's hyperbole disappointed many prospectors.[96] In his 1863 lecture, Macdonald gleefully reported a rumour that Fraser had fled Victoria to avoid being lynched by hundreds of failed prospectors.[97] The gravest allegation against Fraser, made by the former gold-rusher John Emmerson, was that he had exaggerated the region's prospects in order to benefit from his investment in local real estate.[98] This charge seems reasonable as Fraser did become one of Vancouver Island's largest land speculators following his arrival in 1858, and he benefited from a close relationship with James Douglas.[99] Closely following Fraser's arrival in Victoria, Douglas appointed him to the Council of Vancouver Island, where he acted as his "trusted confidant and unofficial advisor."[100] Yet, while it is reasonable to argue that Fraser exaggerated the riches of Vancouver Island and British Columbia, what lies at the heart of his misrepresentations are his characterizations of local First Nations.

Fraser's first articles about the Fraser River gold rush touched on the issue of Aboriginal violence.[101] Writing first from San Francisco, California, Fraser detailed how his American informants considered the threat of Aboriginal violence in British Columbia to be a serious concern.[102] According to Fraser, however, the fears of American miners originated in their inability to mistreat local First Nations on Vancouver Island and in British Columbia in the same manner as they mistreated Aboriginal people in the United States. In other words, Fraser defined Aboriginal violence as an American issue, and he used this subject to critique the national character of Americans. A persistent theme in his correspondence is that Vancouver Island and British Columbia benefitted from the HBC's positive relations with local First Nations.[103] In his first article written in Victoria, he ruminates on the significance of Fort Victoria:

Those plain, whitewashed wooden walls acquired an importance in my eyes when I reflected that this was the place where was concentrated the moral power, the tact, energy, and firmness of purpose by which a few well-instructed Englishmen and Scotchmen rule 80,000 savages, and turn their labours to profitable account. While tribes of these savages are at war with America almost continually, and at this moment, when a fierce and bloody contest is actually going on between them and the Federal forces, whom they have lately beaten, the meanest of the company's servants has a safe passport and a hearty welcome wherever he goes – not a hair of his head will the Indians touch.[104]

In this comparison of British and American policy, Fraser stressed how British "moral power" facilitated positive relations with local First Nations in contrast to what was occurring in the United States. In effect, Fraser celebrated the intertwined legacy of both humanitarianism and British imperialism. Fraser told his metropolitan readers that their British identity guaranteed their security. It would be inaccurate to conclude that Fraser denied the potential threat of British Columbia's Aboriginal population; rather, he minimized the danger by associating Aboriginal hostility with the cruelty and intemperate behaviour of American citizens. This narrative cast First Nations peoples as neutral agents, their hostile or temperate conduct being activated by the conduct of Euro-Americans. It also reveals the innate skill of Euro-Americans like Fraser in discerning the motivations of First Nations peoples and in perceiving their acquiescence to the British colonial project. Fraser amplified this theme several times, particularly during crises in relations between Great Britain and the United States.

For example, during the San Juan Island crisis, when Great Britain and the United States almost came to blows over a disputed island in the Strait of Georgia, Fraser stated that an outbreak of war would precipitate an attack on American territory by 100,000 Aboriginals, who were "burning with revenge, thirsting for their blood."[105] Again, in 1862, Fraser raised the spectre of Aboriginal violence when the American Civil War increased tensions between Great Britain and the United States:

> I seriously trust, however, peace will be maintained, if only to prevent an Indian outbreak. A vast Indian population of warlike "proclivities" is actually thirsting for American blood; and, if hostilities should unhappily break out between the two nations, the Indians would rise to a man. The consequences would be too horrible to dwell upon, and the worst of it would be that we could not control the Indians.[106]

Fraser employed the threat of Aboriginal violence strategically to affirm Vancouver Island's and British Columbia's potential for self-defence in the case of war with the United States. In this context, local First Nations represented powerful, if uncontrollable, allies. Likely, Fraser deployed this spectre of Aboriginal violence to offset local realities: Vancouver Island and

British Columbia were isolated imperial outposts, lacking even the dry-dock facilities needed to repair damaged British naval vessels.[107] The region depended upon the United States for economic supplies, and war would have challenged British defences to the utmost.

Given the dichotomy between British and American Aboriginal policies, it is not surprising that Fraser did not dwell or elaborate upon the Victoria press's fixation with discourses of Aboriginal violence and disorder. Commentary on these themes would have undermined Fraser's positive characterization of the influence of local British policy. Equally important, attention paid to Aboriginal violence and colonists' related anxiety might have deterred emigration. Fraser's first observation of Victoria indicated that "the peace and good order of the place [were] perfectly preserved" by the police commissioner.[108] Again, in *The Times* edition of 19 January 1859, Fraser described the efficiency of Victoria's police, "[who] perambulate the streets much after the fashion of London police; and the peace and good order of the town is perfectly preserved."[109] We know that this description does not parallel the image of Victoria conveyed in the local press. For example, Fraser only briefly mentioned the presence of northern First Nations in Victoria, stressing Douglas's ability to over-awe them and so avoid any conflict.[110] His narratives provide no hint of the long-time local presence of northern First Nations or of how this contributed to the anxiety of colonists and local editors. Fraser exaggerated Victoria's tranquility for effect, and his silence extended to the role of First Nations within the local economy.

In Fraser's narrative of his arrival on Vancouver Island, he notes how the illusion of solitude that marked his steamer's entrance to Esquimalt Harbour dissipated when the canoes of local First Nations came alongside the vessel to transfer cargo to the shore.[111] Here Fraser segued into a commentary on the positive and negative characteristics of First Nations peoples. He contrasted their "harmless" and "industrious" appearance with comments on their immorality and the demoralizing effects of civilization – particularly the corruption of Aboriginal women by "idle ruffians" and Aboriginal men by alcohol abuse. Fraser appraised local Aboriginal peoples by utilizing the familiar discourse of cultural decline – another example of C.L. Higham's thesis that mid-nineteenth-century Euro-Americans perceived First Nations as "wretched Indians," corrupted by vice due to their proximity to Euro-American settlement.[112] However, by accident, Fraser's narrative reveals the participation of local First Nations peoples in the local economy – as wage labourers, farmers, traders in food goods, and agents in the sex trade. Fraser did not intend to highlight the centrality of Victoria's Aboriginal population to the local economy, but his narrative corroborates other contemporary reports. The ubiquitous presence of First Nations peoples in Victoria meant that Fraser could not avoid commenting on them in his account of his arrival in the community. But, aside from this initial description, Fraser paid almost no attention to the presence of First Nations peoples in Victoria.

The Victoria press's support for urban racial segregation was deeply connected to Aboriginal participation in the community's turbulent economy (see Chapter 2). Editors believed that the prevalence of Aboriginal labour prevented potential colonists from remaining in Victoria. Contrary to this, Fraser consistently argued that Vancouver Island and British Columbia were attractive destinations because of the richness of the goldfields and the opportunities within the local economy.[113] He did not deny the high cost of provisions in Victoria, but he stressed that the availability of excellent wages offset the cost of living.[114]

> The recent success of the miners has carried away nearly all the able-bodied men from Victoria, and labor of a common kind has, in consequence, risen to prices far above its value to the employers. All mechanics get $6 a day. Labourers ask $5, and many of them get $3, and some $4. Servants are worth anything, according to the necessities of the helpless master. Forty dollars a-month and "found" is the ordinary rate for a man who knows nothing in particular – who can do nothing well – such as you are accustomed in happy old England, but who will profess to make himself generally useful.[115]

Compare Fraser's description with the *British Colonist*'s in 1860, which notes that the highest wage of Euro-American labourers was $2.50 per day, two dollars per day being the common rate, with most labour conducted by local Aboriginals employed for fifty cents per day or twenty dollars per month.[116]

Fraser cites the availability of Aboriginal labour in only one context. In *The Times*'s 21 September 1861 edition, Fraser notes that, while "white labour" in Victoria earn high wages, "the wages of the Indians are very low, which, together with the fact that there are always plenty of native hands ready to work at outdoor labour, is a great convenience and a great savings to the farmer."[117] The point here is that working-class emigrants could capitalize on Victoria's racialized economy by earning high wages that could then be utilized to purchase cheap Aboriginal labour, thus subsidizing the development of farms. Victoria, it seems, offered an ideal environment for both labour and investment. However, we know from the Victoria press that the local market was not as segregated as Fraser depicted and that both Euro-Americans and local First Nations competed for employment. As a Mr. Bishop complained at a public meeting in Victoria in August 1862, Fraser had not only lied about the richness of the goldfields but had also misrepresented the "facilities for obtaining farm-land and the chances of employment."[118] In consequence, many emigrants felt they had been duped.

Fraser's correspondence reveals how he exploited Vancouver Island's spatial isolation through broad networks of imperial information transmission. In effect, Fraser benefited from a news monopoly, which he employed to stress the economic opportunities on Vancouver Island and in British Columbia. His treatment of local First Nations was carefully crafted to characterize the region in the most positive light. In contrast, the Victoria press, which was attempting to achieve racial segregation, characterized local First Nations as a social problem by repeatedly complaining about Aboriginal violence and social disorder. Fraser's correspondence was crafted in the midst of this social milieu, but one would hardly know it. His divergence from these local narratives of racial antagonism only becomes apparent in the context of a close reading of the Victoria press. Of course, Fraser was not the only writer to elide the local press's version of things.

Guidebooks to Vancouver Island and British Columbia

The *Saturday Review*'s edition of 2 October 1858 provides a pithy summary of Kinahan Cornwallis's guidebook to the Fraser River goldfields:

> There are, in the present day, certain well-marked classes of books, of which all the members resemble each other so much in all essential points that, when we have read the first few pages, we can give a pretty good guess at the contents of the whole volume. Books about gold-diggings belong to this class ... We therefore knew pretty well what Mr. Cornwallis would have to tell before we began to read his book, and our anticipations were pretty accurately realized.[119]

As this passage illustrates, by the mid-nineteenth century guidebooks belonged to a well established literary genre. As historian Dan Davy argues, guidebooks featured narratives infused with "boundless optimism."[120] In the context of New Zealand, Miles Fairburn stresses how guidebooks employed hyperbole to draw potential emigrants, describing New Zealand as an Arcadia of natural abundance.[121] Indeed, Belich suggests that colonial "crusaders" disguised their propaganda through sheer repetition: the publication of numerous guidebooks all repeating the same message allowed more outlandish claims to be subsumed within more objective information.[122] This work reminds us that guidebooks need to be read as sales texts intended to promote a particular destination. One of the ways in which Macdonald broke convention involves how he criticized his subject matter. A critique levelled against Macdonald's rejection of Vancouver Island and British Columbia is that no one else had reached similar conclusions.[123] But this observation ignores the iconoclastic quality of Macdonald's book.

We can rightly imagine, then, that Vancouver Island and British Columbia guidebook writers crafted their narratives according to established templates. This involved providing relevant historical, geographical, meteorological, and commercial information alongside instructions on how best to reach these isolated colonies. Guidebook writers displayed the same spirit of empiricism in characterizing Vancouver Island's and British Columbia's Aboriginal population. Potential emigrants were not necessarily "taken in" by guidebooks as the latter's provision of empirical data likely met readers' expectations; rather, the ability of guidebook writers to veil or conceal negative aspects of Vancouver Island and British Columbia depended upon this region's isolation and the authors' virtual monopoly over the propagation of information in Great Britain.

In this section I draw from twenty-five publications on Vancouver Island and British Columbia, from 1858 to 1866. Seventeen of these were written by prospectors, British naval officers, and colonists with personal experience of the region.[124] The remaining eight were written by metropolitan Britons, who assembled their guidebooks from available information on Vancouver Island and British Columbia.[125] Given the failure of the Victoria press to resonate in Great Britain, for metropolitan Britons guidebooks were the second most important source of information about the region. Certainly, it is no coincidence that all but one of these publications appeared following 1858 as their writers took advantage of the popular interest that the gold rushes had sparked in Great Britain. Given the lack of information regarding the number of publications and editions, it is difficult to gauge the impact of guidebooks in Great Britain. Anecdotally, guidebooks were probably not as significant as was Fraser's correspondence. As we have already seen, the circulation of *The Times* in the mid-nineteenth century was sixty-thousand copies per edition across the British Empire. Fraser's articles were also copied and distributed in many other newspapers, extending their audience across the Empire.[126] In contrast, historian Alexis Weedon suggests that, in the 1850s, books typically featured a print run of one thousand to three thousand copies.[127] Even guidebooks with multiple print runs would not have achieved a similar circulation as *The Times*, nor would their writers have accumulated the same cultural cachet. Nevertheless, the metropolitan press paid attention to the content of guidebooks and summarized their content for its readers. The fact that Vancouver Island's Legislative Assembly sponsored an essay-writing contest that resulted in the publication of Charles Forbes's book *Vancouver Island: Its Resources and Capabilities as a Colony* also signals that colonists perceived guidebooks to be a useful medium for providing information to metropolitan Britons.[128]

Every guidebook writer commented on First Nations. This information, frequently in the form of population estimates and descriptions of Aboriginal culture, sought to prepare prospective emigrants for encounters with local First Nations.[129] In general, writers provided negative characterizations of Aboriginal peoples, emphasizing their treachery, degraded cultures, cruelty, and cowardice.[130] This body of literature built upon earlier representations of First Nations peoples, which had been authored by fur trade officers over the first half of the nineteenth century and published in Great Britain.[131] Joseph Despard Pemberton's guidebook is one of the exceptions to this rule, and it contests the *Illustrated London News*'s contention that local First Nations were the "lowest types of humanity."[132] Pemberton, a resident of Vancouver Island from 1851, whose own diary reveals constant interaction with local First Nations, responded: "[Aboriginal persons] lack neither courage nor intelligence. Some are exceedingly ingenious."[133] But, in general, guidebook writers prepared their readers for cultural difference, characterizing First Nations in terms of an unfavourable binary that identified British culture as the apex of human achievement and First Nations cultures as forms of Aboriginal savagery.

According to Robin Fisher, negative assessments of First Nations often came from uninformed observers whose testimonies were based on preconceived notions of the inferiority of Aboriginal cultures and the demoralizing effects of colonization.[134] These tropes of Indigenous decline and moral degradation were familiar, one-size-fits-all descriptive narratives that were applied across the British Empire. Of course, Fisher is right: the superficial commentary of many guidebook writers was informed by their limited and cursory knowledge. What we must recognize, though, is that guidebook writers gained their cultural expertise through both their proximity to local First Nations and their status as possessors of alleged cultural superiority. According to Marie Louise Pratt, European travel writers described Indigenous peoples within "contact zones" according to the same principles of scientific classification utilized to interpret both the natural world and physical landscapes.[135] This totalizing gaze allowed writers to position Indigenous peoples within systems of racial and cultural knowledge without any dialogue with, or reference to, Indigenous peoples' own beliefs. This is another example of how a stadial notion of cultural development underpinned nineteenth-century assessments of First Nations peoples. Guidebook writers may have known very little about the First Nations cultures they described, but their readers would have assumed that Euro-American writers were implicitly qualified to assess and to describe so-called primitive cultures.

On the topic of Aboriginal violence, many writers confirmed that Vancouver Island's and British Columbia's Aboriginal populations constantly fought each other.[136] However, only Macdonald suggested that the prevalence of Aboriginal violence represented an impediment to emigration. Writers downplayed the significance of Aboriginal violence in several ways. One strategy employed by several writers, as we saw with Fraser, stressed the HBC's record of good relations with local First Nations.[137] The local fur trader Alexander Rattray emphasized how the HBC's legacy of "firmness" had instilled both fear and respect into local First Nations, which, alongside the colonial administration's insistence on First Nations' "strict regard to the laws of the colony and of civilized life," "all combine to render both life and property secure."[138] This suggests that, because of First Nations respect for British authority, Aboriginal violence would not escalate to include local Euro-Americans. Another strategy involved minimizing the threat of Aboriginal violence by stressing the treacherous and cowardly characters of local First Nations.[139] This line of argument suggests that the craven nature of First Nations would prevent their attacking Europeans. This belief informed the advice of several writers, who assured colonists that they should on no account manifest a "want of confidence."[140] Consider the advice of Kinahan Cornwallis:

Courage is a grand thing in first confronting the savage; it inspires immediate respect, whereas the slightest faltering or manifestation of fear leaves the traveller at the mercy of those who can entertain contempt, and detect a want of bravery as readily as any vassal of civilization, and who hold as valueless that which they are not awed by. The best way therefore is to meet the aborigine with a bold fearless front, a steady eye and a defiant look and posture; such self-possession is the white man's only moral defence against the hostility of the Indian, and the safest line of procedure he can adopt when friendly, and especially at a first meeting.[141]

The safety of colonists depended upon a confident facade, an effort defined by the denial of anxiety. Guidebook writers provided a racialized assessment of the threat of Aboriginal violence that downplayed the risk posed to Euro-Americans by emphasizing the connections between their safety and the active performance of cultural superiority.

Former naval officers commented most extensively on Aboriginal violence in Victoria. The narratives of Richard Charles Mayne, C.E. Barrett-Lennard, and Fenton Aylmer capitalized on their own experience in the British navy's security operations in Victoria.[142] This emphasis on Aboriginal violence corresponds to what Elizabeth Vibert notes were the popular themes of "battle, murder, and sudden death" in the travel-writing genre of the eighteenth and nineteenth centuries.[143] Tales of derring-do in the face of the threat of Aboriginal violence allowed these books to function as both adventure stories and guides to potential emigrants. These accounts are of particular interest because they detail the occurrence of Aboriginal violence in Victoria without positing negative assessments of the colony. Indeed, both Barrett-Lennard and Aylmer described the frequent incidence of warfare between battling northern First Nations on the outskirts of Victoria, and their narratives caught the attention of the metropolitan press. For example, the *Saturday Review*'s discussion of several publications on Vancouver Island and in British Columbia in 1862 drew particular attention to Barrett-Lennard's comments on Aboriginal violence.[144] The *Saturday Review* writer notes: "his description of the character and manners of the native population are calculated to give the intending emigrant too unfavourable an impression of his future neighbours."[145] It was no coincidence that Barrett-Lennard's comments garnered attention as he was the only naval officer to assert that local security forces could not stop Aboriginal violence. It is probable that Barret's passage caught the attention of the *Saturday Review* writer: "Until quite recently members of different tribes, at war with one another, would forthwith proceed to extremities on meeting, even in the streets of Victoria itself, and at the present moment the utmost efforts of the authorities are ineffectual to prevent the frequent occurrence of murders in the vicinity of the town."[146] As the *Saturday Review* writer concludes: "the prospects of both colonies are bright, if they will only take care not to fall out with each other, or with the Indians."[147]

It seems that the *Saturday Review*'s guarded optimism regarding the prospects of Vancouver Island and British Columbia stemmed from its comparison of the books by Barrett-Lennard, Macdonald, and Mayne. But it was Mayne's book to which the newspaper gave precedence. Mayne was a gentleman and the son of Sir Charles Mayne, the first commissioner of the London Metropolitan Police. By 1862, the twenty-seven-year-old Mayne was a veteran of fifteen years' service in the British navy and had been garrisoned on Vancouver Island and in British Columbia for four years.[148] Mayne based his guidebook on a personal diary, which he published in Great Britain while promoting Vancouver Island at the London International Exhibition.[149] This book was the product of one facet of his official role as a booster for the region, and it is of particular interest that Mayne explicitly responded to another writer's negative assessments of local First Nations:

> In a recent book on British Columbia one of the many objections urged against the country is said to arise from the danger of Indian aggression upon the colonists. I cannot conclude these remarks without giving this assertion an emphatic contradiction. My own experience – as the reader will have gathered – has led me to form an exactly opposite opinion of the temper and disposition of the Indians.[150]

It seems clear that Mayne is rebutting Macdonald in this passage. Both writers published their guidebooks in 1862, and only Macdonald provided a negative characterization of local First Nations. Yet, while Mayne objected to Macdonald's thesis, his own narrative provides ample evidence of Aboriginal violence, examples of the British navy's intimidation of northern First Nations in Victoria, and the existence of tension between northern First Nations and the colonial administration.[151] From similar evidence sprang different conclusions. The key difference between Mayne and Macdonald lies in their contrasting attitudes towards the British navy's relative power in the region and the benefits of Christianity for First Nations.

While Mayne deployed anecdotes of Aboriginal violence in Victoria to infuse his narrative with a sense of adventure, he did not acknowledge that local First Nations represented an actual military threat; rather, he took white physical superiority for granted, emphasizing his own natural leadership and fearlessness when interacting with local First Nations.[152] Mayne's performance of Victorian manliness could not be easily reconciled with an acknowledgment of settler anxiety regarding the threat of Aboriginal violence. Mayne also believed that local First Nations were valuable human beings who would benefit from the civilizing work of Anglican missionaries.[153]

Throughout his narrative, Mayne celebrates both muscular Christianity and his own participation in Victoria's community of evangelical humanitarians. As historian Robert Hogg argues, this discourse of manliness was particularly popular in the mid-nineteenth century, with its emphasis on Christian principles, manly vigour, and self-control.[154] This theme is exemplified by Mayne's praise for William Duncan's mission work on the Northwest Coast.[155] Whereas Macdonald referenced the Taranaki War as an example of the failure of humanitarian policies of Indigenous administration, Mayne cited the recognition of Maori title in New Zealand as the best policy to implement on Vancouver Island and in British Columbia.[156] In 1862, New Zealand still represented a humanitarian success story for Mayne and functioned as a paradigm for colonial policy. Mayne's and Macdonald's contrasting conclusions hinge upon their attitudes towards Indigenous potential and the benefits of humanitarianism. Mayne's narrative reflects the assumption of British cultural superiority and the belief that the moral and physical degradation of local First Nations could be ameliorated by conversion to Christianity and its civilizing effects. Most colonists probably shared Mayne's beliefs about the cultural inferiority of local First Nations, but they varied in their endorsement of the potential for civilizing First Nations. Most tellingly, the *Saturday Review* found Mayne's humanitarianism more convincing than Macdonald's racial antagonism. Would the *Saturday Review* have reached a different conclusion if it had had better access to the Victoria press?

Guidebook authors addressed the subject of Aboriginal violence circumspectly. Most writers did not comment on reported Aboriginal violence in Victoria, nor did they discuss the anxiety of colonists. The few writers, such as Mayne, who did allude to Aboriginal violence in Victoria did so in order to highlight their own military service. Their purpose and tone in these reflections were very different from Macdonald's. Like Fraser in his correspondence in *The Times*, guidebook writers avoided commenting on the Victoria press's discourses of Aboriginal violence and settler anxiety because they did not want these subjects to resonate in Great Britain. Aboriginal violence and settler anxiety had little place in the guidebook writer's quest to craft positive descriptions of Vancouver Island and British Columbia. Thus, the reported incidence of First Nations violence on the Northwest Coast was not common knowledge in Great Britain in the mid-nineteenth century. Here we see the implications of Simon Potter's general observation: "Certain parts of the empire enjoyed less developed connections with the centre and with each other than did other, more privileged locations."[157] It is useful, then, to close this section with a brief analysis of the California press's coverage of Vancouver Island and British Columbia.

The California Press

The press communities of Vancouver Island and British Columbia were integrated into a broader network of press communities on the west coast of North America, which paid attention to news emerging from the British colonies to the north. Many of the new residents of Vancouver Island and British Columbia hailed from the United States, providing tangible links between the communications networks of the west coast. In this final section, I highlight the *Daily Alta California*'s and the *Sacramento Daily Union*'s coverage of Vancouver Island and British Columbia. The American newspaper historian Edward C. Kimble identifies these newspapers as particularly influential members of the California press.[158] They published numerous articles that commented on Aboriginal violence in Victoria and on the Northwest Coast. The first point to emphasize is that Californian editors interpreted the incidence of Aboriginal violence in Victoria and on the Northwest Coast in the context of American relations with First Nations in Washington Territory. The manner in which local concerns defined Californian papers' interest in the Victoria press illustrates Arjun Appadurai's thesis regarding how information spread by global networks becomes indigenized according to the "imagined worlds" of constituent audiences.[159] In 1856–57, a devastating conflict between the Aboriginal population and local settlers took place in Washington Territory and, according to American accounts, ended inconclusively.[160] In 1858, hostilities reignited.[161] Therefore, when the Fraser River gold rush began in that year, the California press predicted that the invasion by thousands of American prospectors would precipitate a similar war.[162] Similarly, California papers paid particular attention to the presence of northern First Nations in Victoria because of the latter's reputation for raiding American settlements on the coast of the Washington Territory.[163] During the San Juan Island controversy, this focus on the threat of northern First Nations made General William S. Harney's rationale for establishing a military outpost on San Juan Island plausible in the eyes of the California press, but it was rejected out of hand by the Victoria press and by Donald Fraser in *The Times*.[164]

In particular, the articles from the *Daily Alta California*'s own correspondent in Victoria are interesting because he provides an independent perspective on colonists' ambivalent relations with northern First Nations.[165] This correspondent notes how colonists were divided over the benefits of Aboriginal eviction: those who desired their expulsion on the grounds of security and those who valued their labour.[166] In addition, the California press's coverage of Vancouver Island and British Columbia drew upon and commented on the Victoria press's editorial manifestos. The California press, then, commented on many of the issues central to this book: the incidence of Aboriginal violence in Victoria and on the Northwest Coast, the mobility of northern First Nations, the importance of Aboriginal labour in Victoria's economy, settler anxiety, and the horrendous repercussions of eviction for First Nations during the 1862 smallpox epidemic.

While California editors' focus on the threat of Aboriginal violence at the beginning of the Fraser River gold rush may have originated in an attempt to persuade local prospectors not to quit the United States, its coverage of the region was thoroughly grounded by the Victoria press and local correspondents from the region. Moreover, the California press's focus on violence and anxiety in Victoria provides further context for Donald Fraser's articles in *The Times* and for guidebook writers' characterizations of Vancouver Island. California newspapers' depiction of settler relations with local First Nations in Victoria are more accurate than that of either Fraser or guidebook writers because they are infused with narratives that emanated from the Victoria press itself. The narratives of guidebook writers bear little resemblance to the Victoria press's characterizations of settler relations with local First Nations. Given the experience of most guidebook writers in the region, these divergences appear intentional as they would have been familiar with both the situation in Victoria and local editorial perspectives. As the Australian press did for New Zealand, the California press functioned as a selective filter of the Victoria press. However, unlike what Australian newspapers did for New Zealand, California newspapers were not able to make Northwest Coast editorial perspectives resonate in Great Britain.

Conclusion

In this chapter I pursue a number of significant strands in a broad web of connections in order to identify the effects of Vancouver Island's and New Zealand's divergent locations within imperial networks of news transmission.[167] My analysis confirms Simon Potter's argument that mid-nineteenth-century press connections were "diverse, dynamic, multiple, and above all only loosely structured."[168] For example, that *The Times* and the *Saturday Review* did not explicitly endorse any particular New Zealand editor's interpretation of the Taranaki War is not evidence of the failure of colonial newspapers to reach Great Britain. Just the opposite. During the Taranaki War a cacophony of competing perspectives reached Great Britain from both New Zealand and Australia, complicating interpretation. This lack of a unified narrative of the Taranaki War may be the crucial difference between it and what occurred during the Indian Rebellion, when Anglo-Indian newspapers provided a cohesive and racially antagonistic interpretation of the conflict.[169] It seems evident that these multiple viewpoints, alongside the work of lobbyists like Chapman and perhaps Selwyn, influenced the *Saturday Review*'s and *The Times*'s repudiation of colonists. New Zealand had a robust connection to Great Britain in the mid-nineteenth century, challenging any particular newspaper's or press community's ability to exert a monopoly over the interpretation of the Taranaki War.

In addition, *The Times*'s and the *Saturday Review*'s overall responses suggest that editors in New Zealand were right to fear that the metropolitan press might spurn colonial interests in favour of concerns over imperial expenditures on colonial defence. Like Alan Lester, I think that colonial editors infused their editorial perspectives with idealized visions of colonists' British identities. Unlike Lester, though, I think that humanitarian racial discourses were relevant to colonists and the creation of a "trans-imperial discourse of colonialism."[170] Because of New Zealand's robust connection with Great Britain, colonial editors who supported Thomas Gore Browne had to contest not only metropolitan scepticism regarding their relations with Maori but also rival publications from both evangelical humanitarians and dissenting members of New Zealand's press. In this context, defining the war as a defence of Maori rights and British sovereignty was an attempt to overcome metropolitan scepticism regarding colonists' esteem for Maori. What I suggest, however, is that the rhetorical humanitarianism of colonial editors was apparent to metropolitan readers.

In contrast, the metropolitan coverage of Vancouver Island and British Columbia demonstrates that Great Britain did not have meaningful press connections with the region. In addition to emphasizing this comparative underdevelopment of press networks, in this chapter I show that newspaper correspondents' and guidebook writers' failure to characterize settler relations with local First Nations in the same manner as did the Victoria press was intentional. Macdonald was the only writer who drew upon the narratives of Aboriginal violence depicted in the Victoria press, and his invective nullified his conclusions. In order to avoid alienating their readers, Fraser and other guidebook writers characterized settler relations with local First Nations positively. I think the disparity between the Victoria press's accounts of anxiety/violence and the idealized narratives of colonial populists has been ignored because the 1862 smallpox epidemic brought about the sudden removal of northern First Nations from Victoria. In other words, by the time the Victoria press established connections with Great Britain, relations with local First Nations were no longer defined by anxiety.

Conclusion

IN *SETTLER ANXIETY at the Outposts of Empire* I show how, through the use of humanitarian language, colonial newspapers crafted idealized representations of public opinion while, at the same time, forwarding the narrow political and economic interests of their owners and editors. Settler anxiety guided this imperative, shaped both by the perceived threat of Indigenous violence and by metropolitan surveillance of colonial affairs. The resonance of humanitarian racial discourses in New Zealand and Vancouver Island supports the argument that the new imperial history is incorrect in arguing that these discourses were losing their power in the latter half of the mid-nineteenth century. This conclusion echoes the recent work of Damen Salesa, Ann O'Brien, Kevin Grant, and James Heartfield, who each discuss the social and political significance of humanitarian discourses in the second half of the nineteenth century.[1]

Humanitarian themes persisted because they continued to offer a useful frame for settler relations with Indigenous peoples. The use of these themes was an attractive strategy in New Zealand, where colonial leaders were worried about accusations of their having a "nigger despising temper."[2] In this context, the use of humanitarian themes affirmed the benefits of colonization for Maori. In contrast, the use of humanitarian themes by editors on Vancouver Island originated from a combination of local factors: they were used to bolster demands for Aboriginal eviction, to defend black colonists' rights, and to recognize Aboriginal title. Editors in New Zealand voiced stronger and more consistent forms of humanitarian sentiment, but the very presence of humanitarian themes on Vancouver Island, which was beyond the surveillance of metropolitan Britons, is powerful evidence of their connection to British identity during this era. For both colonies, the symbolic role of the press as an embodiment of public opinion and the British Empire's status as an agent of providence ensured that humanitarian language would remain politically useful. It was also well suited to the medium of news print.

The divergent positions of New Zealand and Vancouver Island within imperial networks of news transmission played a significant role in mediating editors' characterizations of Indigenous peoples. In New Zealand, journalists, evangelical humanitarians, and colonial politicians believed that humanitarianism remained influential in Great Britain. They also understood that New Zealand's strong connections to the Australian colonies and the United Kingdom meant that metropolitan Britons could read everything that was reported locally. This is why both opponents and proponents of the Taranaki War crafted their interpretations of the conflict with due deference to Maori treaty rights. But the general mobilization of humanitarianism diminished the points of difference over the Waitara purchase and the Taranaki War. Indeed, metropolitan commentators found it difficult to evaluate competing definitions of precolonial Maori practice. To overcome the additional challenges of Great Britain's spatial and temporal distance from New Zealand, metropolitan commentators depended on the critical analysis of lobbyists and correspondents to verify emerging news.

With no similar expectation of a metropolitan audience, editors in Victoria stressed the incidence of local Aboriginal violence to spur the Crown's removal of local First Nations. This reportage occurred in pursuit of a more sustainable press environment and was grounded in racialized understandings of urban space and the related belief that First Nations peoples belonged in the colonial hinterland. D.G.F. Macdonald wrote about reported Aboriginal violence but, in his warnings about the region, contradicted the ethos of guidebook boosterism. Had editors in Victoria imagined an audience of metropolitan readers, it seems likely that their coverage of Aboriginal violence would have more closely resembled Donald Fraser's inoffensive columns in *The Times*. In both New Zealand and Vancouver Island, settler anxiety over the perceived threat of Indigenous violence was a mercurial force – one that had to be carefully acknowledged in order to avoid transgressing scripts of Victorian manliness, challenging assumptions of European racial superiority, or inciting panic.

To a lesser extent, on Vancouver Island editors' use of humanitarian themes both to appeal to and to critique James Douglas reflected an assumption that humanitarian discourses continued to be a defining feature of British imperial practice and a necessary strategy for conceptualizing amendments to Aboriginal policy. Particularly with regard to demands for the recognition of Aboriginal title, humanitarian language disguised the degree of editors' anxiety over the threat of Aboriginal violence. It is not surprising, then, that support for Aboriginal property rights declined in tandem with diminishing reportage of Aboriginal disorder. Though it is sometimes difficult to discern between the voices of rhetorical and the voices of evangelical humanitarianism, the attention to Indigenous rights in both colonies often implicitly reflected the inability of colonists to employ coercive strategies to achieve local hegemony. In these places of legal pluralism, the writ of law was largely confined to urban centres, while the hinterlands remained Indigenous spaces.

The popularity of humanitarian discourses in New Zealand also had much to do with the legacy of Maori engagement with Christianity, their integration into networks of colonial knowledge, and their military capacity. Christianity was both a marker of "civilization" and a vital social connector. As my analysis of *Te Karere Maori* illustrates, the Crown extolled its covenant-like bond of faith with Maori and claimed to be an agent of divine providence. This vision of racial amalgamation took it for granted that Maori were open to cultural change, but the newspaper's efforts also betrayed anxiety regarding the consequences of Maori knowledge of imperial events. During the Taranaki War, when relations between colonists and Maori were fraught, *Te Karere Maori* sought to reduce the risk of a general war. In this context the use of humanitarian themes veiled the degree of settler anxiety regarding the threat of Maori violence, which was focused on the possibility that Auckland might be attacked. On Vancouver Island, editors assumed that Aboriginal peoples were not integrated into networks of colonial knowledge and so did not try to avoid offending them. Similarly, missionaries like William Duncan were acclaimed for having special influence among local Aboriginal peoples rather than reviled for sabotaging colonialism. In this way, Vancouver Island resembled New Zealand as it had been in the late 1830s and early 1840s.

We have seen how editors on Vancouver Island drew upon the New Zealand wars rather than the Indian Rebellion as a parallel to their own situation. This may reflect several factors, including the fact that the Victoria press was established after the Indian Rebellion, the prominence of the imperial press's coverage of the Taranaki War, New Zealand's similar status as a settler colony, and the experience of local editors in the Australasian press. In contrast, I show the degree to which the Indian Rebellion resonated in New Zealand. Widespread knowledge of the Indian Rebellion informed *Te Karere Maori*'s careful exposition of the conflict to its Maori readers and heightened settler fears of the Taranaki War's potential to become a widespread racial conflict. However, it appears that the New Zealand press deliberately avoided drawing parallels between the Taranaki War and the Indian Rebellion because invoking the violent repression of the "Mutiny" would have contradicted the positive characterizations of settler relations with Maori. This reminds us that each colonial site's response to the Indian Rebellion depended upon local circumstances.[3] By 1869, however, members of New Zealand's House of Representatives felt free to compare Maori violence to the atrocities of the Indian Rebellion.[4] Perhaps the withdrawal of British imperial troops from active service in New Zealand in 1867 created a social space in which comparisons between Maori and rebel Sepoys no longer had the potential to elicit metropolitan interference.[5]

In the case of both New Zealand and Vancouver Island in the 1850s and 1860s, the transmission and interpretation of news continued to depend on conventional forms of transport and the informal networks that bound together editors, correspondents, and colonial lobbyists. Here we are reminded of Harold Innis's emphasis on the unique properties and effects of communication media.[6] Maritime shipping dictated the speed of news transmission, with cut-and-paste journalism facilitating the reproduction of ideas and arguments across the Empire in an environment that lacked adequate context. This argument challenges Simon Potter's contention that, by the mid-nineteenth century, informal networks no longer defined the imperial press system.[7] While I agree with Potter that British colonies often featured uneven connections with both Great Britain and each other, further work is needed in order to test his belief that the mid-nineteenth century was a moment when telegraphic innovation marginalized the relationship between news transmission and the importance of informal networks.[8]

Telegraphic technology heralded a new age of telecommunications, facilitated by what Roland Wenzlhuemer calls the "dematerialization" of information transmission from tangible information carriers to electric impulses capable of near instantaneous transmission across time and space.[9]

What is less clear, though, is how long the transmission of extended and multifaceted press discourses from the colonial periphery remained bound to conventional (i.e., slow-moving) information carriers. The telegraphic era began in Great Britain in the 1840s, but the prominent settler colonies of Canada and Australia remained unconnected to Great Britain by useful submarine telegraphic cables until 1866 and 1871, respectively. This transitional period persisted in New Zealand and Vancouver Island because, at first, telegraphic networks only carried a fraction of the news, and these colonies were initially on the periphery of telegraphic communications networks. For example, at first both colonies benefitted from the faster transmission of telegraphic news to regional press centres – San Francisco for Victoria and Melbourne for New Zealand.[10] News was transmitted nearly instantaneously from the metropole to these places, but then it travelled via newspapers aboard steamers to the colonial periphery. Initially, the first news of value to be carried by telegraphic networks was market prices and shipping information – news that was concise, time sensitive, and economically valuable. Because the use of telegraphic networks was expensive, press agencies such as the Australian Associated Press (1871) and the New Zealand Press Association (1878) were developed to pay for the transmission of general news, which was then exploited by newspapers on the periphery through conventional cut-and-paste journalism.

However, even when both British Columbia and New Zealand were connected via telegraphic networks, the fast flow of information occurred primarily in one direction. The majority of telegraphic news travelled from the metropole outwards. We can imagine, then, that, at least in the early period of telegraphy, the telegraphic news sent from New Zealand and British Columbia would have been in the form of concise headlines rather than long editorials.[11] Thus, the majority of colonial press discourses, the output of many constituent members of colonial press communities, would have continued to travel slowly to the metropole via conventional transportation.[12] So, did the metropolitan reception of colonial news change in the late 1860s and early 1870s when the "staleness" of colonial press discourses became even more pronounced? Can we track changing metropolitan interest in colonial affairs alongside inequalities created by new communications infrastructure, thereby building on Simon Potter's work on the creation of an imperial press monopoly in the late nineteenth century?[13] Subsequent research might test Peter Putnis's hypothesis regarding the conditions under which interpretive monopolies could occur from the mid-nineteenth century on.

In terms of broad debates over "continuity and change" within the British Empire, I suggest that, in the mid-nineteenth century, there was more of the former than the latter.[14] C.A. Bayly argues that this period constitutes a crucial moment when both changing technology and racial attitudes shifted, citing Ronald Hyam's argument that the imperial crises of this period "inaugurated a new era in Imperial history."[15] Similarly, both Catherine Hall and Alan Lester associate this mid-nineteenth-century disjuncture with the decline of humanitarianism and the rise of antagonistic racial discourses. But a close reading of the colonial press in New Zealand and Vancouver Island challenges the pan-imperial applicability of these arguments.

I show how antagonistic racial attitudes were not evenly or consistently publicly adopted in New Zealand and Vancouver Island but, rather, were mediated by colonists' perceptions of their relationship to the metropole and the ongoing political influence of humanitarianism. One could argue that colonists' perceptions of the influence of humanitarianism in Great Britain may have stemmed from a temporal lag between colonies and metropole, whereby colonists' maintenance of humanitarian attitudes reflected their relative ignorance of shifting sentiments in Great Britain. However, the degree to which colonists remained *au fait* with metropolitan public discourses contradicts this theory. Alternatively, colonists in New Zealand and Vancouver Island may have remained self-consciously wedded to humanitarian discourses longer than metropolitan Britons because of their obligation to defend the benefits of colonization and their recognition of Indigenous rights. What seems evident is that the situation in New Zealand and Vancouver Island was very different from Andrew Bank's and Elizabeth Elbourne's description of that in the Cape Colony, where wars between settlers and local Indigenous peoples contributed to the rapid local decline of humanitarianism.[16] The clearest lesson provided by this book is that we cannot assume that shifting racial attitudes in Great Britain were replicated across the Empire in a straightforward fashion.

Certainly, it is evident that humanitarian discourses remained prevalent in New Zealand across the 1860s. For example, Damon Salesa, in his study of the war in Waikato in 1863, argues that colonists came to view violence itself as an agent of racial amalgamation.[17] In this context, Grey's pursuit of dual campaigns – one preparing for a military conflict, the other implementing new institutions for Maori – were not incompatible. George Grey, like Thomas Gore Browne, conceptualized military force as an appropriate tool for protecting the rights of colonists and Maori. This research, like my own, challenges the notion that the British resort to arms in the 1860s marked a symbolic break with humanitarianism. Likewise, throughout this period, settler anxiety related to both metropolitan and Maori surveillance continued apace. James Heartfield illustrates this point by providing evidence that settler politicians like William Fox believed that, in the 1860s, the Aborigines' Protection Society's advocacy had convinced Maori insurgents to prolong the war effort in order to garner metropolitan intervention on their behalf.[18]

Perhaps the most significant example of the ongoing relevance of humanitarian discourses in New Zealand is the Maori Representation Act, 1867. Spearheaded by former chief land commissioner Donald McLean, this legislation enfranchised all Maori men over the age of twenty-one and created four Maori seats within the General Assembly.[19] Here we see how colonists were influenced by the ongoing anxiety over the threat of Maori violence and how they sought to alleviate Maori dissatisfaction by facilitating their participation in government. No other British settler colony extended voting rights to their Indigenous populations in the late nineteenth century. As Tony Ballantyne shows, the popularity of Aryan racial theories in late nineteenth-century New Zealand, which identified the common Indo-centric racial origins of Maori and England's antecedent peoples, continued the legacy of humanitarianism and provided a tangible basis for what colonists perceived to be the privileged status of Maori in comparison to that of other Indigenous peoples.[20]

In the new province of British Columbia, the very opposite occurred, with settlers denying First Nations peoples the right to participate in local government. Humanitarian narratives had not disappeared in this era, but they had changed.[21] We have seen how narratives of sympathy for the plight of Indigenous people on Vancouver Island had the power to elicit both outrage and a rhetorical humanitarian response from Joseph Trutch. By the time Trutch responded to William Sebright Green's complaints near the end of British Columbia's colonial era in 1870, the Crown's official humanitarian narrative had shifted from Douglas's emphasis on the recognition of Aboriginal rights to Trutch's focus on the Crown's responsibility to protect First Nations people as legal minors. Of course both the recognition of Indigenous rights and the protection of Indigenous peoples have always been present in humanitarian discourses. Debates over the creation of both New Zealand and Vancouver Island centred on concerns regarding the protection of local Indigenous peoples. However, in the late 1860s, the most dominant theme – protection – marked the increasing power of the state to intrude upon Indigenous lifeways in both New Zealand and British Columbia. More than anything, this shift was accompanied by settlers' diminishing perception of the ability of Indigenous peoples to violently resist the colonial project.

The continued political utility of humanitarianism in the mid-nineteenth century reveals what Jane Samson terms "the ambiguities of empire."[22] Settler discourses were not monolithic, and the dislocation of Indigenous peoples did not go unquestioned. Humanitarian discourses functioned simultaneously and paradoxically as both a language of critique and as an apologetics for colonialism. This range of sentiment did not simply evaporate in the mid-nineteenth century. Indeed, there are clear similarities between my conclusions and the work of Glenn R. Wilkinson and Gordon Winder, who reveal how British imperialists and Anglophiles continued to describe the British Empire as an agent of both civilization and Christianity into the late nineteenth and mid-twentieth centuries.[23] Here we are reminded of the affinities between humanitarianism and discourses of British "civilization" that were never wholly secular in character.

The broad appeal of humanitarian language lay in its inclusivity and in the common ability of British persons to assess cultural difference according to the principles of stadial theory, discourses of civilization, and the fluidity of racial and cultural categories. Here we must recognize that the prevalence of humanitarian racial discourses reinforced the imposition of racial hierarchies across the British Empire at the same time as Darwinian-inspired notions of immutable racial difference were gathering credibility.[24] Humanitarian themes were less effectual in protecting Indigenous peoples' rights in the late 1850s and early 1860s because both evangelical and rhetorical humanitarians employed common discursive frameworks and often agreed to limit the legal rights of Indigenous peoples on the basis of their perceived lack of cultural sophistication. Humanitarianism, while contentious, continued to be used because it continued to be seen as an effective instrument for shaping both opinion and policy.

Notes

Introduction

1 *Pacific Commercial Advertiser*, 14 April 1861.
2 *British Colonist*, 31 May 1861.
3 *Southern Cross*, 7 September 1860.
4 Kevin Grant, *A Civilised Savagery: Britain and the New Slaveries in Africa, 1884–1926* (New York: Routledge, 2005); Anne O'Brien, "Humanitarianism and Reparation in Colonial Australia," *Journal of Colonialism and Colonial History* 12, 2 (2011), http://muse.jhu.edu/login?auth=0&type=summary&url=/journals/journal_of_colonialism_and_colonial_history/v012/12.2.o-brien.html; James Heartfield, *The Aborigines' Protection Society: Humanitarian Imperialism in Australia, New Zealand, Fiji, Canada, South Africa, and the Congo, 1836–1909* (New York: Columbia University Press, 2011).
5 Ronald Hyam, *Britain's Imperial Century, 1815–1914: A Study of Empire and Expansion* (London: B.T. Batsford, 1976), 70–85; Antoinette Burton, *Burdens of History: British Feminists, Indian Women, and Imperial Culture, 1865–1915* (Chapel Hill: University of North Carolina Press, 1994), 29–30; Alan Lester, *Imperial Networks: Creating Identities in Nineteenth-Century South Africa and Britain* (London: Routledge, 2001), 214; Catherine Hall, *Civilising Subjects: Metropole and Colony in the English Imagination* (Chicago: University of Chicago Press, 2002), 23–27, 54–55, 212.
6 Jill Bender, "Fears of 1857: The British Empire in the Wake of the Indian Rebellion" (PhD diss., Boston College, 2011), 5.
7 Thomas W. Laqueur, "Bodies, Details, and the Humanitarian Narrative," in *The New Cultural History*, ed. Lynn Hunt (Berkeley: University of California Press, 1989), 176–79; Karen Halttunen, "Humanitarianism and the Pornography of Pain in Anglo-American Culture," *American Historical Review* 100, 2 (1995): 303.
8 D.W. Bebbington, *Evangelicalism in Modern Britain: A History from the 1730s to the 1980s* (London: Routledge, 1995), 20–27.
9 Susan Thorne, *Congregational Missions and the Making of an Imperial Culture in 19th-Century England* (Stanford: Stanford University Press, 1999), 23–52.

10 Colin Kidd, *The Forging of Races: Race and Scripture in the Protestant Atlantic World, 1600–2000* (Cambridge: Cambridge University Press, 2006), 59–60.

11 Julie Evans, Patricia Grimshaw, David Phillips, and Shurlee Swain, *Equal Subjects, Unequal Rights: Indigenous People in British Settler Colonies, 1830–1919* (Manchester: Manchester University Press, 2003), 32.

12 Graeme Wynn, "Deplorably Dark and Demoralized Lumberers? Rhetoric and Reality in Early Nineteenth-Century New Brunswick," *Journal of Forest History* 24, 4 (1980): 179–84.

13 Kay Anderson, "White Natures: Sydney's Royal Agricultural Show in Post-Humanist Perspective," *Transactions of the Institute of British Geographers* (n.s.) 28, 4 (2003): 423–25.

14 Andrew Porter, "Trusteeship, Anti-Slavery, and Humanitarianism," in *The Oxford History of the British Empire: The Nineteenth Century*, ed. Andrew Porter (Oxford: Oxford University Press, 1999), 202.

15 Bebbington, *Evangelicalism in Modern Britain*, 71.

16 House of Commons, *Report of the Parliamentary Select Committee on Aboriginal Tribes (British Settlements)* (London: Aborigines' Protection Society, 1837), 104.

17 Kidd, *Forging of Races*.

18 Heartfield, *Aborigines' Protection Society*, 303–4.

19 Elizabeth Elbourne, "The Sin of the Settler: The 1835–36 Select Committee on Aborigines and Debates over Virtue and Conquest in the Early Nineteenth-Century British White Settler Empire," *Journal of Colonialism and Colonial History* 4, 3 (2003): 48.

20 John Scouler, "Dr. John Scouler's Journal of a Voyage to N.W. America [1824–26]," *Quarterly of the Oregon Historical Society* 6, 1 (1905): 176–78, 191–92; D.G.F. Macdonald, *British Columbia and Vancouver Island* (London: Longman, Green, Longman, Roberts & Green, 1862), 128, 130–31; Rachel Standfield, "Warriors and Wanderers: Making Race in the Tasman World, 1769–1840" (PhD diss., University of Otago, 2008), 30.

21 Barry M. Gough, *Gunboat Frontier: British Maritime Authority and Northwest Coast Indians, 1846–1890* (Vancouver: UBC Press, 1984); Angela Ballara, *Taua: "Musket Wars," "Land Wars" or Tikanga? Warfare in Māori Society in the Early Nineteenth Century* (Auckland: Penguin, 2003).

22 C.E. Barrett-Lennard, *Travels in British Columbia: With the Narrative of a Yacht Voyage Round Vancouver's Island* (London: Hurst and Blackett, 1862), 41–42; James Belich, *The New Zealand Wars and the Victorian Interpretation of Racial Conflict: The Maori, the British, and the New Zealand Wars* (Montreal and Kingston: McGill-Queen's University Press, 1986), 21–22.

23 See Jeremy Mouat, "Situating Vancouver Island in the British World, 1846–49," *BC Studies* 145 (Spring 2005): 5–30; Tony Ballantyne, "Humanitarian Narratives: Knowledge and the Politics of Mission and Empire," *Social Sciences and Missions* 24 (2011): 233–64.

24 [John Ward and Edward Gibbon Wakefield], *The British Colonization of New Zealand* (London: John W. Parker, 1837).

25 Ballantyne, "Humanitarian Narratives," 238.

26 Hyam, *Britain's Imperial Century, 1815–1914*, 44–45; Cole Harris, *Making Native Space: Colonialism, Resistance, and Reserves in British Columbia* (Vancouver: UBC Press, 2003), 10–12; Michael Belgrave, *Historical Frictions: Maori Claims and Reinvented Histories* (Auckland: Auckland University Press, 2005), 56–58.

27 Heartfield, *Aborigines' Protection Society*, 126.

28 James Edward Fitzgerald, *An Examination of the Charter and Proceedings of the Hudson Bay Company, with Reference to the Grant of Vancouver Island* (London: Edward Trelawney, 1849); R.M. Martin, *The Hudson's Bay Territories and Vancouver's Island* (London: T. and W. Boone, 1849).

29 See Edward Gibbon Wakefield, *A Letter from Sydney* (London: Joseph Cross, 1829); Edward Gibbon Wakefield, *England and America: A Comparison of the Social and Political State of both Nations*, vols. 1–2 (London: Richard Bentley, 1833).

30 Damon Ieremia Salesa, *Racial Crossings: Race, Intermarriage, and the Victorian British Empire* (Auckland: Oxford University Press, 2011), 27–53.
31 Richard Mackie, "The Colonization of Vancouver Island, 1849–1858," *BC Studies* 96 (Winter 1992–93): 3–40; Philip Temple, *A Sort of Conscience: The Wakefields* (Auckland: Auckland University Press, 2002).
32 Penelope Edmonds, *Urbanizing Frontiers: Indigenous Peoples and Settlers in 19th-Century Pacific Rim Cities* (Vancouver: UBC Press, 2010), 41–43.
33 Harris, *Making Native Space*, 18.
34 Chris Arnett, *The Terror of the Coast: Land Alienation and Colonial War on Vancouver Island and the Gulf Islands, 1849–1863* (Vancouver: Talonbooks, 1999), 30–35; Belgrave, *Historical Frictions*, 44, 69–70.
35 Harris, *Making Native Space*, 17–44.
36 Belgrave, *Historical Frictions*, 69; See also William Martin, *England and the New Zealanders: Remarks Upon a Despatch from the Right Hon. Earl Grey to Governor Grey, Dated to Dec. 23 1846* (Auckland: College Press, 1847).
37 Evans et al., *Equal Subjects*, 184.
38 See Leonore Davidoff and Catherine Hall, *Family Fortunes: Men and Women of the English Middle Class, 1780–1850* (London: Hutchinson, 1987); John Tosh, *A Man's Place: Masculinity and the Middle-Class Home in Victorian England* (New Haven: Yale University Press, 1999); Robert Hogg, *Men and Manliness on the Frontier: Queensland and British Columbia in the Mid-Nineteenth Century* (Basingstoke: Palgrave Macmillan, 2012).
39 Fiona Bateman and Lionel Pilkington, "Introduction," in *Studies in Settler Colonialism: Politics, Identity and Culture*, ed. Fiona Bateman and Lionel Pilkington (Houndsmills, Basingstoke: Palgrave Macmillan, 2011), 1.
40 Harris, *Making Native Space*, 22.
41 Robin Fisher, *Contact and Conflict: Indian-European Relations in British Columbia, 1774–1890* (Vancouver: UBC Press, 1992); Elizabeth Vibert, *Traders' Tales: Narratives of Encounter in the Columbian Plateau, 1807–1846* (Norman: University of Oklahoma Press, 1997); Carol J. Williams, *Framing the West: Race, Gender, and the Photographic Frontier in the Pacific Northwest* (Oxford: Oxford University Press, 2003); Paige Raibmon, *Authentic Indians: Episodes of Encounter from the Late-Nineteenth-Century Northwest Coast* (Durham: Duke University Press, 2005); Renisa Mawani, *Colonial Proximities: Crossracial Encounters and Juridicial Truths in British Columbia, 1871–1921* (Vancouver: UBC Press, 2009).
42 Fisher, *Contact and Conflict*, 150–57; Paul Tennant, *Aboriginal Peoples and Politics: The Indian Land Question in British Columbia, 1849–1989* (Vancouver: UBC Press, 1990), 26–38; Harris, *Making Native Space*, 30–44.
43 Arnett, *Terror of the Coast*, 88–110.
44 Fisher, *Contact and Conflict*, 156–74; Adele Perry, *On the Edge of Empire: Gender, Race, and the Making of British Columbia, 1849–1871* (Toronto: University of Toronto Press, 2001), 119–20.
45 Cole Harris, "How Did Colonialism Dispossess? Comments from an Edge of Empire," *Annals of the Association of American Geographers* 94, 1 (March 2004): 165–82.
46 Lisa Ford, *Settler Sovereignty: Jurisdiction and Indigenous People in America and Australia, 1788–1836* (Cambridge: Harvard University Press, 2010), 2.
47 F. Knight Hunt, *The Fourth Estate: Contributions towards a History of Newspapers and the Liberty of the Press*, vol. 1 (London: David Bogue, 1850), 1.
48 Aled Jones, *Powers of the Press: Newspapers, Power and the Public in Nineteenth Century England* (Aldershot: Scolar Press, 1996), 3.
49 Alexander Andrews, *The History of British Journalism from the Foundation of the Newspaper Press in England to the Repeal of the Stamp Act in 1855, with Sketches of Press Celebrities*, vol. 2 (London: Richard Bentley, 1859), 266, 347; Hunt, *Fourth Estate*, 7–8.

50 Jürgen Habermas, *The Structural Transformation of the Public Sphere: An Inquiry into a Category of Bourgeois Society,* trans. Thomas Burger (Cambridge: MIT Press, 1989), 57–67, 89–95.

51 Jeffrey L. McNairn, *The Capacity to Judge: Public Opinion and Deliberative Democracy in Upper Canada, 1791–1854* (Toronto: University of Toronto Press, 2000), 7.

52 James Grant, *The Newspaper Press: Its Origin – Its Progress – and Present Position,* vol. 2 (London: Tinsley Brothers, 1871), 459–60.

53 *British Colonist,* 11 December 1858, 3 July 1860; *Taranaki Herald,* 2 February 1861.

54 See Gerald J. Baldasty, *The Commercialization of News in the Nineteenth Century* (Madison: University of Wisconsin Press, 1992).

55 Simon Potter, "Webs, Networks, and Systems: Globalization and the Mass Media in the Nineteenth- and Twentieth-Century British Empire," *Journal of British Studies* 46, 3 (2007): 646.

56 Alan Lester and Fae Dussart, "Trajectories of Protection: Protectorates of Aborigines in Early 19th-Century Australia and Aotearoa New Zealand," *New Zealand Geographer* 64, 3 (2008): 217.

57 Harold A. Innis, *Empire and Communications* (Lanham: Rowman and Littlefield, [1950] 2007), 196.

58 Ibid., 138.

59 Jody Berland, *North of Empire: Essays on the Cultural Technologies of Space* (Durham: Duke University Press, 2009), 66–67.

60 Tony Ballantyne, *Orientalism and Race: Aryanism in the British Empire* (Cambridge: Palgrave, 2002), 14–17.

61 Peter Putnis, "The Indian Insurgency of 1857 as a Global Media Event," in *International Association for Mass Communication Research* (The American University in Cairo: University of Canberra, 2007), 10.

62 James W. Carey, *Communication as Culture: Essays on Media and Society* (Boston: Unwin Hyman, 2009), 11–28.

63 Ibid., 12–13.

64 Ibid., 12–13, 17.

65 Gordon M. Winder, "Imagining World Citizenship in the Networked Newspaper: La Nación Reports the Assassination at Sarajevo, 1914," *Historical Social Science Research* 35, 1 (2010): 162.

66 Yrjö Kaukiainen, "The Improvements of Communication in International Freight Markets, c.1830-70," in *Information, Media and Power through the Ages,* ed. Hiram Morgan, 137–51 (Dublin: University College Dublin Press, 2001).

67 Ibid., 146.

68 C.A. Bayly, *Empire and Information: Intelligence Gathering and Social Communication in India, 1780–1870* (Cambridge: Cambridge University Press, 1996), 318–19.

69 Potter, "Webs, Networks, and Systems," 629–31.

70 Kirsten McKenzie, *Scandal in the Colonies: Sydney and Cape Town, 1820–1850* (Melbourne: Melbourne University Press, 2004), 12.

71 Peter Gibbons, "Non-Fiction," in *Oxford History of New Zealand Literature in English,* ed. Terry Sturm (Auckland: Oxford University Press, 1998), 38.

72 Carey, *Communication as Culture,* 14.

73 Bernard Porter, *The Lion's Share: A Short History of British Imperialism* (London: Longman, 1975), 116, 363; Bernard Porter, *The Absent-Minded Imperialists: What the British Really Thought about Empire* (Oxford: Oxford University Press, 2004), 37, 104, 225.

74 Tony Ballantyne and Antoinette Burton, "Postscript: Bodies, Genders, Empires: Reimagining World Histories," in *Bodies in Contact: Rethinking Colonial Encounters in World History,*

ed. Tony Ballantyne and Antoinette Burton (Durham; London: Duke University Press, 2005), 416.

75 Hall, *Civilising Subjects;* Lester, *Imperial Networks;* Zoë Laidlaw, *Colonial Connections, 1815–45: Patronage, the Information Revolution and Colonial Government* (Manchester and New York: Manchester University Press, 2005); Julie Evans, *Edward Eyre: Race and Colonial Governance* (Dunedin: University of Otago Press, 2005).

76 Evans et al., *Equal Subjects;* Alan Lester and David Lambert, eds., *Colonial Lives across the British Empire: Imperial Careering in the Long Nineteenth Century* (Cambridge: Cambridge University Press, 2006); Ballantyne, *Orientalism and Race;* James Belich, *Replenishing the Earth: The Settler Revolution and the Rise of the Anglo-World, 1783–1939* (Oxford: Oxford University Press, 2009); Lester, *Imperial Networks;* Edmonds, *Urbanizing Frontiers;* Phillip Buckner, ed., *Canada and the British Empire* (Oxford: Oxford University Press, 2010); Hogg, *Men and Manliness on the Frontier.*

77 Tony Ballantyne, "Archives, Empires and Histories of Colonialism," *Archifacts* (April 2004): 24–25, 29.

78 Arnett, *Terror of the Coast,* 12.

Chapter 1: A Short History

1 See Bonnie L. Pitblado, "A Tale of Two Migrations: Reconciling Recent Biological and Archaeological Evidence for the Pleistocene Peopling of the Americas," *Journal of Archaeological Research* 19, 4 (2011): 327–75.

2 Robert J. Muckle, *The First Nations of British Columbia* (Vancouver: UBC Press, 1998), 17–18.

3 John Douglas Belshaw, *Becoming British Columbia: A Population History* (Vancouver: UBC Press, 2009), 24.

4 Muckle, *First Nations of British Columbia,* 33.

5 Penelope Edmonds, *Urbanizing Frontiers: Indigenous Peoples and Settlers in 19th-Century Pacific Rim Cities* (Vancouver: UBC Press, 2010), 90.

6 Muckle, *First Nations of British Columbia,* 39.

7 Ibid., 55–56.

8 Ibid., 7.

9 Belshaw, *Becoming British Columbia,* 20.

10 Atholl Anderson, "Origins, Settlement and Society of Pre-European South Polynesia," in *The New Oxford History of New Zealand,* ed. Gyselle Byrnes (Auckland: Oxford University Press, 2009), 27.

11 See D.G. Sutton et al., "The Timing of the Human Discovery and Colonization of New Zealand," *Quaternary International* 184 (2008): 109–21.

12 Philippa Mein Smith, *A Concise History of New Zealand* (Cambridge: Cambridge University Press, 2005), 6.

13 Anderson, "Origins, Settlement and Society," 34–35.

14 Ibid., 42; Ian Pool, "From Waka to Tiriti: The Maori Population until 1840," in *Te Iwi Maori: Population Past, Present and Projected* (Auckland: University of Auckland Press, 1991), 58.

15 Ann Parsonson, "The Pursuit of Mana," in *The Oxford History of New Zealand,* ed. W.H. Oliver with B.R. Williams (Oxford: Clarendon Press, 1981), 141.

16 See Parsonson, "Pursuit of Mana."

17 See Anne Salmond, *Two Worlds: First Meetings between Maori and Europeans, 1642–1772* (Auckland: Penguin Books, 1991); Barry M. Gough, *Fortune's a River: The Collision of Empires in Northwest America* (Madeira Park: Harbour Publishing Company, 2008); Daniel W. Clayton, *Islands of Truth: The Imperial Fashioning of Vancouver Island* (Vancouver: UBC Press, 2000).

18 James Gibson, *Otter Skins, Boston Ships, and China Goods: The Maritime Fur Trade of the North-west Coast, 1785–1841* (Montreal and Kingston: McGill-Queen's University Press, 1992), 22.

19 Ibid., 299–310.

20 Ibid., 87–88.

21 Clayton, *Islands of Truth*, 150–51.

22 Gibson, *Otter Skins*, 270–71.

23 See Lyndsay Head, "Land, Authority and the Forgetting of Being in Early Colonial Maori History" (PhD diss., University or Canterbury, 2006).

24 Tony Ballantyne, *Entanglements of Empire: Missionaries, Māori, and the Question of the Body* (Durham: Duke University Press, 2014), 1.

25 See Wilson Duff, *The Indian History of British Columbia* (Victoria: Royal British Columbia Museum, 1997); Cole Harris, "Voices of Smallpox around the Strait of Georgia," in *The Resettlement of British Columbia: Essays on Colonialism and Geographical Change*, 3–30 (Vancouver: UBC Press, 1997); Robert T. Boyd, *The Coming of the Spirit of Pestilence* (Seattle: University of Washington Press, 1999).

26 Belshaw, *Becoming British Columbia*, 27. James Daschuk's *Clearing the Plains: Disease, Politics of Starvation, and the Loss of Aboriginal Life* (Regina: University of Regina Press, 2013) reveals how tuberculosis was present in precontact America and was exacerbated by the introduction of Western diseases.

27 Muckle, *First Nations of British Columbia*, 60.

28 Keith Thor Carlson, *The Power of Place, the Problem of Time: Aboriginal Identity and Historical Consciousness in the Cauldron of Colonialism* (Toronto: University of Toronto Press, 2010), 92.

29 Ibid., 112.

30 Harris, "Voices of Smallpox," 30.

31 *British Columbian*, 2 December 1865.

32 James Belich, *Making Peoples: A History of the New Zealanders, from Polynesian Settlement to the End of the Nineteenth Century* (Honolulu: University of Hawaii Press, 2001), 174.

33 Recently, Angella Ballara's *Taua: Musket Wars, Land Wars or Tikanga? Warfare in Maori Society in the Early Nineteenth Century* (Auckland: Penguin Books, 2003) has challenged this perspective.

34 Belich, *Making Peoples*, 159.

35 Smith, *Concise History of New Zealand*, 38.

36 See Bronwyn Elsmore, *Mana from Heaven: A Century of Maori Prophets in New Zealand* (Auckland: Moana Press, 1989); Judith Binney, "Ancestral Voices: Maori Prophet Leaders," in *The Oxford Illustrated History of New Zealand*, ed. Keith Sinclair, 153–85 (Auckland: Oxford University Press, 1990).

37 Harrison M. Wright, *New Zealand, 1769–1840: Early Years of Western Contact* (Cambridge: Harvard University Press, 1959), 141.

38 Wright, *New Zealand;* J.M.R. Owens, "Christianity and the Maoris to 1840," *New Zealand Journal of History* 2, 1 (1968): 18–40; Judith Binney, "Christianity and the Maoris to 1840: A Comment," *New Zealand Journal of History* 3, 2 (1969): 143–65; K.R. Howe, "The Maori Response to Christianity in the Thames-Waikato Area, 1833–1840," *New Zealand Journal of History* 7, 1 (1973): 28–46; Damon Salesa, "Korero: A Reflection on the Work of Judith Binney," *New Zealand Journal of History* 38, 2 (2004): 272–98.

39 Wright, *New Zealand*, 141–65; Keith Sinclair, *A History of New Zealand* (London: Oxford University Press, 1961), 29–31.

40 Belich, *Making Peoples*, 217–23.

41 Judith Binney, *Redemption Songs: A Life of Te Kooti Arikirangi Te Turuki* (Auckland: Auckland University Press, 1995).

42 Raeburn Lange, "Indigenous Agents of Religious Change in New Zealand, 1830–1860," *Journal of Religious History* 24, 3 (2000): 280–87.

43 Shaunnagh Dorsett, "'Destitute of the Knowledge of God': Maori Testimony before the New Zealand Courts in the Early Crown Colony Period," in *Past Law, Present Histories*, ed. Diane Kirkby (Canberra: Australian National University Press, 2012), 57.

44 See Nancy Wright, "The Problems of Aboriginal Evidence in Early Colonial New South Wales," in *Law, History, Colonialism: The Reach of Empire*, ed. D. Kirkby and C. Coleborne, 140–55 (Manchester: Manchester University Press, 2001); Russell Smandych, "Contemplating the Testimony of 'Others': James Stephen, the Colonial Office, and the Fate of Australian Aboriginal Evidence Acts, Circa 1839–1849," *Legal History* 10 (2006): 97–143.

45 Reginald Good, "Regulating Indian and Chinese Civic Identities in British Columbia's 'Colonial Contact Zone,' 1858–1887," *Canadian Journal of Law and Society* 26, 1 (2001): 72.

46 Adele Perry, "Changing Intimacies, Changing Empire," in *Colonial Family: Intimacy, Mobility and Power in the Nineteenth-Century Imperial World* (Cambridge: Cambridge University Press, 2015).

47 Susan Neylan, "Prophets, Revivals, and Evangelists," in *The Heavens Are Changing: Nineteenth-Century Protestant Missions and Tsimshian Christianity* (Montreal and Kingston: McGill-Queen's University Press, 2003), 175–209.

48 See Vincent J. McNally, *The Lord's Distant Vineyard: A History of the Oblates and the Catholic Community in British Columbia* (Edmonton: University of Alberta Press, 2000).

49 See Richard Somerset Mackie, *Trading beyond the Mountains: The British Fur Trade on the Pacific, 1793–1843* (Vancouver: UBC Press, 1997).

50 Adele Perry, *On the Edge of Empire: Gender, Race, and the Making of British Columbia, 1849–1871* (Toronto: University of Toronto Press, 2001), 13.

51 Cole Harris, "Strategies of Power in the Cordilleran Fur Trade," in Harris, *Resettlement of British Columbia*, 31–67.

52 Edmonds, *Urbanizing Frontiers*, 30–32.

53 Belich, *Making Peoples*, 132.

54 Ibid., 188.

55 Jim McAloon, "The New Zealand Economy, 1792–1914," in *The New Oxford History of New Zealand*, ed. Gyselle Byrnes, 203–6 (Auckland: Oxford University Press, 2009).

56 See Hazel Petrie, *Chiefs of Industry: Maori Tribal Enterprise in Early Colonial New Zealand* (Auckland: Auckland University Press, 2006); Paul Monin, "Maori Economies and Colonial Capitalism," in *The New Oxford History of New Zealand*, ed. Gyselle Byrnes, 125–46 (Auckland: Oxford University Press, 2009).

57 Dan Davy, "Lost Tailings: Gold Rush Societies and Cultures in Colonial Otago, New Zealand, 1861–1911" (PhD diss., University of Otago, 2013).

Chapter 2: Violence and Eviction on Vancouver Island

1 *British Colonist*, 11 July 1862.

2 *The Press*, 17 June 1862.

3 Ibid., 28 April 1862.

4 *British Colonist*, 28 April 1862.

5 John S. Lutz, *Makúk: A New History of Aboriginal-White Relations* (Vancouver: UBC Press, 2008), 179.

6 First *Victoria Gazette* (June 1858–November 1859), *Vancouver Island Gazette* (July–September 1858), *Newsletter for Vancouver Island and New Caledonia* (September 1858), *Le Courier de la Nouvelle Caledonie* (September–October 1858), *British Colonist* (December 1858–1980), *New Westminster Times and Vancouver Island Guardian* (September 1859–March 1860), second

Victoria Gazette (December 1859–September 1860), *The Press* (March 1861–October 1862, *Victoria Daily Chronicle* (October 1862–June 1866).

7 Edward C. Kemble, *A History of California Newspapers, 1846–1858*, ed. Helen Harding, 114–31 (Los Gatos: Talisman Press, 1962).

8 Ibid., 130.

9 First *Victoria Gazette*, 25 June 1858.

10 Daniel P. Marshall, "Claiming the Land: Indians, Goldseekers, and the Rush to British Columbia" (PhD diss., University of British Columbia, 2000), 172.

11 First *Victoria Gazette*, 30 December 1858.

12 R.A.J. McDonald and H. Keith Ralston, "De Cosmos, Amor," Dictionary of Canadian Biography Online, http://www.biographi.ca/en/search.php.

13 Margaret Ross, "Amor Decosmos, a British Columbia Reformer" (MA thesis, University of British Columbia, 1931), 6.

14 George Woodcock, *Amor De Cosmos: Journalist and Reformer* (Toronto: Oxford University Press, 1975), 14–15.

15 Robin Fisher, *Contact and Conflict: Indian-European Relations in British Columbia, 1774–1890* (Vancouver: UBC Press, 1992), 110–11.

16 *British Colonist*, 11 December 1858.

17 Ross, "Amor Decosmos," 4–5; Wild, *Amor De Cosmos,* 18; Woodcock, *Amor De Cosmos,* 4–5.

18 Jean Barman, *The West beyond the West: A History of British Columbia* (Toronto: University of Toronto Press, 1996), 80–81.

19 See Jeffrey L. McNairn, *The Capacity to Judge: Public Opinion and Deliberative Democracy in Upper Canada, 1791–1854* (Toronto: University of Toronto Press, 2000).

20 *British Colonist*, 9 April 1859.

21 D.G.F. Macdonald, *British Columbia and Vancouver Island* (London: Longman, Green, Longman, Roberts & Green, 1862), 278–79; *British Colonist*, 9 April 1859.

22 McDonald and Ralston, "De Cosmos."

23 Wild, *Amor De Cosmos,* 94, 114.

24 Charles Forbes, *Vancouver Island: Its Resources and Capabilities as a Colony* (Victoria: The Colonial Government, 1862), 34.

25 *British Colonist*, 11 December 1860.

26 This measure is achieved by dividing the *British Colonist*'s combined weekly output of four thousand editions by its six weekly publications, garnering a speculative figure of 667 newspapers per edition. I then divide 667 newspapers per edition by *The Press*'s estimate of Victoria's population of three thousand Euro-American colonists in 1861, showing that the *British Colonist* published sufficient newspapers for 22 percent of local residents.

27 First *Victoria Gazette*, 28 July 1859, 30 July 1859, 2 August 1859, 22 October 1859.

28 Hugh Doherty, "The First Newspapers on Canada's West Coast: 1858–1863," Victoria's Victoria, web.uvic.ca/vv/articles/doherty/newspaper.html.

29 Second *Victoria Gazette*, 23 December 1859, 30 December 1859, 2 January 1860, 9 January 1860, 11 January 1860, 13 January 1860, 10 February 1860.

30 H. Keith Ralston, "McClure, Leonard," Dictionary of Canadian Biography Online, http://www.biographi.ca/en/search.php; Sydney G. Pettit, "King, Edward Hammond," Dictionary of Canadian Biography Online, http://www.biographi.ca/en/search.php.

31 Doherty, "First Newspapers on Canada's West Coast."

32 Ralston, "McClure."

33 David William Higgins, "Miscellaneous material," BCA, M/H53.

34 First *Victoria Gazette*, 14 August 1858, 22 October 1858, 25 November 1858, 30 December 1858, 9 April 1859, 12 July 1859, 6 August 1859.

35 Daniel Marshall, "No Parallel: American Miners-Soldiers at War with the Nlaka'pamux of the Canadian West," in *Parallel Destinies: Canadian-American Relations West of the Rockies,*

ed. John M. Findlay and Ken S. Coates, 31-79 (Seattle and London: University of Washington Press, 2002)

36 Barman, *West beyond the West*, 90–91.
37 Doherty, "First Newspapers on Canada's West Coast."
38 Lutz, *Makúk*, 50–51.
39 Ibid., 75.
40 Penelope Edmonds, *Urbanizing Frontiers: Indigenous Peoples and Settlers in 19th-Century Pacific Rim Cities* (Vancouver: UBC Press, 2010).
41 Lutz, *Makúk*, 83.
42 Douglas to Russell, 21 August 1855, CO 305/6 no. 10048, *Vancouver Island: 1855–1857*, vol. 3, Colonial Despatches of British Columbia, ed. James Hendrickson (Victoria: University of Victoria, 1988), 28–29.
43 Rear Admiral R.L. Baynes to the Secretary of the Admiralty, 21 February 1860, "Great Britain/Admiralty Papers," BCA, GR 1309, box 2, vol. 2, file 1.
44 Adele Perry, "'Is Your Garden in England, Sir': James Douglas's Archive and the Politics of Home," *History Workshop Journal* 70 (Autumn 2010): 69–72.
45 Douglas to Russell, 21 August 1855, CO 305/6 no. 10048, *Vancouver Island: 1855–1857*, 28–29; Douglas to Labouchere, 10 April 1856, CO 305/7 no. 5814, *Vancouver Island: 1855–1857*, 97–98; Douglas to Labouchere, 22 July 1856, CO 305/7 no. 9300 *Vancouver Island: 1855–1857*, 105–6; Douglas to Labouchere, 20 August 1856, CO 305/7 no. 9708, *Vancouver Island: 1855–1857*, 109; Douglas to Labouchere, 20 October 1856, CO 305/7 no. 11582, *Vancouver Island: 1855–1857*, 114; Douglas to Labouchere, 5 May 1857, CO 305/8 no. 6331, *Vancouver Island: 1855–1857*, 191–92; Douglas to Newcastle, 7 July 1860, CO 305/14 no. 8319, *Vancouver Island: 1860*, vol. 6, Colonial Despatches of British Columbia, ed. James Hendrickson, 37–40 (Victoria: University of Victoria, 1988); Douglas to Newcastle, 8 August 1860, CO 305/14 no. 9267, *Vancouver Island: 1860*, 43.
46 Douglas to Newcastle, 7 July 1860, CO 305/14 no. 8319, *Vancouver Island: 1860*, 37–40.
47 Lutz, *Makúk*, 169.
48 See Jean Barman, "Taming Aboriginal Sexuality: Gender, Power, and Race in British Columbia, 1850–1900," *BC Studies* 115/16 (Autumn/Winter 1997–98): 237–66; Jean Barman, "Aboriginal Women on the Streets of Victoria," in *Contact Zones: Aboriginal and Settler Women in Canada's Colonial Past*, ed. Katie Pickles and Myra Rutherdale, 205–27 (Vancouver: UBC Press, 2005); Patrick A. Dunae, "Geographies of Sexual Commerce and the Production of Prostitutional Space: Victoria, British Columbia, 1860–1914," *Journal of the Canadian Historical Association* 19, 1 (2008): 115–42.
49 Perry, *Edge of Empire*.
50 Renisa Mawani, *Colonial Proximities: Crossracial Encounters and Juridicial Truths in British Columbia, 1871–1921* (Vancouver: UBC Press, 2009), 5.
51 Cole Harris, "Strategies of Power in the Cordilleran Fur Trade," in *The Resettlement of British Columbia: Essays on Colonialism and Geographical Change*, 31–67 (Vancouver: UBC Press, 1997).
52 Mawani, *Colonial Proximities*, 6–7.
53 Douglas to Labouchere, 10 April 1856, CO 305/7 no. 5814, *Vancouver Island: 1855–1857*, 97.
54 Ibid., 22 July 1856, CO 305/7 no. 9300, *Vancouver Island: 1855–1857*, 106.
55 Douglas to Russell, 21 August 1855, CO 305/6 no. 10048, *Vancouver Island: 1855–1857*, 28–29; Douglas to Rear-Admiral Robert Baynes, 3 August 1860, "Vancouver Island/Colonial Correspondence Outward," BCA, C/AA/30.1J/1A, vol. 2.
56 See Patrick Wolfe, *Settler Colonialism and the Transformation of Anthropology: The Politics and Poetics of an Ethnographical Event* (London: Cassell, 1999), 3, 27.
57 *British Colonist*, 6 September 1861.
58 Edmonds, *Urbanizing Frontiers*, 184–229.

59 Barry M. Gough, *Gunboat Frontier: British Maritime Authority and Northwest Coast Indians, 1846–90* (Vancouver: UBC Press, 1984); Tina Loo, *Making Law, Order, and Authority in British Columbia, 1821–1871* (Toronto: University of Toronto Press, 1994); Marshall, "Claiming the Land."

60 The Victoria press reported that twenty Aboriginal women had been murdered in Victoria between 1858 and 1862.

61 *British Colonist*, 15 January 1859, 21 January 1860; second *Victoria Gazette*, 20 February 1860; *British Colonist*, 14 April 1860, 7 July 1860.

62 *British Colonist*, 14 April 1860.

63 First *Victoria Gazette*, 1 February 1859; *British Colonist*, 24 June 1859; first *Victoria Gazette*, 12 October 1858; *British Colonist*, 19 August 1859, 24 April 1860; second *Victoria Gazette*, 25 April 1860; *British Colonist*, 29 May 1860; second *Victoria Gazette*, 30 May 1860, 13 June 1860, 25 June 1860; *British Colonist*, 3 July 1860, 5 July 1860; second *Victoria Gazette*, 9 July 1860; *British Colonist*, 10 July 1860, 12 July 1860, 6 August 1861; second *Victoria Gazette*, 29 September 1860; *British Colonist*, 15 June 1861; *The Press*, 30 June 1861; *British Colonist*, 6 August 1861; *The Press*, 5 September 1861, 27 December 1861.

64 *The Press*, 27 December 1861.

65 Second *Victoria Gazette*, 30 May 1860; *British Colonist*, 5 July 1860, 30 August 1862.

66 Second *Victoria Gazette*, 25 April 1860.

67 Macdonald, *British Columbia and Vancouver Island*, 330.

68 *British Colonist*, 29 November 1862.

69 First *Victoria Gazette*, 1 February 1859; *British Colonist*, 26 January 1860; second *Victoria Gazette*, 12 March 1860; *British Colonist*, 13 March 1860, 29 May 1860, 19 February 1861.

70 *British Colonist*, 26 January 1860.

71 Paige Raibmon, *Authentic Indians: Episodes of Encounter from the Late-Nineteenth-Century Northwest Coast* (Durham: Duke University Press, 2005), 9.

72 Second *Victoria Gazette*, 29 September 1860. George E. Nias, the editor of the second *Victoria Gazette*, acknowledged this fact in his paper's final editorial, entitled "City Morals." Here, he reversed his earlier support for Aboriginal eviction, stating that demands to "banish the Indians," "drive them to their natives forests," and "separate the husbands from the wives," had "a radical rottenness in their first principles."

73 *British Colonist*, 29 May 1860, 19 February 1861, 18 April 1861; *The Press*, 17 June 1862.

74 *British Colonist*, 29 May 1860.

75 See Crawford Kilian, *Go Do Some Great Thing: The Black Pioneers of British Columbia* (Vancouver: Douglas and McIntyre, 1978).

76 First *Victoria Gazette*, 24 February 1859; *British Colonist*, 26 March 1859, 8 June 1859, 13 March 1860, 19 February 1861.

77 *British Colonist*, 19 February 1861.

78 C.L. Higham, *Noble, Wretched and Redeemable: Protestant Missionaries to the Indians in Canada and the United States, 1820–1900* (Albuquerque/Calgary: University of New Mexico Press/University of Calgary Press, 2000), 31–36, 41–56.

79 Ibid., 56–57.

80 *British Colonist*, 1 June 1859; second *Victoria Gazette*, 18 May 1860, 1 June 1860; *British Colonist*, 26 October 1860, 19 February 1861; *The Press*, 27 August 1861

81 *British Colonist*, 20 September 1861.

82 Ibid., 5 June 1860.

83 Second *Victoria Gazette*, 18 May 1860.

84 *The Press*, 27 May 1862.

85 Roberta L. Bagshaw, ed., *No Better Land: The 1860 Diaries of the Anglican Colonial Bishop George Hills* (Victoria: Sono Nis Press, 1996), 55–56.

86 Robert T. Boyd, *The Coming of the Spirit of Pestilence* (Seattle: University of Washington Press, 1999), 22.
87 Ibid., 262.
88 Ibid., 229–30.
89 See J.R. Smith, *The Speckled Monster: Smallpox in England, 1670–1970, with Particular Reference to Essex* (Essex: Essex Record Office, 1987).
90 Boyd, *Coming of the Spirit of Pestilence*, 185, 196–99.
91 *British Colonist*, 19 March 1862.
92 Ibid., 26 March 1862; *The Press*, 27 March 1862.
93 *British Colonist*, 26 March 1862.
94 *The Press*, 28 March 1862; *British Colonist*, 28 March 1862; *The Press*, 31 March 1862; *British Colonist*, 1 April 1862.
95 Ibid., 28 March 1862.
96 Ibid., 1 April 1862.
97 Boyd, *Coming of the Spirit of Pestilence*, 22.
98 *The Press*, 27 March 1862.
99 Ibid., 27 March 1862.
100 Ibid.
101 *British Colonist*, 26 April 1862.
102 Dorothy Blakey Smith, ed., *The Reminiscences of Doctor John Sebastian Helmcken* (Vancouver: UBC Press, 1975), 187.
103 F.A. Garrett, "A.C. Garrett Reminiscences," BCA, MSS E/B/G19; Garrett also argues that there was a shortage of vaccine material in Victoria during the 1862 smallpox epidemic, which hampered efforts to vaccinate local Aboriginals, but there is no mention of this shortage in the press.
104 Douglas to Barclay, 16 May 1853, "Letters to Hudson's Bay Company on Vancouver Island Colony, 1850–55," BCA, A/C/20/Vi2A.
105 *British Colonist*, 27 March 1862, 28 March 1862. The *British Colonist* reported that large numbers of Euro-Americans sought vaccination from local doctors following the arrival of smallpox.
106 Boyd, *Coming of the Spirit of Pestilence*, 182.
107 *The Press*, 27 April 1862.
108 Ibid., 27 April 1862.
109 *British Colonist*, 28 April 1862.
110 *The Press*, 28 April 1862; *British Colonist*, 28 April 1862.
111 *British Colonist*, 28 April 1862.
112 Ibid., 28 April 1862.
113 *British Colonist*, 4 January 1859; *The Press*, 5 September 1861; Pemberton to Young, 12 September 1861, "Colonial Correspondence," BCA, GR1372, BO1356, F1385.
114 *British Colonist*, 30 April 1862; *The Press*, 30 April 1862; *British Colonist*, 1 May 1862; *The Press*, 1 May 1862.
115 *British Colonist*, 16 June 1862. Lekwungen people maintained a strict quarantine on Discovery Island, killing northern First Nations persons who attempted to land on the island.
116 *British Colonist*, 30 April 1862.
117 *The Press*, 28 May 1862.
118 Ibid., 11 May 1862; *British Colonist*, 12 May 1862; *The Press*, 13 May 1862; *British Colonist*, 13 May 1862, 14 May 1862, 15 May 1862.
119 *The Press*, 15 May 1862; *British Colonist*, 15 May 1862, 7 June 1862, 12 June 1862.
120 See Tom Swanky, *The True Story of Canada's "War" of Extermination on the Pacific* (Burnaby, BC: Dragon Heart Enterprises, 2012).

121 *British Colonist*, 12 June 1862.

122 *British Colonist*, 9 January 1863, 21 April 1863; *Evening Express*, 16 June 1863.

Chapter 3: New Zealand's Humanitarian Extremes

1 *Taranaki Herald*, 21 April 1860.

2 Jane Maria Richmond to Emily Atkinson, 23 April 1860, *The Richmond-Atkinson Papers*, vol. 1, ed. G.H. Scholefield (Wellington: R.E. Owen, Government Printer, 1960), 569–70.

3 *Taranaki Herald*, 28 April 1860, 5 May 1860, 12 May 1860.

4 Ibid., 28 April 1860.

5 Ibid.

6 Frances Porter and W.H. Oliver, "Richmond, James Crowe-Biography," *Dictionary of New Zealand Biography, Te Ara-the Encyclopedia of New Zealand*, http://www.teara.govt.nz/remap_url.php?src=en/biographies/1t10/1.

7 J.C. Richmond to Mary Richmond, 12 May 1860, *Richmond-Atkinson Papers*, 581–82.

8 J.C. Richmond to C.W. Richmond, 12 May 1860, *Richmond-Atkinson Papers*, 579–81.

9 8 April 1860, "Journal of Henry Sewell," Alexander Turnbull Library (ATL), QMS-1783.

10 James Belich, *Making Peoples: A History of the New Zealanders, from Polynesian Settlement to the End of the Nineteenth Century* (Honolulu: University of Hawaii Press, 2001), 156–64.

11 *Taranaki Herald*, 17 July 1858.

12 Frederick Alonzo Carrington, *The Land Question of Taranaki, with Suggestions for Improving the Condition of the Aboriginal Inhabitants and Developing the Resources of New Zealand* (New Plymouth: Taranaki News Office, 1860), 5.

13 Hazel Petrie, *Chiefs of Industry: Maori Tribal Enterprise in Early Colonial New Zealand* (Auckland: Auckland University Press, 2006), 240–41.

14 *Taranaki Herald*, 16 January 1858, 23 January 1858, 30 January 1858, 6 February 1858, 13 February 1858, 20 February 1858, 27 February 1858, 20 March 1858, 17 April 1858, 24 April 1858, 8 May 1858, 19 June 1860, 8 January 1859.

15 Thomas Gore Browne to C.W. Richmond, 6 February 1858, *Richmond-Atkinson Papers*, 344.

16 Mark Francis, *Governors and Settlers: Images of Authority in the British Colonies* (Canterbury: Palgrave Macmillan, 1992), 213.

17 *Te Karere Maori*, 31 March 1859.

18 Gore Browne to E. Bulwer Lytton, 29 March 1859, no. 1, *Correspondence and Papers Relating to the Maori Uprisings in New Zealand, 1861*, vol. 12 (Shannon: Irish University Press, 1970), 1–2.

19 J.S. Tullett, *The Industrious Heart: A History of New Plymouth* (New Plymouth: New Plymouth City Council, 1981), 173.

20 Ross Harvey, "Economic Aspects of Nineteenth-Century New Zealand Newspapers," *Bibliographical Society of Australia and New Zealand Bulletin* 17, 2 (1993): 62.

21 Registrar General, *Statistics of New Zealand for 1858* (Auckland: W.C. Wilson, 1859), no. 9; Registrar General, *Statistics of New Zealand for 1862* (Auckland: New Zealander Printing Office, 1863), no. 1.

22 Registrar General, *Statistics of New Zealand for 1858*, no. 1. The figure of 2.5 colonists per edition of the *Taranaki Herald* is achieved by dividing the total number of colonists aged eighteen years of age and over (1,242 colonists) by the *Taranaki Herald*'s circulation in 1862 (five hundred copies).

23 Ibid., no. 2. This figure is achieved by dividing the number of newspapers (five hundred per week) by the number of households in Taranaki (680).

24 Harvey, "Economic Aspects of Nineteenth-Century New Zealand Newspapers," 62.

25 Registrar General, *Statistics of New Zealand for 1859* (Auckland: W.C. Wilson, 1860), no. 30; Registrar General, *Statistics of New Zealand for 1860* (Auckland: W.C. Wilson, 1861), no. 29.

26 Registrar General, *Statistics of New Zealand for 1860*, no. 29.

27 Registrar General, *Statistics of New Zealand for 1861* (Auckland: W.C. Wilson, 1862), no. 58; Registrar General, *Statistics of New Zealand for 1862*, no. 46. In 1861, 23,948 newspapers were despatched from New Plymouth: 7,378 to the United Kingdom, 2,414 to Australian colonies, 13,877 to other parts of New Zealand, and 279 to "All other places." In 1862, following the Taranaki War's close, the number of despatched newspapers fell to 14,341: 5,451 to the United Kingdom, 595 to Australian colonies, and 7,299 to other New Zealand provinces.

28 The figure of 38 percent is reached by dividing the number of newspapers despatched from New Plymouth in 1860 (21,549) by the estimated number of newspapers published by the *Taranaki Herald* in 1860 (fifty-two thousand).

29 *Taranaki Herald*, 8 January 1859, 19 February 1859, 26 February 1859, 12 March 1859, 3 September 1859, 22 October 1859, 29 October 1859, 3 December 1859, 7 January 1860, 18 February 1860, 25 February 1860, 3 March 1860, 17 March 1860.

30 Ibid., 3 September 1859.

31 Ibid., 22 October 1859.

32 Ibid.

33 Ibid., 3 December 1859.

34 Thomas Buddle, *The Maori King Movement in New Zealand with a Full Report of the Native Meetings Held at Waikato, April and May, 1860* (Auckland: The "New Zealander" Office, 1860); William Swainson, *New Zealand and the War* (London: Smith, Elder and Co., 1862); John Eldon Gorst, *The Maori King; or, the Story of Our Quarrel with the Natives of New Zealand* (London: Macmillan and Co., 1864).

35 Browne to Newcastle, 27 April 1860, no. 14, *Correspondence and Papers Relating to the Maori Uprisings in New Zealand, 1861*, 121–22.

36 *Taranaki Herald*, 8 May 1858. The *Herald* had previously reported in 1858 that Wiremu Kingi Te Rangitake had been approached by the Kingitanga and that he had rejected their overtures.

37 *Taranaki Herald*, 8 May 1858.

38 J.C. Richmond to C.W. Richmond, 23 October 1859, *Richmond-Atkinson Papers*, 494.

39 William White, ed., *Memorials of Sergeant William Marjouram, Royal Artillery; Including Six Years' Service During the Late Maori War* (London: James Nisbet and Co., 1862), 175; Mary Martin to Miss Palmer, 28 August 1860, *Extracts of Letters from New Zealand on the War Question: With an Article from the New Zealand Spectator of November 3rd, 1860* (London: F.J. Wilson, 1861), 15–16.

40 *Taranaki Herald*, 18 February 1860.

41 Ibid., 25 February 1860.

42 Thomas Gore Browne to Gordan Gairdner, 27 February 1860, "Sir Thomas Gore Browne Letterbook," ATL, QMS-0284.

43 Robert Clinton Hughes, diary, Puke Ariki (PA), ARC2001-140; William King Wakefield, Correspondence, PA, ARC2001-391; Rawson Family, correspondence, PA, ARC2001-99; Hugh Ronalds, Correspondence, PA, ARC2002-161.

44 Henry Butler Stoney, *Taranaki: A Tale of the War* (Auckland: W.C. Wilson, 1861), 105–6.

45 Hugh Ronalds, correspondence, PA, ARC2002-161.

46 James Belich, *The New Zealand Wars and the Victorian Interpretation of Racial Conflict: The Maori, the British, and the New Zealand Wars* (Montreal and Kingston: McGill-Queen's University Press, 1986), 76–116.

47 *Richmond-Atkinson Papers*, 674–75.

48 Donald McLean to Browne, 5 March 1860, memoranda, ANZ, MA-1-832-1861/21.

49 Belich, *New Zealand Wars*, 113–16.

50 Donald McLean to the Native Secretary, 16 April 1860, memoranda, ANZ, MA-1-831-1860/34; Belich, *New Zealand Wars*, 89–91.

51 *Taranaki Herald*, 16 June 1860.

52 Ibid., 16 June 1860.

53 Emily Richmond to Jane Maria Atkinson, 22 June 1860, *Richmond-Atkinson Papers*, 596–97.

54 Belich, *New Zealand Wars*, 91–98. British forces were repulsed by Maori defenders with thirty-three killed at the battle of Puketakauere.

55 *Taranaki Herald*, 14 July 1860.

56 Ibid., 21 July 1860.

57 Ibid.

58 Ibid., 7 April 1860, 1 December 1860, 27 April 1861.

59 Ibid., 7 April 1860.

60 Ibid., 6 April 1861, 27 April 1861.

61 For example, see H.A. Atkinson to C.W. & Emily Richmond, 6 April 1860, *Richmond-Atkinson Papers*, 551–54; H.A. Atkinson to A.S. Atkinson, 11 November 1860, ibid., 652; H.A. Atkinson to A.S. Atkinson, 16 April 1861, ibid., 703.

62 Peter Putnis, "The Indian Insurgency of 1857 as a Global Media Event," in *International Association for Mass Communication Research* (The American University in Cairo: University of Canberra, 2007).

63 Jill Bender, "Fears of 1857: The British Empire in the Wake of the Indian Rebellion" (PhD diss., Boston College, 2011), 66.

64 *Taranaki Herald*, 6 February 1858, 27 February 1858.

65 Ibid., 27 February 1858.

66 White, *Memorials of Sergeant William Marjouram*, 175–76.

67 Ibid., 176.

68 *Taranaki Punch*, 31 October 1860, 7 November 1860, 21 November 1860, 5 December 1860, 19 December 1860, 2 January 1861, 16 January 1861, 30 January 1861, 13 February 1861, 27 February 1861, 13 March 1861, 27 March 1861, 19 June 1861, 3 July 1861, 17 July 1861, 7 August 1861.

69 Henry Freer Rawson, *Taranaki Punch*, PA, ARC2002-538.

70 *Taranaki Herald*, 3 November 1860; *Nelson Examiner*, 24 November 1860; *Lyttelton Times*, 28 November 1860, 20 March 1861.

71 *Lyttelton Times*, 20 March 1861.

72 *Taranaki Punch*, 27 February 1861.

73 Phil Parkinson and Penny Griffith, "The Maori Messenger = Te Karere Maori (1855–1861)," in *Books in Māori, 1815–1900: An Annotated Bibliography* (Auckland: Reed Publishing, 2004), 749–51.

74 *Te Karere Maori*, July 1855.

75 Lachy Paterson, *Colonial Discourses: Niupepa Māori 1855–1863* (Dunedin: Otago University, 2006), 12. Paterson offers the most in-depth study of *Te Karere Maori*.

76 In 1861, *Te Karere Maori* was rebranded as *Te Manuhiri Tuarangi*, or the *Maori Intelligencer*. *Te Manuhiri Tuarangi*, though, was swiftly renamed *Te Karere Maori* in 1861, lasting until 1863, when the war in Waikato began.

77 Ross Harvey, "Economic Aspects of Nineteenth-Century New Zealand Newspapers," *Bibliographical Society of Australia and New Zealand Bulletin* 17, 2 (1993): 59. It is not known when *Te Karere Maori*'s circulation was reduced.

78 Registrar General, *Statistics of New Zealand for 1858* (Auckland: W.C. Wilson, 1859), no. 10.

79 In 1857, New Zealand's leading newspaper, the *New Zealander*, published one edition for every ten adult colonists in Auckland.

80 *New Zealander*, 25 May 1859.

81 Paterson, *Colonial Discourses*, 37–48; Tony Ballantyne, "Teaching Maori about Asia: Print Culture and Community Identity in Nineteenth-Century New Zealand," in *Asia in the Making of New Zealand*, ed. Brian Moloughney (Auckland: Auckland University Press, 2006), 21–23; Walter Brodie, *Remarks on the Past and Present State of New Zealand, Its Government, Capabilities, and Prospects* (London: Whittaker and Co., 1845), 109–10.

82 Ballantyne, "Teaching Maori about Asia," 19; Arthur Saunders Thomson, *The Story of New Zealand: Past and Present – Savage and Civilized*, vol. 2 (London: John Murray, 1859), 297.

83 Thomas Henry Smith and Frederick Whitaker to Thomas Gore Browne, 22 March 1860, memoranda, ANZ, MA-1-831-1860/23; Donald McLean to the Native Secretary, 20 April 1860, memoranda, ANZ, MA-1-831-1860/42.

84 Native Secretary, memoranda, ANZ, MA-24-8/16.

85 *Te Karere Maori*, 14 July 1860, 31 July 1860, 1 September 1860; Lachy Paterson, "The Kohimārama Conference of 1860: A Contextual Reading," *Journal of New Zealand Studies* 12 (2011): 29–46.

86 *Auckland Examiner*, 30 March 1859; *New Zealander*, 25 May 1859, 31 August 1859; *Auckland Weekly Register*, 17 March 1860; *Auckland Examiner*, 4 April 1860, 11 April 1860; *Taranaki Herald*, 15 December 1860; *Southern Cross*, 19 February 1861.

87 Ross Harvey, "David Burn and *The Maori Messenger*," *Script & Print* 37, 2 (2013): 69–87.

88 David Burn, 11 January 1856, diary, State Library of New South Wales (SLNSW), microfilm-CY 1094.

89 11 January 1856, diary, State Library of New South Wales (SLNSW), microfilm-CY 1094; Burn to the Native Secretary, "General Inwards Correspondence to the Colonial Secretary," ANZ, IA-1-222-1861/2131.

90 Burn to the Native Secretary, 7 October 1861, "General Inwards Correspondence to the Colonial Secretary," ANZ, IA-1-222-1861/2131.

91 D.H. Borchardt, "Burn, David (1799–1875)," *Australian Dictionary of Biography*, vol. 1 (Melbourne: Melbourne University Press, 1966). David Burn emigrated to Auckland from New South Wales in 1847. He was first employed by William Brown's *Southern Cross* and then began editing *Te Karere Maori* in 1849. By 1855, Burn was employed by John Williamson's *New Zealander*, the primary rival of the *Southern Cross*. In addition to his duties as a journalist, Burn was employed by Williamson, then the superintendent of Auckland province, in his electoral campaigns.

92 Burn to the Colonial Secretary, 7 October 1861, "General Inwards Correspondence to the Colonial Secretary," ANZ, IA-1-222-1861/2131.

93 Paterson, *Colonial Discourses*, 49–67.

94 Ibid., 49–50.

95 *Te Karere Maori*, 1 September 1855.

96 Ibid., 1 September 1855.

97 Ibid., 30 August 1856.

98 David Burn, 1 July and 4 September 1856, diary.

99 *Te Karere Maori*, 30 June 1859.

100 Lyndsay Head, "Land, Authority and the Forgetting of Being in Early Colonial Maori History" (PhD diss., University or Canterbury, 2006), 2.

101 Michael J. Stevens, "Muttonbirds and Modernity in Murihiku: Continuity and Change in Kāi Tahu Knowledge" (PhD diss., University of Otago, 2009), 15–16.

102 Gauri Viswanathan, *Outside the Fold: Conversion, Modernity, and Belief* (Princeton: Princeton University Press, 1998), 122.

103 Ibid., 122.

104 Bronwyn Elsmore, *Mana from Heaven: A Century of Maori Prophets in New Zealand* (Tauranga: Moana Press, 1989).

105 See Thomas Buddle, *The Maori King Movement in New Zealand* (Auckland: 'New Zealander' Office, 1860).

106 *Te Karere Maori*, 28 February 1857, 31 March 1857, 30 June 1857, 15 September 1857, 15 December 1857, 31 May 1858, 16 August 1858, [?] January 1860.

107 Keith Sinclair, *The Origins of the Maori Wars* (Wellington: New Zealand University Press, 1961), 41; Alan Ward, *A Show of Justice: Racial "Amalgamation" in Nineteenth-Century New Zealand* (Toronto: University of Toronto Press, 1974), 92.

108 *Auckland Examiner*, 30 March 1859, 4 April 1860, 11 April 1860; *Taranaki Herald*, 15 December 1860; *Southern Cross*, 19 February 1861; John Eldon Gorst, *The Maori King* (London: Macmillan and Co., 1864), 52–53.

109 Damon Ieremia Salesa, *Racial Crossings: Race, Intermarriage, and the Victorian British Empire* (Auckland: Oxford University Press, 2011); Angela Wanhalla, *Matters of the Heart: A History of Interracial Marriage in New Zealand* (Auckland: Auckland University Press, 2013).

110 [John Ward, Edward Gibbon Wakefield, and Edward Jerningham Wakefield], *The British Colonization of New Zealand* (London: John W. Parker, 1837).

111 Salesa, *Racial Crossings*, 43.

112 *Te Karere Maori*, 30 June 1859.

113 Ibid., 31 March 1856.

114 Ibid., 31 August 1859.

115 *Te Karere Maori*, 31 August 1859.

116 James Belich, *Making Peoples: A History of New Zealanders, from Polynesian Settlement to the End of the Nineteenth Century* (Honolulu: University of Hawaii Press, 2001), 247–72.

117 *New Zealander*, 31 August 1859; *Southern Cross*, 6 September 1859, 13 September 1859; *Te Karere Maori*, 30 September 1859.

118 Hazel Petrie, *Chiefs of Industry: Māori Tribal Enterprise in Early Colonial New Zealand* (Auckland: Auckland University Press, 2006), 253–60; Paul Monin, "Maori Economies and Colonial Capitalism," in *The New Oxford History of New Zealand*, ed. Gyselle Byrnes (Auckland: Oxford University Press, 2009), 133.

119 McLean to Browne, 6 March 1861, no. 12, enclosure no. 1, *Correspondence and Other Papers Relating to New Zealand, 1862–64*, vol. 13 (Shannon: Irish University Press, 1970), 39; Browne to Newcastle, 26 September 1861, no. 41, ibid., 99–101.

120 *Southern Cross*, 17 May 1859.

121 Paterson, *Colonial Discourses*, 111–22; *Appendices to the Journal of the House of Representatives* (1860), E-1C, 17. F.D. Fenton, resident magistrate of Waikato, recorded in his journal on 29 July 1859: "I have heard mention made of the Romans and their bridges, and of the consequent subjugation of England."

122 *Te Karere Maori*, 15 March 1859, 31 July 1857, 30 November 1857.

123 Ibid., 1 January 1855, 1 June 1855.

124 David W. McIntyre, *The Journal of Henry Sewell, 1853–7*, vol. 2 (Christchurch: Whitcoulls Publishers, 1980), 242–43, 251.

125 Thomas Gore Browne to Herman Merivale, 2 July 1856, "Sir Thomas Gore Browne Letterbook."

126 Browne to Labouchere, 18 February 1858, CO 209/145.

127 *Te Karere Maori*, 30 June 1858, 15 July 1858, 31 December, 1858, 15 June 1859.

128 Ballantyne, "Teaching Maori about Asia," 22–23.

129 *Te Karere Maori*, 30 June 1858.

130 Ibid.

131 Ibid., 31 May 1860.

132 Ibid., 30 April 1860.

133 Ibid., 30 June 1860.

134 Selwyn to the Native Secretary, 15 February 1861, memoranda, ANZ, MA-1-832-1861/21.

135 Donald McLean to Thomas Gore Browne, 5 March 1861, memoranda, ANZ, MA-1-832-1861/21.

Chapter 4: Aboriginal Title and the Victoria Press

1 *Victoria Daily Chronicle*, 3 July 1864, 5 August 1864, 10 January 1866.
2 *British Columbian*, 4 June 1864.
3 *British Colonist*, 3 May 1863, 4 July 1863.
4 *Victoria Daily Chronicle*, 5 August 1864.
5 Ibid., 6 May 1863.
6 Tony Ballantyne, "Genesis 1:28 and the Languages of Colonial Improvement in Victorian New Zealand," *Victorian Review* 37, 2 (2011): 10–11.
7 Genesis 1:28 (King James Version).
8 *Victoria Daily Chronicle*, 5 August 1864.
9 Hamar Foster and Alan Grove, "'Trespassers on the Soil': United States v. Tom and a New Perspective on the Short History of Treaty Making in Nineteenth-Century British Columbia," *BC Studies* 138/39 (Summer/Autumn 2003): 53.
10 Raymond Frogner, "'Innocent Legal Fictions': Archival Convention and the *North Saanich Treaty* of 1852," *Archivaria* 70 (Fall 2010): 45–94.
11 Second *Victoria Gazette*, 13 April 1860; Frogner, "'Innocent Legal Fictions,'" 81.
12 Frogner, "'Innocent Legal Fictions,'" 77.
13 P.G. McHugh, *Aboriginal Title: The Modern Jurisprudence of Tribal Land Rights* (Oxford: Oxford University Press, 2011), 26.
14 Douglas to Newcastle, 25 March 1861, CO 305/17 no. 4779, Colonial Despatches of Vancouver Island and British Columbia, 1846–1871, http://bcgenesis.uvic.ca/getDoc.htm?id=V61024.scx.
15 Robin Fisher, *Contact and Conflict: Indian-European Relations in British Columbia, 1774–1890* (Vancouver: UBC Press, 1992), 66–69, 151–60; Paul Tennant, *Aboriginal Peoples and Politics: The Indian Land Question in British Columbia, 1849–1989* (Vancouver: UBC Press, 1990), 26–38; Cole Harris, *Making Native Space: Colonialism, Resistance, and Reserves in British Columbia* (Vancouver: UBC Press, 2003), 18–44.
16 Foster and Grove, "'Trespassers on the Soil,'" 51–84.
17 Chris Arnett, *The Terror of the Coast: Land Alienation and Colonial War on Vancouver Island and the Gulf Islands, 1849–1863* (Vancouver: Talonbooks, 1999), 88–110.
18 Douglas to Labouchere, 6 September 1856, CO 305/7 no. 10152, *Vancouver Island: 1855–1857*, vol. 3, Colonial Despatches of British Columbia, ed. James Hendrickson (Victoria: University of Victoria Press, 1988), 112.
19 Douglas to Barclay, 16 May 1850, "Letters to Hudson's Bay Company on Vancouver Island, 1850–55," BCA, A/C/20/Vi2A.
20 John Lutz, *Makúk: A New History of Aboriginal-White Relations* (Vancouver: UBC Press, 2008), 66–68.
21 Douglas to Labouchere, 20 October 1856, CO 305/7 no. 11582, "Census of the Indian population of Vancouver Island, 1856," Colonial Despatches of Vancouver Island and British Columbia, 1846–1871, http://bcgenesis.uvic.ca/getDoc.htm?id=V56024.scx.
22 Douglas to Lytton, 25 May 1859, CO 305/10 no. 6949, *Vancouver Island: 1859*, vol. 5, Colonial Despatches of British Columbia, ed. James Hendrickson (Victoria: University of Victoria Press, 1988), 21–22.
23 Ibid.
24 *British Colonist*, 3 March 1860.
25 Ibid., 7 March 1861.
26 William A. Young to Joseph Despard Pemberton, 3 December 1861; Young to Henry Peers, Edward Stamp et al., 9 December 1861, "Colonial Secretary of Vancouver Island's Correspondence," C/AA/30.1J/3, BCA.

27 Cole Harris, "How Did Colonialism Dispossess? Comments from an Edge of Empire," *Annals of the Association of American Geographers* 94, 1 (2004): 169.

28 Edmond Hope Verney to Commodore John W.S. Spencer, 10 May 1863, *Vancouver Island Letters of Edmond Hope Verney, 1862–65,* ed. Allan Pritchard (Vancouver: UBC Press, 1996), 211.

29 William A.G. Young to Governor Frederick Seymour, 19 November 1866, "Memorandum for the information of His Excellency the Governor," BCA, Vancouver Island, Colonial Secretary's Correspondence Outward, 11 September 1865–29 November 1866, C/AA/30.1J/6.

30 *British Colonist*, 20 March 1861; *The Press*, 19 April, 1861; *British Colonist*, 17 May 1862; *The Press*, 19 May 1862; *British Colonist*, 20 May 1862, 13 September 1862; *Evening Express*, 29 April 1863; *Victoria Daily Chronicle*, 12 May 1863, 26 September 1863, 27 September 1863; *British Colonist*, 18 February 1864, 5 July 1864; *Victoria Daily Chronicle*, 16 July 1864; *Vancouver Island Times*, 8 May 1865; *British Colonist*, 13 November 1866.

31 *British Colonist*, 4 July 1859.

32 *British Colonist*, 4 July 1859, 8 July 1859; second *Victoria Gazette*, 4 April 1860, 13 April 1860; *British Colonist*, 22 August 1860, 7 March 1861, 8 March 1861; *The Press*, 1 April 1862; *British Colonist*, 13 September 1862; *Victoria Daily Chronicle*, 6 May 1863; *British Colonist*, 12 May 1863, 28 May 1863; *Victoria Daily Chronicle*, 11 June 1863; *British Colonist*, 2 August 1863; *Victoria Daily Chronicle*, 7 August 1863; *British Colonist*, 2 October 1863, 12 May 1864; *Evening Express*, 23 July 1864; *Victoria Daily Chronicle*, 5 August 1864; *British Colonist*, 12 October 1864; *Vancouver Island Times*, 20 April 1865.

33 Tennant, *Aboriginal Peoples and Politics*, 25.

34 *British Colonist*, 24 March 1860.

35 Ibid., 24 March 1860.

36 Ibid., 30 June 1860.

37 Robert L. Smith, "Kennedy, Sir Arthur Edward," Dictionary of Canadian Biography Online, vol. 11, 2003, http://www.biographi.ca/en/bio/kennedy_arthur_edward_11E.html.

38 Robert Louis Smith, "Governor Kennedy of Vancouver Island and the Politics of Union" (MA thesis, University of Victoria, 1970). My assessment of the political conflict between Kennedy and the Legislative Assembly of Vancouver Island draws extensively on Smith's analysis.

39 Douglas to Newcastle, 12 February 1864, "Resolution of the House of Assembly," CO 305/22 no. 2905, Colonial Despatches of Vancouver Island and British Columbia, 1846–1871, http://bcgenesis.uvic.ca/getDoc.xml?id=V64003.scx.

40 Jane Samson, "British Authority or 'Mere Theory?' Colonial Law and Native People on Vancouver Island," *Western Legal History* 11, 1 (1999): 45.

41 Kennedy to Cardwell, 1 October 1864, CO 305/23 no. 10589, Colonial Despatches of Vancouver Island and British Columbia, 1846–1871, http://bcgenesis.uvic.ca/getDoc.xml?id=V64180.scx.

42 *Victoria Daily Chronicle*, 23 August 1864.

43 William A.G. Young to Governor Frederick Seymour, 19 November 1866, "Memorandum for the information of His Excellency the Governor."

44 *Victoria Daily Chronicle*, 22 February 1865.

45 Second *Victoria Gazette*, 13 April 1860. Emphasis in original.

46 Ibid., 13 April 1860.

47 Ibid. Emphasis in original.

48 Ibid., 1 April 1862.

49 Douglas to Newcastle, 25 March 1861, CO 305/17 no. 4779, *Vancouver Island: 1861*, vol. 7, Colonial Despatches of British Columbia, ed. James Hendrickson (Victoria: University of Victoria, 1988), 23–24.

50 Ibid.
51 *The Press*, 1 April 1862.
52 *British Colonist*, 4 July 1859, 8 July 1859, 22 August 1860.
53 Ibid., 22 August 1860.
54 Ibid.
55 Ibid., 8 March 1861.
56 Ibid., 22 August 1862.
57 Ibid., 17 December 1862.
58 Arnett, *Terror of the Coast*, 310–11.
59 See Gray H. Whaley, *Oregon and the Collapse of Illahee: US Empire and the Transformation of an Indigenous World, 1792–1859* (Chapel Hill: University of North Carolina Press, 2010).
60 Petition of the Legislative Assembly, 25 March 1861, CO 305/17 no. 4779, Colonial Despatches of Vancouver Island and British Columbia, 1846–1871, http://bcgenesis.uvic.ca/getDoc. htm?id=V61024.scx.
61 Jane Samson, "British Voices and Indigenous Rights: Debating Aboriginal Legal Status in Nineteenth-Century Australia and Canada," *Cultures of the Commonwealth: Essays and Studies* 2 (Winter 1996–97): 11.
62 Lutz, *Makúk*, 339n118.
63 *British Colonist*, 7 November 1864, 20 July 1865.
64 Samson, "British Authority," 46–47.
65 See Laura Benton, *Law and Colonial Cultures: Legal Regimes in World History, 1400–1900* (Cambridge: Cambridge University Press, 2002).
66 *Evening Express*, 12 May 1863.
67 Ibid., 29 April 1863.
68 *British Colonist*, 12 May 1864.
69 *Vancouver Island Times*, 20 April 1865.
70 *British Columbian*, 19 December 1861, 27 February 1862, 30 April 1862, 3 May 1862, 21 May 1861, 21 June 1862.
71 Ibid., 21 June 1862.
72 Ibid., 28 June 1862.
73 Ibid., 13 June 1863.
74 Ibid., 23 July 1864.
75 Ibid., 2 December 1865.
76 *Victoria Daily Chronicle*, 22 May 1865.
77 *Vancouver Daily Post*, 20 December 1865.
78 F.W. Chesson to E. Bulwer Lytton, 10 August 1858, 8017 NA, CO 6/26, Colonial Despatches of Vancouver Island and British Columbia, 1846–1871, http://bcgenesis.uvic.ca/getDoc. htm?id=V585MI22_A.scx&search=aborigines%27%20%20society#searchHit1.
79 *Vancouver Daily Post*, 20 December 1865.
80 *Vancouver Island Times*, 12 December 1864.
81 *Victoria Daily Chronicle*, 20 December 1865.
82 *British Columbian*, 21 May 1864.
83 W. Sebright Green, "The Indians of Vancouver Island," *The Colonial Intelligencer or, Aborigines' Friend* (London: Aborigines' Protection Society, 1 December 1869), 191–93. Emphasis in original.
84 Joseph W. Trutch, 13 January 1870, "Memorandum refuting the charges in Sebright Green's report on the conditions of the Indians on Vancouver island, with explanation," in *Papers Connected with the Indian Land Question, 1850–75* (Victoria: R. Wolfenden, 1875), app. B.
85 For an extended discussion of Trutch, see Robin Fisher, "Joseph Trutch and Indian Land Policy," *BC Studies* 12 (Winter 1971/72): 3–33.

86 Harris, *Making Native Space*, 265.
87 See Megan Harvey, "Story People: Stó:lō-State Relations and Indigenous Literacies in British Columbia, 1864–1874," *Journal of the Canadian Historical Association* 24, 1 (2013): 51–88.

Chapter 5: The Auckland Press at War

1 D.B. Waterson, "Firth, Josiah Clifton-Biography," *Dictionary of New Zealand Biography, Te Ara-the Encyclopedia of New Zealand*, http://www.teara.govt.nz/remap_url.php?src=en/biographies/1f7/1.
2 *New Zealander*, 5 May 1860.
3 *Southern Cross*, 22 May 1860; *New Zealander*, 23 May 1860.
4 *Southern Cross*, 22 May 1860.
5 Ibid.; *New Zealander*, 23 May 1860. Carleton argued that only 450 colonists had been in attendance, while the *New Zealander* estimated the crowd's size at between eight and nine hundred.
6 D.B. Waterson, "Williamson, John-Biography," *Dictionary of New Zealand Biography, Te Ara-the Encyclopedia of New Zealand*, http://www.teara.govt.nz/remap_url.php?src=en/biographies/1f7/1.
7 G.M. Main, *The Newspaper Press of Auckland* (Auckland: Wilsons and Horton, 1890); R.C.J. Stone, "Brown, William-Biography," *Dictionary of New Zealand Biography, Te Ara-the Encyclopedia of New Zealand*, http://www.teara.govt.nz/remap_url.php?src=en/biographies/1b37/1; R.C.J. Stone, "Campbell, John Logan-Biography," *Dictionary of New Zealand Biography, Te Ara-the Encyclopedia of New Zealand*, http://www.teara.govt.nz/remap_url.php?src=en/biographies/1c3/1.
8 D.B. Silver, "Carleton, Hugh Francis-Biography," *Dictionary of New Zealand Biography, Te Ara-the Encyclopedia of New Zealand*, http://www.teara.govt.nz/en/biographies/1c5.
9 *Auckland Examiner*, 22 October 1857; F.B. Smith, "Southwell, Charles-Biography," *Dictionary of New Zealand Biography, Te Ara-the Encyclopedia of New Zealand*, http://www.teara.govt.nz/remap_url.php?src=en/biographies/1s17/1.
10 Anonymous, "Auckland Newspaper Press," *The Cyclopedia of New Zealand, Auckland Provincial District* (Christchurch: Cyclopedia Company, Limited, 1902), 267–68. During the 1850s, Auckland featured several additional very short-lived newspapers: the *Pensioner Settlements Gazette* (1851), the *Auckland Temperance Telegraph* (1854), the *Independent* (1859), and the *Telegraph* (September 1859-February 1860).
11 Main, *Newspaper Press of Auckland*, 2.
12 Registrar General, *Statistics of New Zealand for 1860* (Auckland: W.C. Wilson, 1861), no. 29; Registrar General, *Statistics of New Zealand for 1861* (Auckland: W.C. Wilson, 1862), no. 1. In 1861, 57 percent of Auckland's European population was over sixteen years of age. If Auckland, in 1860, featured the same demographic proportions, each colonist in 1860 might have received and despatched twenty-three newspapers and eighteen letters per year.
13 Registrar General, *Statistics of New Zealand for 1860*, no. 28, no. 29.
14 Registrar General, *Statistics of New Zealand for 1859* (Auckland: W.C. Wilson, 1860), no. 30; Registrar General, *Statistics of New Zealand for 1860*, no. 29; Registrar General, *Statistics of New Zealand for 1861*, no. 58. In 1859, Auckland colonists despatched 136,798 newspapers, increasing to 177,839 in 1860 and 238,642 in 1861.
15 Registrar General, *Statistics of New Zealand for 1859*, no. 1; Registrar General, *Statistics of New Zealand for 1861*, no. 1; Registrar General, *Statistics of New Zealand for 1862* (Auckland: New Zealander Printing Office, 1863), no. 46.
16 See Ross Harvey, "The Power of the Press in Colonial New Zealand: More Imagined Than Real," *Bibliographical Society of Australia and New Zealand Bulletin* 20, 2 (1996): 130–45;

Patrick Day, *The Making of the New Zealand Press: A Study of the Organizational and Political Concerns of New Zealand Newspaper Controllers, 1840–1880* (Wellington: Victoria University Press, 1990). Both Harvey and Day argue that the New Zealand press in the mid-nineteenth century was elitist rather than populist in its orientation and that it did not achieve widespread popularity until the mid-to-late 1860s.

17 Harvey, "Power of the Press in Colonial New Zealand," 143; Main, *Newspaper Press of Auckland*, 2. Main details that the *Trumpeter and Universal Advertiser* was an "advertising sheet," published in conjunction with the *Auckland Examiner* in 1857. This detail hints that the *Auckland Examiner* also may have had a circulation of four hundred in 1857.

18 William Brown to John Logan Campbell, 18 April 1860, "William Brown Correspondence," Auckland War Memorial Museum Library (AWMML), John Logan Campbell Collections, MSS 51, file 60.

19 Registrar General, *Statistics of New Zealand for 1858* (Auckland: W.C. Wilson, 1859), no. 1;

20 This measure is achieved by matching the Auckland press's circulation per edition of 3,261 against 4,117 houses and buildings in Auckland province.

21 Harvey, "Economic Aspects of Nineteenth-Century New Zealand Newspapers," 59.

22 *Auckland Examiner*, 20 December 1860, 27 December 1860.

23 David Burn, 7 February 1857, diary, SLNSW, microfilm-CY 1094; Harvey, "Economic Aspects of Nineteenth Century New Zealand Newspapers," 59.

24 Brown to Campbell, 18 April 1860, "William Brown Correspondence."

25 Ibid., 24 December 1860.

26 Registrar General, *Statistics of New Zealand for 1860*, no. 29.

27 This comparison is achieved by comparing the average weekly number of newspapers despatched from Auckland in 1860 (177,839/52 = 3,420) to the Auckland press's total weekly production (two thousand editions from the *New Zealander* + 542 from the *Southern Cross* + 1,500 from the *Auckland Weekly Register* + 500 from the *Auckland Examiner* = 4,541).

28 J.E. Traue, "The Public Library Explosion in Colonial New Zealand," *Libraries and the Cultural Record* 42, 2 (2007): 152

29 Ibid., 157–60.

30 Jeremiah Rankin, "Science and Civic Culture in Colonial Auckland" (MA thesis, University of Auckland, 2006), 45; Registrar General, *Statistics of New Zealand for 1861*. The Mechanics' Institute's importance in Auckland is evidenced by the fact that, in 1861, 13 percent of male colonists in Auckland city were members.

31 Rankin, "Science and Civic Culture in Colonial Auckland," 49. The Mechanics' Institute's membership between 1857 and 1864: 300 in 1857, 400 in 1858, 330 in 1859, 400 in 1860, 290 in 1861, 310 in 1862, 290 in 1863, and 490 in 1864.

32 Ibid., 109.

33 *Auckland Weekly Register*, 14 February 1859; *New Zealander*, 28 April 1860: The Mechanics' Institute's reading room featured twenty-one newspapers, eleven from New Zealand, seven from Great Britain, and three from Australia; the Young Men's Christian Association carried twenty-three newspapers, including three copies of the *Southern Cross* and two copies of the *New Zealander*.

34 Rankin, "Science and Civic Culture in Colonial Auckland," 110. Rankin indicates that the reading room featured a daily average attendance of fifty persons.

35 R.D. McGarvey, "Local Politics in the Auckland Province, 1853–62" (MA thesis, University of New Zealand, 1954), 47. Franchise requirements entailed that any male over twenty-one years of age, excepting criminals and aliens, could vote if they could claim: (1) six months possession of a freehold property valued at fifty pounds per year or a leasehold of not less than three years valued at ten pounds per year, (2) or six months occupation of a tenement of the annual value of ten pounds within the town or five pounds elsewhere. Maori were

not qualified to vote unless they could prove the possession of a Crown grant to their land.

36 H.J. Hanham, "The Political Structure of Auckland, 1853–76" (MA thesis, University of New Zealand, 1950), 36. Hanham notes that the number of eligible voters in 1861 was reduced from the mid-1850s following electoral reform in the late 1850s, which purged Auckland's electoral rolls and lessened the opportunity for electoral fraud.

37 Ibid., 33–35, fig. 14, 52. The figure of 90 percent is reached by taking the number of electoral votes cast in Auckland's twelve electoral districts (4,508) and matching this sum to the number of adult males within the electoral districts (6,695). Thus 67 percent of the total number of adult males in Auckland province were represented by electors. However, only 75 percent, or 5,021, local adult males were eligible to vote, indicating that 90 percent of eligible voters were represented by electors. This figure is slightly inflated, though, because colonists who possessed property qualifications in several electoral districts had a plural vote. It is difficult to ascertain the number of plural votes cast in Auckland elections.

38 "The 1852 Constitution and Responsible Government," *An Encyclopaedia of New Zealand 1966,* http://www.teara.govt.nz/en/1966/history-constitutional/page-4.

39 "The Provincial Period, 1853–76," *An Encyclopaedia of New Zealand 1966,* http://www.teara.govt.nz/en/1966/history-constitutional/page-5.

40 R. Stone, "Auckland Party Politics in the Early Years of the Provincial System, 1853–58," *New Zealand Journal of History* 14, 2 (1980): 159.

41 McGarvey, "Local Politics in the Auckland Province," 186–87.

42 Ibid., 186–87.

43 Stone, "Brown, William-Biography."

44 Stone, "Auckland Party Politics in the Early Years," 174.

45 McGarvey, "Local Politics in the Auckland Province," 189.

46 Hanham, "Political Structure of Auckland," 32–33.

47 McGarvey, "Local Politics in the Auckland Province," 179.

48 Harold J. Whitwell, "The Forty Acre System" (MA thesis, University of New Zealand, 1954), 112, 161. According to Whitwell, Williamson's "Forty Acre System" was inaugurated through the Waste Lands Act, 1858. In 1859, 3,860 "Forty Acre Men" arrived in Auckland, buoying Auckland's urban population of 6,285. Fifteen thousand Forty Acre Men arrived in Auckland over ten years.

49 *Victoria Daily Press,* 18 October 1865.

50 James Belich, *Replenishing the Earth: The Settler Revolution and the Rise of the Anglo-World, 1783–1939* (Oxford: Oxford University Press, 2009), 87.

51 *Auckland Weekly Register,* 7 February 1857, 23 May 1857, 30 May 1857; *New Zealander,* 12 March 1859, 16 March 1859; *Auckland Weekly Register,* 5 April 1858; *New Zealander,* 16 November 1859, 7 December 1859; *Auckland Weekly Register,* 27 December 1858, 8 August 1859; *New Zealander,* 14 March 1860.

52 Main, *Newspaper Press of Auckland,* 2–3; G.H. Scholefield, *Newspapers in New Zealand* (Wellington: Reed, 1958), 80.

53 *Auckland Examiner,* 29 October 1857.

54 *Southern Cross,* 23 September 1859, 30 September 1859, 11 October 1859, 18 October 1859, 24 February 1860, 23 March 1860, 1 May 1860, 25 May 1860, 28 August 1860, 1 September 1860, 23 September 1860.

55 *Auckland Examiner,* 11 December 1856.

56 Ibid., 16 October 1858, 20 October 1858, 23 October 1858, 30 October 1858, 27 November 1858, 1 December 1858, 4 December 1858, 8 December 1858, 18 December 1858, 26 February 1858.

57 John Stenhouse, "Churches, State and the New Zealand Wars: 1860–1872," *Journal of Law and Religion* (1998–99): 483–507; John Stenhouse, "Imperialism, Atheism, and Race: Charles Southwell, Old Corruption, and the Maori," *Journal of British Studies* 44 (2005): 754–74; John Stenhouse, "Religion and Society," in *The New Oxford History of New Zealand*, ed. Gyselle Byrnes, 323–56 (Auckland: Oxford University Press, 2009).

58 *Auckland Examiner*, 25 December 1856, 1 January 1857, 8 January 1857, 2 July 1857, 15 July 1858, 16 September 1858, 12 February 1859, 23 July 1859, 7 September 1859.

59 Ibid., 7 May 1857, 25 June 1857, 26 March 1859, 30 March 1859, 12 October 1859.

60 28 July 1860, "Diary of Thomas Gore Browne [Harriet Browne]," ANZ. Though identified within ANZ records as the diary of Thomas Gore Browne, the majority of entries were written by Harriet Louisa Browne.

61 *Auckland Examiner*, 1 January 1857, 7 January 1858, 11 March 1858, 9 September 1858, 16 September 1858, 20 August 1859.

62 Ibid., 1 January 1857.

63 Ibid., 15 June 1859.

64 Catherine Hall, *Civilising Subjects: Metropole and Colony in the English Imagination, 1830–1867* (Chicago: University of Chicago Press, 2002), 347–63.

65 Peter Mandler, "The Problem with Cultural History," *Cultural and Social History* 1, 1 (2004): 96–97.

66 Day, *Making of the New Zealand Press*, 94.

67 Hanham, "Political Structure of Auckland," 91–92.

68 *Southern Cross*, 4 February 1859

69 Vaughan Wood, Tom Brooking, and Peter Perry, "Pastoralism and Politics: Reinterpreting Contests for Territory in Auckland Province, New Zealand, 1853–1864," *Journal of Historical Geography* 34, 2 (2008): 227, 233–34.

70 Ibid., 224.

71 Ibid., 239–40.

72 Hanham, "Political Structure of Auckland," 304.

73 *Auckland Examiner*, 1 January 1857, 5 March 1857, 2 April 1857; *Southern Cross*, 16 June 1857, 20 April 1858, 4 February 1859, 11 February 1859; *Auckland Examiner*, 12 February 1859; *Southern Cross*, 25 February 1859, 8 March 1859, 22 March 1859, 25 March 1859, 8 April 1859, 31 May 1859, 3 June 1859, 7 June 1859; *Auckland Examiner*, 8 June 1859; *Southern Cross*, 10 June 1859; *Auckland Examiner*, 15 June 1859; *Southern Cross*, 17 June 1859, 21 June 1859, 24 June 1859; *Auckland Examiner*, 25 June 1859; *Southern Cross*, 28 June 1859; *Auckland Examiner*, 6 July 1859; *Southern Cross*, 8 July 1859, 12 July 1859, 15 July 1859, 26 July 1859, 12 August 1859, 16 August 1859; *Auckland Examiner*, 27 August 1859; *Southern Cross*, 30 August 1859, 21 October 1859, 9 December 1859, 30 December 1859.

74 *Southern Cross*, 24 May 1859, 3 June 1859, 10 June 1859, 16 August 1859, 30 August 1859.

75 Ibid., 5 June 1857, 5 February 1858, 29 June 1858, 10 May 1859, 24 May 1859.

76 Ibid., 20 April 1858.

77 Francis Canavan, *The Political Economy of Edmund Burke: The Role of Property in His Thought* (New York: Fordham University Press, 1995), 29.

78 *Southern Cross*, 20 April 1858.

79 *Auckland Weekly Register*, 7 February 1857, 14 February 1857, 28 February 1857, 7 March 1857, 28 March 1857, 4 January 1858; *New Zealander*, 6 January 1858, 13 January 1858; *Auckland Weekly Register*, 5 April 1858; *New Zealander*, 16 October 1858; *Auckland Weekly Register*, 27 December 1858; *New Zealander*, 1 January 1859; *Auckland Weekly Register*, 3 January 1859; *New Zealander*, 12 January 1859, 23 February 1859; *Auckland Weekly Register*, 8 August 1859; *New Zealander*, 16 November 1859, 11 January 1860.

80 *New Zealander*, 6 February 1858, 12 January 1859, 5 February 1859, 23 February 1859, 2 March 1850, 5 March 1859, 12 March 1859, 16 March 1859, 23 March 1859, 21 May 1859, 28 May 1859, 4 June 1859, 8 June 1859, 11 June 1859, 22 June 1859, 30 July 1859, 3 August 1859, 20 August 1859, 31 August 1859.

81 *Auckland Weekly Register*, 14 February 1857, 7 September 1857, 4 January 1858, 5 April 1858, 27 December 1858, 8 August 1859.

82 *New Zealander*, 2 March 1859, 12 March 1859.

83 Ibid., 12 March 1859, 16 March 1859.

84 Ibid., 20 August 1859.

85 Ibid., 16 March 1859, 20 August 1859.

86 Ibid., 22 June 1859.

87 *Southern Cross*, 21 June 1859.

88 Browne to Gordon Gairdner, 26 July 1859, "Sir Thomas Gore Browne Letterbook," ATL.

89 *Auckland Examiner*, 4 April 1860, 7 April 1860, 11 April 1860, 14 April 1860, 18 April 1860, 21 April 1860, 23 April 1860, 5 May 1860, 9 May 1860, 16 May 1860, 30 May 1860.

90 Ibid., 23 April 1860.

91 Smith, "Southwell, Charles-Biography."

92 *New Zealander*, 27 February 1860; *Southern Cross*, 28 February 1860, 13 March 1860, 20 March 1860, 23 March 1860; *New Zealander*, 28 March 1860; *Southern Cross*, 3 April 1860, 27 April 1860; *New Zealander*, 5 May 1860, 16 May 1860, 23 May 1860.

93 *Southern Cross*, 28 February 1860, 6 March 1860; *New Zealander*, 17 March 1860; *Southern Cross*, 26 June 1860, 14 August 1860.

94 *New Zealander*, 27 February 1860; *Southern Cross*, 28 February 1860; *New Zealander*, 17 March 1860; *Southern Cross*, 23 March 1860.

95 *New Zealander*, 28 March 1860.

96 *Southern Cross*, 28 February 1860, 26 March 1860, 2 April 1860, 20 April 1860, 27 April 1860, 28 April 1860, 15 May 1860, 25 May 1860.

97 *Southern Cross*, 28 April 1860, 1 May 1860, 8 May 1860, 25 May 1860, 6 July 1860, 21 August 1860, 28 August 1860, 7 September 1860.

98 *Southern Cross*, 7 September 1860.

99 Browne to Chichester Fortescue, 3 November 1860, "Sir Thomas Gore Browne Letterbook." Browne revealed how the *Wellington Advertiser*, the *Wellington Independent*, and the *Wellington Spectator* all criticised his Maori policy and wartime administration.

100 *Southern Cross*, 1 May 1860, 25 May 1860.

101 Brown to Campbell, 9 March 1860; 25 June 1860, "William Brown Correspondence."

102 *Southern Cross*, 9 November 1860.

103 Ibid., 1 January 1861.

104 Stone, "Campbell, John Logan-Biography."

105 R.C.J. Stone, *The Father and His Gift: John Logan Campbell's Later Years* (Auckland: Auckland University Press, 1987), 31–34.

106 Brown to Campbell, 25 July 1860, "William Brown Correspondence."

107 *Southern Cross*, 19 April 1861.

108 *Southern Cross*, 26 March 1861, 2 April 1861, 12 April 1861, 16 April 1861, 19 April 1861, 23 April 1861, 14 May 1861, 21 May 1861, 28 May 1861, 7 June 1861, 11 June 1861, 18 June 1861, 23 July 1861, 24 December 1861.

109 Ibid., 18 June 1861.

110 *New Zealander*, 20 March 1861, 23 March 1861, 3 April 1861, 17 April 1861, 20 April 1861, 27 April 1861, 25 May 1861, 3 July 1861, 20 July 1861, 31 July 1861, 28 September 1861, 6 November 1861, 16 November 1861, 4 December 1861, 7 December 1861.

111 Ibid., 5 May 1860.
112 William White, ed., *Memorials of Sergeant William Marjouram, Royal Artillery; Including Six Years' Service During the Late Maori War* (London: James Nisbet and Co., 1862), 175.
113 *Auckland Examiner*, 12 February 1859.
114 Ibid., 19 May 1860.
115 Ibid., 23 April 1860.
116 23 April 1860, "Journal of Henry Sewell, 1859–1866, vol. 1," ATL, QMS-1783.
117 Rev. R. Maunsell to C.W. Richmond, 15 November 1860, *The Richmond-Atkinson Papers*, vol. 1, ed. G.H. Scholefield (Wellington: R.E. Owen, Government Printer, 1960), 657; Browne to Newcastle, 24 April 1860, no. 12, *Correspondence and Papers Relating to the Maori Uprisings in New Zealand, 1861*, vol. 12 (Shannon: Irish University Press, 1970), 30; Browne to Newcastle, 2 October 1860, no. 48, ibid., 143; Browne to Newcastle, 3 November 1860, no. 52, ibid., 162; Browne to Newcastle, 8 November 1860, no. 54, ibid., 167; Browne to Newcastle, 6 March 1861, no. 12, ibid., 39; 17 October 1860, "Diary of Thomas Gore Browne," ANZ, ADCZ 17006 W5431/3; 25 October 1860, ibid.; 1 November 1860, ibid.; 18 February 1861, "Diary of Thomas Gore Browne," ANZ, ADCZ 17006 W5431/4; 19 February 1861, ibid.; 28 February 1861, "Diary of Harriet Louisa Browne," ANZ, ADCZ 17007 W5431/7; Browne to Gordon Gairdner, 9 October 1860, "Sir Thomas Gore Browne Letterbook"; Donald McLean to Browne, 5 March 1861, memoranda, ANZ, M-1-832-1861/21.
118 Browne to Newcastle, 31 December 1860, "Sir Thomas Gore Browne Letterbook"; Jan Pilditch, ed., *The Letters and Journals of Reverend John Morgan*, vol. 2 (Glasgow: Grimsay Press, 2010), 559–631.
119 23 April 1860, "Journal of Henry Sewell."
120 *Southern Cross*, 26 January 1860, 6 April 1860; *New Zealander*, 7 April 1860; *Southern Cross*, 10 April 1860; *New Zealander*, 11 April 1860; *Auckland Examiner*, 23 April 1860; *Southern Cross*, 4 May 1860, 8 May 1860, 15 May 1860, 18 May 1860, 22 May 1860, 29 May 1860; *New Zealander*, 13 June 1860; *Southern Cross*, 26 June 1860, 29 June 1860, 2 October 1860, 9 October 1860, 20 November 1860, 5 March 1861, 8 March 1861.
121 *Southern Cross*, 6 April 1860.
122 *New Zealander*, 7 April 1860.
123 Ibid., 7 April 1860, 11 April 1860.
124 Ibid., 11 April 1860.
125 *Auckland Examiner*, 21 April 1860.
126 *Southern Cross*, 24 April 1860.
127 Ibid., 13 March 1860, 24 April 1860.
128 *Aotearoa, or The Maori Recorder*, January 1861.
129 Browne to Newcastle, 25 April 1860, no. 37 (Miscellaneous), "Original Correspondence [relating to New Zealand], 1830–1922," Hocken Collections (HC), 10122.
130 The intention of the New Zealand Bill was to reform the administration of New Zealand's Native affairs; the proposed legislation would have removed the Crown's monopoly on Maori land sales, but it would have maintained the Colonial Executive's control over Maori policy. The New Zealand Bill garnered considerable criticism and was withdrawn.
131 *Wellington Independent*, 9 October 1860.
132 *Southern Cross*, 9 October 1860.
133 30 September 1860, "Journal of Henry Sewell."
134 *New Zealander*, 20 April 1861.
135 Julie Evans, Patricia Grimshaw, and David Phillips, *Equal Subjects, Unequal Rights: Indigenous Peoples in British Settler Colonies, 1830–1910* (Manchester: Manchester University Press, 2003), 81.

Chapter 6: Colonial Humanitarians?

1 12 October 1861, "Diary of Thomas Gore Browne," ADCZ 17006 W5431/4, ANZ.
2 Browne to Newcastle, 16 May 1861, no. 25, *Correspondence and Other Papers Relating to New Zealand, 1862–64,* vol. 13 (Shannon: Irish University Press, 1970), 49–50; Browne to Newcastle, 27 June 1861, no. 26, *Correspondence and Papers Relating to the Maori Uprisings in New Zealand, 1861,* vol. 12 (Shannon: Irish University Press, 1970), 68–73.
3 Browne to Newcastle, 16 May 1861, no. 25, *Correspondence and Other Papers Relating to New Zealand, 1862–64,* 49–50; Browne to Newcastle, 27 June 1861, no. 26, *Correspondence and Papers Relating to the Maori Uprisings in New Zealand, 1861,* 68–73.
4 29 July 1861, "Diary of Harriet Browne," ANZ, ADCZ 17007 W5431/7.
5 Ibid.
6 *New Zealander,* 31 July 1861, 17 August 1861; *Southern Cross,* 27 September 1861.
7 Browne to Newcastle, 29 August 1860, no. 40, *Correspondence and Papers Relating to the Maori Uprisings in New Zealand, 1861,* 121–22; Browne to Gordon Gairdner, 18 October 1856, "Sir Thomas Gore Browne Letterbook, 1855–1861," QMS-0284, ATL; Browne to Gairdner, 24 February 1859, ibid.
8 12 October 1861, "Diary of Thomas Gore Browne."
9 See Zoë Laidlaw, *Colonial Connections, 1815–1845: Patronage, the Information Revolution, and Colonial Government* (Manchester: Manchester University Press, 2005); Julie Evans, *Edward Eyre: Race and Colonial Governance* (Dunedin: Otago University Press, 2005).
10 Charlotte Macdonald, "Between Religion and Empire: Sarah Selwyn's Aotearoa/New Zealand, Eton and Lichfield, England, 1840s-1900," *Journal of the Canadian Historical Association* 19, 2 (2008): 46.
11 24 September 1860, "Diary of Thomas Gore Browne [Harriet Browne]," ANZ, ADCZ 1706 W5431/3; 30 October 1860, ibid.; 6 January 1861, ibid.; 2 June 1861, "Diary of Harriet Browne," ANZ. Harriet Louisa wrote the entries in Gore Browne's 1860 diary from 9 July 1860 to 25 January 1861.
12 Gore Browne to Gordon Gairdner, 18 October 1856, "Sir Thomas Gore Browne Letterbook."
13 Mark Francis, *Governors and Settlers: Images of Authority in the British Colonies, 1820–60* (Canterbury: Canterbury University Press, 1992), 213–37.
14 John Stenhouse, "Churches, State and the New Zealand Wars: 1860–1872," *Journal of Law and Religion* (1998–99): 484.
15 Browne to Newcastle, [3 December 1860?], "Sir Thomas Gore Browne Letterbook."
16 Sarah Selwyn to M.A.P., 30 August 1860, *Extracts of Letters from New Zealand on the War Question: With an Article from the New Zealand Spectator of November 3rd, 1860* (London: F.J. Wilson, 1861), 15–16.
17 3 July 1860, 6 July 1860, Parliamentary Debates, Commons, 3rd series, vol. 159 (1860), cols. 1326–29, 1518–20; Brown to Campbell, 25 July 1860, "William Brown Correspondence," John Logan Campbell Collection, AWMML, MS 51, F60, Auckland War Memorial Museum Library; 23 August 1860, "Diary of Thomas Gore Browne [Harriet Browne]."
18 23 August 1860, "Diary of Thomas Gore Browne [Harriet Browne]."
19 *New Zealand Gazette,* 25 January 1861.
20 Arthur S. Thomson, *The Story of New Zealand: Past and Present – Savage and Civilized,* vol. 2 (London: John Murray, 1859), 297; *Southern Cross,* 24 April 1860.
21 *Southern Cross,* 29 January 1861.
22 31 January 1861, "Diary of Harriet Louisa Browne."
23 William Martin, *The Taranaki Question* (Auckland: Melanesian Press, 1860).
24 Ibid., prefacing remarks.
25 Harriet Louisa Browne, *Narrative of the Waitara Purchase and the Taranaki War,* ed. W.P. Morrell (Dunedin: University of Otago Press, 1965), 47.

26 F.D. Bell, F. Whitaker, and T.G. Browne, *Notes on Sir William Martin's Pamphlet Entitled the Taranaki Question* (Auckland: New Zealand Government, 1861); C.W. Richmond, *Memorandum on the Taranaki Question: Reviewing a Pamphlet by Sir William Martin, D.C.L., Late Chief Justice of New Zealeand [sic], on the Same Subject* (Auckland, 1861).

27 Browne to Newcastle, 4 December 1860, no. 55, *Correspondence and Papers Relating to the Maori Uprisings in New Zealand, 1861*, 169–255; 13 December 1860, "Diary of Thomas Gore Browne [Harriet Browne]."

28 Browne to Belhaven, 3 December 1860, "Sir Thomas Gore Browne Letterbook."

29 Browne to Newcastle, 4 December 1860, no. 55, *Correspondence and Papers Relating to the Maori Uprisings in New Zealand, 1861*, 171.

30 Browne to the Duke of Newcastle, [no date], "Sir Thomas Gore Browne Letterbook."

31 Browne to Herman Merivale, 15 October 1856, "Sir Thomas Gore Browne Letterbook."

32 Browne to Newcastle, 25 May 1860, no. 19, *Correspondence and Papers Relating to the Maori Uprisings in New Zealand, 1861*, 48; Browne to Newcastle, 25 May 1860, no. 21, ibid., 60; Browne to Newcastle, 28 June 1860, no. 27, ibid., 77–79; Browne to Newcastle, 7 September 1860, no. 45, ibid., 127–28; Browne to Newcastle, 31 October 1860, no. 50, ibid., 152–59.

33 Browne to Newcastle, 28 May 1860, no. 23, ibid., 66; Browne to Newcastle, 31 August 1860, no. 42, ibid., 124–25; Browne to Newcastle, 22 October 1860, no. 49, ibid., 151.

34 Browne to Newcastle, 28 April 1860, no. 16, ibid., 45; Browne to Newcastle, 25 May 1860, no. 21, ibid., 60–61.

35 Browne to Fortescue, 3 November 1860, "Sir Thomas Gore Browne Letterbook."

36 Browne to Gairdner, 28 May 1860, ibid.

37 Browne to Sewell, 13 June 1859, ibid.

38 6 March 1861, "Diary of Harriet Louisa Browne."

39 25 February 1861, ibid.; 6 March 1861, ibid.

40 Browne to Newcastle, 9 September 1860, "Sir Thomas Gore Browne Letterbook."

41 See Karen M. Morin, "(Anti?) Colonial Women Writing War," *New Zealand Geographer* 56, 1 (2000): 22–29; Karen M. Morin and Lawrence D. Berg, "Gendering Resistance: British Colonial Narratives of Wartime New Zealand," *Journal of Historical Geography* 27, 2 (2001): 196–222.

42 Mary Martin, 21 May 1860, *Extracts of Letters from New Zealand on the War Question*, 5–7.

43 Caroline Abraham, 24 April 1860, ibid., 1–4.

44 Morin and Berg, "Gendering Resistance," 211.

45 8 August 1860, "Diary of Thomas Gore Browne [Harriet Browne]"; 23 August 1860, ibid.; 9 September 1860, ibid.; 24 September 1860, ibid.; 4 October 1860, ibid.; 14 October 1860, ibid.; 25 October 1860, ibid.; 6 January 1861, ibid.; 26 January 1861, "Diary of Harriet Browne"; 25 February 1861, ibid.; 28 February 1861, ibid.; 2 June 1861, ibid.; 2 July 1861, ibid.

46 *Auckland Examiner*, 4 April 1860, 11 April 1860, 21 April 1860.

47 Browne to Newcastle, [n.d.] "Sir Thomas Gore Browne Letterbook"; Jan Pilditch, ed., *The Letters and Journals of Reverend John Morgan*, vol. 2 (Glasgow: Grimsay Press, 2010), 559–99.

48 Frederick Alonzo Carrington, *The Land Question of Taranaki, with Suggestions for Improving the Condition of the Aboriginal Inhabitants and Developing the Resources of New Zealand* (New Plymouth: Taranaki News Office, 1860), 14.

49 Ibid., 5, 25.

50 J.S. Tullett, "Carrington, Frederic Alonzo-Biography," *Dictionary of New Zealand Biography, Te Ara-the Encyclopedia of New Zealand*, http://www.teara.govt.nz/remap_url.php?src=en/biographies/1c7/1.

51 Octavius Hadfield, *One of England's Little Wars. A Letter to the Right Hon. The Duke of Newcastle, Secretary of State for the Colonies* (London: Williams & Norgate, 1860), 7, 20–21.

52 Fox, *War in New Zealand*, 5, 44.
53 Martin, *Taranaki Question*, 1–10.
54 Bell, Whitaker, and Browne, *Notes on Sir William Martin's Pamphlet*, 5; Richmond, *Memorandum on the Taranaki Question*, 2–3.
55 James Busby, *Remarks Upon a Pamphlet Entitled "the Taranaki Question," by Sir William Martin, D.C.L., Late Chief Justice of New Zealand* (Auckland: Philip Kunst, Southern Cross Office, 1860), 3–11; George Clarke, *Remarks Upon a Pamphlet by James Busby, Esq. Commenting Upon a Pamphlet Entitled the 'Taranaki Question,' by Sir William Martin, D.C.L., Late Chief Justice of New Zealand* (Auckland: Philip Kunst, 1861), 6–14.
56 Hadfield, *One of England's Little Wars*, 7–9, 12; Fox, *War in New Zealand*, 26–27, 33; Martin, *Taranaki Question*, 13, 19–20, 23; Clarke, *Remarks Upon a Pamphlet by James Busby, Esq.*, 6–14, 19.
57 Martin, *The Taranaki Question*, 1.
58 Ibid., 23–24.
59 Bell, Whitaker, and Browne, *Notes on Sir William Martin's Pamphlet*, 24–25.
60 Edward Harold Browne, *The Case of the War in New Zealand* (Cambridge: Deighton, Bell, and Co., 1860), 9–11; Bell, Whitaker, and Browne, *Notes on Sir William Martin's Pamphlet*, 21; Richmond, *Memorandum on the Taranaki Question*, 3–5.
61 Browne, *Case of the War in New Zealand*, 29, 35–36, 41–44; Bell, Whitaker, and Browne, *Notes on Sir William Martin's Pamphlet*, 27–28, 92; Richmond, *Memorandum on the Taranaki Question*, 2–3.
62 Michael Belgrave, *Historical Frictions: Maori Claims and Reinvented Histories* (Auckland: Auckland University Press, 2005), 235.
63 Ibid., 230.
64 Ibid., 235–40.
65 11 May 1861, "Diary of Harriet Browne."
66 Belgrave, *Historical Frictions*, 261.
67 Waitangi Tribunal, *The Taranaki Report: Kaupapa Tautahi: Wai 143: Muru Me Te Raupata = the Muru and Raupatu of the Taranaki Land and People,* (Wellington: Waitangi Tribunal, 1996), 1.6, 3.6, 3.8.
68 Ibid., 3.6.
69 Browne to Gairdner, 27 September 1857, "Sir Thomas Gore Browne Letterbook."
70 *Southern Cross*, 21 June 1859.
71 Richmond, *Memorandum on the Taranaki Question*, 2; Bell, Whitaker, and Browne, *Notes on Sir William Martin's Pamphlet*, 9.
72 24 July 1860, "Diary of Thomas Gore Browne [Harriet Browne]."
73 24 July 1860, Ibid.
74 James Belich, *The New Zealand Wars and the Victorian Interpretation of Racial Conflict: The Maori, the British, and the New Zealand Wars* (Montreal and Kingston: McGill-Queen's University Press, 1986), 76–80.
75 Damen Ward, "Territory, Jurisdiction, and Colonial Governance: 'A Bill to Repeal the British Constitution,' 1856–60," *Journal of Legal History* 33, 3 (2012): 313–33.
76 Ibid., 331.
77 Clarke, *Remarks Upon a Pamphlet by James Busby, Esq.*, 3–5, 14, 19, 21–22; Bell, Whitaker, and Browne, *Notes on Sir William Martin's Pamphlet*, 28; Fox, *War in New Zealand*, 26–27; Hadfield, *Second Year of One of England's Little Wars*, 22; Martin, *Taranaki Question*, 10, 13; Martin, *Remarks on 'Notes Published for the New Zealand Government,' January 1861: And on Mr. Richmond's Memorandum on the Taranaki Question, December 1860* (Auckland: Melanesian Press, 1861), 3; Richmond, *Memorandum on the Taranaki Question*, 1, 3.
78 Martin, *Taranaki Question*, 10.

79 Ibid., 9–10.
80 Mark Hickford, *Lords of the Land: Indigenous Property Rights and the Jurisprudence of Empire* (Oxford: Oxford University Press, 2011), 420–34.
81 William Martin, *England and the New Zealanders: Remarks Upon a Despatch from the Right Hon. Earl Grey to Governor Grey, Dated to Dec. 23 1846* (Auckland: College Press, 1847).
82 Busby, *Remarks Upon a Pamphlet Entitled "the Taranaki Question,"* 7.
83 Ibid., 7.
84 Ibid., 5.
85 Lindsey MacDonald, "The Political Philosophy of Property Rights" (PhD diss., Canterbury University, 2009), 158.
86 Ibid., 11, 13–14.
87 Clarke, *Remarks Upon a Pamphlet by James Busby, Esq.*, 3.
88 Ibid., 5.
89 Ibid., 4.
90 Browne to Busby, 21 December 1860, "Sir Thomas Gore Browne Letterbook."
91 Browne, *Case of the War in New Zealand*, 25.
92 Browne to Newcastle, 4 December 1860, no. 55, *Correspondence and Papers Relating to the Maori Uprisings in New Zealand, 1861*, 169–96; *Southern Cross*, 3 July 1860.
93 Hickford, *Lords of the Land*, 382–85.
94 Roberta L. Bagshaw, ed., *No Better Land: The 1860 Diaries of the Anglican Colonial Bishop George Hills* (Victoria: Sono Nis Press, 1996), 117; Peter Murray, *The Devil and Mr. Duncan* (Victoria: Sono Nis Press, 1985), 57.
95 William Duncan, 30 July 1860, Journal, BCA, MS 2758, AO 1715.
96 Robin Fisher, *Contact and Conflict: Indian-European Relations in British Columbia, 1774–1890* (Vancouver: UBC Press, 1992), 119–25.
97 William Duncan, *The British Columbia Mission, or, Metlahkatlah* (London: Church Missionary House, 1871), 5.
98 *Church Missionary Intelligencer*, July 1856.
99 Eugene Stock, *Metlakahtla and the North Pacific Mission of the Church Missionary Society* (London: Seeley, Jackson, & Halliday, 1880), 17.
100 William Duncan, 20 June 1857, Journal.
101 Murray, *Devil and Mr. Duncan*, 29.
102 Jean Usher, *William Duncan of Metlakatla: A Victorian Missionary in British Columbia* (Ottawa: National Museum of Man, 1974), 39.
103 William Duncan, 20 June 1857, Journal.
104 Usher, *William Duncan of Metlakatla*, 29.
105 Ibid., 47–48.
106 Ibid., 52, 63–64.
107 Robert T. Boyd, *The Coming of the Spirit of Pestilence* (Seattle: University of Washington Press, 1999), 196–99.
108 Susan Neylan, *The Heavens Are Changing: Nineteenth-Century Protestant Missions and Tsimshian Christianity* (Montreal and Kingston: McGill-Queen's University Press, 2003), 135, 211.
109 R.C. Mayne, *Four Years in British Columbia and Vancouver Island* (London: John Murray, 1862), 211; Matthew Macfie, *Vancouver Island and British Columbia: Their History, Resources, and Prospects* (London: Longman, Green, Longman, Roberts, and Green, 1865), 482–86.
110 Stock, *Metlakahtla and the North Pacific Mission of the Church Missionary Society*; Henry Solomon Wellcome, *The Story of Metlakahtla* (London: Saxon & Co., 1887); John William Arctander, *The Apostle of Alaska: The Story of William Duncan* (New York: Fleming H. Revell Company, 1909).

111 Murray, *Devil and Mr. Duncan*; Adele Perry, "The Autocracy of Love and the Legitimacy of Empire: Intimacy, Power and Scandal in Nineteenth Century Metlakahtlah," *Gender and History* 16, 2 (2004): 261–88.

112 Usher, *William Duncan of Metlakatla*; Clarence Bolt, *Thomas Crosby and the Tsimshian: Small Shoes for Feet Too Large* (Vancouver: UBC Press, 1992); Neylan, *Heavens Are Changing*.

113 Neylan, *Heavens Are Changing*, 5.

114 Bagshaw, *No Better Land*, 55–56, 101, 117.

115 Ibid., 117.

116 Douglas to Newcastle, 18 February 1860, CO 60/7 no. 3622, *British Columbia: 1860*, vol. 3, Colonial Despatches of British Columbia, ed. James Hendrickson (Victoria: University of Victoria, 1988), 22–23.

117 Mayne, *Four Years in British Columbia and Vancouver Island*, 210.

118 William Duncan, 12 June 1860, Journal; 13 June 1860, ibid.; 14 June 1860, ibid.; 16 June 1860, ibid.; 17 June 1860, ibid.; 18 June 1860, ibid.

119 29 May 1860, ibid. This journal entry details Duncan's consultation with Bishop Hills: "Had a long talk about the Mission and the Indians. He approved entirely of my plans for carrying on the work of the Mission and promised at once to write officially to the Governor on the subject."

120 9 July 1860, ibid. (Elijah at Mount Carmel, 1 Kings 18); 16 July 1860, ibid. (Sodom and Gomorrah, Genesis 18–19); 23 July 1860, ibid. (the Barren fig tree, Matthew 21:18–21); 5 August 1860, ibid. (Jonah/2 Chronicles 33); 10 August 1860, ibid. (Daniel 5).

121 21 June 1860, ibid.; Duncan to Douglas, 22 June 1860, "Colonial Correspondence," BCA, GR1372, BO1326, F498.

122 Duncan to Douglas, 22 June 1860, "Colonial Correspondence."

123 Usher, *William Duncan of Metlakatla*, 57.

124 Bagshaw, *No Better Land*, 96–97.

125 Ibid., 63. Hills's diary reveals that the Indian Improvement Committee was initiated by himself, Captain Prevost, Dr. Tolmie, Mr. Finlayson, Captain Gossett, Mr. Wood, Charles Fraser, Mr. McKay, and Revs. Dowson and Dundas, all prominent members of Victoria's colonial society.

126 William Duncan, 21 June 1860, Journal.

127 Douglas to Newcastle, 7 July 1860, CO 305/14 no. 8319, *Vancouver Island: 1860*, vol. 6, Colonial Despatches of British Columbia. ed. James Hendrickson (Victoria: University of Victoria), 37–40.

128 Ibid.

129 Ibid.

130 Douglas to Baynes, 3 August 1860, "Vancouver Island/Colonial Correspondence Outward," BCA, C/AA/30.1J/1A, vol. 2.

131 Ibid.

132 Douglas to Baynes, 3 August 1860, "Vancouver Island/Colonial Correspondence Outward"; Douglas to Newcastle, 7 July 1860, CO 305/14 no. 8319, *Vancouver Island: 1860*, 37–40.

133 Douglas to Newcastle, 7 July 1860, CO 305/14 no. 8319, ibid., 37–40.

134 Adele Perry, *Colonial Family: Intimacy, Mobility and Power in the Nineteenth-Century Imperial World* (Cambridge: Cambridge University Press, 2015), 135–39.

135 Ibid., 138.

136 William Duncan, 22 June 1860, Journal; 24 June 1860, ibid.; 25 June 1860, ibid.; 30 June 1860, ibid.; 1 July 1860, ibid.; 2 July 1860, ibid.; 9 July 1860, ibid.; 23 July 1860, ibid.

137 25 June 1860, ibid.

138 *British Colonist*, 30 June 1860.

139 Ibid., 3 July 1860.

140 William Duncan, 30 June 1860, Journal; 2 July 1860, ibid.

141 30 June 1860, ibid.

142 2 July 1860, ibid.

143 23 July 1860, ibid.

144 Mayne, *Four Years in British Columbia and Vancouver Island*, 78.

145 Duncan, *British Columbia Mission*, 53–54.

146 See George Lang, *Making Wawa: The Genesis of Chinook Jargon* (Vancouver: UBC Press, 2008).

147 John S. Lutz, *Makúk: A New History of Aboriginal-White Relations* (Vancouver: UBC Press, 2008), 193.

148 Ibid., x-xi.

149 Ibid., 301.

150 Usher, *William Duncan of Metlakatla*, 24–25.

151 Bagshaw, *No Better Land*; Society for the Propagation of the Gospel in Foreign Parts, "British Columbia Papers, 1858–1861," BCA, H/A/So2/vol. 1. Bishop Hills's diary and correspondence by A.C. Garrett detail their use of Chinook *wawa* in favour of other Aboriginal languages.

152 *British Colonist*, 23 June 1860. Regarding Duncan's translation of Douglas: "One of the Hyters complained that his people did not understand the Simpsean language; and addressed those of his tribe present, saying that Governor Douglas was telling the Simpsean and Tongas tribes to exterminate the Hyters."

153 William Duncan, 9 August 1860, Journal.

154 19 June 1860, ibid. In this entry Duncan details how Aboriginal peoples from Nass and Fort Rupert had requested him to live in their communities, how Douglas had asked him to remain in Victoria, and how Ts'msyen persons had urged him "to commence a village for the better disposed (or wise people as they say) that they may at once be enabled to improve and practice what they are taught." These comments reflect the multiple demands on Duncan and the Ts'msyen impetus for the foundation of Metlakatla.

155 2 August 1860, ibid.

156 Murray, *Devil and Mr. Duncan*, 99.

157 Bagshaw, *No Better Land*, 24–25.

158 Duncan to Douglas, 25 October 1860, "Colonial Correspondence."

159 Garrett to Douglas, 16 April 1861, "Colonial Correspondence," BCA, GR1372, BO1356, F1385.

160 *British Colonist*, 15 April 1861; *The Press*, 16 April 1861.

161 Pemberton to Douglas, 16 April 1861, "Colonial Correspondence," BCA, GR1372, BO1356, F1385.

162 *British Colonist*, 20 April 1860.

163 Ibid., 20 April 1860.

164 William Young to Pemberton, [?] June 1861, "Vancouver Island/Colonial Correspondence Outward," BCA, C/AA/30.1J/2A, vol. 2, 182B-183A.

165 Ibid.

166 *British Colonist*, 20 July 1861.

167 Ibid., 20 July 1861.

168 Ibid., 23 July 1861, 26 July 1861, 1 August 1861, 7 August 1861.

169 Ibid., 15 August 1861.

170 Pemberton to Douglas, 1 September 1861, "Colonial Correspondence."

171 *British Colonist*, 5 September 1861.

172 *The Press*, 5 September 1861.

173 Ibid., 5 September 1861.

174 Pemberton to Douglas, 13 September 1861, "Colonial Correspondence."

175 Ibid.

176 Willam Young to A.C. Garrett, 7 August 1860, "Vancouver Island/Colonial Correspondence Outward," BCA, C/AA/30.1J/1A, vol. 2.
177 Second *Victoria Gazette*, 4 July 1860.
178 *British Colonist*, 20 October 1862.
179 Ibid., 14 September 1859, 19 April 1860, 17 May 1860, 14 September 1860, 5 October 1860, 11 October 1860, 12 October 1860, 13 October 1860, 16 October 1860, 14 March 1861, 20 March 1861, 10 April 1861, 3 May 1861, 8 August 1861, 13 August 1861, 14 October 1861.
180 Bolt, *Thomas Crosby and the Tsimshian*, 44, 77, 82, 84.

Chapter 7: The Imperial Press

 1 D.G.F. Macdonald, *British Columbia and Vancouver Island* (London: Longman, Green, Longman, Roberts and Green, 1862), 299.
 2 Ibid., 28–29, 224, 391.
 3 Ibid., 70.
 4 Ibid., 29, 54, 56, 65, 221, 229, 314–15, 378, 469, 489, 501–2.
 5 William Mark, *Cariboo: A True and Correct Narrative* (Stockton: M. Weight, 1863); John Emmerson, *British Columbia and Vancouver Island: Voyages, Travels, and Adventures* (London: W. Ainsley, 1865).
 6 George F.G. Stanley, *Mapping the Frontier: Charles Wilson's Diary of the Survey of the 49th Parallel, 1858–1862, while Secretary of the British Boundary Commission* (Seattle: University of Washington Press, 1970), 2; H. Barry Cotton, "The Retribution of D.G.F. Macdonald C.E.," *BC Historical News* 32, 1 (1998/99): 14–15; Stella Higgins, "Colonial Vancouver Island and British Columbia as Seen through British Eyes, 1849–1871" (MA thesis, University of Victoria, 1972), 10.
 7 D.G.F. Macdonald, *Lecture on British Columbia and Vancouver's Island* (London: Longman, Green, Longman, Roberts & Green, 1863); John Martin, "Macdonald, Duncan George Forbes (1827/28–1884)," *Oxford Dictionary of National Biography*, http://www.teara.govt.nz/remap_url.php?src=en/biographies/1c7/1.
 8 Macdonald, *British Columbia and Vancouver Island*, 299.
 9 William Swainson, *New Zealand and Its Colonization* (London: Smith, Elder and Co., 1859), 65–66; Macdonald, *British Columbia and Vancouver Island*, 298–99.
10 Macdonald, *British Columbia and Vancouver Island*, 161; John Roebuck, 13 March 1862, *Hansard's Parliamentary Debates, Third Series*, vol. 165 (London: Cornelius Buck, 1862), 1448–49.
11 Macdonald, *British Columbia and Vancouver Island*, 131–32, 169–70, 328–30, 357–58.
12 Ibid., 328–29.
13 James Belich, *Replenishing the Earth: The Settler Revolution and the Rise of the Anglo-World, 1783–1939* (Auckland: Oxford University Press, 2009).
14 For example, between 24 August 1860 and 30 June 1862 the *Southern Cross* published thirty-one metropolitan articles on the Taranaki War and ten leading articles commenting on metropolitan coverage of the war.
15 *Southern Cross*, 15 February 1861.
16 Simon Potter, "Empire and the English Press, C. 1857–1914," in *Newspapers and Empire in Ireland and Britain: Reporting the British Empire, c. 1857–1921*, ed. Simon Potter (Dublin: Four Courts Press, 2004), 47; Alan Lester, "British Settler Discourse and the Circuits of Empire," *History Workshop Journal* 1, 54 (2002): 24–48.
17 *Taranaki Herald*, 2 February 1861; *Southern Cross*, 15 February 1861.
18 James Grant, *The Newspaper Press: Its Origin – Its Progress – and Present Position*, vol. 2 (London: Tinsley Brothers, 1871), 459–60.

19 *The Times, The History of* The Times, *the Tradition Established, 1841–1884* (London: The Office of *The Times,* 1939), 147.

20 Glenn R. Wilkinson, *Depictions and Images of War in Edwardian Newspapers, 1899–1914* (Houndsmills, Basingstoke: Palgrave Macmillan, 2003), 6–7.

21 Henry Richard Fox Bourne, *English Newspapers: Chapters in the History of Journalism,* vol. 2 (London: Chatto, 1887), 232.

22 Aled Jones, *Powers of the Press: Newspapers, Power and the Public in Nineteenth Century England* (Aldershot: Scolar Press, 1996), 109–10.

23 Bourne, *English Newspapers,* 232.

24 Grant, *Newspaper Press,* 321.

25 Ibid., 4, 26.

26 *The Times, A Newspaper History, 1785–1935* (London: *The Times* Publishing Company, Limited, 1935), 139–42.

27 Ibid., 142.

28 Grant, *Newspaper Press,* 53–54.

29 *Southern Cross,* 11 February 1858, 24 August 1860; *Taranaki Herald,* 2 February 1861.

30 *Taranaki Herald,* 2 February 1861

31 James W. Carey, *Communication as Culture: Essays on Media and Society* (Boston: Unwin Hyman, 2009), 12–13, 17.

32 Geoffrey Hamilton, "Delane, John Thadeus (1817–1879)," *Oxford Dictionary of National Biography,* http://www.oxforddnb.com/view/article/7440?docPos=1.

33 *The Times, History of* The Times, 320–25.

34 Ibid., 166.

35 A.J. Harrop, *England and the Maori Wars* (London: Whitcombe and Tombs, 1937); James Belich, *The New Zealand Wars and the Victorian Interpretation of Racial Conflict: The Maori, the British, and the New Zealand Wars* (Montreal and Kingston: McGill-Queen's University Press, 1986).

36 *Saturday Review,* 26 May 1860, 2 June 1860; *The Times,* 18 June 1860.

37 *The Times,* 13 June 1860, 18 June 1860, 14 September 1860, 17 September 1860.

38 Ibid., 13 June 1860.

39 Ibid., 13 June 1860, 18 June 1860.

40 *Southern Cross,* 24 August 1860.

41 *The Times,* 10 October 1860.

42 Ibid., 14 November 1860.

43 Ibid., 17 November 1860.

44 Ibid., 20 November 1860, 23 November 1860.

45 Octavius Hadfield, *A Sequel to "One of England's Little Wars": Being an Account of the Real Origin of the War in New Zealand, Its Present Stage, and the Future Prospects of the Colony* (London: Williams and Norgate, 1861), 2.

46 Articles from *The Times*'s Melbourne correspondent: 14 September 1860, 14 November 1860, 15 November 1860, 18 December 1860, January 14 1861, 18 March 1861, 13 April 1860, 13 May 1861, 16 August 1861, 16 September 1861, 16 December 1861.

47 22 November 1861, "Diary of Thomas Gore Browne," ANZ, ADCZ 17006 W5431/4.

48 D.G. Edwards, "Chapman, Henry Samuel-Biography," *Dictionary of New Zealand Biography, Te Ara-the Encyclopedia of New Zealand,* http://www.teara.govt.nz/remap_url.php?src=en/biographies/1c14/1.

49 19 December 1860, "Diary of Thomas Gore Browne [Harriet Browne]," ANZ, ADCZ, W5431/3.

50 K.R. Miller, "Henry Samuel Chapman, Colonizer and Colonist" (MA thesis, University of New Zealand, 1956); Peter Spiller, *The Chapman Legal Family* (Wellington: Victoria University Press, 1992).

51 Miller, "Henry Samuel Chapman," 4, 7, 36; Spiller, *Chapman Legal Family*, 21–23, 29.

52 Miller, "Henry Samuel Chapman," 102, 114; Spiller, *Chapman Legal Family*, 35.

53 Lucy Brown et al., "Foreign Correspondent," in *Dictionary of Nineteenth-Century Journalism*, ed. Laurel Brake and Marysa Demoor (London: Academia Press, 2009), 224–25.

54 *The Times*, 21 November 1860.

55 Ibid., 21 November 1860, 23 May 1861.

56 Catherine Hall, *Civilising Subjects: Metropole and Colony in the English Imagination, 1830–1867* (Chicago: University of Chicago Press, 2002), 358.

57 *The Times*, 23 May 1861.

58 Ibid., 14 February 1861, 23 May 1861, 28 August 1861, 30 August 1861.

59 Ibid., 16 August 1861.

60 Ibid., 28 August 1861.

61 Ibid., 30 August 1861.

62 Ibid., 16 December 1861.

63 Ibid., 13 June 1860 (Sydney correspondent); 7 August 1860 (*Sydney Morning Herald*); 13 September 1860 (*Sydney Morning Herald*); 17 October 1860 (*Sydney Morning Herald*); 14 November 1860 (Melbourne correspondent; Sydney correspondent); 15 November 1861 (Melbourne correspondent); 18 December 1860 (Melbourne correspondent); 14 January 1861 (Melbourne correspondent); 18 March 1861 (Melbourne correspondent); 13 April 1861 (Melbourne correspondent); 13 May 1861 (Melbourne correspondent); 14 June 1861 (Melbourne *Argus*); 16 August 1861 (Melbourne correspondent); 16 September 1861 (Melbourne correspondent); 16 December 1861 (Melbourne correspondent).

64 *The Times*, 10 October 1860 (*Wanganui Chronicle*); 1 November 1860 (*Statistics of New Zealand*); 20 December 1860 (Auckland correspondent; New Plymouth correspondent); 18 June 1861 (*Taranaki Herald*); 24 October 1861 (*New Zealand Examiner*).

65 Registrar General, *Statistical Register of New South Wales for the Year 1861* (Sydney: Thomas Richards, 1862), 181; Registrar General, *Statistics of New Zealand for 1861* (Auckland: W.C. Wilson, 1862), no. 58.

66 Kerry Powell, "The Saturday Review," in *British Literary Magazines: The Victorian and Edwardian Age, 1837–1913*, ed. Alvin Sullivan, 379–83 (London: Greenwood Press, 1984).

67 Barbara Quinn Schmidt, "Cook, John Douglas (1808? –1868)," *Oxford Dictionary of National Biography*, http://oxforddnb.com/index/101006145.

68 *Taranaki Herald*, 2 February 1861; *Southern Cross*, 15 February 1861.

69 *Saturday Review*, 25 August 1860.

70 Ibid.

71 James Heartfield, *The Aborigines' Protection Society: Humanitarian Imperialism in Australia, New Zealand, Fiji, Canada, South Africa, and the Congo, 1836–1909* (New York: Columbia University Press, 2011), 63.

72 Thomas Buddle, *The Maori King Movement in New Zealand with a Full Report of the Native Meetings Held at Waikato, April and May, 1860* (Auckland: The 'New Zealander' Office, 1860); *Southern Cross*, 8 June 1860, 12 June 1860.

73 *Saturday Review*, 3 November 1860.

74 Ibid., 3 November 1860.

75 Ibid., 9 February 1861.

76 Ibid., 8 December 1860.

77 Ibid., 26 April 1862.

78 Ibid., 25 August 1860, 3 November 1860, 8 December 1860.

79 Ibid., 21 September 1861.

80 R.H. Hutton to C.W. Richmond, *The Richmond-Atkinson Papers*, vol. 1, ed. G.H. Scholefield (Wellington: R.E. Owen, Government Printer, 1960), 713.

81 G.C. Boase, H.C.G. Matthew, "Selwyn, Sir Charles Jasper (1813–1869)," *Oxford Dictionary of National Biography*, http://www.oxforddnb.com/index/101025064; Schmidt, "Cook, John Douglas (1808?-1868)."

82 Charles Selwyn, 11 April 1862, *Hansard's Parliamentary Debates, Third Series*, vol. 162 (London: Cornelius Buck, 1862), 488–98.

83 *Saturday Review*, 8 December 1860.

84 *Taranaki Herald*, 2 February 1861; *Southern Cross*, 15 February 1861.

85 *Southern Cross*, 5 November 1861.

86 Ibid., 5 November 1861.

87 Earl of Carnarvon, 14 June 1860, *Hansard's Parliamentary Debates, Third Series*, vol. 159 (London: Cornelius Buck, 1860), 417–18; Lord Alfred Churchill; Chichester Fortescue, 15 June 1860, ibid., 524–25; Charles Adderley; Chichester Fortescue, 13 March 1862, *Hansard's Parliamentary Debates, Third Series*, 1445–46.

88 Harrop, *England and the Maori Wars*, 70, 111, 117–18

89 William Carew Hazlitt, *British Columbia and Vancouver Island* (London: G. Routledge & Co., 1858), 134–49; *The Handbook of British Columbia and Emigrant's Guide to the Gold Fields*, (London: W. Oliver, [1862]), 3–7, 137–70, 172, 179; Robert Michael Ballantyne, *Handbook to the New Gold Fields* (Edinburgh: A. Strahan, 1858.), 2, 11, 28, 46–47, 57–66, 107, 110, 111; William Carew Hazlitt, *The Great Gold Fields of Cariboo* (London: Routledge, Wanre and Routledge, 1862), 99, 138–56.

90 Mark, *Cariboo*, 3; Matthew Macfie, *Vancouver Island and British Columbia: Their History, Resources, and Prospects* (London: Longman, Green, Longman, Roberts, and Green, 1865), 75; Charles Alfred Bayley, "Early Life on Vancouver Island [1878]," BCA, E/B/B34.2, 20.

91 Macfie, *Vancouver Island and British Columbia*, 75.

92 *British Colonist*, 10 June 1862, 26 June 1862. The *Otago Daily Times* carried an article by Donald Fraser in its edition on 18 December 1861.

93 *British Colonist*, 26 June 1862.

94 *Otago Daily Times*, 18 December 1861, 2 June 1862, 28 June 1862, 14 August 1862, 25 August 1862, 24 September 1862, 17 October 1862, 10 November 1862, 15 December 1862.

95 James Hendrickson, "Fraser, Donald," *Dictionary of Canadian Biography Online*, http://www.biographi.ca/en/search.php.

96 Mark, *Cariboo*, 3, 30, 34; Emmerson, *British Columbia and Vancouver Island*, 52; *British Colonist*, 5 August 1862.

97 Macdonald, *Lecture on British Columbia and Vancouver's Island*, 46.

98 Emmerson, *British Columbia and Vancouver Island*, 95.

99 *Government Gazette*, 30 September 1861, 19 October 1861. Property tax assessments reveal that Fraser owned 683 acres in Victoria and the neighbouring districts of North and South Saanich, including over one hundred lots within Victoria itself.

100 Hendrickson, "Fraser, Donald."

101 *The Times*, 4 August 1858, 5 August 1858, 12 October 1858, 30 November 1858, 1 December 1858, 25 December 1858.

102 Ibid., 4 August 1858.

103 Ibid., 4 August 1858, 27 August 1858, 6 February 1862.

104 Ibid., 27 August 1858.

105 Ibid., 27 September 1859.

106 Ibid., 6 February 1862.

107 R.C. Mayne, *Four Years in British Columbia and Vancouver Island* (London: John Murray, 1862), 24–25.

108 *The Times*, 27 August 1858.

109 Ibid., 19 January 1859.

110 Ibid., 4 October 1860.

111 Ibid., 27 August 1858.

112 C.L. Higham, *Noble, Wretched and Redeemable: Protestant Missionaries to the Indians in Canada and the United States, 1820–1900* (Albuquerque/Calgary: University of New Mexico Press/University of Calgary Press, 2000), 31–60.

113 *The Times*, 17 February 1859, 28 June 1859, 8 September 1859, 1 November 1859, 30 January 1860, 4 October 1860, 8 August 1861, 5 February 1862, 6 February 1862, 15 August 1862.

114 Ibid., 17 February 1859, 3 June 1859, 28 June 1859, 26 July 1859, 21 September 1861, 6 February 1862, 25 March 1862.

115 Ibid., 3 June 1859.

116 *British Colonist*, 5 June 1860.

117 Ibid:, 21 September 1861.

118 Ibid., 5 August 1862.

119 *Saturday Review*, 2 October 1858.

120 Dan Davy, "Selling Australia: New South Wales Emigration Manuals and Scottish Perceptions of Australia, 1820–1850" (MSc, University of Edinburgh, 2007), 34, 49–54.

121 Miles Fairburn, *The Ideal Society and Its Enemies: The Foundations of Modern New Zealand Society, 1850–1900* (Auckland: Auckland University Press, 1989), 20–26.

122 James Belich, *Making Peoples: A History of the New Zealanders, from Polynesian Settlement to the End of the Nineteenth Century* (Honolulu: University of Hawaii Press, 2001), 279–87.

123 Higgins, "Colonial Vancouver Island and British Columbia," 71.

124 Grant W. Couquhoun, "Description of Vancouver Island, by Its First Colonist," *Journal of the Royal Geographical Society* 27 (1851): 268–320; Kinahan Cornwallis, *The New El Dorado: Or, British Columbia* (London: Thomas Cautley Newby, 1858); Henry De Groot, *British Columbia: Its Condition and Prospects, Soil, Climate, and Mineral Resources, Considered* (San Francisco: Alta California's job office, 1859); Fenton Aylmer, *A Cruise in the Pacific: From the Log of a Naval Officer*, vol. 2 (London: Hurst and Blackwett, 1860); Joseph Despard Pemberton, *Facts and Figures Relating to Vancouver Island and British Columbia Showing What to Expect and How to Get There* (London: Longman, Green, Longman, and Roberts, 1860); A Returned Digger, *The Newly Discovered Gold Fields of British Columbia* (London: Darton & Hodge, 1862); C.E. Barrett-Lennard, *Travels in British Columbia: With the Narrative of a Yacht Voyage Round Vancouver's Island* (London: Hurst and Blackett, 1862); Charles Forbes, *Vancouver Island: Its Resources and Capabilities as a Colony* (Victoria: The Colonial Government, 1862); A.J. Langley, *A Glance at British Columbia and Vancouver's Island in 1861* (London: Robert Harwick, 1862); Anonymous, *London International Exhibition, Catalogue of the Vancouver Contribution with a Short Account of Vancouver Island and British Columbia* (London, 1862); Macdonald, *British Columbia and Vancouver Island;* Mayne, *Four Years in British Columbia and Vancouver Island;* Alexander Rattray, *Vancouver Island and British Columbia: Where They Are; What They Are; and What They May Become* (London: Smith, Elder, 1862); Mark, *Cariboo;* Macdonald, *Lecture on British Columbia and Vancouver's Island;* Macfie, *Vancouver Island and British Columbia;* Emmerson, *British Columbia and Vancouver Island.*

125 Ballantyne, *Handbook to the New Gold Fields;* John Domer, *New British Gold-Fields: A Guide to British Columbia and Vancouver Island* (London: William Henry Angel, 1858); Hazlitt, *British Columbia and Vancouver Island;* W. Parker Snow, *British Columbia, Emigration and Our Colonies Considered Practically* (London: Piper, Stephenson, and Spence, 1858); Hazlitt, *The Great Gold Fields of Caribou;* Edward Graham Alston, *Handbook to Vancouver Island and British Columbia* (London: F. Alger, 1862); Anonymous, *The Handbook of British Columbia and Emigrant's Guide to the Gold Fields* (London: W. Oliver, 1862); J.D. Churchill and J. Cooper, *British Columbia and Vancouver Island Considered as a Field for Commercial Enterprise* (London: Rees and Collin, 1866).

126 See Gethin Matthews, "Gold Fever: The Stampede from South Wales to British Columbia in 1862," *North American Journal of Welsh Studies* 5, 2 (2005): 54–83.

127 Alexis Weedon, *Victorian Publishing: The Economics of Book Production for a Mass Market, 1836–1916* (Aldershot; Burlington: Ashgate, 2003), 49.

128 *British Colonist*, 20 June 1862.

129 Alston, *Handbook to Vancouver Island and British Columbia*, 4; Returned Digger, *Newly Discovered Gold Fields of British Columbia*, 54; Ballantyne, *Handbook to the New Gold Fields*, 77–78; Churchill, *British Columbia and Vancouver Island*, 2; Cornwallis, *New El Dorado*, 30; Domer, *New British Gold-Fields*, 20; Forbes, *Vancouver Island*, 25; Couquhoun, "Description of Vancouver Island," 293; Anonymous, *London International Exhibition*, 1; Macdonald, *British Columbia and Vancouver Island*, 327; Macfie, *Vancouver Island and British Columbia*, 429, 488; Mayne, *Four Years in British Columbia and Vancouver Island*, 243, 250; Pemberton, *Facts and Figures Relating to Vancouver Island and British Columbia*, 132; Rattray, *Vancouver Island and British Columbia*, 13. Estimates of Vancouver Island's Aboriginal population ranged between ten thousand and twenty thousand, and British Columbia's between thirty thousand and sixty thousand. They were based upon guesswork.

130 Returned Digger, *Newly Discovered Gold Fields of British Columbia*, 54; Aylmer, *Cruise in the Pacific*, 98; Ballantyne, *Handbook to the New Gold Fields*, 78; Barrett-Lennard, *Travels in British Columbia*, 41–44, 59; Domer, *New British Gold-Fields*, 24; Emmerson, *British Columbia and Vancouver Island*, 24; Forbes, *Vancouver Island*, 25; Couquhoun, "Description of Vancouver Island," 296. Anonymous, *Handbook of British Columbia*, 25–27; Hazlitt, *British Columbia and Vancouver Island*, 189–90; Macfie, *Vancouver Island and British Columbia*, 458. Mark, *Cariboo*, 23; Macdonald, *British Columbia and Vancouver Island*, 17, 70, 127, 131–33, 136, 140, 169, 187–88, 199.

131 See Elizabeth Vibert, *Traders' Tales: Narratives of Cultural Encounters in the Columbian Plateau, 1807–1846* (Norman: University of Oklahoma Press, 1997).

132 Pemberton, *Facts and Figures Relating to Vancouver Island and British Columbia*, 128.

133 Ibid., 130–31. See also "Pemberton Family," BCA, MS-1295.

134 Robin Fisher, *Contact and Conflict: Indian-European Relations in British Columbia, 1774–1890* (Vancouver: UBC Press, 1992), 73–94.

135 Marie Louise Pratt, *Imperial Eyes: Travel Writing and Transculturation* (New York: Routledge, 1992), 15–107.

136 Aylmer, *Cruise in the Pacific*, 88–89, 98; Barrett-Lennard, *Travels in British Columbia*, 41–42; De Groot, *British Columbia*, 9; Domer, *New British Gold-Fields*, 23; Emmerson, *British Columbia and Vancouver Island*, 130; Forbes, *Vancouver Island*, 20, 25; Couquhoun, "Description of Vancouver Island," 296. Anonymous, *Handbook of British Columbia*, 27; Macfie, *Vancouver Island and British Columbia*, 470; Mayne, *Four Years in British Columbia and Vancouver Island*, 73; Macdonald, *British Columbia and Vancouver Island*, 131; Macdonald, *Lecture on British Columbia and Vancouver's Island*, 47–48.

137 Mayne, *Four Years in British Columbia and Vancouver Island*, 354.

138 Rattray, *Vancouver Island and British Columbia*, 172–73.

139 Aylmer, *Cruise in the Pacific*, 98; Domer, *New British Gold-Fields*, 24.

140 Forbes, *Vancouver Island*, 25; Mayne, *Four Years in British Columbia and Vancouver Island*, 50.

141 Cornwallis, *New El Dorado*, 223.

142 Aylmer, *Cruise in the Pacific*, 88–89, 153–58; Barrett-Lennard, *Travels in British Columbia*, 41–42, 59–66; Mayne, *Four Years in British Columbia and Vancouver Island*, 73–78, 190.

143 Vibert, *Traders' Tales*, 98.

144 *Saturday Review*, 25 October 1862.

145 Ibid., 25 October 1862.

146 Barrett-Lennard, *Travels in British Columbia*, 41–42.

147 *Saturday Review*, 25 October 1862.
148 Clive Emsley, "Mayne, Sir Richard (1796–1868)," *Oxford Dictionary of National Biography*, http://www.oxforddnb.com/view/article/18444/18445; James Cowan, *The New Zealand Wars: A History of the Maori Campaigns and the Pioneering Period*, vol. 1 (Wellington: W.A.G. Skinner, 1922), 322. Following Mayne's promotion to the rank of commander he was transferred to New Zealand, where he was severely wounded at the battle of Rangiriri on 20 November 1863.
149 Richard Charles Mayne, "Journal of Admiral Richard Charles Mayne, 17 February 1857–31 December 1860," BCA, E/B/M45.
150 Mayne, *Four Years in British Columbia and Vancouver Island*, 423.
151 Ibid., 73–78, 190–93, 210, 216.
152 Ibid., 99–102, 190–211.
153 Ibid., 337.
154 Robert Hogg, *Men and Manliness on the Frontier: Queensland and British Columbia in the Mid-Nineteenth Century* (Basingstoke: Palgrave Macmillan, 2012), 2.
155 Mayne, *Four Years in British Columbia and Vancouver Island*, 305–52. Mayne's chapter, "Religious and Educational Condition of the Colonies," drew extensively on Duncan's own journal, describing Duncan as the "foremost" Protestant missionary on the Northwest Coast.
156 Ibid., 164–65.
157 Simon Potter, "Webs, Networks, and Systems: Globalization and the Mass Media in the Nineteenth and Twentieth-Century British Empire," *Journal of British Studies* 46, 3 (2007): 646.
158 Edward C. Kemble, *A History of California Newspapers, 1846–1858*, ed. Helen Harding (Los Gatos: Talisman Press, 1962), 29, 88–97.
159 Arjun Appadurai, *Modernity at Large: Cultural Dimensions of Globalization* (Minneapolis: University of Minnesota Press, 1996), 32–33.
160 *Sacramento Daily Union*, 10 June 1858.
161 Ibid., 1 January 1858, 10 June 1858, 14 June 1858; *Daily Alta California*, 2 July 1858.
162 Ibid., 5 April 1858, 24 April 1858, 26 May 1858, 10 June 1858, 14 June 1858; *Daily Alta California*, 2 July 1858.
163 *Sacramento Daily Union*, 1 January 1858; *Daily Alta California*, 6 April 1858; *Sacramento Daily Union*, 26 May 1858; *Daily Alta California*, 23 June 1858, 2 July 1858; *Sacramento Daily Union*, 2 July 1858, 2 May 1859, 30 July 1859, 13 July 1859, 1 October 1859; *Daily Alta California*, 21 November 1859; *Sacramento Daily Union*, 30 April 1860, 13 June 1860.
164 *British Colonist*, 5 August 1859; *Sacramento Daily Union*, 13 August 1859; *Daily Alta California*, 21 November 1859; *The Times*, 28 December 1859.
165 *Daily Alta California*, 21 May 1860, 29 May 1860, 3 June 1860, 4 July 1860, 14 July 1860, 1 August 1860, 18 August 1860, 11 September 1860, 11 November 1860, 7 February 1861, 29 March 1861, 13 May 1862, 13 July 1862.
166 *Daily Alta California*, 21 May 1860, 3 June 1860.
167 Potter, "Webs, Networks, and Systems," 641.
168 Ibid., 634.
169 Ibid., 629.
170 Lester, "British Settler Discourse and the Circuits of Empire," 25.

Conclusion

1 Kevin Grant, *A Civilised Savagery: Britain and the New Slaveries in Africa, 1884–1926* (New York: Routledge, 2005); Anne O'Brien, "Humanitarianism and Reparation in Colonial

Australia," *Journal of Colonialism and Colonial History* 12, 2 (2011), http://dx.doi.org/10.1353/cch.2011.0016; Damon Ieremia Salesa, *Racial Crossings: Race, Intermarriage, and the Victorian British Empire* (Auckland: Oxford University Press, 2011); James Heartfield, *The Aborigines' Protection Society: Humanitarian Imperialism in Australia, New Zealand, Fiji, Canada, South Africa, and the Congo, 1836–1909* (New York: Columbia University Press, 2011).

2 *Saturday Review*, 25 August 1860, 3 November 1860, 8 December 1860.

3 See, for example, Jill C. Bender, "Mutiny or Freedom Fight? The 1857 Indian Mutiny and the Irish Press," in *Newspapers and Empire in Ireland and Britain: Reporting the British Empire, c. 1857–1921*, ed. Simon Potter, 92–108 (Dublin: Four Courts Press, 2004).

4 *Wanganui Herald*, 1 March 1883. This edition featured extracts from the House of Representatives in June 1869, where Edward Stafford, the former premier during the Taranaki War in 1860, states: "Every atrocity of the Sepoy rebellion has been paralleled and outdone in the raids, burnings, violations, tortures, murders, and cannibalism of the last nine months in New Zealand, and with less provocation or excuse."

5 James Belich, *The New Zealand Wars and the Victorian Interpretation of Racial Conflict: The Maori, the British, and the New Zealand Wars* (Montreal and Kingston: McGill-Queen's University Press, 1986), 211.

6 Harold Innis, *Empire and Communications* (Lanham: Rowman and Littlefield, 2007), 138.

7 Simon Potter, "Webs, Networks, and Systems: Globalization and the Mass Media in the Nineteenth- and Twentieth-Century British Empire," *Journal of British Studies* 46, 3 (2007): 629–35.

8 Ibid., 628–30.

9 Roland Wenzlhuemer, "The Dematerialization of Telecommunication," *Journal of Global History* 2, 3 (2007): 349.

10 See Eric Pawson and Neil Quigley, "The Circulation of Information and Frontier Development: Canterbury 1850–1890," *New Zealand Geographer* 38, 2 (1982): 65–76; Cole Harris, "The Struggle with Distance," in *The Resettlement of British Columbia: Essays on Colonialism and Geographical Change* (Vancouver: UBC Press, 1997), 161–93. San Francisco was connected to the eastern United States in 1861; Australia to the rest of the world in 1872.

11 Kevin G. Barnhurst and John Nerone, *The Form of News: A History* (New York: Guilford Press, 2001), 103–5.

12 Alex Nalbach, "'The Software of Empire': Telegraphic News Agencies and Imperial Publicity, 1865–1914," in *Imperial Co-Histories: National Identities and the British and Colonial Press*, ed. Julie F. Codell (Madison: Fairleigh Dickinson University Press, 2003), 71.

13 See Simon Potter, *News and the British World: The Emergence of an Imperial Press System, 1876–1922* (Oxford: Oxford University Press, 2003).

14 C.A. Bayly, "The Second British Empire," in *The Oxford History of the British Empire, Historiography*, ed. Robin W. Winks, 60–64 (Oxford; New York: Oxford University Press, 1999).

15 Ibid., 64; Ronald Hyam, *Britain's Imperial Century, 1815–1914: A Study of Empire and Expansion* (London: B.T. Batsford, 1976), 70–85.

16 Andrew Bank, "Losing Faith in the Civilizing Mission: The Premature Decline of Humanitarian Liberalism at the Cape, 1840–60," in *Empire and Others: British Encounters in with Indigenous Peoples, 1600–1850* (London: UCL Press, 1999); Elizabeth Elbourne, *Blood Ground: Colonialism, Missions, and the Contest for Christianity in the Cape Colony and Britain, 1799–1853* (Montreal and Kingston: McGill-Queen's University Press, 2002).

17 Salesa, *Racial Crossings*, 175–78.

18 Heartfield, *Aborigines' Protection Society*, 149–51.

19 Julie Evans, Patricia Grimshaw, and David Phillips, *Equal Subjects, Unequal Rights: Indigenous People in British Settler Colonies, 1830–1919* (Manchester: Manchester University Press, 2003), 63–87.

20 See Tony Ballantyne, *Orientalism and Race: Aryanism in the British Empire* (Cambridge: Palgrave, 2002).

21 Evans, Grimsahw, and Phillips, *Equal Subjects, Unequal Rights*, 55.

22 Jane Samson, "British Voices and Indigenous Rights: Debating Aboriginal Legal Status in Nineteenth-Century Australia and Canada," *Cultures of the Commonwealth: Essays and Studies* 2 (Winter 1996–97): 15.

23 Glenn R. Wilkinson, *Depictions and Images of War in Edwardian Newspapers, 1899–1914* (Houndsmills, Basingstoke: Palgrave Macmillan, 2003), 17–29; Gordon M. Winder and M. Schmitt, "Geographical Imaginaries in the *New York Times'* reports of the assassinations of Mahatma Gandhi (1948) and Indira Gandhi (1984)," *Journal of Historical Geography* (2014), http://dx.doi.org/10.1016/j.jhg.2014.03.001.

24 C.A. Bayly, *Imperial Meridian: The British Empire and the World, 1780–1830* (London: Longman, 1989), 7.

Bibliography

Archival Sources

Bayley, Charles Alfred. "Early Life on Vancouver Island." BCA, MSS E/B/B34.2.
Brown, William. "William Brown Correspondence." AWMML, John Logan Campbell Collections, MSS 51, file 60.
Browne, Harriet Louisa. "Diary of Harriet Louisa Browne, 26 January 1861–21 January 1862." ANZ, ADCZ 17007 W5431/7.
Browne, Thomas Gore. "Diary of Thomas Gore Browne, 28 February 1860–25 January 1861." ANZ, ADCZ 1706 W5431/3.
–. "Diary of Thomas Gore Browne, 1 January 1861–3 December 1861." ANZ, ADCZ 17006 W5431/4.
–. "Sir Thomas Gore Browne Letterbook, 1855–1861." ATL, QMS-0284.
Burn, David. Diary, 1855–1858. SLNSW, CY 1094.
Bushby, Arthur Thomas. Diary, 1860. BCA, MSS 811/A861.
Colonial Office. "Original Correspondence [relating to New Zealand], 1830–1922," HC, 10122.
Colonial Secretary of New Zealand. "General Inwards Correspondence to the Colonial Secretary, 1861." ANZ, IA-1-222-1861/1861/1946-2156.
Colonial Secretary of Vancouver Island. "Correspondence Outwards, 14 September 1859–21 September 1860." BCA, C/AA/30.1J/1A, vols. 1–2.
–. "Correspondence Outwards, 28 September 1860–13 August 1861." BCA, C/AA/30.1J/2A, vols. 1–2.
–. "Correspondence Outwards, 15 August 1861–24 March 1863." BCA, C/AA/30.1J/3.
–. "Miscellaneous Letters, 24 March 1863–20 September 1864." BCA, C/AA/30.1J/4.
Douglas, James. "Letters to Hudson's Bay Company on Vancouver Island Colony, 1850–1855." BCA, A/C/20/Vi2A.
–. "Letters to Hudson's Bay Company on Vancouver Island, 11 December 1855–8 July 1859." BCA, A/C/20/Vi3A.
Duncan, William. Journal. BCA, MS 2758, AO 1715.
Garrett, F.A. "A.C. Garrett Reminiscences." BCA, MSS E/B/G19.

Grayling, William Irwin. "Journal of Events of the War at Tarameika." PA, ARC2001-48.
Great Britain. "Admiralty Papers, 1858–1860." BCA, GR 1309, box 2, vol. 2, file 1.
Hughes, Robert Clinton. Diary, 1860–69. PA, ARC2001-140.
Mayne, R.C. "Journal of Admiral Richard Charles Mayne, 17 February 1857–31 December 1860." BCA, MSS E/B/M45A.
Native Secretary of New Zealand. Memoranda, 1859–63. ANZ, RG-16036.
Pemberton family. "Diaries and Reminiscences." BCA, MSS 1295.
Rawson family. Letters, 1856–69. PA, ARC2001-99.
Ronald, Hugh. Letters, 1853–69. PA, ARC2002-161.
Sewell, Henry. "Journal of Henry Sewell, 1859–1866." ATL, QMS-1783.
Society for the Propagation of the Gospel in Foreign Parts. "British Columbia Papers, 1858–1861." BCA, H/A/So2/vol. 1.
Vancouver Island. "Colonial Correspondence, 1857–1872." BCA, GR 1372.
Vancouver Island. Volunteer Rifle Corps. Correspondence. BCA, O/B/V26.
Victoria Police Department. "Victoria Gaol Records, 1859–1863." BCA, GR 0308, vols. 1–2.
Victoria Volunteer Rifle Corps. "Papers Connected with Vancouver Island Volunteer Rifle Corps, 1861–1862." BCA, C/AA/30.1/M58, box 1, file 2.
Wakefield, William King. Letters, 1860–69. PA, ARC2001-391.
Woolsey, John. "Account of an Indian Battle at Victoria Harbour, 1859." BCA, F/54/W88.

Periodicals

Argus (1860–62)
Auckland Examiner (1856–60)
Auckland Weekly Register (1857–60)
British Colonist (1858–66)
British Columbian (1861–66)
Church Missionary Intelligencer (1856)
Daily Alta California (1858–62)
Daily Evening Express (1863–65)
Evening Telegraph (1866)
Government Gazette (1861)
Illustrated London News (1860–62)
New Zealand Gazette (1861)
New Zealander (1858–62)
Otago Daily Times (1862)
Pacific Commercial Advertiser (1861)
Sacramento Daily Union (1858–62)
Saturday Review (1858–62)
Southern Cross (1858–62)
Sydney Morning Herald (1860–62)
Taranaki Herald (1857–62)
Taranaki News (1858–62)
Taranaki Punch (1860–61)
Te Karere Maori (1855–60)
The Press (1861–62)
The Times (1858–62)
Vancouver Island Times (1864–65)
Victoria Daily Chronicle (1862–66)
Victoria Gazette (1858–60)

Primary Published Sources

Alston, Edward Graham. *Handbook to Vancouver Island and British Columbia*. London: F. Alger, 1862.

Amphlett, James. *The Newspaper Press, in Part of the Last Century, and up to the Present Period of 1860*. London: Whittaker & Co., 1860.

Andrews, Alexander. *The History of British Journalism from the Foundation of the Newspaper Press in England to the Repeal of the Stamp Act in 1855, with Sketches of Press Celebrities*, vol. 2. London: Richard Bentley, 1859.

Anonymous. *The Handbook of British Columbia and Emigrant's Guide to the Gold Fields*. London: W. Oliver, 1862.

Anonymous. *London International Exhibition, Catalogue of the Vancouver Contribution with a Short Account of Vancouver Island and British Columbia*. London, 1862.

Appendices to the Journal of the House of Representatives of New Zealand. Auckland, 1860.

A Returned Digger. *The Newly Discovered Gold Fields of British Columbia*. London: Darton & Hodge, 1862.

Aylmer, Fenton. *A Cruise in the Pacific: From the Log of a Naval Officer*, vol. 2. London: Hurst and Blackwett, 1860.

Bagshaw, Roberta L., ed. *No Better Land: The 1860 Diaries of the Anglican Colonial Bishop George Hills*. Victoria: Sono Nis Press, 1996.

Ballantyne, Robert Michael. *Handbook to the New Gold Fields*. Edinburgh: A. Strahan, 1858.

Barrett-Lennard, C.E. *Travels in British Columbia: With the Narrative of a Yacht Voyage Round Vancouver's Island*. London: Hurst and Blackett, 1862.

Bell, F.D., F. Whitaker, and T.G. Browne. *Notes on Sir William Martin's Pamphlet Entitled the Taranaki Question*. Auckland: New Zealand Government, 1861.

Bourne, Henry Richard Fox. *English Newspapers: Chapters in the History of Journalism*, vol. 2. London: Chatto, 1887.

Brodie, Walter. *Remarks on the Past and Present State of New Zealand, Its Government, Capabilities, and Prospects*. London: Whittaker and Co., 1845.

Brown, R.C. *Klatassen and Other Reminiscences of Missionary Life in British Columbia*. London: Society for Promoting Christian Knowledge, 1873.

Browne, Edward Harold. *The Case of the War in New Zealand*. Cambridge: Deighton, Bell and Co., 1860.

Browne, Harriet Louisa. *Narrative of the Waitara Purchase and the Taranaki War*, edited by W.P. Morrell. Dunedin: University of Otago Press, 1965.

Buddle, Thomas. *The Maori King Movement in New Zealand with a Full Report of the Native Meetings Held at Waikato, April and May, 1860*. Auckland: The "New Zealander" Office, 1860.

Busby, James. *Remarks Upon a Pamphlet Entitled "the Taranaki Question," by Sir William Martin, D.C.L., Late Chief Justice of New Zealand*. Auckland: Philip Kunst, Southern Cross Office, 1860.

Carey, Robert. *Narrative of the Late War in New Zealand*. London: Richard Bentley, 1863.

Carrington, Frederick Alonzo. *The Land Question of Taranaki, with Suggestions for Improving the Condition of the Aboriginal Inhabitants and Developing the Resources of New Zealand*. New Plymouth: Taranaki News Office, 1860.

Churchill, J.D., J. Cooper. *British Columbia and Vancouver Island Considered as a Field for Commercial Enterprise*. London: Rees and Collin, 1866.

Clarke, George, Sr. *Remarks Upon a Pamphlet by James Busby, Esq. Commenting Upon a Pamphlet Entitled the "Taranaki Question," by Sir William Martin, D.C.L., Late Chief Justice of New Zealand*. Auckland: Philip Kunst, 1861.

Clarke, George, Jr. *Notes on Early Life in New Zealand*. Hobart: J. Walch and Sons, 1903.

Cornwallis, Kinahan. *The New El Dorado: Or, British Columbia*. London: Thomas Cautley Newby, 1858.

Correspondence and Other Papers Relating to New Zealand, 1862–64, vol. 13, British Parliamentary Papers. Shannon: Irish University Press, 1970.

Correspondence and Papers Relating to the Maori Uprisings in New Zealand, 1861, vol. 12, British Parliamentary Papers. Shannon: Irish University Press, 1969.

Couquhoun, Grant W. "Description of Vancouver Island, by Its First Colonist." *Journal of the Royal Geographical Society* 27: 268–320.

De Groot, Henry. *British Columbia: Its Condition and Prospects, Soil, Climate, and Mineral Resources, Considered*. San Francisco: Alta California's job office, 1859.

Domer, John. *New British Gold-Fields: A Guide to British Columbia and Vancouver Island*. London: William Henry Angel, 1858.

Duncan, William. *The British Columbia Mission, or, Metlahkatlah*. London: Church Missionary House, 1871.

Emmerson, John. *British Columbia and Vancouver Island: Voyages, Travels, and Adventures*. London: W. Ainsley, 1865.

Extracts of Letters from New Zealand on the War Question: With an Article from the New Zealand Spectator of November 3rd, 1860. London: F.J. Wilson, 1861.

Firth, Josiah Clifton. *Nation Making, a Story of New Zealand: Savagism v. Civilization*. London: Longmans, Green, and Co., 1890.

Fitzgerald, James Edward. *An Examination of the Charter and Proceedings of the Hudson Bay Company, with Reference to the Grant of Vancouver Island*. London: Edward Trelawney, 1849.

Forbes, Charles. *Vancouver Island: Its Resources and Capabilities as a Colony*. Victoria: The Colonial Government, 1862.

Fox, William. *The Six Colonies of New Zealand*. London: John W. Parker and Son, 1851.

–. *The War in New Zealand*. London: Williams and Norgate, 1860.

Gorst, John Eldon. *The Maori King; or, the Story of Our Quarrel with the Natives of New Zealand*. London: Macmillan and Co., 1864.

Grant, James. *The Newspaper Press: Its Origin – Its Progress – and Present Position*, vol. 2. London: Tinsley Brothers, 1871.

Green, W. Sebright. "The Indians of Vancouver Island." *The Colonial Intelligencer or, Aborigines' Friend*. London: Aborigines' Protection Society, 1 December 1869: 191–93.

Hadfield, Octavius. *One of England's Little Wars. A Letter to the Right Hon. The Duke of Newcastle, Secretary of State for the Colonies*. London: Williams & Norgate, 1860.

–. *A Sequel to 'One of England's Little Wars': Being an Account of the Real Origin of the War in New Zealand, Its Present Stage, and the Future Prospects of the Colony*. London: Williams and Norgate, 1861.

–. *The Second Year of One of England's Little Wars*. London: Williams and Norgate, 1861.

Hansard's Parliamentary Debates, Third Series, vol. 159. London: Cornelius Buck, 1860.

Hansard's Parliamentary Debates, Third Series, vol. 162. London: Cornelius Buck, 1862.

Hansard's Parliamentary Debates, Third Series, vol. 165. London: Cornelius Buck, 1860–62.

Hazlitt, William Carew. *British Columbia and Vancouver Island*. London: G. Routledge & Co., 1858.

–. *The Great Gold Fields of Caribou*. London: Routledge, Wanre and Routledge, 1862.

Hendrickson, James, ed. *British Columbia: 1860*, vol. 3 of Colonial Despatches of British Columbia. Victoria: University of Victoria, 1988.

Hendrickson, James, ed. *Vancouver Island: 1852–1863*, vols. 1–9 of Colonial Despatches of British Columbia. Victoria: University of Victoria, 1988.

House of Commons. *Report of the Parliamentary Select Committee on Aboriginal Tribes (British Settlements)*. London: Aborigines' Protection Society, 1837.

Humanities Computing and Media Centre, University of Victoria. "The Colonial Despatches of Vancouver Island and British Columbia 1846–1871." bcgenesis.uvic.ca.

Hunt, F. Knight. *The Fourth Estate: Contributions Towards a History of Newspapers and the Liberty of the Press*, vol. 1. London: David Bogue, 1850.

Kemble, Edward C. *A History of California Newspapers, 1846–1858*, ed. Helen Harding. Los Gatos: Talisman Press, 1962. First published 1858 by the *Sacramento Daily Union*.

Langley, A.J. *A Glance at British Columbia and Vancouver's Island in 1861*. London: Robert Harwick, 1862.

Macdonald, D.G.F. *British Columbia and Vancouver Island*. London: Longman, Green, Longman, Roberts & Green, 1862.

–. *Lecture on British Columbia and Vancouver's Island*. London: Longman, Green, Longman, Roberts & Green, 1863.

Macfie, Matthew. *Vancouver Island and British Columbia: Their History, Resources, and Prospects*. London: Longman, Green, Longman, Roberts, and Green, 1865.

Mark, William. *Cariboo: A True and Correct Narrative*. Stockton: M. Weight, 1863.

Martin, R.M. *The Hudson's Bay Territories and Vancouver's Island*. London: T. and W. Boone, 1849.

Martin, William. *England and the New Zealanders: Remarks Upon a Despatch from the Right Hon. Earl Grey to Governor Grey, Dated to Dec. 23 1846*. Auckland: College Press, 1847.

–. *The Taranaki Question*. Auckland: Melanesian Press, 1860.

–. *Remarks on 'Notes Published for the New Zealand Government,' January 1861: And on Mr. Richmond's Memorandum on the Taranaki Question, December 1860*. Auckland: Melanesian Press, 1861.

Mayne, R.C. *Four Years in British Columbia and Vancouver Island*. London: John Murray, 1862.

McIntyre, David W., ed. *The Journal of Henry Sewell, 1853–7*, vols. 1–2. Christchurch: Whitcoulls Publishers, 1980.

Pemberton, Joseph Despard. *Facts and Figures Relating to Vancouver Island and British Columbia Showing What to Expect and How to Get There*. London: Longman, Green, Longman, and Roberts, 1860.

Pilditch, Jan, ed. *The Letters and Journals of Reverend John Morgan*, vols. 1–2. Glasgow: The Grimsay Press, 2010.

Pritchard, Allan, ed. *Vancouver Island Letters of Edmond Hope Verney, 1862–65*. Vancouver: UBC Press, 1996.

Rattray, Alexander. *Vancouver Island and British Columbia: Where They Are; What They Are; and What They May Become*. London: Smith, Elder, 1862.

Registrar General. *Statistical Register of New South Wales for the Year 1861*. Sydney: Thomas Richards, 1862.

Registrar General. *Statistics of New Zealand for 1858*. Auckland: W.C. Wilson, 1859.

–. *Statistics of New Zealand for 1859*. Auckland: W.C. Wilson, 1860.

–. *Statistics of New Zealand for 1860*. Auckland: W.C. Wilson, 1861.

–. *Statistics of New Zealand for 1861*. Auckland: W.C. Wilson, 1862.

–. *Statistics of New Zealand for 1862*. Auckland: New Zealander Printing Office, 1863.

–. *Statistics of New Zealand for 1864*. Auckland: W.C. Wilson, 1866.

Richmond, C.W. *Memorandum on the Taranaki Question: Reviewing a Pamphlet by Sir William Martin, D.C.L., Late Chief Justice of New Zealeand [sic], on the Same Subject*. Auckland, 1861.

Scholefield, G.H., ed. *The Richmond-Atkinson Papers*, vol. 1. Wellington: R.E. Owen, Government Printer, 1960.

Sewell, Henry. *The New Zealand Native Rebellion: Letter to Lord Lyttelton*. Auckland: Henry Sewell, 1864.

Smith, Dorothy Blakey, ed. *The Reminiscences of Doctor John Sebastian Helmcken*. Vancouver: UBC Press, 1975.

Snow, W. Parker. *British Columbia, Emigration and Our Colonies Considered Practically*. London: Piper, Stephenson, and Spence, 1858.

Stanley, George F.G., ed. *Mapping the Frontier: Charles Wilson's Diary of the Survey of the 49th Parallel, 1858–1862, While Secretary of the British Boundary Commission*. Seattle: University of Washington Press, 1970.

Stoney, Henry Butler. *Taranaki: A Tale of the War*. Auckland: W.C. Wilson, 1861.

Swainson, William. *New Zealand and Its Colonization*. London: Smith, Elder and Co., 1859.

–. *New Zealand and the War*. London: Smith, Elder and Co., 1862.

Taylor, Richard. *Te Ika a Maui, or New Zealand and Its Inhabitants*. London, 1855.

Thomson, Arthur Saunders. *The Story of New Zealand: Past and Present – Savage and Civilized*, vol. 2. London: John Murray, 1859.

Trutch, Joseph W. "Memorandum refuting the charges in Sebright Green's report on the conditions of the Indians on Vancouver Island, with explanation." In *Papers Connected with the Indian Land Question, 1850–75*. Victoria: R. Wolfenden, 1875.

Wakefield, Edward Gibbon. *A Letter from Sydney*. London: Joseph Cross, 1829.

–. *England and America: A Comparison of the Social and Political State of both Nations*, vols. 1–2. London: Richard Bentley, 1833.

–. *The British Colonization of New Zealand; Being an Account of the Principles, Objects, and Plans of the New Zealand Association*. London: John W. Parker, 1837.

White, William, ed. *Memorials of Sergeant William Marjouram, Royal Artillery; Including Six Years' Service During the Late Maori War*. London: James Nisbet and Co., 1862.

Secondary Published Sources

Adams, John. *Old Square-Toes and His Lady: The Life of James and Amelia Douglas*. Victoria: Horsdal and Schubert, 2001.

Anderson, Atholl. "Origins, Settlement and Society of Pre-European South Polynesia." In *The New Oxford History of New Zealand*, ed. Gyselle Byrnes, 21–46. Auckland: Oxford University Press, 2009.

Anderson, Benedict. *Imagined Communities: Reflections on the Origin and Spread of Nationalism*. London: Verso, 1991.

Anderson, Kay. "White Natures: Sydney's Royal Agricultural Show in Post-Humanist Perspective." *Transactions of the Institute of British Geographers* (n.s.) 28, 4 (2003): 423–25.

Anonymous. "Auckland Newspaper Press." In *The Cyclopedia of New Zealand, Auckland Provincial District*. Christchurch: Cyclopedia Company, Limited, 1902.

Appadurai, Arjun. *Modernity at Large: Cultural Dimensions of Globalization*. Minneapolis: University of Minnesota Press, 1996.

Arctander, John William. *The Apostle of Alaska: The Story of William Duncan*. New York: Fleming H. Revell Company, 1909.

Arnett, Chris. *The Terror of the Coast: Land Alienation and Colonial War on Vancouver Island and the Gulf Islands, 1849–1863*. Vancouver: Talonbooks, 1999.

Baldasty, Gerald J. *The Commercialization of News in the Nineteenth Century*. Madison: University of Wisconsin Press, 1992.

Ballantyne, Tony. *Orientalism and Race: Aryanism in the British Empire*. Cambridge: Palgrave, 2002.

–. "Archives, Empires and Histories of Colonialism." *Archifacts* (April 2004): 21–36.

–. "Christianity, Colonialism and Cross-Cultural Communication: New Perspectives on New Zealand History." In *Christianity, Modernity and Culture*, ed. John Stenhouse, 23–57. Adelaide: ATF Press, 2005.

–. "Teaching Maori about Asia: Print Culture and Community Identity in Nineteenth-Century New Zealand." In *Asia in the Making of New Zealand*, ed. Brian Moloughney, 13–35. Auckland: Auckland University Press, 2006.

–. "The State, Politics, and Power, 1769–1893." In *The New Oxford History of New Zealand*, ed. Gyselle Byrnes, 99–124. Auckland: Oxford University Press, 2009.

–. "Information, Intelligence, Empire: Rethinking the Mid-Nineteenth Century Crisis in the British Empire." Paper presented at *Eclipse of Empires: Colonial Resistance, Metropolitan Decline, and Imperial Crises in the 19th and 20th Centuries*. Institut Universitari d'Història Jaume Vicens Vives, 3 June 2010.

–. "Humanitarian Narratives: Knowledge and the Politics of Mission and Empire." *Social Sciences and Missions* 24 (2011): 233–64.

–. "Genesis 1:28 and the Languages of Colonial Improvement in Victorian New Zealand." *Victorian Review* 37, 2 (2011): 9–13.

–. *Entanglements of Empire. Missionaries, Māori, and the Question of the Body*. Durham: Duke University Press, 2014.

Ballantyne, Tony, and Antoinette Burton, "Postscript – Bodies, Genders, Empires: Reimagining World Histories." In *Bodies in Contact: Rethinking Colonial Encounters in World History*, ed. Tony Ballantyne and Antoinette Burton, 405–24. Durham: Duke University Press, 2005.

Ballara, Angela. *Taua: "Musket Wars," "Land Wars" or Tikanga? Warfare in Māori Society in the Early Nineteenth Century*. Auckland: Penguin, 2003.

Bancroft, Hubert Howe. *History of British Columbia, 1792–1887*. The History Company, 1887.

Bank, Andrew. "Losing Faith in the Civilizing Mission: The Premature Decline of Humanitarian Liberalism at the Cape, 1840–60." In *Empire and Others: British Encounters in with Indigenous Peoples, 1600–1850*, 364–83. London: UCL Press, 1999.

Banner, Stuart. *Possessing the Pacific: Land, Settlers, and Indigenous People from Australia to Alaska*. Cambridge: Harvard University Press, 2007.

Barman, Jean. *The West beyond the West: A History of British Columbia*. Toronto: University of Toronto Press, 1996.

–. "Taming Aboriginal Sexuality: Gender, Power, and Race in British Columbia, 1850–1900." *BC Studies* 115/16 (Autumn/Winter 1997–98): 237–66.

–. "Aboriginal Women on the Streets of Victoria." In *Contact Zones: Aboriginal and Settler Women in Canada's Colonial Past*, ed. Katie Pickles and Myra Rutherdale, 205–27. Vancouver: UBC Press, 2005.

Barnhurst, Kevin G., and John Nerone. *The Form of News: A History*. New York: Guilford Press, 2001.

Bateman, Fiona, and Lionel Pilkington. "Introduction." In *Studies in Settler Colonialism: Politics, Identity and Culture*, 1–9. Houndsmills, Basingstoke: Palgrave Macmillan, 2011.

Bayly, C.A. *Imperial Meridian: The British Empire and the World, 1780–1830*. London: Longman, 1989.

–. *Empire and Information: Intelligence Gathering and Social Communication in India, 1780–1870*. Cambridge: Cambridge University Press, 1996.

–. "The Second British Empire." In *The Oxford History of the British Empire, Historiography*, ed. Robin W. Winks, 54–72. Oxford: Oxford University Press, 1999.

Bebbington, D.W. *Evangelicalism in Modern Britain: A History from the 1730s to the 1980s*. London: Routledge, 1995.

Beck, Murray J. "Howe, Joseph." *Dictionary of Canadian Biography Online.* http://www.biographi.ca/en/bio.php?BioId=39171.

Belgrave, Michael. *Historical Frictions: Maori Claims and Reinvented Histories.* Auckland: Auckland University Press, 2005.

Belich, James. *The New Zealand Wars and the Victorian Interpretation of Racial Conflict: The Maori, the British, and the New Zealand Wars.* Montreal and Kingston: McGill-Queen's University Press, 1986.

–. *Making Peoples: A History of the New Zealanders, from Polynesian Settlement to the End of the Nineteenth Century.* Honolulu: University of Hawaii Press, 2001.

–. *Replenishing the Earth: The Settler Revolution and the Rise of the Anglo-World, 1783–1939.* Auckland: Oxford University Press, 2009.

Belshaw, John Douglas. *Becoming British Columbia: A Population History.* Vancouver: UBC Press, 2009.

Bender, Jill C. "Mutiny or Freedom Fight? The 1857 Indian Mutiny and the Irish Press." In *Newspapers and Empire in Ireland and Britain: Reporting the British Empire, c. 1857–1921,* ed. Simon Potter, 92–108. Dublin: Four Courts Press, 2004.

–. "Fears of 1857: The British Empire in the Wake of the Indian Rebellion." PhD diss., Boston College, 2011.

Benton, Laura. *Law and Colonial Cultures: Legal Regimes in World History, 1400–1900.* Cambridge: Cambridge University Press, 2002.

Berland, Jody. *North of Empire: Essays on the Cultural Technologies of Space.* Durham: Duke University Press, 2009.

Binney, Judith. "Christianity and the Maoris to 1840: A Comment." *New Zealand Journal of History* 3, 2 (1969): 143–65.

–. "Ancestral Voices: Maori Prophet Leaders." In *The Oxford Illustrated History of New Zealand,* ed. Keith Sinclair, 153–84. Auckland: Oxford University Press, 1990.

–. *Redemption Songs: A Life of Te Kooti Arikirangi Te Turuki.* Auckland: Auckland University Press, 1995.

Black, Jeremy. *A Military History of Britain from 1775 to the Present.* Santa Barbara: Praeger, 2006.

Boase, G.C., and H.C.G. Matthew. "Selwyn, Sir Charles Jasper (1813–1869)." *Oxford Dictionary of National Biography.* http://www.oxforddnb.com/index/101025064/.

Bolt, Clarence. *Thomas Crosby and the Tsimshian: Small Shoes for Feet Too Large.* Vancouver: UBC Press, 1992.

Borchardt, D.H. "Burn, David (1799–1875)." *Australian Dictionary of Biography,* vol. 1. Melbourne: Melbourne University Press, 1966.

Boyd, Robert T. *The Coming of the Spirit of Pestilence.* Seattle: University of Washington Press, 1999.

Brown, Lucy, et al. "Foreign Correspondent." *Dictionary of Nineteenth-Century Journalism,* ed. Laurel Brake, Marysa Demoor, 224–25. London: Academia Press, 2009.

Buckner, Phillip, ed. *Canada and the British Empire.* Oxford: Oxford University Press, 2010.

Burton, Antoinette. *Burdens of History: British Feminists, Indian Women, and Imperial Culture, 1865–1915.* Chapel Hill: University of North Carolina Press, 1994.

Canavan, Francis. *The Political Economy of Edmund Burke: The Role of Property in His Thought.* New York: Fordham University Press, 1995.

Carey, James W. *Communication as Culture: Essays on Media and Society,* 3rd ed. Boston: Unwin Hyman, 2009.

Carlson, Keith Thor. *The Power of Place, the Problem of Time: Aboriginal Identity and Historical Consciousness in the Cauldron of Colonialism.* Toronto: University of Toronto Press, 2010.

Carpenter, Samuel. D. "History, Law and Land: The Languages of Native Policy in New Zealand's General Assembly, 1858–62." MA thesis, Massey University, 2008.

Clayton, Daniel. *Islands of Truth: The Imperial Fashioning of Vancouver Island*. Vancouver: UBC Press, 2000.

Colvin, Gina Maree. "The Soliloquy of Whiteness: Colonial Discourse and New Zealand's Settler Press 1839–1873." PhD thesis, University of Canterbury, 2009.

Cotton, H. Barry. "The Retribution of D.G.F. Macdonald C.E." *BC Historical News* 32, 1 (1998/99): 14–15.

Cowan, James. *The New Zealand Wars: A History of the Maori Campaigns and the Pioneering Period*, vol. 1. Wellington: W.A.G. Skinner, 1922.

Curteis, G.H. *Bishop Selwyn of New Zealand, and of Lichfield, a Sketch of His Life and Work, with Some Further Gleanings from His Letters, Sermons, and Speeches*. London: Kegan Paul, Trench & Co., 1889.

Dalton, B.J. *War and Politics in New Zealand, 1855–1870*. Sydney: Sydney University Press, 1967.

Daschuk, James. *Clearing the Plains: Disease, Politics of Starvation, and the Loss of Aboriginal Life*. Regina: University of Regina Press, 2013.

Davidoff, Leonore, and Catherine Hall. *Family Fortunes: Men and Women of the English Middle Class, 1780–1850*. London: Hutchinson, 1987.

Davy, Dan. "Selling Australia: New South Wales Emigration Manuals and Scottish Perceptions of Australia, 1820–1850." MSc, University of Edinburgh, 2007.

–. "Lost Tailings: Gold Rush Societies and Cultures in Colonial Otago, New Zealand, 1861–1911." PhD diss, University of Otago, 2013.

Day, Patrick. *The Making of the New Zealand Press: A Study of the Organizational and Political Concerns of New Zealand Newspaper Controllers, 1840–1880*. Wellington: Victoria University Press, 1990.

Doherty, Hugh. "The First Newspapers on Canada's West Coast." http://hughdoherty.tripod.com/victoria.htm.

Dorsett, Shaunnagh. "'Destitute of the Knowledge of God': Maori Testimony before the New Zealand Courts in the Early Crown Colony Period." In *Past Law, Present Histories*, ed. Diane Kirkby, 39–60. Canberra: ANU ePress, 2012.

Duff, Wilson. *The Indian History of British Columbia*. Victoria: British Columbia Provincial Museum, 1964.

Dunae, Patrick A. "Geographies of Sexual Commerce and the Production of Prostitutional Space: Victoria, British Columbia, 1860–1914." *Journal of the Canadian Historical Association* 19, 1 (2008): 115–42.

Edmonds, Penelope. *Urbanizing Frontiers: Indigenous Peoples and Settlers in 19th-Century Pacific Rim Cities*. Vancouver: UBC Press, 2010.

Edwards, D.G. "Chapman, Henry Samuel-Biography." *Dictionary of New Zealand Biography, Te Ara-the Encyclopedia of New Zealand*. http://www.teara.govt.nz/remap_url.php?src=en/biographies/1c14/1.

Elbourne, Elizabeth. *Blood Ground: Colonialism, Missions, and the Contest for Christianity in the Cape Colony and Britain, 1799–1853*. Montreal and Kingston: McGill-Queen's University Press, 2002.

–. "The Sin of the Settler: The 1835–36 Select Committee on Aborigines and Debates over Virtue and Conquest in the Early Nineteenth Century British White Settler Empire." *Journal of Colonialism and Colonial History* 4, 3 (2003). http://muse.jhu.edu/login?auth=0&type=summary&url=/journals/journal_of_colonialism_and_colonial_history/v004/4.3elbourne.html.

Elsmore, Bronwyn. *Mana from Heaven: A Century of Maori Prophets in New Zealand.* Tauranga: Moana Press, 1989.

Emsley, Clive. "Mayne, Sir Richard, 1796–1868." *Oxford Dictionary of National Biography.* http://www.oxforddnb.com/view/article/18444/18445.

Evans, John H. *Churchman Militant: George Augustus Selwyn Bishop of New Zealand and Lichfield.* Wellington: Allen and Unwin, 1964.

Evans, Julie, Patricia Grimshaw, and David Phillips. *Equal Subjects, Unequal Rights: Indigenous People in British Settler Colonies, 1830–1919.* Manchester: Manchester University Press, 2003.

Evans, Julie. *Edward Eyre: Race and Colonial Governance.* Dunedin: University of Otago Press, 2005.

Fairburn, Miles. *The Ideal Society and Its Enemies: The Foundations of Modern New Zealand Society 1850–1900.* Auckland: Auckland University Press, 1989.

Fisher, Robin. "Joseph Trutch and Indian Land Policy." *BC Studies* 12 (Winter 1971/72): 3–33.

–. *Contact and Conflict: Indian-European Relations in British Columbia, 1774–1890.* Vancouver: UBC Press, 1992 [1977].

Ford, Lisa. *Settler Sovereignty: Jurisdiction and Indigenous People in America and Australia, 1788–1836.* Cambridge: Harvard University Press, 2010.

Foster, Hamar, and Alan Gove. "'Trespassers on the Soil': United States v. Tom and a New Perspective on the Short History of Treaty Making in Nineteenth-Century British Columbia." *BC Studies* 138/39 (Summer/Autumn 2003): 51–84.

Francis, Mark. *Governors and Settlers: Images of Authority in the British Colonies.* Canterbury: Palgrave Macmillan, 1992.

Frogner, Raymond. "'Innocent Legal Fictions': Archival Convention and the North Saanich Treaty of 1852." *Archivaria* 70 (Fall 2010): 45–94.

Gibbons, Peter. "Non-Fiction." *Oxford History of New Zealand Literature in English*, ed. Terry Sturm, 21–118. Auckland: Oxford University Press, 1998.

Gibson, James. *Otter Skins, Boston Ships, and China Goods: The Maritime Fur Trade of the Northwest Coast, 1785–1841.* Montreal and Kingston: McGill-Queen's University Press, 1992.

Good, Reginald. "Regulating Indian and Chinese Civic Identities in British Columbia's 'Colonial Contact Zone,' 1858–1887." *Canadian Journal of Law and Society* 26, 1 (2001): 69–88.

Gough, Barry M. *Gunboat Frontier: British Maritime Authority and Northwest Coast Indians, 1846–1890.* Vancouver: UBC Press, 1984.

–. *Fortune's a River: The Collision of Empires in Northwest America.* Madeira Park: Harbour, 2008.

Grant, Kevin. *A Civilised Savagery: Britain and the New Slaveries in Africa, 1884–1926.* New York: Routledge, 2005.

Grant, Susannah. "God's Governor: George Grey and Racial Amalgamation in New Zealand 1845–1853." PhD diss., University of Otago, 2005.

Grimshaw, Michael Patrick. "Fouling the Nest: The Conflict between the 'Church Party' and Settler Society during the New Zealand Wars, 1860–1865." PhD diss., University of Otago, 1999.

Guha, Ranajit. "Not at Home in Empire." *Critical Inquiry* 23, 3 (1997): 482–93.

Habermas, Jürgen. *The Structural Transformation of the Public Sphere: An Inquiry into a Category of Bourgeois Society.* Trans. Thomas Burger. Cambridge: MIT Press, 1989.

Hall, Catherine. *Civilising Subjects: Metropole and Colony in the English Imagination, 1830–1867.* Chicago: University of Chicago Press, 2002.

Hall, Catherine, and Keith McClelland, eds. *Race, Nation and Empire: Making Histories, 1750 to the Present.* Manchester: Manchester University Press, 2010.

Halttunen, Karen. "Humanitarianism and the Pornography of Pain in Anglo-American Culture." *American Historical Review* 100, 2 (1995): 303–34.

Hamilton, Geoffrey. "Delane, John Thadeus (1817–1879)." *Oxford Dictionary of National Biography*. http://www.oxforddnb.com/view/article/7440?docPos=1.

Hanham, H.J. "The Political Structure of Auckland, 1853–76." MA thesis, University of New Zealand, 1950.

Harring, Sidney L. *White Man's Law: Native People in Nineteenth-Century Canadian Jurisprudence*. Toronto: Osgoode Society for Canadian Legal History, 1998.

Harris, Cole. *The Resettlement of British Columbia: Essays on Colonialism and Geographical Change*. Vancouver: UBC Press, 1997.

–. *Making Native Space: Colonialism, Resistance, and Reserves in British Columbia*. Vancouver: UBC Press, 2003.

–. "How Did Colonialism Dispossess? Comments from an Edge of Empire." *Annals of the Association of American Geographers* 94, 1 (2004): 165–82.

Harris, Douglas C. *Fish, Law, and Colonialism: The Legal Capture of Salmon in British Columbia*. Toronto: University of Toronto Press, 2001.

Harrop, A.J. *England and the Maori Wars*. London: Whitcombe and Tombs, 1937.

Harvey, Megan. "Story People: Stó:lō-State Relations and Indigenous Literacies in British Columbia, 1864–1874." *Journal of the Canadian Historical Association* 24, 1 (2013): 51–88.

Harvey, Ross. "Circulation Figures of Some Nineteenth-Century New Zealand Newspapers." *Archifacts* (1988/4 & 1989/1): 20–29.

–. "The Bibliography of Nineteenth-Century New Zealand Newspapers." *New Zealand Journal of Serials Librarianship* 2, 2 (1991): 19–33.

–. "Economic Aspects of Nineteenth Century New Zealand Newspapers." *Bibliographical Society of Australia and New Zealand Bulletin* 17, 2 (1993): 55–78.

–. "The Power of the Press in Colonial New Zealand: More Imagined Than Real?" *Bibliographical Society of Australia and New Zealand Bulletin* 20, 2 (1996): 130–45.

–. "Newspaper Archives in Australia and New Zealand." *Media History* 5, 1 (1999): 71–80.

–. "David Burn and the *Maori Messenger*." *Script and Print* 37, 2 (2013): 69–87.

Hatch, F.J. "The British Columbia Police, 1858–1871." MA thesis, University of British Columbia, 1955.

Head, Lyndsay. "Land, Authority and the Forgetting of Being in Early Colonial Maori History." PhD diss., University of Canterbury, 2006.

Heartfield, James. *The Aborigines' Protection Society: Humanitarian Imperialism in Australia, New Zealand, Fiji, Canada, South Africa, and the Congo, 1836–1909*. New York: Columbia University Press, 2011.

Hendrickson, James. "Blanshard, Richard." *Dictionary of Canadian Biography Online*. http://www.biographi.ca/en/search.php.

–. "Fraser, Donald." *Dictionary of Canadian Biography Online*. http://www.biographi.ca/en/search.php.

Hibbert, Christopher. *The Illustrated London News: Social History of Victorian Britain*. London: Angus and Robertson, 1975.

Hickford, Mark. *Lords of the Land: Indigenous Property Rights and the Jurisprudence of Empire*. Oxford: Oxford University Press, 2011.

Higgins, Stella. "Colonial Vancouver Island and British Columbia as Seen through British Eyes, 1849–1871." MA thesis, University of Victoria, 1972.

Higham, C.L. *Noble, Wretched and Redeemable: Protestant Missionaries to the Indians in Canada and the United States, 1820–1900*. Albuquerque/Calgary: University of New Mexico Press/University of Calgary Press, 2000.

Hill, Richard. *Policing the Colonial Frontier: The Theory and Practice of Coercive Social and Racial Control in New Zealand, 1767–1867*, vols. 1–2. Wellington: VR Ward, 1986.

Hogg, Robert. *Men and Manliness on the Frontier: Queensland and British Columbia in the Mid-Nineteenth Century*. Houndsmills, Basingstoke: Palgrave Macmillan, 2012.

Howe, K.R. "The Maori Response to Christianity in the Thames-Waikato Area, 1833–1840." *New Zealand Journal of History* 7, 1 (1973): 28–46.

Hyam, Ronald. *Britain's Imperial Century, 1815–1914: A Study of Empire and Expansion*. London: B.T. Batsford, 1976.

Innis, Harold A. *Empire and Communications*. Lanham: Rowman and Littlefield, 2007. First published in 1950 by Clarendon Press.

Jolly, Margaret. "Specters of Inauthenticity." In *Voyaging through the Contemporary Pacific*, ed. David and Geoffrey M. White Hanlon, 274–97. Lanham: Rowman and Littlefield, 2000.

Jones, Aled. *Powers of the Press: Newspapers, Power and the Public in Nineteenth-Century England*. Aldershot: Scolar Press, 1996.

Kaukiainen, Yrjö. "The Improvements of Communication in International Freight Markets, C.1830-70." In *Information, Media and Power through the Ages*, ed. Hiram Morgan, 137–52. Dublin: University College Dublin Press, 2001.

Keenan, Danny. *Wars without End: The Land Wars in Nineteenth-Century New Zealand*. Auckland: Penguin, 2009.

Kidd, Colin. *The Forging of Races: Race and Scripture in the Protestant Atlantic World, 1600–2000*. Cambridge: Cambridge University Press, 2006.

Kilian, Crawford. *Go Do Some Great Thing: The Black Pioneers of British Columbia*. Vancouver: Douglas and McIntyre, 1978.

Knafla, Louis A., and Haijo Westra, eds. *Aboriginal Title and Indigenous Peoples: Canada, Australia, and New Zealand*. Vancouver: UBC Press, 2010.

Laidlaw, Zoë. *Colonial Connections, 1815–45: Patronage, the Information Revolution and Colonial Government*. Manchester: Manchester University Press, 2005.

Lambert, David, and Alan Lester, eds. *Colonial Lives across the British Empire: Imperial Careering in the Long Nineteenth Century*. Cambridge: Cambridge University Press, 2006.

Lang, George. *Making Wawa: The Genesis of Chinook Jargon*. Vancouver: UBC Press, 2008.

Lange, Raeburn. "Indigenous Agents of Religious Change in New Zealand, 1830–1860." *Journal of Religious History* 24, 3 (October 2000): 280–87.

Laqueur, Thomas W. "Bodies, Details, and the Humanitarian Narrative." In *The New Cultural History*, ed. Lynn Hunt, 176–204. Berkeley: University of California Press, 1989.

Lee, Alan J. *The Origins of the Popular Press, 1855–1914*. London: Croom Helm, 1976.

Lennard, Guy. *Sir William Martin: The Life of the First Chief Justice of New Zealand*. Christchurch: Whitcombe and Tombs, 1961.

Lester, Alan. *Imperial Networks: Creating Identities in Nineteenth- Century South Africa and Britain*. London: Routledge, 2001.

–. "British Settler Discourse and the Circuits of Empire." *History Workshop Journal* 1, 54 (2002): 24–48.

Lester, Allan, and Fae Dussart. "Trajectories of Protection: Protectorates of Aborigines in Early 19th-Century Australia and Aotearoa New Zealand." *New Zealand Geographer* 64, 3 (2008): 205–20.

Lethbridge, Christopher. *The Wounded Lion: Octavius Hadfield, 1814–1904*. Christchurch: Caxton Press, 1993.

Limbrick, Warren E., ed. *Bishop Selwyn in New Zealand, 1841–68*. Palmerston North: Dunmore Press, 1983.

—. "Selwyn, George Augustus-Biography." *Dictionary of New Zealand Biography, Te Ara-the Encyclopedia of New Zealand.* http://www.teara.govt.nz/remap_url.php?src=en/biographies/1s5/1.

Loo, Tina. *Making Law, Order, and Authority in British Columbia, 1821–1871.* Toronto: University of Toronto Press, 1994.

Lutz, John. "Inventing an Indian War: Canadian Indians and American Settlers in the Pacific West, 1854–1864." *Journal of the West* 38, 3 (1998): 7–13.

—. "Work, Sex, and Death on the Great Thoroughfare: Annual Migrations Of 'Canadian Indians' to the American Pacific Northwest." In *Parallel Destinies: Canadian-American Relations West of the Rockies,* ed. J.M. Findlay and Ken Coates, 80–103. Seattle/Montreal-Kingston: University Washington Press/McGill-Queen's University Press, 2002.

—. *Makúk: A New History of Aboriginal-White Relations.* Vancouver: UBC Press, 2008.

Macdonald, Charlotte. "Between Religion and Empire: Sarah Selwyn's Aotearoa/New Zealand, Eton and Lichfield, England, 1840s–1900." *Journal of the Canadian Historical Association* 19, 2 (2008): 43–75.

Macdonald, Lindsey. "The Political Philosophy of Property Rights." PhD diss., Canterbury University, 2009.

Mackie, Richard. "The Colonization of Vancouver Island, 1849–1858." *BC Studies* 96 (Winter 1992–93): 3–40.

—. *Trading beyond the Mountains: The British Fur Trade on the Pacific, 1793–1843.* Vancouver: UBC Press, 1997.

Main, G.M. *The Newspaper Press of Auckland.* Auckland: Wilsons and Horton, 1890.

Mandler, Peter. "The Problem with Cultural History." *Cultural and Social History* 1, 1 (2004): 94–117.

Marshall, Daniel Patrick. "Claiming the Land: Indians, Goldseekers, and the Rush to British Columbia." PhD diss., University of British Columbia, 2000.

—. "No Parallel: American Miner-Soldiers at War with the Nlaka'pamux of the Canadian West." In *Parallel Destinies: Canadian-American Relations West of the Rockies.* Seattle/Montreal and Kingston: University of Washington Press/McGill-Queen's University Press, 2002.

Martin, John. "Macdonald, Duncan George Forbes (1827/8–1884)." *Oxford Dictionary of National Biography.* http://www.oxforddnb.com/index/101017431/.

Matthews, Gethin. "Gold Fever: The Stampede from South Wales to British Columbia in 1862." *North American Journal of Welsh Studies* 5, 2 (2005): 54–83.

Mawani, Renisa. *Colonial Proximities: Crossracial Encounters and Juridicial Truths in British Columbia, 1871–1921.* Vancouver: UBC Press, 2009.

McAloon, Jim. "The New Zealand Economy, 1792–1914." In *The New Oxford History of New Zealand,* ed. Giselle Byrnes, 197–218. Auckland: Auckland University Press, 2006.

McDonald, R.A.J., and H. Keith Ralston. "De Cosmos, Amor." *Dictionary of Canadian Biography Online.* http://www.biographi.ca/en/search.php.

McGarvey, R.D. "Local Politics in the Auckland Province, 1853–62." MA thesis, University of New Zealand, 1954.

McHugh, P.G. *Aboriginal Societies and the Common Law: A History of Sovereignty, Status, and Self-Determination.* Oxford: Oxford University Press, 2004.

—. *Aboriginal Title: The Modern Jurisprudence of Tribal Land Rights.* Oxford: Oxford University Press, 2011.

McKenzie, Kirsten. *Scandal in the Colonies: Sydney and Cape Town, 1820–1850.* Melbourne: Melbourne University Press, 2004.

—. "The Daemon behind the Curtain: William Edwards and the Theatre of Liberty." *South African Historical Journal* 61, 3 (2009): 482–505.

McLuhan, Marshall. *The Gutenberg Galaxy: The Making of the Typographic Man*. London: Routledge, 1967.

—. *Understanding Media: The Extensions of Man*, ed. Lewis H. Lapham. Cambridge: MIT Press, 1999.

McNairn, Jeffrey. *The Capacity to Judge: Public Opinion and Deliberative Democracy in Upper Canada, 1791–1854*. Toronto: University of Toronto Press, 2000.

McNally, Vincent J. *The Lord's Distant Vineyard: A History of the Oblates and the Catholic Community in British Columbia*. Edmonton: University of Edmonton Press, 2000.

McNeill, R. *The Press, 1861–1961: The Story of a Newspaper*. Christchurch: Christchurch Press, 1963.

Mein Smith, Philippa. *A Concise History of New Zealand*. Cambridge: Cambridge University Press, 2005.

Miller, K.R. "Henry Samuel Chapman, Colonizer and Colonist." MA thesis, University of New Zealand, 1956.

Monin, Paul. "Maori Economies and Colonial Capitalism." In *The New Oxford History of New Zealand*, ed. Gyselle Byrnes, 125–46. Auckland: Oxford University Press, 2009.

Morin, Karen M. "(Anti?) Colonial Women Writing War." *New Zealand Geographer* 56, 1 (2000): 22–29.

Morin, Karen M., and Lawrence D. Berg. "Gendering Resistance: British Colonial Narratives of Wartime New Zealand." *Journal of Historical Geography* 27, 2 (2001): 196–222.

Morrell, W. P. *British Colonial Policy in the Age of Peel and Russell*. Oxford: Clarendon Press, 1930.

—. *The Anglican Church in New Zealand*. Dunedin: Anglican Church of the Province of New Zealand, 1973.

Mouat, Jeremy. "Situating Vancouver Island in the British World, 1846–49." *BC Studies* 145 (Spring 2005): 5–30.

Muckle, Robert J. *The First Nations of British Columbia*. Vancouver: UBC Press, 1998.

Murray, Peter. *The Devil and Mr. Duncan*. Victoria: Sono Nis, 1985.

Nalbach, Alex. "'The Software of Empire': Telegraphic News Agencies and Imperial Publicity, 1865–1914." In *Imperial Co-Histories. National Identities and the British and Colonial Press*, ed. Julie F. Codell, 68–94. Madison: Fairleigh Dickinson University Press, 2003.

Nerone, John. "Newspapers and the Public Sphere." In *A History of the Book in America*, ed. Scott E. Casper et al., 230–47. Chapel Hill: The University of North Carolina Press, 2007.

Neylan, Susan. *The Heavens Are Changing: Nineteenth-Century Protestant Missions and Tsimshian Christianity*. Montreal and Kingston: McGill-Queen's University Press, 2003.

O'Brien, Anne. "Humanitarianism and Reparation in Colonial Australia." *Journal of Colonialism and Colonial History* 12, 2 (2011). http://muse.jhu.edu/login?auth=0&type=summary&url=/journals/journal_of_colonialism_and_colonial_history/v012/12.2.0-brien.html.

Oettli, Peter H. *God's Messenger: J.F. Riemenschneider and Racial Conflict in 19th-Century New Zealand*. Wellington: Huia Publishers, 2008.

Oliver, W.H. "The Future behind Us: The Waitangi Tribunal's Retrospective Utopia." In *Histories, Power and Loss: Uses of the Past – A New Zealand Commentary*, ed. Andrew Sharp and Paul McHugh, 9–30. Wellington: Bridget Williams Books, 2001.

Orange, Claudia. *The Treaty of Waitangi*. Wellington: Bridget William Books, 1987.

Ormsby, Margaret A. *British Columbia: A History*. Vancouver: Macmillan, 1958.

Owens, J.M.R. "Christianity and the Maoris to 1840." *New Zealand Journal of History* 2, 1 (1968): 18–40.

Parkinson, Phil, and Penny Griffith. *Books in Māori, 1815–1900: An Annotated Bibliography*. Auckland: Reed Publishing, 2004.

Parsonson, Ann. "The Pursuit of Mana." In *The Oxford History of New Zealand*, ed. W.H. Oliver with B.R. Williams, 140–67. Oxford: Clarendon Press, 1981.

Paterson, Lachy. *Colonial Discourses: Niupepa Māori, 1855–1863*. Dunedin: Otago University Press, 2006.

—. "The Kohimārama Conference of 1860: A Contextual Reading," *Journal of New Zealand Studies* 12 (2011): 29–46.

Pawson, Eric, and Neil Quigley. "The Circulation of Information and Frontier Development: Canterbury, 1850–1890." *New Zealand Geographer* 38, 2 (October 1982): 46–96.

Perry, Adele. "'Fair Ones of a Purer Caste': White Women and Colonialism in Nineteenth-Century British Columbia." *Feminist Studies, Inc.* 23, 3 (1987): 501–24.

—. *On the Edge of Empire: Gender, Race, and the Making of British Columbia, 1849–1871*. Toronto: University of Toronto Press, 2001.

—. "The State of Empire: Reproducing Colonialism in British Columbia." *Journal of Colonialism and Colonial History* 2, 2 (2001). https://muse.jhu.edu/journals/journal_of_colonialism_and_colonial_history/v002/2.2perry.html.

—. "The Autocracy of Love and the Legitimacy of Empire: Intimacy, Power and Scandal in Nineteenth Century Metlakahtlah." *Gender and History* 16, 2 (2004): 261–88.

—. "'Is Your Garden in England, Sir': James Douglas's Archive and the Politics of Home." *History Workshop Journal* 70 (Autumn 2010): 67–85.

—. *Colonial Family: Intimacy, Mobility and Power in the Nineteenth-Century Imperial World*. Cambridge: Cambridge University Press, 2015.

Petrie, Hazel. *Chiefs of Industry: Māori Tribal Enterprise in Early Colonial New Zealand*. Auckland: Auckland University Press, 2006.

Pettit, Sydney G. "King, Edward Hammond." *Dictionary of Canadian Biography Online*. http://www.biographi.ca/en/search.php.

Pilton, J.W. "Negro Settlement in British Columbia, 1858–1871." MA thesis, University of British Columbia, 1951.

Pitblado, Bonnie L. "A Tale of Two Migrations: Reconciling Recent Biological and Archaeological Evidence for the Pleistocene Peopling of the Americas." *Journal of Archaeological Research* 19, 4 (2011): 327–75.

Pool, Ian. *Te Iwi Maori: Population Past, Present and Projected*. Auckland: University of Auckland Press, 1991.

Porter, Andrew. "Trusteeship, Anti-Slavery, and Humanitarianism." In *The Oxford History of the British Empire: The Nineteenth Century*. Oxford: Oxford University Press, 1999.

Porter, Bernard. *The Lion's Share: A Short History of British Imperialism*. London: Longman, 1975.

—. *The Absent-Minded Imperialists: What the British Really Thought about Empire*. Oxford: Oxford University Press, 2004.

Porter, Frances, and W.H. Oliver. "Richmond, James Crowe-Biography." *Dictionary of New Zealand Biography, Te Ara-the Encyclopedia of New Zealand*. http://www.teara.govt.nz/remap_url.php?src=en/biographies/1r10/1.

Potter, Simon. *News and the British World: The Emergence of an Imperial Press System*. Oxford: Oxford University Press, 2003.

—. "Empire and the English Press, c. 1857–1914." In *Newspapers and Empire in Ireland and Britain: Reporting the British Empire, c. 1857–1921*, 39–61. Dublin: Four Courts Press, 2004.

—. "Webs, Networks, and Systems: Globalization and the Mass Media in the Nineteenth- and Twentieth-Century British Empire." *Journal of British Studies* 46, 3 (2007): 621–46.

Powell, Kerry. "The Saturday Review." *British Literary Magazines: The Victorian and Edwardian Age, 1837–1913*, ed. Alvin Sullivan, 379–83. London: Greenwood Press, 1984.

Pratt, Marie Louise. *Imperial Eyes: Travel Writing and Transculturation*. London: Routledge, 1992.

Pruner, Jacqueline F. "Aboriginal Title and Extinguishment Not So Clear and Plain: A Comparison of the Current Maori and Haida Experiences." *Pacific Rim Law and Policy Journal Association* 1 (2005): 253–89.

Putnis, Peter. "The Indian Insurgency of 1857 as a Global Media Event." In *International Association for Mass Communication Research 25th Conference Proceedings*, 185–90. Canberra: University of Canberra, 2007.

Raibmon, Paige. *Authentic Indians. Episodes of Encounter from the Late-Nineteenth-Century Northwest Coast*. Durham: Duke University Press, 2005.

Ralston, H. Keith. "McClure, Leonard." *Dictionary of Canadian Biography Online*. http://www.biographi.ca/en/search.php.

Rankin, Jeremiah. "Science and Civic Culture in Colonial Auckland." MA thesis, University of Auckland, 2006.

Reimer, Chad. *Writing British Columbia History, 1784–1958*. Vancouver: UBC Press, 2009.

Reynolds, Henry. *Frontier: Aborigines, Settlers and Land*. St. Leonards: Allen and Unwin, 1987.

Reynolds, James I. "Recent Developments in Aboriginal Law in the United States, Australia and New Zealand: Lessons for Canada?" *Advocate* 62 (2004): 59–71.

Ross, Margaret. "Amor Decosmos, a British Columbia Reformer." MA thesis, University of British Columbia, 1931.

Rutherford, James. *Sir George Grey, K.C.B.* London: Cassell, 1961.

Salesa, Damon Ieremia. "Korero: A Reflection on the Work of Judith Binney." *New Zealand Journal of History* 38, 2 (2004): 272–98.

–. *Racial Crossings: Race, Intermarriage, and the Victorian British Empire*. Auckland: Oxford University Press, 2011.

Salmond, Anne. *Two Worlds: First Meetings between Maori and Europeans, 1642–1772*. Auckland: Viking, 1993.

Samson, Jane. "British Voices and Indigenous Rights: Debating Aboriginal Legal Status in Nineteenth Century Australia and Canada." *Cultures of the Commonwealth: Essays and Studies* 2 (Winter 1996–97): 5–16.

–. "British Authority or 'Mere Theory?' Colonial Law and Native People on Vancouver Island." *Western Legal History* 11, 1 (1999): 39–63.

Schmidt, Barbara Quinn. "Cook, John Douglas (1808? –1868)." *Oxford Dictionary of National Biography*. http://oxforddnb.com/index/101006145/.

Scholefield, G.H. *Newspapers in New Zealand*. Wellington: Reed, 1958.

Scouler, John. "Dr. John Scouler's Journal of a Voyage to N.W. America [1824–26]." *Quarterly of the Oregon Historical Society* 6, 1 (1905): 159–205.

Silver, D.B. "Carleton, Hugh Francis-Biography." *Dictionary of New Zealand Biography, Te Ara-the Encyclopedia of New Zealand*. http://www.teara.govt.nz/en/biographies/1c5.

Sinclair, Keith. *The Origins of the Maori Wars*. Wellington: New Zealand University Press, 1961.

–. *A History of New Zealand*. London: Oxford University Press, 1961.

Smandych, Russell. "Contemplating the Testimony of 'Others': James Stephen, the Colonial Office, and the Fate of Australian Aboriginal Evidence Acts, circa 1839–1849." *Legal History* 10 (2006): 97–143.

Smith, F.B. "Southwell, Charles-Biography." *Dictionary of New Zealand Biography, Te Ara-the Encyclopedia of New Zealand*. http://www.teara.govt.nz/remap_url.php?src=en/biographies/1s17/1.

Smith, J.R. *The Speckled Monster: Smallpox in England, 1670–1970, with Particular Reference to Essex*. Essex: Essex Record Office, 1987.

Smith, Robert Louis. "Governor Kennedy of Vancouver Island and the Politics of Union." MA thesis, University of Victoria, 1970.

Spiller, Peter. *The Chapman Legal Family*. Wellington: Victoria University Press, 1992.

Standfield, Rachel. "Warriors and Wanderers: Making Race in the Tasman World, 1769–1840." PhD thesis, University of Otago, 2008.

Stenhouse, John. "Churches, State and the New Zealand Wars: 1860–1872." *Journal of Law and Religion* 13, 2 (1998–99): 483–507.

–. "Imperialism, Atheism, and Race: Charles Southwell, Old Corruption, and the Maori." *Journal of British Studies* 44 (2005): 754–774.

–. "Religion and Society." *The New Oxford History of New Zealand*, ed. Gyselle Byrnes, 323–56. Auckland: Oxford University Press, 2009.

Steven, Margaret. *Trade, Tactics and Territory: Britain in the Pacific, 1783–1823* Melbourne: Melbourne University Press, 1983.

Stevens, Michael J. "Muttonbirds and Modernity in Murihiku: Continuity and Change in Kāi Tahu Knowledge." PhD diss., University of Otago, 2009.

Stock, Eugene. *Metlakahtla and the North Pacific Mission of the Church Missionary Society*. London: Seeley, Jackson, & Halliday, 1880.

Stoler, Ann Laura, and Frederick Cooper. "Between Metropole and Colony: Rethinking a Research Agenda." In *Tensions of Empire: Colonial Cultures in a Bourgeois World*, 1–58. Berkeley: University of California Press, 1997.

Stone, R.C.J. "Auckland Party Politics in the Early Years of the Provincial System, 1853–58.'" *New Zealand Journal of History* 14, 2 (1980): 153–78.

–. *The Father and His Gift: John Logan Campbell's Later Years*. Auckland: Auckland University Press, 1987.

–. "Brown, William-Biography." *Dictionary of New Zealand Biography, Te Ara-the Encyclopedia of New Zealand*. http://www.teara.govt.nz/remap_url.php?src=en/biographies/1b37/1.

–. "Campbell, John Logan-Biography." *Dictionary of New Zealand Biography, Te Ara-the Encyclopedia of New Zealand*. http://www.teara.govt.nz/remap_url.php?src=en/biographies/1c3/1.

Stonier-Newman, Lynne, *Policing a Pioneer Province: The BC Provincial Police 1858–1950*. Madeira Park: Harbour, 1991.

Sutton, D.G., et al. "The Timing of the Human Discovery and Colonization of New Zealand." *Quaternary International* 184 (2008): 109–21.

Swanky, Tom. *The True Story of Canada's "War" of Extermination on the Pacific*. Burnaby, BC: Dragon Heart Enterprises, 2012.

Temple, Philip. *A Sort of Conscience: The Wakefields*. Auckland: Auckland University Press, 2002.

Tennant, Paul. *Aboriginal Peoples and Politics: The Indian Land Question in British Columbia, 1849–1989*. Vancouver: UBC Press, 1990.

Thackray, W.S. "Keeping the Peace on Vancouver Island: The Colonial Police and the Royal Navy, 1850–1866." MA thesis, University of Victoria, 1982.

Thorne, Susan. *Congregational Missions and the Making of an Imperial Culture in 19th-Century England*. Stanford: Stanford University Press, 1999.

The Times: The History of the Times, the Tradition Established, 1841–1884. London: The Office of *The Times*, 1939.

The Times: A Newspaper History, 1785–1935. London: *The Times* Publishing Company, Ltd., 1935.

Tosh, John. *A Man's Place: Masculinity and the Middle-Class Home in Victorian England*. New Haven: Yale University Press, 1999.

Traue, J.E. "The Public Library Explosion in Colonial New Zealand." *Libraries and the Cultural Record* 42, 2 (2007): 151–64.

Tullett, J.S. *The Industrious Heart: A History of New Plymouth*. New Plymouth: New Plymouth City Council, 1981.

—. "Carrington, Frederic Alonzo-Biography." *Dictionary of New Zealand Biography, Te Ara-the Encyclopedia of New Zealand*. http://www.teara.govt.nz/remap_url.php?src=en/biographies/1c7/1.

University of Victoria, "Who Killed William Robinson? Race, Justice and Settling the Land." http://www.canadianmysteries.ca/sites/robinson/murder/castofcharacters/1672en.html.

Usher, Jean. *William Duncan of Metlakatla: A Victorian Missionary in British Columbia*. Ottawa: National Museum of Man, 1974.

Vibert, Elizabeth. *Traders' Tales: Narratives of Encounter in the Columbian Plateau, 1807–1846*. Norman: University of Oklahoma Press, 1997.

Viswanathan, Gauri. *Outside the Fold: Conversion, Modernity, and Belief*. Princeton: Princeton University Press, 1998.

Waitangi Tribunal. *The Taranaki Report: Kaupapa Tautahi: Wai 143: Muru Me Te Raupata = the Muru and Raupatu of the Taranaki Land and People*. Wellington: Waitangi Tribunal, 1996.

Wanhalla, Angela. *Matters of the Heart: A History of Interracial Marriage in New Zealand*. Auckland: Auckland University Press, 2013.

Ward, Alan. "The Origins of the Anglo-Maori Wars: A Reconsideration." *New Zealand Journal of History* 1, 2 (1967): 148–70.

—. *A Show of Justice: Racial "Amalgamation" in Nineteenth-Century New Zealand*. Toronto: University of Toronto Press, 1974.

Ward, Damon. "Territory, Jurisdiction, and Colonial Governance: A Bill to Repeal the British Constitution." *Journal of Legal History* 33, 3 (2012): 313–33.

Wards, Ian. "Fitzroy, Robert-Biography." *Dictionary of New Zealand Biography, Te Ara-the Encyclopedia of New Zealand*. http://www.teara.govt.nz/remap_url.php?src=en/biographies/1f12/1.

Waterson, D.B. "Firth, Josiah Clifton-Biography." *Dictionary of New Zealand Biography, Te Ara-the Encyclopedia of New Zealand*. http://www.teara.govt.nz/remap_url.php?src=en/biographies/1f7/1.

—. "Williamson, John-Biography." *Dictionary of New Zealand Biography, Te Ara-the Encyclopedia of New Zealand*. http://www.teara.govt.nz/remap_url.php?src=en/biographies/1w28/1.

Weedon, Alexis. *Victorian Publishing: The Economics of Book Production for a Mass Market, 1836–1916*. Aldershot: Ashgate, 2003.

Wellcome, Henry Solomon. *The Story of Metlakahtla*. London: Saxon & Co., 1887.

Wenzlhuemer, Roland. "The Dematerialization of Telecommunication." *Journal of Global History* 2, 3 (2007): 345–72.

Whaley, Gray H. *Oregon and the Collapse of Illahee. US Empire and the Transformation of an Indigenous World, 1792–1859*. Chapel Hill: UNC Press, 2010.

White, Richard. *The Middle Ground: Indians, Empires, and Republics in the Great Lakes Region, 1650–1815*. Cambridge: Cambridge University Press, 1991.

Whitwell, Harold J. "The Forty Acre System." MA thesis, University of New Zealand, 1954.

Wild, Roland. *Amor De Cosmos*. Toronto: Ryerson Press, 1958.

Wilkinson, Glenn R. *Depictions and Images of War in Edwardian Newspapers, 1899–1914*. Houndsmills, Basingstoke: Palgrave Macmillan, 2003.

Williams, Carol J. *Framing the West: Race, Gender, and the Photographic Frontier in the Pacific Northwest*. Oxford: Oxford University Press, 2003.

Winder, Gordon M. "Imagining World Citizenship in the Networked Newspaper." *Historical Social Science Research* 35, 1 (2010): 140–66.

Winder, Gordon M., and M. Schmitt. "Geographical Imaginaries in the *New York Times'* Reports of the Assassinations of Mahatma Gandhi (1948) and Indira Gandhi (1984)." *Journal of Historical Geography* (2014), http://dx.doi.org/10.1016/j.jhg.2014.03.001.

Wolfe, Patrick. *Settler Colonialism and the Transformation of Anthropology: The Politics and Poetics of an Ethnographical Event.* London: Cassell, 1999.

Wood, Vaughan, Tom Brooking, and Peter Perry, "Pastoralism and Politics: Reinterpreting Contests for Territory in Auckland Province, New Zealand, 1853–1864." *Journal of Historical Geography* 34, 2 (2008): 220–41.

Woodcock, George. *Amor De Cosmos: Journalist and Reformer.* Toronto: Oxford University Press, 1975.

Wright, Harrison M. *New Zealand, 1769–1840: Early Years of Western Contact.* Cambridge: Harvard University Press, 1959.

Wright, Nancy. "The Problems of Aboriginal Evidence in Early Colonial New South Wales." In *Law, History, Colonialism: The Reach of Empire*, ed. D. Kirkby and C. Coleborne, 140–55. Manchester: Manchester University Press, 2001.

Wynn, Graeme. "Deplorably Dark and Demoralized Lumberers? Rhetoric and Reality in Early Nineteenth-Century New Brunswick." *Journal of Forest History* 24, 4 (1980): 179–84.

Young, Robert. *Colonial Desire: Hybridity in Theory, Culture and Race.* London: Routledge, 1995.

Zaffaroni, Irene Genevieve Marie. "The Great Chain of Being: Racism and Imperialism in Colonial Victoria, 1858–1871." MA thesis, University of Victoria, 1987.

Index

Abolitionism, 5, 7–8, 60, 196
Aborigines' Protection Society, 60, 123, 126, 227
Abraham, Caroline, 163–64
Abraham, Charles, 158
Ahuriri, NZ, 96
Anderson, Atholl, 29
Aotearoa, NZ: early European settlement, 36–38; European exploration and maritime trade, 29–31, 73; history (pre-contact), 25, 27–29; map, 28(f); population (pre-contact), 29, 32
Appadurai, Arjun, 217
Arminianism, 6
Arnett, Chris, xii, 15, 106, 117
Atkinson, Jane Maria, 70
Auckland, NZ, 36, 75, 96; military garrison, 148, 151; Provincial Council, 129, 132, 137; photo, 132(f); political culture, 136–38; population, 133–34; postal records, 133, 135; settler anxiety, 151; superintendency, 132
Auckland Examiner, 131–35; anti-clericalism, 138–40, 145, 164; "Blood for Blood," 152–55; circulation, 133–34; collapse, 145, 156; criticism of Thomas Gore Browne, 139, 145, 149–50, 152, 164; critique of the *New Zealander*, 138; Direct Purchase Movement, 141; Indian Rebellion, 149–50; Kingitanga, 149–50; popularity, 140;

pre-war manifesto, 138; racial amalgamation, 140, 145; racial vitriol, 139–40; threat of Maori violence, 149–50
Auckland Mechanics' Institute, 135–36
Auckland press, 131–56; circulation, 132–36; colonial public opinion, 131; criticism of Thomas Gore Browne, 139; effects of staffing, 147–48; endorsement of the *Taranaki Herald*, 155; humanitarianism, 144, 147; Indian Rebellion, 129, 149; metropolitan audience, 134–35, 155–56; "Monster Meeting," 129–31; political manifestos, 136–44; promotion of Maori rights, 155; public opinion, 156; Taranaki War, 145–56, 155
Auckland Weekly Register, 89, 131–33, 135; circulation, 134; criticism of Hugh Carleton, 143; pre-war manifesto, 138, 143
Auckland Young Men's Christian Association, 135–36
Australian Associated Press, 225
Australian colonial press, 19, 22, 77, 190, 198–99
Australian colonies, 225
Aylmer, Fenton, 214

Ballantyne, Tony, xi, 11, 19, 21–22, 31, 97, 227
Banfield, William, 118
Bank, Andrew, 226

Cross, 132, 136–38, 148; humanitarian
rhetoric, 141–44; Maori readers, 153;
metropolitan surveillance, 130–31;
opposition to the Taranaki War, 146–48,
155; responsible government, 154–55
Carlson, Keith, xii, 31–32
Carlyle, Thomas, 139–40
Carrington, Frederick Alonzo, 164–65
Chapman, Henry Samuel: correspondent
for *The Times*, 195–98, 201, 203, 219; ties
to the Wellington political establishment,
195–96
Chapman's Almanac, 148
Chatham Islands, 4
Chee-al-thuc (King Freezy), 64, 66. *See
also* Lekwungen First Nation
China, 30
Chinook *wawa*, 27, 105, 179–80, 182
Christianity: Aboriginal, 35, 62, 215; civil-
ization discourse, 7, 91–95, 216, 228;
Indigenous, 7–8, 33–35, 186; Maori,
33–34, 37, 91–95, 100, 139, 144, 153, 173,
187, 223; missions in New Zealand, 33;
missions on Northwest Coast, 34–35,
173–75, 187; muscular, 216
Church Missionary Intelligencer, 173
Church Missionary Society (CMS): New
Zealand, 11–12, 33, 130, 151, 164, 170;
Northwest Coast, 35, 159, 170, 172–74,
179–80, 184
civilization discourse, 6–7, 9, 34, 59, 72, 87,
90–95, 103–4, 139, 142–44, 216, 223, 228
Clarke, George, Sr., 74, 165, 170, 172; chief
protector of the Aborigines, 170
Clayoquot Sound, 118
Coast Salish First Nation, 31, 105, 120
Coles, John, 110
Colonial Evidence Act, 34, 116
Colonial Intelligencer, 126
Colonial Office, 8; New Zealand, 11–12,
79–80, 89, 94, 96–97, 154–57, 162–64,
171, 186, 201, 203; perceptions of control
over New Zealand and Vancouver
Island, 14, 100, 155–56; Vancouver Island
and British Columbia, 12, 42, 49–53, 59,
104–6, 107, 110–11, 113–16, 123, 126, 159,
175, 177–78, 184, 186–87
Columbia District, 11, 35–36
communications networks, 158, 162, 191,
195–96; between New Zealand and

Great Britain, 156, 187, 219–20, 222–25;
between Vancouver Island and Great
Britain, 62, 123, 187, 189, 203–4, 210–
11, 219–20, 222–25; circulation, 211–12;
conventional (slow) forms of transport,
224, 226; links between California press,
Victoria press, and Great Britain, 217–19;
Maori connections, 87, 97, 100; North-
west Coast, 55
Connolly, William, 49
Constitution Act, 136, 160
Constitutional Party, 132, 136–38, 141
Cook, James, 9, 25, 30, 73
Cook, John Douglas, 199
Coromandel Peninsula, 37
Cornwallis, Kinahan, 210, 213–14
Cowichan district, 106–9, 112–13, 115–16,
118
Cowichan First Nation, 103, 106–9, 111–12,
114–15, 117, 119, 122, 125–27
Cridge, Edward, 35, 176
Crimean War, 96–97, 100
culture of sensibility, 6
Cutfield, George, 77

Daily Alta California, 217–18
Davis, C.O., 89, 97. *See also Te Karere
Maori*
Davy, Dan, xii, 210–11
Day, Patrick, 140
De Cosmos, Amor, 43–44, 46–47, 58,
60, 62, 67, 113–16, 185. *See also British
Colonist*
de la Bodega y Quadra, Juan Francisco, 31
Delane, John Thadeus, 193
disease: Maori and First Nations, 30–33,
38–39; smallpox, 15, 31–32, 39, 41, 63–68,
117, 126, 174
Dorsett, Shaunnagh, 34
Douglas, Amelia, *née* Connolly, 49
Douglas, James: Aboriginal title and treaty-
making, 13–14, 104–10, 112–16, 121, 125–
27, 227; Chinook *wawa*, 179–80, 182;
Colonial Office, 42, 49–52, 104–6, 113,
159, 175, 177–78, 184, 187; criticism of
Douglas, 35, 41, 43–47, 54, 56, 60, 111,
119–20, 185, 223; Donald Fraser, 206,
208; eviction of northern First Nations,
14, 51–53, 56, 64, 68, 176–77, 179; Fort
Victoria, 48; fur trade career, 49, 51;

Great Britain, 6–9, 11–12, 14, 17–18, 20, 22, 37, 43, 58, 60, 73, 77–78, 81, 95–97, 100, 123, 125, 131, 133, 135, 137–40, 146–47, 154–56, 160–62, 165, 168, 171, 173, 189–204, 207, 211–12, 215, 217, 219–20, 222, 224–26

Green, W. Sebright, 126–27, 227

Grey, George, 13, 82, 88, 136–37, 148–49, 157–58, 160, 178, 198, 203, 226

Grey, Henry George, 136, 169–70

guidebooks, 22, 44, 204, 210–18; fears of war with First Nations, 57; First Nations violence, 57, 188–90, 213–17, 220, 222; genre conventions, 210–11; portrait of First Nations, 18, 204, 212–18, 220; praise for William Duncan, 174, 179

Hadfield, Charles, 194–95

Hadfield, Octavius, 130, 146–47, 158, 163, 165, 186, 194–95

Haida First Nation, 27, 48, 178–80, 182–83

Haisla First Nation, 27, 48

Hall, Catherine, 5, 21, 226

Hamilton, Geoffrey, 193

Handywood, Tom, 181

hapu, 29, 32–34, 75, 79, 166, 168

Harney, William S., 218

Harris, Cole, 14–15, 32, 106, 108

Harrop, A.J., 193

Harvey, Ross, xii, 89, 134

Head, Lyndsay, 92

Heartfield, James, 11, 200, 221, 227

Heiltsuk First Nation, 27, 48

Helmcken, John Sebastian, 65–66, 111–12

Hickford, Mark, 172

Higgins, David W., 46, 102, 122. *See also British Colonist; Victoria Daily Chronicle*

Higham, C.L., 61, 208

Hills, George, 172, 175–76, 181, 185

Hobson, William, 11

Hogg, Robert, 216

Hope, A.J.B Beresford, 199

House of Commons Select Committee on New Zealand, 12

Howe, Joseph, 43

Hudson's Bay Company (HBC), 66; Aboriginal title, 11–13, 104–6, 110–11, 113, 127; criticism of the HBC, 34–35, 43–44, 46; fur trade operations, 35–36, 42, 48–49, 51, 64, 173, 178; humanitarian debates over foundation of Vancouver

Island, 11–12; positive relations with First Nations, 206–7, 213; systematic colonization, 12

humanitarianism: British imperialism, 8, 20–21, 177–78, 186–87, 189, 199–203, 207, 219, 223, 228; in the colonial press, 13–14, 58–62, 71–73, 80, 85, 87, 99, 101–4, 116, 120–22, 138–56, 185, 196, 199–203, 221–22; criticism of, 85–87, 129–31, 139–40, 145, 185, 189; debates over Maori rights and civilization, 11, 20, 34, 71–73, 80–82, 87, 93, 131, 221; decline in popularity, 5, 9, 119, 221, 226; discourses, 5, 14, 127, 172, 226–28; emphasis on protection of Indigenous peoples, 11, 127, 227–28; evangelical humanitarianism, 8–9, 22, 37, 80, 85, 102–4, 146–48, 157–87, 198, 215–16, 223; eviction of First Nations from Victoria, 58–62; origins, 5–9; persistence and political utility, 5–6, 163, 221–23, 226, 228; racial amalgamation, 93–95; rhetorical humanitarianism, 8–9, 42, 58–62, 72, 80–81, 120–22, 141–42, 144, 168, 177–78, 183–84, 200, 219–21, 223; settler anxiety, 9, 38, 123, 131, 149–56, 221, 223–24

Hunt, F. Knight, 16–17

Hutton, R.H., 201

Hyam, Ronald, 5, 226

Illustrated London News, 212

Indian Improvement Committee, 59, 176, 180, 184

Indian Rebellion (1857), 3–4, 5–7, 19–20, 68, 83–85, 97–98, 100, 129, 149–51, 156, 219, 223–24

Indigenous (modern use of), 23

Indigenous title: First Nations, 13–14, 104–10, 112–16, 121, 125–27, 227; Maori, 11–13, 37, 74–76, 79–80, 87, 105, 141–45, 147, 156, 161–62, 164–72, 186, 199–200, 216

Innis, Harold, 18–19, 224

iwi, 29, 32–33, 73–75, 79, 83, 96, 166

Jenner, Edward, 65

kakahu, 33

Kemp Deed, 105

Kennedy, Arthur, 15, 110–12, 118, 125, 127

Kimble, Edward C., 217

159, 172–87, 216, 223; northern First
Nations, 14–15, 39, 41, 48–52, 66–68,
64, 116, 159, 175–83, 208, 215, 218, 220;
threat of First Nations violence, 117–22,
217–18
North Saanich Treaty, 105
North West Company, 35
Nova Scotia, 43
Nuu-chah-nulth First Nation, 27
Nuxalk First Nation, 27, 48

O'Brien, Ann, 221
Occasional Discourse on the Negro Question,
139
Ogden Point, 67
Oregon, 106
Oregon Treaty, 11, 35–36, 48, 106
Otago Daily Times, 205
Otago gold rush, 37, 204
Otaki, 163
Oweekeno First Nation, 27

pa, 29, 70, 80, 82
Pacific Commercial Advertiser, 3–4
pakeha, 36–37, 76, 91, 94–95, 149
pamphlet war, 146, 158–59, 164–72; invasion
of Taranaki by Waikato *iwi*, 165–66;
Maori land tenure, 165–67; Maori rights
and the Treaty of Waitangi, 158–59, 165–
66, 169–71, 186; Robert Fitzroy and the
New Zealand Company, 165–66; Te
Rangitake versus Te Teira, 165–67
Parliamentary Select Committee on
Aboriginal Tribes, 11
Paterson, Lachy, xii, 89, 96
Pemberton, Augustus, 39, 41, 66–68, 119,
176, 179, 181–84
Pemberton, Joseph Despard, 212
Perry, Adele, xi–xii, 15, 49, 51, 65, 174, 178
Petrie, Hazel, 75
Pheney, Richard, 76–77
Plymouth Company, 165
Potlatch, 27, 30, 48
Potter, Simon, 21, 191, 217, 219, 224–25
Pratt, Marie Louise, 213
The Press, 39, 183; Aboriginal title, 113;
criticism of Douglas, 46, 60; initiation,
45–46; smallpox, 65–67; threat of war
with First Nations, 56; urban segrega-
tion, 64

Prevost, James Charles: comparison of
Ts'msyen people to Maori, 173; Fort
Simpson, 173–74
Progress Party, 132, 136–38, 140–42
Puget Sound, 54
Puke Kowhatu *hapu*, 75
Puketakauere *pa*, 82
Putnis, Peter, 19, 225–26

Raibmon, Paige, 15, 59
rangatira, 11, 29, 31, 81, 88, 90, 94, 124, 166–
77, 170, 172
Rattray, Alexander, 213
Rawson, Henry Freer, 85, 87. *See also
Taranaki Punch*
*Report of the Parliamentary Select Commit-
tee on Aboriginal Tribes*, 7–8, 11
Richmond, C.W., 70, 75, 161, 165, 201
Richmond, James Crowe, 72–73, 76. *See
also Taranaki Herald*
Richmond, Maria, 72
Robson, Ebenezar, 120
Robson, John, 120–22, 124. *See also British
Columbian*
Roebuck, John, 189
Rogers, Frederick, 203
Roman Catholic Church, 33, 35, 92
Royal Charlie, 178–79
Royal Navy, Vancouver Island, 67, 107–8,
117–18, 173, 182–83
Royal Proclamation, 116, 124

Sacramento Daily Union, 217–19
Salesa, Damon, 12, 94, 221, 226–27
Samson, Jane, 116, 118, 228
San Francisco, 36, 39, 42–43, 47, 65, 205–6,
225
San Juan Island controversy, 45, 204, 207,
218
Santhal insurrection, 5
Saturday Review, 191; BC gold rush guidebooks, 210, 214–16; circulation, 199;
criticism of Thomas Gore Browne, 199–
201; criticism of George August Selwyn,
201–2; initiation and editorial manifesto,
199; New Zealand Bill, 199; New Zealand
press, 201; Taranaki War, 199–203, 219;
Waitara purchase, 199–200
Schmidt, Barbara Quinn, 199
scientific racial theory, 5, 138–39, 213

71–73, 78–88, 98–101, 124, 130–31, 145–56, 190–203, 224; metropolitan press coverage, 193–203, 219–20, 224; opposition, 70–73, 129, 146–48, 157–72, 186, 194–98, 201–3, 222; support, 70, 72, 74–75, 129–31, 145–46, 162–68, 170–72, 193–94, 198–201, 222; termination, 148

Te Ati Awa *iwi*, 70, 74–76, 147, 166, 171; agricultural success at Waitara, 75; inter-*hapu* conflict, 75; membership in the Anglican Church, 158; Taranaki War, 83, 98, 151

Te Hokioi o Niu Tireni e Rere Atu Na, 99. *See also* Kingitanga

Te Ika a Maui, 27

Te Karere Maori, 22, 73; British Empire's providential role, 87, 91–92, 99, 223; circulation, 87–88, 99; Crimean War, 96–97; history of England and stadial theory, 87, 90–91, 94–96, 103; Indian Rebellion, 97–98, 224; Kohimarama conference, 88; Maori anxiety, 95, 223; Maori cultural sophistication, 82, 98–99; Maori Christianity, 91–93, 100; Maori integration within networks of colonial knowledge, 96–98, 100, 153, 224; mission statement, 87; racial amalgamation, 87, 91, 93–95, 131, 144, 223; *Taranaki Punch*, 86–87; Taranaki War, 98–99; ties to the New Zealand press, 89

Te Kohia *pa*, 80

Te Kooti Arikirangi Te Turuki, 34

Te Rangitake, Wiremu Kingi, 70, 75–76, 79–82, 99, 141–42, 145–47, 152, 158, 165–72, 193, 197; membership in the Anglican Church, 158

Te Wai Pounamu, 27

Te Waka o Te Iwi, 97

Te Wherowhero, Potatau, 79, 149. *See also* Kingitanga

telegraphic communications, introduction, 20–21, 224–25

Tennant, Paul, 106

The Times: Australian press, 198–99; British Columbia, 189–90, 204–10, 216–18, 222; British military defeat in New Zealand, 196–97; circulation, 191–93, 199, 212; coverage of the Taranaki War, 193–98, 202–3, 219; foreign correspondents, 36, 195–96; Melbourne correspondent,

194–98, 219; political orientation, 193; representation of public opinion, 20; rhetorical humanitarianism, 197–98; Sydney correspondent, 194

Thompson, Arthur S., 88

Tlingit First Nation, 27, 48, 182–83

Tolmie, William Fraser, 110, 182

Towne, James W., 42–43, 45. *See also Victoria Gazette*

Traue, J.E., 135

treaties: Oregon, 11, 36; Vancouver Island, 13, 48, 105–6, 108, 113–15, 121, 125, 180; Waitangi, 11, 13, 33; 164–65, 169–71

Treaty of Waitangi, 11–13, 33, 80, 116, 124, 140, 164–66, 169–71, 186, 199–200

Trumpeter and Universal Advertiser, 133

Trutch, Joseph, 126–27, 227

Tsilhqot'in First Nation, 27, 117–18

Ts'msyen First Nation, 27, 67, 173–75, 178–80, 183, 185, 187

Tugwell, Lewen Street, 180–81

Tugwell, Mary Wild, 180–81

Tullett, J.S., 77

Unsworn Testimony Ordinance, 34

Usher, Jean (Friesen), 173–74, 176, 180

United States, 60

Vancouver Island: comparisons with New Zealand, 9–16, 18–22, 61–62, 69, 123–25, 178, 180, 185–89, 204, 221–28; Council, 206; early colonial history, 11–13, 35–36, 38, 48–52; Legislative Assembly, 44, 65–66, 107, 109–16, 122, 127, 182, 212; map, 40(f); map of New Zealand and Vancouver Island, 10(f); postal records, 58; settler anxiety, 13, 49–52; union with British Columbia, 125

Vancouver Island: Its Resources and Capabilities as a Colony, 212

Vancouver Island Times, 120, 122–23

Venn, Henry, 180

Vibert, Elizabeth, 15, 214

Victoria: black settler community, 60, 221; Fort Victoria, 34–36, 48–49, 107, 206–7; Gaol, 55; gold rush economy, 42–43, 47, 51, 116, 209–10; Grand Jury reports, 55–56; Indigenous space, 48; judiciary, 54; photo of Victoria from the Songhees Reserve, 49(f); Police Department, 39,

Printed and bound in Canada by Friesens
Set in Garamond by Artegraphica Design Co. Ltd.
Copy editor: Joanne Richardson
Cartographer: Eric Leinberger